Securing Google Cloud Platform

*Implementing cloud security by leveraging
native GCP services and modern principles*

Deepam Kanjani

bpb

www.bpbonline.com

First Edition 2026

Copyright © BPB Publications, India

ISBN: 978-93-65893-939

LIMITS OF LIABILITY AND DISCLAIMER OF WARRANTY

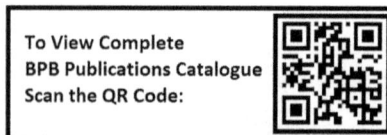

To View Complete
BPB Publications Catalogue
Scan the QR Code:

Dedicated to

"Security, like trust, is built quietly - layer by layer."

Thanks to everyone who believed in this book even before the pages took shape. Your support, love, and grounding presence helped me finish what I once thought I could not begin.

To my family, friends, mentors, and everyone who stood by me during my difficult times, a heartfelt thanks.

About the Author

Deepam Kanjani is an experienced security professional with over 15 years of expertise in cybersecurity, cloud platforms, and secure software development. His work encompasses enterprise security architecture, threat modelling, incident response, and automation-driven security design, particularly in modern cloud environments such as Google Cloud. He specialises in the software supply chain, AI, data and cloud security.

Over the years, he has led product security programs, built threat detection pipelines, and assisted engineering teams in integrating security into everything from CI/CD workflows to zero trust initiatives. His approach combines technical expertise with a builder's mindset, emphasising clarity, usability, and impact over complexity.

Deepam actively contributes to the global security community through conference talks, mentoring, and open-source security tools. He is passionate about coaching the next generation of engineers and security leaders, helping them navigate the real-world challenges of cloud security with confidence and purpose.

He believes that good security is not just about tools and policies, but also about how people think.

About the Reviewers

❖ **Karan Rajoria** is a cloud security analyst specializing in security operations. He brings hands-on experience in securing cloud-native environments through proactive threat detection, incident response, and vulnerability management.

With a strong grasp of cloud architecture and security best practices, Karan has worked closely with cross-functional teams to design and implement scalable security frameworks. He holds multiple cloud security certifications and currently works at EY, supporting enterprise clients in building resilient and compliant infrastructures on the cloud.

❖ **Sourabh Mahajan** brings nearly two decades of industry experience as a technical architect and technology innovator with a specialization in Salesforce and enterprise solutions known for translating complex technical requirements into scalable, real world systems. He blends business acumen with hands on expertise in emerging technologies and digital transformation. He holds multiple Salesforce certificates, including Health Cloud, Sales Cloud and Service Cloud Professional and is a certified Salesforce application and data architect.

Sourabh specializes in Salesforce ecosystems, enterprise architecture, CRM strategy, and cloud transformation. Sourabh possesses an innate ability to translate business concepts into development requirements, earning the trust of his clients and leading them to successful project completions.

Acknowledgement

I want to thank a few people for their constant support, encouragement, and belief throughout the journey of writing this book. While the content may focus on securing cloud systems, this book is built on very human foundations, patience, curiosity, late nights, and people who kept me grounded through it all.

First and foremost, I want to thank my family, especially my mother, whose faith in me never wavered even when she did not fully understand the technical details. To my sisters, thank you for being my sounding boards, my critics, and my peace, and to my two lovely nieces, your joy reminds me why the world is worth protecting.

This book is dedicated to my father. His quiet strength, integrity, and presence continue to guide me, even in his absence.

I am also grateful to the technical communities, mentors, and peers who challenged my ideas, corrected my blind spots, and shared their experiences so generously. Your contributions, often shared freely in blogs, discussions, or open-source projects, became the sparks I needed to keep going. To the days, when friends who brainstormed ideas on how something could be done better in GCP than other tools.

I am deeply grateful to the remarkable tools and AI-powered resources that have facilitated this journey. Their support and assistance made each step easier, transforming daunting tasks into manageable milestones along the way.

My heartfelt thanks to the editorial team at BPB Publication for their constant support, flexibility, and patience. Your support in constantly enhancing the book's quality made the writing process far less scary and much more meaningful.

A special thank you to the technical reviewers for their kind technical scrutiny and feedback that helped sharpen the edges of this work.

Finally, to every reader, whether you are securing your first cloud workload or solving challenging architectural problems. I hope this book helps you pause, question, and build with intent. Every chapter ends with a short story on making something complex simple; I hope you make life that way.

Preface

I still remember staring at my first IAM policy in Google Cloud - five lines long, deceptively simple, and wide open to the internet. No alarms, no audit trails, just access. That moment changed how I viewed cloud security forever.

What began as curiosity became a career. Over the years, I have worked with teams across industries, designing controls, investigating incidents, teaching developers, debating defaults, and trying to answer one big question: How do we make cloud security both usable and practical?

This book is my response to that question. It is not just my perspective, but a collection of lessons, stories, and patterns shaped by real-world deployments of Google Cloud. It takes you from the basics of IAM, network, and data protection to advanced domains like DevSecOps, compliance, monitoring, and incident response. Each chapter builds on the last but is written so you can pick up any topic independently.

You do not need to read this cover to cover. If you are new to GCP security, start with the IAM, data, and network security chapters. If you have hands-on experience in automation, containers, or DevSecOps, jump directly to chapters 5, 6, or 12. If you are mapping strategy or compliance, chapters 7, 9, and 10 will be most relevant. And if you want to test your readiness for real-world use cases or certification, chapter 12 is your blueprint.

By the end, you will not only understand Google Cloud's security features but also know how to apply them in practice, bridging the gap between certification knowledge and real-world cloud security. This book is designed to serve practitioners, architects, and leaders alike: whether you are securing your first project, scaling an enterprise deployment, or aligning your controls with compliance.

Chapter 1: Introduction to Google Cloud Platform Security - Understand the core principles of GCP security, from the shared responsibility model to the foundational differences that make Google Cloud unique.

Chapter 2: IAM and Access Control - Learn how roles, policies, and service accounts interact in Google Cloud. Build strong identity controls using least privilege, resource hierarchy, and audit capabilities.

Chapter 3: Data Security and Encryption - Explore data protection using Cloud KMS, CMEK, CSEK, Cloud HSM, and DLP. Learn how to apply encryption consistently across storage, databases, and analytics pipelines.

Chapter 4: Network Security in GCP - Secure your networks using VPCs, firewall rules, Cloud Armor, Shared VPCs, and VPC SC. Understand hybrid connectivity and segmentation to reduce risk.

Chapter 5: Automating Security in DevOps Pipelines - Integrate security into CI/CD using IaC, from all the instances of policy as code, tfsec, and secret management. Shift left without slowing down deployments.

Chapter 6: Securing Containerized Workloads GKE - Secure Kubernetes workloads on GKE—harden nodes, manage identity, scan and sign images, and apply pod-level policies for compliance and resilience.

Chapter 7: Compliance, Auditing, and Continuous Monitoring - Build a compliant cloud using Cloud Logging, Monitoring, Access Transparency, and real-time policy enforcement with Forseti and Policy Analyzer.

Chapter 8: Threat Detection using SCC and Chronicle - Use Security Command Center and Chronicle to detect misconfigurations, identify active threats, and correlate signals across your environment.

Chapter 9: Hybrid and Multi-Cloud Security with Anthos - Manage policy, security, and governance across Google Cloud, AWS, and on-prem using Anthos. Unify operations with tools like Istio, Config Management, and Gatekeeper.

Chapter 10: Zero Trust and BeyondCorp Enterprise - Go beyond VPNs with zero trust access. Implement BeyondCorp Enterprise, enforce identity-aware controls, and design posture-based security models.

Chapter 11: Incident Response and Forensics in GCP - Prepare for incidents in a dynamic cloud using automated detection, log correlation, snapshotting, and evidence collection across ephemeral workloads.

Chapter 12: Real-world Cloud Security - Apply everything through scenario-based implementations. This final chapter connects security blueprints with certification prep, long-term strategy, and scalable patterns.

In the pages ahead, you will find more than just checklists and service descriptions.

You'll find a mindset that evolves and is deeply tied to how people build in the cloud.

Code Bundle and Coloured Images

Please follow the link to download the
Code Bundle and the *Coloured Images* of the book:

https://rebrand.ly/95d6e7

The code bundle for the book is also hosted on GitHub at
https://github.com/bpbpublications/Securing-Google-Cloud-Platform.
In case there's an update to the code, it will be updated on the existing GitHub repository.

We have code bundles from our rich catalogue of books and videos available at
https://github.com/bpbpublications. Check them out!

Errata

We take immense pride in our work at BPB Publications and follow best practices to ensure the accuracy of our content to provide with an indulging reading experience to our subscribers. Our readers are our mirrors, and we use their inputs to reflect and improve upon human errors, if any, that may have occurred during the publishing processes involved. To let us maintain the quality and help us reach out to any readers who might be having difficulties due to any unforeseen errors, please write to us at: errata@bpbonline.com

Your support, suggestions and feedbacks are highly appreciated by the BPB Publications' Family.

At www.bpbonline.com, you can also read a collection of free technical articles, sign up for a range of free newsletters, and receive exclusive discounts and offers on BPB books and eBooks. You can check our social media handles below:

| *Instagram* | *Facebook* | *Linkedin* | *YouTube* |

Get in touch with us at: business@bpbonline.com for more details.

Piracy

If you come across any illegal copies of our works in any form on the internet, we would be grateful if you would provide us with the location address or website name. Please contact us at business@bpbonline.com with a link to the material.

If you are interested in becoming an author

If there is a topic that you have expertise in, and you are interested in either writing or contributing to a book, please visit www.bpbonline.com. We have worked with thousands of developers and tech professionals, just like you, to help them share their insights with the global tech community. You can make a general application, apply for a specific hot topic that we are recruiting an author for, or submit your own idea.

Reviews

Please leave a review. Once you have read and used this book, why not leave a review on the site that you purchased it from? Potential readers can then see and use your unbiased opinion to make purchase decisions. We at BPB can understand what you think about our products, and our authors can see your feedback on their book. Thank you!

For more information about BPB, please visit www.bpbonline.com.

Join our Discord space

Join our Discord workspace for latest updates, offers, tech happenings around the world, new releases, and sessions with the authors:

https://discord.bpbonline.com

Table of Contents

CHAPTER 1

Introduction to Google Cloud Platform Security

Introduction

This book is designed to empower you with the knowledge to leverage Google Cloud securely, while also guiding you in creating a scalable and secure infrastructure that enterprises can genuinely depend on. Your journey into this essential area enriches your understanding and enhances the security landscape for many.

In this opening chapter, we will explore why securing workloads on the **Google Cloud Platform (GCP)** is essential in an era of accelerated cloud adoption. We begin by examining the constantly evolving threat landscape and the necessity for robust, scalable defenses when migrating critical applications to the cloud.

Next, we will be comparing GCP's security approach with that of other major providers, highlighting Google's global infrastructure, shared responsibility model, and built-in security features, which are essential for deploying a strong foundation.

We will conclude by discussing how to set up your first secure GCP project, including establishing baseline configurations, logging, monitoring, and compliance measures from the outset. By the end, you will be equipped with fundamental concepts and ready to progress toward more advanced GCP security practices in subsequent chapters.

Structure

In this chapter, we will discuss the following topics:

- Setting the stage
- Case studies in cloud security incidents
- GCP versus other cloud providers
- GCP shared responsibility model
- Key security features of GCP
- Setting up your first secure GCP project
- Compliance overview in Google Cloud Platform
- Complex made simple

Objectives

This chapter aims to provide readers with a comprehensive understanding of the essential elements required for securing workloads on GCP. By examining the evolving cybersecurity threat landscape and contrasting GCP's security methods with industry standards, it offers a methodical approach to establishing secure GCP projects. Along the way, the chapter emphasizes the ongoing transition to cloud platforms, highlighting the advantages of cloud migration while stressing the necessity of strong security measures to ensure compliance and prevent misconfigurations. Furthermore, it offers insights into Google's *shared fate* security model, illustrating how Google and its customers work together to maintain a secure environment. Ultimately, readers will gain a thorough understanding of cloud security best practices, equipping them to effectively navigate and address the complexities of modern cloud security challenges.

Setting the stage

Over the last decade, finance, healthcare, startups, and other organizations have transformed their IT strategies, shifting from costly on-premises data centers to public cloud platforms. GCP stands out for its services, including VMs, container orchestration, serverless computing, and managed data analytics.

A report from *Accenture* shows that 86% of companies grew their cloud initiatives over two years, spending over $10 billion monthly.

Initially, these migrations focused on *reducing operational overhead*, but today's drivers/ motivations also include:

- **Scalability**: Instantly match resource usage to demand fluctuations.
- **Cost optimization**: Pay-as-you-go models eliminate enormous upfront costs and idle capacity expenses.

- **Global reach**: Deploy data and apps nearer to end users, enhancing performance and lowering latency.

However, while agility brings advantages, it also introduces new security challenges. Quickly spinning up numerous virtual machines or containers may lead to misconfiguration unless robust measures are in place, making cloud security engineers indispensable.

Google employs a unique approach to security, leveraging its *shared fate* concept. In the following sections, we will explore this concept to gain a deeper understanding of both Google's and customers' responsibilities regarding security.

Evolving threat landscape

Cyber threats target not only on-premises servers but also cloud-based workloads. As a GCP security professional responsible for safeguarding enterprise deployments and ensuring compliance, you must thoroughly understand how Google secures its infrastructure. Attackers can exploit the following:

- **Misconfigured cloud resources:** Firewalls, public buckets, or APIs exposing sensitive data.

- **Compromised credentials:** Poorly protected keys or passwords allow unauthorized access.

- **Insider threats:** Individuals with excessive privileges inadvertently (or maliciously) leak data.

- **Supply chain attacks:** Malicious packages, compromised dependencies, or tampered CI/CD pipelines leading to trusted software becoming an attack vector.

- **Zero-day exploits:** Attackers leveraging unknown vulnerabilities in cloud services, libraries, or operating systems before patches are available.

With cloud adoption accelerating, security must be *proactive*, anticipating threats, and *reactive*, rapidly detecting and addressing attacks.

Google's mission to create the most trusted cloud environment drives its commitment to security. The company has implemented multiple layers of protection for its infrastructure, data, and users. Rather than relying on a single technology, Google employs a progressive approach to security, embodying the principle of defense in depth. For instance:

- Google has built its infrastructure to be multi-tenant; it is managed, hardened, and operated by Google.

- Non-human identities (also known as service accounts) and human identities (user accounts) are cryptographically authenticated, and only authorized binaries are allowed to run.

- You can choose to run on a private, end-to-end encrypted network. Google also ensures security by default, implementing **Transport Layer Security (TLS)** for all externally exposed **application programming interfaces (APIs)** across its entire network.

These are compelling examples of how Google, leveraging its vast scale, is committed to establishing comprehensive end-to-end provenance while significantly enhancing its security posture and trustworthiness.

Business drivers for Google Cloud Platform security

Keeping data secure and reliable is extremely important, and GCP is committed to this mission. GCP uses a variety of security measures to reduce risks and protect sensitive information from new threats. This includes strong authentication processes for people and machines, as well as advanced encryption techniques.

GCP's comprehensive security system helps businesses protect their assets, stay compliant with regulations, and ensure smooth operations. Features like end-to-end encryption and proactive threat detection are built into its core functions, making security an integral part of what GCP offers.

Protecting brand reputation and customer trust

A data breach can erase years of trust and damage your public image. High-profile incidents often result in:

- **Financial penalties**: Under **General Data Protection Regulation (GDPR)**, **Health Insurance Portability and Accountability Act (HIPAA)**, or the **Digital Operational Resilience Act (DORA)**, organizations may face significant fines for failing to protect customer data. DORA, currently being assessed by many EU organizations, specifically enforces **Information and Communication Technology (ICT)** risk management and operational resilience requirements for financial institutions, adding another layer of regulatory accountability for cloud deployments.
- **Legal consequences**: Lawsuits, enforcement actions, or criminal investigations.
- **Customer attrition**: Clients switching to providers are perceived as being more secure.

GCP offers robust security mechanisms such as *encryption by default, IAM controls*, and *advanced threat detection*. To help you maintain and demonstrate a secure environment.

Maintaining business continuity

Downtime can be catastrophic for critical or crown-jewel applications for the enterprise. A robust GCP security setup helps in the following:

- **Minimise outage risks**: Guarding against DDoS, ransomware, and unauthorized modifications. At a scale where it can absorb volumetric attacks by default.

- **Enhance resilience**: Google's global infrastructure and redundancy improve fault tolerance, which is contingent on correct security configurations. This includes, but is not limited to, having 24/7 security operations to detect threats and respond to security incidents.

Meeting regulatory and compliance obligations

You may face frameworks like HIPAA, PCI-DSS, GDPR, or FedRAMP, depending on your industry or location. Typically required are the following:

- **Data encryption** (at rest, in transit)
- **Identity management and logging** (access control, auditing)
- **Detailed audit records** (who accessed what and when)

GCP's certifications (**International Organization for Standardization (ISO), System and Organization Controls (SOC), and Payment Card Industry Data Security Standard (PCI-DSS)**) facilitate compliance, provided you configure and manage resources correctly.

Unique challenges and opportunities in GCP

Navigating the regulatory landscape requires a keen understanding of legal requirements and best practices for security and data protection. The following are the key points highlighting how GCP aids organizations in achieving these objectives:

- **Tools and certifications**: GCP offers various tools and certifications to help enterprises meet regulatory demands.

- **Versatile security configurations**: Organizations can easily align with different regulatory frameworks through GCP's security options.

- **Data encryption**: Encryption of data at rest and in transit is fundamental to protecting sensitive information from unauthorized access.

- **Identity management**: Enhanced access control measures through identity management and logging capabilities allow for auditing and monitoring activities in the cloud.

- **Compliance certifications**: GCP's certifications (ISO, SOC, PCI-DSS) ensure compliance with international security standards, demonstrating Google's commitment to security.

- **Optimizing security configurations**: In addition to compliance, organizations should leverage GCP's strengths to tackle the unique challenges of multi-tenant and distributed environments.

Multi-tenant and distributed environment

GCP data centers host multiple customers on shared hardware. Ensuring your data remains isolated from others is both a *challenge* and an *opportunity*:

- **Challenge**: Guarantee strict data isolation despite shared infrastructure.
- **Opportunity**: Google's secure hardware (Titan chips), robust networking, and identity solutions provide strong built-in protections.

At the heart of Google Cloud's security infrastructure lies the Titan chip, a purpose-built hardware root of trust designed to safeguard server integrity and prevent unauthorized access. This chip plays a crucial role in establishing a secure foundation for Google's cloud services, ensuring that every layer of computing, from boot processes to data encryption, is built on a trusted hardware base. The following figure shows the Titan chip:

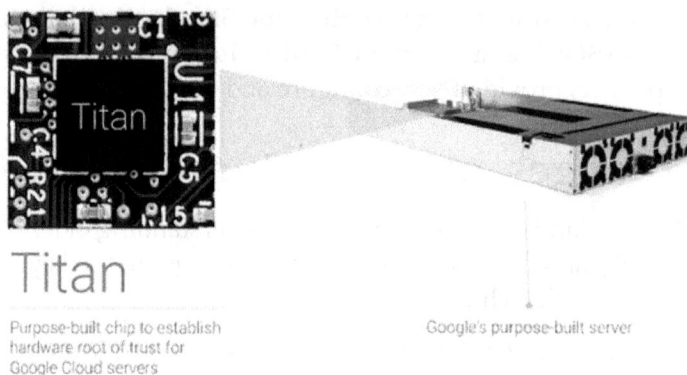

Titan

Purpose-built chip to establish
hardware root of trust for
Google Cloud servers

Google's purpose-built server

Figure 1.1: Photograph of Titan inside Google's purpose-built server

Greater access to advanced security tools

Adopting GCP grants your security team immediate access to Google's internal security frameworks:

- **Security Command Center (SCC)**, which includes central asset discovery, vulnerability scanning, and threat detection;
- **BeyondCorp,** Google's zero trust approach focusing on user and device context.
- **Customer-Managed Encryption Keys (CMEK)** for enhanced encryption key management control.

Cloud-native DevOps workflows

Rapid creation and teardown of workloads help and hinder security:

- **Continuous delivery**: Faster feature releases but risk of misconfigurations if neglected.

- **IaC (Terraform)**: Enforces consistent policies at scale.
- **DevSecOps**: Embeds security checks early in pipelines.

Cost and impact of security breach

Even minor incidents can escalate in the cloud, such as:

- **Data leakage:** Exposed customer data can lead to lawsuits, fines, and reputational harm.
- **Service interruptions:** Ransomware or malicious insiders may halt operations.
- **Regulatory fallout:** Non-compliance can result in heavy penalties.

Setting the tone for secure GCP deployment

The following information outlines key considerations for a secure and resilient GCP environment, focusing on efficient workload management, the consequences of a security breach, and the essential distinction between proactive and reactive security measures:

- **Creating and managing workloads efficiently:** Regarding GCP deployments, there are several advantages, such as:
  - **Continuous delivery**: Releases features faster but can lead to misconfigurations if not managed well.
  - **Infrastructure as Code (IaC) (Terraform):** Helps maintain consistent policies across large systems.
  - **DevSecOps**: Integrates security checks early in the development process.
- **Cost and effects of a security breach:** In terms of GCP deployments, there can be a significant impact on organizations, some of which extend to the following:
  - **Data leaks**: Exposed customer information can lead to lawsuits, fines, and damage to reputation.
  - **Service disruptions**: Ransomware or insider threats can stop operations unexpectedly.
  - **Regulatory consequences**: Failing to comply can result in significant penalties.
- **Proactive versus reactive security:** The following explains the key differences between proactive and reactive security in the context of GCP deployments:
  - **Proactive security**: Aims to stop incidents before they happen.
  - **Reactive security**: Focuses on identifying and responding to threats after they occur.

Proactive versus reactive security

While reactive security focuses on *detecting and responding* to threats *after* they occur, *proactive security* aims to *prevent* incidents *before* they happen. In *cloud environments*, these two approaches must work seamlessly together.

The following are proactive measures:

- **Vulnerability scanning**: Regularly scan your GCP resources, such as VMs, Kubernetes clusters, and storage buckets, for known issues or misconfigurations. Early identification and remediation ensure that weak points are addressed well before attackers can exploit them.

- **Patch management:** Keeps operating systems, third-party libraries, and container images up-to-date with the latest security patches. This minimizes the window for zero-day exploits and high-severity vulnerabilities.

- **IaC validation**: Policy as code frameworks (for example, OPA and Terraform validations) can enforce secure defaults in deployments and prevent insecure configurations from reaching production.

- **Continuous education**: Training developers and DevOps teams on secure coding and configuration best practices is crucial. A well-informed team is the most effective first line of defense.

The following are the reactive controls:

- **Intrusion detection and threat intelligence**: Real-time alerting on suspicious activities, such as abnormal network traffic or unauthorized role assignments, helps security teams swiftly contain breaches.

- **Incident response playbooks**: These clearly define workflows for escalation, evidence collection (logs, snapshots), and recovery. A well-rehearsed plan reduces the time it takes to contain and remediate incidents.

- **Real-time monitoring**: Tools such as SCC, Cloud Monitoring, and Cloud Logging, along with integrated SIEM solutions, continuously track resource usage and security events. Cloud Logging captures logs from various Google Cloud services, supporting *auditing, troubleshooting, and security analysis* while enabling alerting on suspicious patterns. Any unexpected spike, irregular login pattern, or misconfiguration triggers alerts for prompt investigation.

- **Post-incident reviews**: Analyzing breaches or near-misses thoroughly provides insights into root causes and long-term prevention strategies, enhancing proactive and reactive tactics.

The following is why both matter:

- **Proactive** strategies significantly reduce your attack surface by identifying vulnerabilities early and blocking potential intrusion pathways.

- **Reactive** measures ensure that when threats surface, despite proactive efforts, robust detection, containment, and recovery capabilities are ready to minimize their impact.

Striking the right *balance* between these two models in GCP is essential to *maintaining a resilient security posture* that safeguards data, applications, and business operations throughout the cloud lifecycle.

Given the shortened time to compromise, robust security from the start is paramount.

Culture of security

Securing cloud workloads involves more than deploying firewalls or enabling encryption. The *organizational culture* must also embrace and promote best practices at every level, from executive leadership to frontline developers and IT operators:

- **Training:** Fostering a culture of security should be a foundational priority. The following concepts focus on how enterprises should scale their training objectives:

  o **Shared responsibility**: Everyone who interacts with cloud environments, including DevOps engineers, application developers, and IT admins, plays a crucial role in security. Formal workshops, lunch-and-learn sessions, and targeted training modules can give each group the necessary knowledge.

  o **Security champions**: Identifying *security champions* within each team ensures that someone advocates for secure coding, design reviews, and vulnerability assessments. This fosters a positive feedback loop where teams learn from real examples and enhance their approach.

- **Policies:** To effectively instill a culture of security, consider the following essential strategies:

  o **Identity management**: Clear policies define how user identities, groups, and service accounts are created, managed, and decommissioned. This consistency helps prevent orphaned credentials and privileges.

  o **Data classification**: Defining tiers of data sensitivity (public, internal, confidential, or regulated) clarifies how data must be encrypted, logged, and accessed.

  o **Incident handling**: Pre-prepared playbooks, contact lists, and escalation paths facilitate swift and assured responses. Policies also promote a no-blame culture that encourages teams to report issues promptly.

- **Automation:** The following are some quick wins to set immediate security guardrails:

  o **IaC**: Tools like Terraform and Cloud Deployment Manager allow you to define security configurations once and then version, review, and replicate them. This eliminates manual drift and ensures repeatable, secure deployments.

- ○ **Continuous integration/continuous delivery (CI/CD)**: Incorporating security scanners (SAST, DAST) into Cloud Build or Jenkins pipelines can identify vulnerabilities early, long before production.

- ○ **Configuration management**: Automated scripts and policy as code frameworks, such as Open Policy Agent, further minimize human error while ensuring consistent enforcement throughout the entire cloud stack.

Organizations cultivate a strong security culture by integrating *training, policies, and automation* into daily operations. Instead of viewing security as a mere add-on, every technical and non-technical contributor embraces security as a collective mission, ensuring that GCP deployments are resilient and compliant over the long term.

Case studies in cloud security incidents

Implementing these quick wins by enforcing MFA, aligning IAM with least-privilege standards, and utilizing SCC's scanning capabilities will quickly reduce your cloud's attack surface and establish a security-focused tone for all future GCP workflows. The following are some examples of real-world incidents and the lessons learned from them:

- **Open storage buckets:** The misconfiguration left data in storage buckets publicly accessible.
  - ○ **Lesson**: Apply deny-by-default policies; never expose buckets publicly without a strong need/business case.

- **Accidental exposure of credentials:** Developers push secrets or keys to public Git repos.
  - ○ **Lesson**: Implement secrets management (Secret Manager) and code scanning for sensitive data.

- **DDoS attacks on public APIs:** Attackers flood endpoints, aiming for denial of service or inflated costs.
  - ○ **Lesson**: Use Cloud Armor, rate limiting, or external DDoS solutions if needed.

GCP versus other cloud providers

As more organizations move to the cloud, comparing the security approaches of major public cloud providers such as GCP, **Amazon Web Services** (**AWS**), and Microsoft Azure is essential. Each has its strengths, and understanding their unique features can help you make informed decisions about your cloud security strategy.

GCP takes a security-first approach with services like Cloud **Identity and Access Management** (**IAM**), which offers detailed RBAC. GCP's IAM roles include primitive, predefined, or custom roles and service accounts, ensuring flexibility and precision in managing permissions. GCP offers robust network controls through a **Virtual Private Cloud** (**VPC**) with subnets, routes, and firewall rules.

On the other hand, AWS provides IAM users, groups, roles, and policies, enabling detailed permission management. It also includes VPCs with security groups and subnets, ensuring secure resource segmentation. AWS's encryption capabilities are extensive, offering tools like the **Key Management Service (KMS)** for data protection.

Microsoft Azure has Azure **Active Directory (AD)** for identity management and **role-based access control (RBAC)** for permission management. Azure's virtual networks and security groups offer strong network isolation and segmentation. Azure also provides comprehensive encryption options, ensuring data security at rest and in transit.

While their implementations differ, all three providers share common security principles, such as least privilege and using virtual networks for resource isolation. By understanding these similarities and differences, organizations can better tailor their security practices to their chosen cloud platform and enhance their overall security posture.

Comparing security approaches

When assessing the security measures of major cloud providers like GCP, AWS, and Azure, it is essential to examine the unique features and strengths that each contributes. GCP emphasizes a security-first approach with detailed RBAC through its IAM services and robust network controls utilizing VPCs. However, AWS offers extensive encryption capabilities and granular permission management via IAM users, groups, roles, and policies. Meanwhile, Azure excels in identity management through Azure AD and provides strong network isolation using its virtual networks and network security groups. Understanding these distinct features enables organizations to make more informed decisions and tailor their security strategies to suit their cloud environments.

Common ground

All major public cloud providers, such as GCP, AWS, and Microsoft Azure, operate under a shared responsibility model. This framework clarifies which part of the provider's stack secures (for example, physical data centers, network infrastructure, hypervisors) and which aspects the user must ensure (for example, VM configurations, access policies, data encryption). While each cloud has its naming conventions and specialized services, they all offer core security capabilities:

- **IAM:** When exploring IAM across major cloud providers, one finds:

    o **Granular role-based controls**: Each provider offers fine-grained permissions. AWS provides IAM users, groups, roles, and policies; Azure features RBAC and Azure AD; GCP utilizes IAM roles (primitive, predefined, or custom) and service accounts.

    o **Principle of least privilege**: Best practices emphasize providing only the minimum necessary permissions in all cloud environments.

- **Network controls:** The network controls across all environments have capabilities that assist users in scaling their workloads:

  o **Virtual networks**: AWS utilizes VPCs, including subnets and security groups; Azure offers virtual networks and network security groups; and GCP provides VPCs with subnets, routes, and firewall rules.

  o **Segmentation and isolation**: Isolating resources (by project or subscription) is a universal strategy. Connectivity products (for example, load balancers and NAT gateways) secure inbound and outbound flows.

- **Encryption:** Encryption across all three providers for in-rest, in-transit, and KMS:

  o **Data at rest**: All three cloud providers encrypt stored data by default, typically using provider-managed keys. However, users can choose to have more control through KMS solutions: AWS KMS, Azure Key Vault, or Google Cloud KMS (CMEK).

  o **Data in transit**: TLS and SSL are the standard for communication with cloud services. Traffic within internal data centers is also commonly encrypted.

  o **KMS variants**: Each provider allows you to create and manage your encryption keys and oversee their lifecycle as needed.

By sharing these baseline security functionalities (IAM, network isolation, encryption), the big three clouds enable consistent security postures across multi-cloud or hybrid strategies, provided organizations correctly configure each platform's controls.

Key differentiators

Despite many similarities, each cloud differentiates itself with unique specialties, tools, and default governance approaches:

- **Scope of services:** While these shared capabilities provide a solid foundation for cloud security, each provider also offers unique advantages in terms of service scope and security tools:

  o **AWS** boasts the most extensive catalog of services, ranging from container orchestration (Amazon **Elastic Container Service (ECS)**, Amazon **Elastic Kubernetes Service (EKS)**) to niche offerings such as machine learning endpoints (SageMaker) and serverless databases. Its ecosystem can address nearly any workload, although it introduces complexity in service selection and governance.

  o **Azure** provides deep integration with Microsoft Office 365, Windows Server, and on-premises AD. It often appeals to enterprises heavily invested in the Microsoft stack that seek straightforward hybrid or identity bridging.

- o **GCP** is renowned for its *data analytics* offerings, such as BigQuery and Dataflow, machine learning capabilities like Vertex AI, and container orchestration with Google Kubernetes Engine. Additionally, Google's internal innovations, including Borg and Colossus, influence GCP's focus on high-performance computing, containers, and big data solutions.

- **Security tools:** In tailoring cloud security strategies, it is crucial to understand how each provider's security tools align with their unique services and governance frameworks:

  - o **GCP's SCC** centralizes asset discovery, vulnerability scanning, threat detection, and compliance checks. Its deep integration with GCP's data analytics heritage and optional advanced features, such as container threat detection, can streamline large-scale or container-driven environments.

  - o **The AWS Security Hub** aggregates findings from various AWS security services (GuardDuty and Inspector) into a unified dashboard. It tightly aligns with AWS's broad ecosystem, including CloudWatch and Config rules.

  - o **Azure Security Center** monitors Azure resources such as VMs, containers, and apps; it detects potential misconfigurations and integrates with Azure Sentinel for SIEM capabilities.

- **Implementation details:** When choosing a cloud provider, it is essential to consider the unique implementation details that can significantly impact governance, scalability, and security. Each provider offers a distinct approach to organizing and managing resources:

  - o **GCP's resource hierarchy (Org | Folder | Project):** It offers a *top-down* approach that simplifies the application of organization-level constraints through the Organization Policy Service and facilitates resource usage monitoring. This structure can *enhance* governance in large enterprises, especially in multi-department setups.

  - o **AWS's multi-account patterns**: It is common practice to separate environments using multiple AWS accounts or organizational units, necessitating cross-account roles or consolidated billing setups.

  - o **Azure's subscription and resource groups**: Azure organizes workloads into subscriptions under a tenant, while resource groups cluster related services. The interaction of RBAC with AD groups can vary in complexity depending on existing usage within the Microsoft ecosystem.

These differences matter as the organizations planning a multi-cloud or hybrid approach must understand each provider's unique strengths and default configurations. GCP might be a natural fit for big data or container-heavy environments; AWS might suit broad service coverage with robust ecosystem integration; and Azure seamlessly fits Microsoft-centric shops or Microsoft-focused or Microsoft-service heavy environments. Even purely GCP-based teams benefit from knowing how GCP's approach to identity, networking, and data security stands out, ultimately shaping a more tailored, secure deployment strategy.

GCP's global infrastructure and edge network

A core aspect of GCP security and performance is its global backbone, the massive, privately managed network that supports data transfers between GCP regions. By reducing dependence on the public internet, Google mitigates exposure to common internet-based risks (for example, eavesdropping and congestion-related slowdowns) while providing more consistent latency and robust capacity.

Private global fiber network

GCP's global infrastructure's robustness significantly enhances its security and performance capabilities, setting it apart from other cloud providers.

Google's investment in undersea cables and private fiber backbones is a testament to its commitment to maintaining a reliable and secure network. These strategic undersea cables, such as Dunant, Equiano, and Grace Hopper, connect continents and enable the management of vast bandwidth capacities.

- **Strategic undersea cables and backbone links:** The following explains how Google invests in its undersea and backbone link network:

  o **Undersea cables**: Google invests heavily in trans-oceanic routes (like Dunant, Equiano, and Grace Hopper) to link continents and manage enormous bandwidth.

  o **Private fiber backbones**: Even on land, Google's owned and leased fibre routes offer end-to-end control, enabling them to bypass the unpredictability of public internet routing and peering.

- **Reduced exposure:** This robust infrastructure not only supports high-performance data transfers but also significantly enhances security elements, making GCP a strong contender for enterprises with stringent security requirements:

  o **Controlled routing**: Since traffic between GCP data centers primarily travels on Google's internal network, the potential points of interception or attack on the public internet are significantly reduced.

  o **Encrypted inter-data center traffic**: Internal links generally employ encryption, reducing the risk of on-path adversaries.

- **High performance:** The seamless integration of security and performance across GCP's infrastructure is further evidenced by the following benefits:

  o **Optimised paths**: GCP can deliver consistent throughput and lower latency by dynamically directing traffic along less congested internal routes.

- o **Predictable quality**: Enterprises that rely on real-time services (for example, video streaming and financial transactions) experience fewer jitter-spikes and capacity bottlenecks.

- **Redundancy:** Additionally, Google's extensive network infrastructure provides several key advantages for enterprises seeking both performance and security:

  - o **Multiple circuits and cable systems**: Google uses parallel routes and backup links to ensure load balancing and failover.

  - o **Resilience to cable failures**: Automatic rerouting mitigates physical disruptions (storms, cable cuts), reducing potential downtime for regional or global workloads.

It matters for security because, compared to typical public internet routes, a more tightly controlled backbone reduces the risk of amplifying **distributed denial-of-service** (**DDoS**) attacks or man-in-the-middle attacks on inter-region traffic. When paired with encryption, this approach provides *performance* and *security* benefits for mission-critical applications.

Edge points of presence

GCP leverages strategic edge **points of presence** (**PoPs**) to deliver content and enhance security measures. These PoPs serve as localized gateways for content delivery, providing several advantages:

- **Local gateways for content delivery:** GCP leverages strategic edge PoPs to deliver content and enhance security measures efficiently. These PoPs serve as localized gateways for content delivery, providing several advantages:

  - o **Cloud Content Delivery Network (CDN)**: Distributed cache servers are located near major internet exchange points worldwide. This localizes content, reduces user latency, and minimizes the risk of malicious traffic traveling deep into GCP's network.

  - o **Load balancing**: Global load balancers can utilize these PoPs to terminate user connections near their geographic origin.

- **DDoS mitigation:** One of the most significant aspects of Google's infrastructure is its robust security measures, particularly in DDoS mitigation:

  - o **Cloud Armor**: Deployed at or near these PoPs, Cloud Armor filters high volumes of malicious traffic (such as DDoS floods) before it reaches core GCP resources (Compute Engine, GKE, etc.).

  - o **Scaling at the edge**: These PoPs manage substantial traffic volumes, enhancing defense systems and avoiding overload in the primary data centers.

It matters for security as by *absorbing or blocking* malicious traffic at the edges of PoPs, legitimate application resources stay protected from volumetric DDoS assaults or mass scanning attempts. This approach is crucial to GCP's layered defense strategy, which halts threats before they impact primary workloads.

Regional versus multi-regional deployments

Ensuring content's secure and efficient delivery is paramount in the rapidly evolving cloud computing landscape. To address these critical needs, GCP has developed an intricate network of edge PoPs:

1. **Regional deployments:** GCP leverages strategic edge PoPs to deliver content and enhance security measures efficiently. These PoPs serve as localized gateways for content delivery, providing several advantages:

   - **Per-region control**: You can choose specific regions (for example, us-east1, europe-west1) for resource placement, ensuring compliance with **data residency** or **latency** requirements.

   - **Regulatory compliance**: For instance, EU-based data may be stored within European regions to meet **GDPR** obligations, and healthcare workloads may reside in specific US East zones to ensure HIPAA compliance.

2. **Multi-regional services:** GCP optimizes for high availability and data security and offers multi-regional services designed to enhance resilience and performance across a wide geographic area:

   - **Redundancy and high availability**: GCP services, such as multi-regional Cloud Storage, replicate data across several regions within a wide geographic area. This guarantees minimal downtime, even if an entire region becomes unavailable.

   - **Global latency reduction**: Certain multi-regional configurations assist in distributing read and write loads, enhancing user experience globally.

It matters for security as you might prefer *regional* deployments for strict compliance (for example, storing data only within a single EU country) or *multi-regional* options for high availability and resilience. In both scenarios, *Google's global backbone* ensures that traffic stays on secure links, and *edge PoPs* protect data from attacks closer to user origins. Balancing compliance, cost, and user experience is crucial for designing a robust data placement strategy across GCP's extensive infrastructure.

Native security advantages of Google Cloud Platform

While all major cloud providers share core security concepts such as IAM, network isolation, and encryption, GCP differentiates itself with internally developed technologies that extend security from hardware components to advanced zero trust frameworks. These built-in capabilities can significantly bolster an organization's security posture when adequately leveraged.

Google-grade security

In the ever-evolving landscape of cloud computing, securing infrastructure and ensuring regulatory compliance are paramount. GCP stands out with its advanced security features and strategic deployment options. In the following, we explore the key components that fortify GCP's robust security framework:

- **Titan keys (Physical 2FA):** Titan keys provide a crucial physical layer of authentication, further bolstering GCP's security framework:

    o **Hardware root of trust**: Titan Security Keys provide a phishing-resistant MFA solution. By requiring the physical presence of a USB, **Near Field Communication (NFC)**, or Bluetooth token, attackers cannot compromise credentials by stealing passwords alone.

    o **Integration with GCP**: Administrators can require privileged users to use Titan Key, ensuring robust protection for tasks such as console logins and sensitive API interactions.

- **Titan M (pixel phones):** As organizations increasingly adopt cloud-based solutions, the importance of robust security mechanisms cannot be overstated. Among the many features of GCP, integrating advanced hardware and policy-based controls plays a significant role in safeguarding sensitive data and operations.

    o **Secure element on mobile**: The Titan M chip embedded in modern Pixel devices securely stores cryptographic keys, manages verified boot, and guarantees app integrity. This provides an additional layer of hardware-backed security for mobile endpoints that employees utilize.

    o **Use cases**: Corporate fleets of Pixel devices can integrate with Google Workspace or Cloud Identity policies to restrict device-based approvals or sign-ins and prevent unauthorized use.

- **Assured Workloads:** GCP offers a comprehensive security framework tailored to the diverse needs of modern enterprises, particularly those operating in highly regulated industries. Among the myriad features designed to enhance security and compliance, Assured Workloads stands out as a pivotal solution:

    o **Compliance-focused**: Assured Workloads enforces compliance mandates (such as FedRAMP, CJIS, and HIPAA) by restricting data locations, administrative access, and developer workflows to approved regions.

- **Policy enforcement**: By implementing organizational policies and specialized workloads, you can automatically ensure that only U.S. citizens oversee certain workloads or that data remains within a specific region, critical for regulated industries like government or healthcare.

It matters as these *Google-grade security features* minimize reliance on solely software-based defenses, providing hardware-backed trust (Titan) and compliance-based configurations (Assured Workloads). They diminish the risk of credential theft or region-based data law violations, allowing you to develop secure cloud solutions from the ground up.

Built-in zero trust BeyondCorp

In the ever-evolving cybersecurity landscape, robust solutions are imperative to protect sensitive data and maintain compliance. GCP offers a range of advanced security mechanisms designed to meet these needs:

- **Identity-Aware Proxy (IAP):** To enhance security within the GCP, one pivotal feature is the IAP, which offers several advantages over traditional security models:

  - **No VPN required**: Unlike traditional perimeter security models (VPN for *internal* applications), IAP is positioned before an application or service, necessitating that each request be authenticated and authorized at the application level.

  - **Fine-grained controls**: By checking user identity, device context, and other factors, IAP ensures that only legitimate, policy-compliant sessions are processed, minimizing lateral movement risks even within GCP.

- **Context-aware access:** Leveraging advanced features within GCP is essential for maintaining a robust security posture and ensuring continuous compliance. One critical component in achieving this is implementing context-aware access controls, which provide a dynamic and adaptive approach to security:

  - **Device, location, security posture**: BeyondCorp's zero trust approach continuously assesses whether a user's device complies with established security standards (for example, OS version and patches). It may also consider geo-location rules to increase compliance or mitigate threats.

  - **Adaptive policies**: Implement flexible rules (block read/write actions from unauthorized devices or provide limited read-only access if a device lacks an OS update).

It matters as the traditional perimeter defenses assume that everything inside a corporate network is *trusted*. BeyondCorp in GCP reverses this assumption, *treating all traffic as potentially hostile* unless verified. Such zero trust frameworks significantly reduce the impact of breaches, preventing compromised accounts or rogue actors from moving freely within your environment.

Security Command Center

The SCC in GCP is a comprehensive security management tool, helping organizations maintain a strong defensive posture against evolving threats. This centralized system offers several critical features:

- **Unified security dashboard:** To further streamline security operations and enhance visibility across your cloud infrastructure, GCP offers a unified security dashboard through its SCC:

  - **Asset discovery** automatically enumerates all your GCP resources, such as projects, VMs, and storage buckets, so you can see what is deployed across the organization.

  - **Vulnerability scanning identifies misconfigurations** (e.g., open firewall ports and overly permissive IAM) and flags potential exposures.

  - **Threat detection**: SCC Premium consolidates signals from container threat detection, Event Threat Detection, and more, emphasizing active attacks or suspicious behavior.

  - **Incident response and automation:** SCC integrates **Security Orchestration, Automation, and Response (SOAR)** capabilities, allowing teams to automatically trigger remediation workflows, quarantine suspicious resources, and route critical alerts to Slack, PagerDuty, or SOAR pipelines for rapid containment and response.

- **Deep ecosystem integration:** When choosing GCP as your cloud service provider, several strategic considerations can enhance your organization's efficiency and security posture. Some of the key advantages are:

  - **GCP services** integrate with Cloud Storage, Compute Engine, Kubernetes Engine, BigQuery, and more to assess security posture continuously.

  - **Alerting** generates actionable findings that can be incorporated into **Cloud Monitoring**, **Pub/Sub**, or SIEM solutions, allowing security teams to respond quickly.

This is important because SCC unifies various security signals under *a single pane of glass*. Instead of managing separate dashboards for network vulnerabilities, misconfigured buckets, or suspicious IAM changes, you gain a comprehensive view of your GCP environment. This minimizes blind spots and speeds up incident response, which are key benefits for any security-conscious organization.

Strategic considerations when choosing GCP

Leveraging GCP's robust security and integration features, organizations can significantly enhance their operational efficiency and security posture. By integrating the GCP with Google Workspace, businesses can streamline their user management and enforce consistent security policies across all their tools and platforms.

Integration with Google Workspace

When choosing GCP as your cloud service provider, several strategic considerations can enhance your organization's efficiency and security posture. One of the key advantages is:

- **Seamless user management and single sign-on (SSO):** By choosing GCP and integrating it with Google Workspace, organizations can benefit from centralized user management and enhanced security measures:

  - Organisations can manage users and permissions from a single administrative console by integrating GCP with Google Workspace (formerly G Suite). This enables employees to use the same credentials for Gmail, Drive, and other Workspace applications as they do for GCP services.

  - The integrated IAM framework and Google Workspace user directories enable centralized and consistent policy enforcement across all Google services.

- **Unified policy enforcement and security:** The following are the key advantages of integrating GCP with Google Workspace:

  - When Google Workspace connects to GCP, administrators can enforce consistent security policies, implement **multi-factor authentication** (**MFA**), and manage devices across productivity tools and cloud resources.

  - The *GCP Access Context Manager* can use attributes such as user location, device security status, or IP address to implement context-aware access policies across Workspace apps and GCP resources, enhancing your organization's security posture.

- **Streamlined collaboration and productivity:** Integrating GCP with Google Workspace provides several strategic advantages for organizations. The following are the key benefits that include:

  - Development and operations teams can collaborate in real-time on documents, spreadsheets, and presentations directly related to projects hosted in GCP. This reduces feedback loops and streamlines project management.

  - Existing Workspace groups (DevOps, Data Science, and Finance) can be directly mapped to IAM roles, ensuring that the right individuals can access the appropriate cloud resources without manual reconfiguration.

Cost and pricing model

Integrating GCP with Google Workspace offers a range of comprehensive benefits that enhance user management, security, collaboration, and cost-efficiency. In the following, we explore the key advantages and strategic implications of this powerful integration:

- **Flexible pricing options:** The following points discuss various flexible pricing options considered under the GCP benefits and pricing model:

  o **Sustained-use discounts**: GCP automatically offers discounts without upfront payments for workloads that operate for a substantial portion of the billing month. This is especially advantageous for continuous production systems.

  o **Committed use discounts**: By committing to a specific usage level (for example, CPU, memory) for a defined term, you can obtain significantly lower rates than on-demand pricing. This arrangement is ideal for predictable, long-term workloads like databases or core applications.

  o **Preemptible VMs** are transient compute instances that are available at a significant discount. They are well-suited for batch processing, data analytics, or fault-tolerant workloads that can endure occasional interruptions.

- **Cost as a security consideration:** Budget constraints can affect how organisations implement security controls:

  o By leveraging GCP's discounts and cost-optimization tools (such as Cloud Billing reports and budgets/alerts), organisations can balance the need for robust security with financial prudence. This may involve strategically determining which services (for example, threat intelligence feeds and advanced DDoS protection) should always be on rather than on demand.

- **Tools to manage and optimize spend:** There are several tools available to manage and optimize spend in GCP:

  o **Cloud billing and cost management**: GCP offers dashboards and detailed cost breakdowns by project, label, or resource. This visibility enables teams to identify and address cost anomalies swiftly.

  o **Recommendations through the recommender APIs**: GCP's intelligent recommendations can suggest rightsizing compute resources, eliminating unused IP addresses, or removing idle resources to optimize spending.

Specific regulatory compliance support

As a platform, Google also supports its customers with regulatory compliance by providing a range of compliance attestations and specialized compliance and data governance tools.

- **Broad compliance attestations:** The platform in itself has a host of compliance certifications:

    o GCP adheres to international and industry-specific standards as of August 2025, including **ISO 27001**, **SOC 1/2/3**, **PCI-DSS**, **HIPAA**, and **FedRAMP** for government workloads. These attestations confirm that GCP's physical and logical controls meet stringent security requirements.

    o These certifications can significantly improve an organization's compliance efforts, as much of the foundational infrastructure is already certified. Google also works on continuous-certification attestations.

- **Specialised compliance and data governance tools:** GCP also provides users with the correct set of governance tools to enable them with the necessary frameworks:

    o **Assured Workloads:** It allows organizations in highly regulated sectors (such as government, financial services, and healthcare) to configure their cloud environments to meet specific compliance requirements (for example, data residency and restricted administrator access). It automates guardrails to ensure workloads remain compliant throughout their lifecycle.

    o **Cloud Data Loss Prevention (DLP)** helps identify, classify, and manage sensitive information (such as PII and PCI) by scanning data at rest or in motion. It can also mask or redact sensitive fields before they are stored or shared.

    o **VPC Service Controls**: This system creates security perimeters around GCP resources to mitigate data exfiltration risks. It ensures that sensitive data remains in designated regions or within specific project boundaries to meet locality and privacy requirements.

- **Practical benefits for regulated industries:** Many customers can avoid the overhead of managing compliance certifications themselves, which accelerates their time to market or development cycles:

    o Organisations subject to GDPR, HIPAA, PCI-DSS, or other regulations can reduce overhead by leveraging GCP's built-in compliance features. Pre-configured templates and policy guidelines can accelerate the development and deployment of compliant workloads.

    o Audit, Access Transparency, and activity logs provide comprehensive reporting for internal governance and external auditors.

GCP shared responsibility model

Under GCP, Google and the customer share security and compliance responsibilities. Google secures and manages the core infrastructure, such as the physical data centers, networking, and hardware while customers are responsible for appropriately configuring and managing their applications, data, identity, and access controls, and any services they develop on GCP. This division of responsibilities clarifies who protects what, aiding customers in maintaining secure and compliant workloads in the cloud.

Defining shared responsibility

Shared responsibility in GCP means that Google secures and manages the underlying cloud infrastructure (physical data centers, hardware, and networking). At the same time, customers are responsible for securing their applications, data, and access controls on top of that infrastructure. This ensures both parties understand and fulfill their respective roles in maintaining security and compliance.

Core rationale to leverage shared responsibility model

In a traditional on-premises environment, organizations are responsible for end-to-end security, including physical facilities, networking, hardware, virtualization, operating systems, and application stacks. In contrast, with cloud services like GCP, Google manages security and operations for the underlying infrastructure, such as data centers, physical servers, networking hardware, and hypervisors, while customers control how they configure and secure their applications, data, and higher-level services:

- **Provider responsibilities**: Google Cloud is responsible for maintaining secure data centers, managing physical hardware, patching the host operating system, and ensuring the global infrastructure meets compliance standards.

- **Customer responsibilities**: You are responsible for configuring and securing all aspects above the infrastructure layer. This encompasses application logic, access control (IAM), network configurations (VPC/firewalls), data encryption policies, and logging or monitoring.

This division enables organizations to transfer essential security responsibilities to Google while maintaining precise control over their deployments.

The following are the benefits:

- **Clear role division**: The shared responsibility model clearly defines which elements are managed by Google Cloud and which responsibilities fall on customers. This clarity minimises confusion and ensures that critical tasks such as patching, backups, and access control are covered adequately.

- **Reduced on-prem overhead:** By letting Google Cloud manage physical security, hardware maintenance, and core infrastructure patching, organisations can lower operational overhead and concentrate on business-critical activities and innovation.

- **Flexible custom configurations:** Customers can define application-layer security, data encryption strategies, and network topologies. This control allows teams to tailor security measures to compliance requirements, risk profiles, and performance needs.

Layers of model

Google provides diverse services on its cloud platform to cater to various needs. These include traditional **Infrastructure-as-a-Service (IaaS)** options like Google Compute Engine, managed databases as part of its **Platform-as-a-Service (PaaS)** offerings, and **Software-as-a-Service (SaaS)** solutions. By implementing a clear division of responsibility between the customer and the provider, Google ensures that users can choose the level of management that best fits their requirements, making cloud computing accessible and efficient for everyone. The different layers of the model are as follows:

- **Physical infrastructure:** Google manages the hypervisor, while customers maintain secure configurations of virtual machines. The responsibilities are split as follows:

  o **Provider (Google Cloud) responsibility**: Security of data centers, including gates, guards, perimeter monitoring, surveillance systems, servers, networking cables, power supplies, and cooling systems.

  o **Customer involvement**: Generally minimal at this layer, except for comprehending compliance reports and validating the physical security posture for audits.

- **Virtualisation layer:** Google provides managed services, and customers securely configure them to meet operational and compliance needs. The responsibilities are split as follows:

  o **Provider (Google Cloud) responsibility**: Maintaining and updating the hypervisor, host OS, and container orchestration for services such as **Google Kubernetes Engine (GKE)**.

  o **Customer responsibility includes** patching guest operating systems within virtual machines, managing containers at the application level (container images, dependencies, libraries), and configuring container orchestration at the cluster level.

- **Service configurations:** The responsibilities for the service configurations are split as follows:

  o **Customer responsibility includes** configuring IAM, setting up firewall rules, enabling encryption at rest and in transit (KMS, CMEKs), defining key rotation policies, and enforcing network segmentation (VPC Service Controls).

  o **Provider (Google Cloud) support**: Tools (such as IAM, Cloud KMS, and SCC) suggest best practices for streamlining these configurations.

- **Applications and data:** Customers are fully responsible for securing their applications, encrypting data, and managing access controls. The responsibilities are split as follows:

  o **Customer responsibility**: Developing secure code, managing runtime security for workloads, securing APIs, handling data classification, overseeing ingestion and egress, adhering to data residency requirements, and ensuring proper logging.

o **Provider (Google Cloud) support**: Services such as Cloud Logging, Cloud Monitoring, Cloud DLP, and integrated scanning tools to facilitate the implementation of best practices. Refer to the following figure:

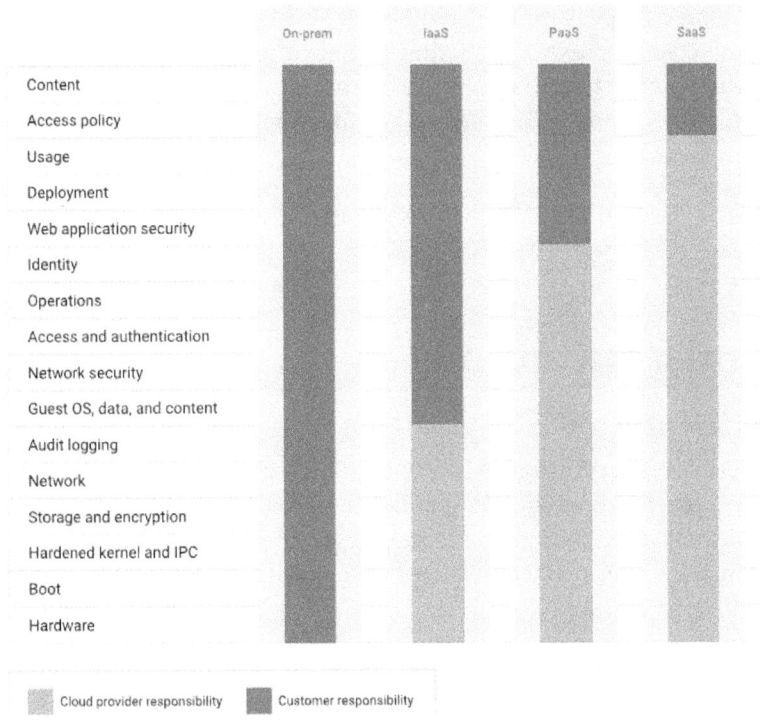

	On-prem	IaaS	PaaS	SaaS
Content				
Access policy				
Usage				
Deployment				
Web application security				
Identity				
Operations				
Access and authentication				
Network security				
Guest OS, data, and content				
Audit logging				
Network				
Storage and encryption				
Hardened kernel and IPC				
Boot				
Hardware				

Cloud provider responsibility   Customer responsibility

Figure 1.2: Google Cloud's shared security responsibility (IaaS)

Google has recently adopted a mindset of shared fate rather than shared responsibility. The premise is to implement a shared fate model for risk management in conjunction with customers. While Google has traditionally been an active partner in helping customers deploy and utilize Google Cloud, it aims to engage with customers from day one by supporting them in implementing security best practices and providing assurance that it will assist not only during cloud adoption but also if challenges arise and help is needed.

Impact on governance and compliance

- **The ownership structure:** Within GCP, organizations must clarify roles such as applying critical patches, running vulnerability scans, and maintaining encryption keys. For example, Google automatically patches host operating systems, but customers must patch guest OSs and dependencies within their containers or VMs.

- **Regulatory transparency:** The following is the shared responsibility regarding regulatory transparency between Google and customers:

    o Google publishes certifications and attestations (for example, ISO 27001, SOC 2, PCI DSS, HIPAA, and FedRAMP). These documents demonstrate that GCP's underlying infrastructure meets relevant compliance controls.

    o Customer responsibility involves ensuring that workloads are appropriately architected (for example, using the correct data residency or data encryption features) and that configurations align with internal policies and external regulations. Tools like *Assured Workloads* help establish guardrails for regulated workloads.

Since GCP addresses specific compliance layers, audits can be more streamlined; however, organisations must still show proper configurations and data handling at both the application and network layers.

Common misconceptions

The following are the misconceptions:

- **Google secures everything:** While Google secures its infrastructure and provides robust security tools, customers still retain ownership of the configuration and security of their applications, data, and higher-level services. For instance, failing to set up IAM roles properly can lead to vulnerabilities, even with a secure underlying infrastructure.

- **On-prem processes will not change:** Traditional on-premises security approaches (e.g., perimeter firewalls and manual patch cycles) may not easily translate to a cloud-native environment. GCP provides distributed services with ephemeral instances, making automation and policy as code vital for effective governance.

- **Encryption is set-and-forget**: Encrypting data at rest and during transit is crucial, but managing keys is equally essential. Automated key rotations, secure storage of encryption keys, and continuous validation are necessary to maintain strong encryption practices and meet compliance requirements.

Practical strategies to align responsibilities

Organizations can align responsibilities in GCP by clearly defining accountability for each security aspect, establishing robust access controls through IAM best practices, and automating key processes to maintain secure configurations. In addition, continuous monitoring and auditing of logs and configurations help detect potential threats early and ensure compliance, while ongoing education and training ensure team members stay updated on the latest security and operational best practices. The following are practical strategies to align these responsibilities:

- **Responsible, Accountable, Consulted, Informed (RACI) matrix:** By mapping out each layer of the shared responsibility model, you can establish who handles tasks such as patching, logging, incident response, encryption key management, and configuration updates. This ensures each team understands its role to prevent gaps or overlaps in coverage.

- **Automate best practices:** Automate the creation and configuration of cloud resources using **Infrastructure-as-Code** (**IaC**) tools such as Terraform and Deployment Manager. Implement policy as code (for example, using tools like Open Policy Agent and HashiCorp Sentinel) to enforce consistent security baselines across various environments.

- **Security baseline definition:** Document standard VPC configurations, including subnets, firewall rules, IAM roles and permissions, and encryption. One should also establish a baseline, which facilitates the consistent application of changes across projects and environments while reducing misconfigurations.

- **Continuous monitoring:** Utilise **SCC**, **Cloud Logging**, **Cloud Monitoring**, and third-party tools to identify anomalies, ensure compliance, and receive real-time alerts.

Key security features of GCP

GCP's *built-in security arsenal* includes IAM, VPC, default encryption, and SCC. They offer a *comprehensive, layered approach* to cloud security:

- **IAM**: Ensures the principle of least privilege by providing fine-grained access to users, service accounts, and groups.

- **VPC**: Offers logical isolation, firewall rules, and network controls to protect resources at the network layer.

- **Encryption defaults**: Automatically encrypts data at rest on Google-managed infrastructure, providing options for custom key management.

- **SCC**: This tool offers visibility into assets, vulnerabilities, and threats across your GCP environment, serving as a *single pane of glass* for cloud security operations.

By adopting these tools collectively, organizations can significantly reduce misconfigurations, unauthorized access, and data exposure risks.

Identity and Access Management

GCP IAM determines which identities (users, service accounts, or groups) can perform specific actions on designated resources. It adopts a zero trust philosophy by default: access is not granted until explicitly configured.

The following are the roles:

- **Primitive roles (owner, editor, viewer):** These are general permissions designed mainly for initial GCP use or small-scale projects. These roles may grant excessive access and are not ideal for production environments.

- **Predefined roles**: Specific roles for services with detailed permissions (for example, Compute Admin, Storage Object Viewer, BigQuery Data Editor, Cloud Functions Developer). Google updates and maintains these to align with evolving service functionalities, ensuring that permissions remain granular and aligned with the principle of least privilege.

- **Custom roles**: You can select permissions tailored to specific organizational needs. This flexibility helps uphold the principle of least privilege, granting only the permissions that a user or service account needs.

The following are the principles for service accounts:

- **Purpose**: Service accounts represent machine or application identities, allowing workloads such as VMs or containers to securely access other GCP services (e.g., using the Pub/Sub API).

- **Short-lived tokens**: GCP's OAuth2 token flow ensures that tokens are ephemeral, reducing the risk of compromised credentials.

- **Avoid JSON keys**: Storing or distributing JSON keys on disk can pose security risks. Use the built-in Google credential flow or Workload Identity Federation to eliminate long-lived credentials whenever feasible.

The following principles are of OS login:

- **Connecting SSH to IAM**: By enabling OS Login, organisations can control SSH access to virtual machines using IAM identities instead of having separate user accounts on each instance.

- **Centralised auditing**: SSH access logs can be linked to specific IAM accounts, simplifying the auditing process by identifying who accessed which VM, when, and from where.

The following are best practices for IAM implementation in GCP:

- Adopt the principle of *least privilege* and assign the most restricted roles possible to minimise lateral movement and accidental privilege escalation.

- Rotate or avoid using *long-lived credentials*; prefer ephemeral tokens or service account impersonation.

- Implement MFA and context-aware access (through Access Context Manager) for high-risk actions.

Virtual Private Cloud

VPC is GCP's foundational networking construct. It provides a logically isolated, software-defined network where you host your GCP resources (VMs, containers, and serverless services).

The following is the subnet architecture:

- **IP range planning**: Subnets can be regional or global (in the case of serverless VPC connectors). Planning IP address ranges carefully is essential to avoid collisions, particularly when employing hybrid connectivity options (for example, VPN or Cloud Interconnect).

- **Global versus regional subnets**: GCP provides global VPCs that enable the creation of subnets across various regions within a single VPC. This strategy can streamline cross-region networking, yet you might still require distinct subnets for improved segmentation or compliance needs.

The following are the firewall rules:

- **Deny-by-default**: GCP's firewall rules deny inbound connections from the internet unless explicitly permitted, significantly reducing the attack surface.

- **Explicitly allow traffic**: Administrators should define discrete rules for traffic that must be permitted (for example, SSH from an internal IP range, HTTPs from the Internet).

- **Ingress and Egress rules**: Refine both inbound and outbound access to manage data flow and minimize the risk of data exfiltration or lateral movement.

- **Target rules:** Firewall rules can specify target instances or service accounts, applying the rule only to the intended workloads within the VPC. This allows granular enforcement, ensuring that only designated resources are subject to specific firewall rules while others remain unaffected.

The following are the principles for implementing Shared VPCs:

- **Centralisation of network policy**: Shared VPC allows multiple projects to use a single, centrally managed VPC, making it easier for network and security teams to set consistent firewall rules and routing policies across the organization.

- **Separation of duties**: Resource owners manage resources in their projects, while a dedicated networking or security team can own the Shared VPC host project and ensure standardized network controls are enforced organization-wide.

The following are the best practices for implementing VPCs:

- Implement distinct subnets or projects for development, staging, and production to prevent accidental cross-environment access.

- Implement VPC Service Controls to enhance data exfiltration protection, particularly for sensitive information in services like BigQuery, Cloud Storage, or Pub/Sub.

- Regularly review firewall rules and automate the scanning for overly permissive rules or unnecessary open ports.

- **Use network tags:** Apply firewall rules to specific instances using network tags rather than applying them to all instances in a network. This allows precise control over which workloads are subject to specific security policies, improving both security posture and operational manageability.

Encryption defaults

GCP automatically implements *encryption* to safeguard data at-rest and in-transit, providing a strong security baseline for all services.

The following are the best practices for the data in-transit:

- **Automatic encryption**: All data stored in GCP (for example, Cloud Storage, Persistent Disks, BigQuery) is automatically encrypted with Google-managed keys, minimising risk in the event of physical media compromise.

- **CMEK**: For stricter compliance or internal key management policies, you can utilise Cloud KMS to retain control over encryption keys. You oversee key rotation, usage permissions, and lifecycle management while GCP handles the underlying encryption process.

The following are the best practices for key management:

- **SSL/TLS by default**: Communication between GCP services and clients is secured with TLS. For instance, accessing Cloud Storage or BigQuery endpoints from the public internet uses HTTPS.

- **Mutual TLS**: Advanced scenarios may require **mutual TLS (mTLS)** within a service mesh (for example, Istio on GKE) to authenticate the client and server, further securing internal microservices communication.

The following are the key management tips:

- **Automate key rotation:** Implement policies that comply with industry or regulatory standards.

- **Restrict key access**: Utilize IAM roles for Cloud KMS (e.g., CryptoKey Encrypter/ Decrypter) to control which users or services can access the keys.

- **Monitor essential usage logs**: Activate Cloud Logging for KMS to track how and when keys are accessed.

Security Command Center

SCC is a centralized dashboard that offers visibility into your GCP organisation's assets, vulnerabilities, and threats. Below are the capabilities SCC offers its consumers:

- **Asset discovery**: SCC automatically scans and catalogs GCP resources such as projects, buckets, and Compute Engine instances. This inventory identifies *rogue* assets or shadow IT and ensures that everything is under governance.

- **Vulnerability scanning:** Built-in Web Security Scanner can detect common vulnerabilities (e.g., cross-site scripting) in App Engine, GKE, or other web applications. SCC also surfaces issues like overly broad IAM roles, open firewall ports, or unencrypted storage and provides actionable remediation steps.

- **Threat detection:** SCC offers a host of features in the Premium tier for additional support for Threat Detection, such as:

    o **Premium features**: The upgraded tier (SCC Premium) provides real-time threat detection, **indicators of compromise** (**IoCs**), and curated threat intelligence directly in the SCC dashboard.

    o **Integration with SIEM**: SCC findings can be integrated into third-party **security information and event management** (**SIEM**) tools, providing a more comprehensive view of enterprise security.

- **Operational value:** SCC consolidates security intelligence from GCP services into a single console, simplifying complexity and accelerating response times. Also, findings can be setup to initiate Cloud Functions or Cloud Workflows for automated remediation steps, such as revoking permissions or quarantining instances.

Setting up your first secure GCP project

To set up your first GCP project, we should identify and avoid common pitfalls or mistakes:

- **Broad default permissions**: When GCP resources are created with overly permissive roles, malicious actors or accidental misconfigurations can easily cause security incidents.

- **Unmonitored resources**: New projects frequently neglect the logging, monitoring, and alerting processes, resulting in unnoticed intrusions or configuration drifts.

Some standard best practices that help set up the project are:

    o **Simplifying compliance:** Establishing a secure baseline makes it easier to comply with internal policies (for example, your company's security policy) and external requirements (for example, GDPR, PCI-DSS). A well-structured project architecture also prepares you for audits by ensuring consistent guardrails.

    o **Consistent security across environments:** Creating a consistent, secure project template guarantees that development, testing, and production environments adopt shared security practices. This consistency minimizes human error, accelerates new project launches, and builds stakeholder confidence.

Instructions for setting up a secure GCP project

When setting up a secure GCP project, create a well-structured project hierarchy and enable only essential APIs. Next, IAM roles and service accounts should be configured to enforce the principle of least privilege, network segmentation (VPCs and firewall rules) should be implemented, and logging and monitoring should be enabled to track activity. Finally, use encryption for data at rest and in transit, establish auditing with Cloud Audit Logs, and continuously scan and monitor resources for vulnerabilities to maintain a robust security posture. The following steps can be leveraged to set up the project:

1. **Create and organize the project:** To do so, *Access the Google Cloud Console*.

   You must sign in at **console.cloud.google.com** with an account that has permission to create new projects (for example, resource manager.projects.create).

2. **Choose the correct folder (if using an organization node):** From the project selector dropdown (top-left), pick the organization you want to create the project.

   If folders are set up, select the folder corresponding to the department or environment for which you are creating the project (for example, development, production, analytics).

3. **Create a new project: Follow these steps:**

   a. Click **New Project** (usually near the project selector).

   b. **Name** your project clearly (e.g., dev-ecommerce).

   c. Optionally set a **custom Project ID** or use the auto-generated one.

   d. Click **Create** to finalize.

Configure essential settings

One should start with basic settings to set up a secure GCP project. The following are the region selection and resource locations:

1. **Identify compliance requirements:**

   a. Check if your data must be stored in a particular geographic area (for example, the EU for GDPR or certain US regions for HIPAA).

   b. Know these requirements beforehand.

2. **Set default region (where applicable):**

   a. For services like Cloud Storage or BigQuery, choose a region close to your main user base *or* one that meets compliance.

   b. For example, use **us-central1** for North America or **europe-west1** for Europe.

Establish basic security guardrails

Start by setting up fundamental security measures to protect your GCP environment from the ground up.

The following is the IAM policy configuration:

1. **Properly configuring IAM policies:** It is crucial to enforce the principle of least privilege and maintain secure access control.

2. **Remove primitive roles:** To reduce unnecessary permissions and tighten security, broad Owner, Editor, or Viewer roles should be eliminated.

   a. Navigate to **IAM & Admin | IAM** in the Console.

   b. If any users or groups have an *Owner, Editor,* or *Viewer* at the project level, *remove or downgrade* them to more granular roles depending on your use-case.

3. **Assign appropriate roles:** Use specific IAM roles tailored to each user's responsibilities, minimizing overprivileged accounts:

   a. Add principals (users, groups, or service accounts) with roles that reflect their responsibilities. For example, a DevOps user might get **roles/compute.admin** to manage VMs but not broad **Editor** privileges.

   b. Click **Add**, enter the principal's email, select **+ Add Another Role** if multiple roles are needed, and click **Save**.

4. **Use groups for team access:** Manage permissions more efficiently by assigning roles to Google Groups rather than individuals. Instead of assigning roles to individuals, create or use existing Google Groups (**devops@company.com**) so that new or departing team members' group membership automatically grants or revokes permissions.

The following are the configurations of audit logs:

1. **Audit logs:** They provide crucial visibility into operations and security events, helping detect anomalies and meet compliance needs.

2. **Check current settings:** Verify that default logs are enabled to capture all critical activity:

   a. Go to **IAM & Admin | Audit Logs**.

   b. Ensure **Admin Activity** logs are **ON** (default).

3. **Enable Data Access logs:** Track read or write actions on sensitive resources to quickly spot unauthorized usage:

   a. Locate the services storing sensitive data (for example, BigQuery, Cloud Storage).

   b. Turn on **Data Access logs** for these services to track read or write operations.

4. **Export logs:** Store logs for long-term analysis and incident response by routing them to external storage:

   a. Navigate to **Logging** | **Logs Router.**

   b. For long-term analysis, create a sink to export logs to a **Cloud Storage** bucket, **BigQuery** dataset, or **Pub/Sub** topic.

   c. Name the sink (for example, export-audit-logs) | choose the destination | **Create Sink**.

The following are the steps to enable monitoring:

1. **Set up monitoring:** To monitor your system's health in real-time and detect performance or security issues early.

2. **Access Cloud Monitoring**: Begin by navigating to the Cloud Monitoring console to configure observability. Go to **Monitoring** in the Console (or via the top-left menu).

3. **Set up uptime checks:** Confirm your services are running by continuously checking their availability and performance:

   a. Under **Uptime Checks**, create a check for your public-facing services (e.g., your website's HTTPS endpoint).

   b. Provide a name, URL, protocol, and check frequency.

   c. Save the uptime check.

4. **Create alerting policies:** Define and receive instant notifications if critical metrics exceed acceptable thresholds:

   a. In the **Alerts** section, choose **Create Policy**.

   b. Define conditions (for example, CPU usage | 80% for five minutes).

   c. Specify notification channels (email, SMS, or Slack).

   d. Review and **Save**.

Network and resource setup

Properly segmenting networks and configuring resources helps contain threats and manage traffic securely. The following are the steps in creating a dedicated VPC:

1. **Go to VPC network**: To start your custom network setup, access the VPC Networks page in the GCP console. In the console, click **VPC network** | **VPC networks** | **Create VPC**.

2. **Plan IP ranges:** Use carefully chosen private IP address ranges to avoid overlaps with on-prem or other cloud networks.

a. Use unique RFC 1918 addresses (for example, 10. x.x.x, 192.168.x.x) for each subnet (RFC 1918 defines specific IPv4 address ranges reserved for private networks, which are not publicly routable on the internet).

b. Make sure they do not overlap with on-prem or other VPC networks.

3. **Restrict firewall rules:** Limit inbound and outbound network traffic to only necessary, reducing the attack surface:

a. Default inbound is typically *denied*.

b. Create explicit firewall rules to *allow* only trusted source IPs or subnets for ports you need (for example, *TCP 22* for SSH).

The following are the steps using OS login:

1. **Implement OS login:** To centralize authentication and streamline SSH access management.

2. **Enable OS login:** This option turns on OS Login at the project level, eliminating the need for manual SSH key distribution:

a. Go to **Compute Engine** | **Metadata** | **Enable OS Login**.

b. Add **enable-oslogin=TRUE** under **Project metadata** if not already present.

3. **Tie VM access to IAM**: Rely on IAM identities for SSH access to maintain a clear audit trail and revoke privileges easily. Now, each SSH login is associated with a user's IAM identity. No local SSH key management is needed.

The following are the steps to testing connectivity:

1. **Validate your network:** To set up by confirming that permitted connections work and blocked ones fail.

2. **Launch a test VM**: Spin up a small instance to check if firewall rules and VPC configurations are correct.

a. **Launch a test VM:** Create a small instance (for example, e2-micro) in the newly created subnet.

b. **Check the network tags:** Ensure the network tags match firewall rules for SSH (if applicable).

3. **Attempt SSH:** Test legitimate access paths and confirm untrusted IPs are denied:

a. SSH from a trusted IP range will confirm that access works.

b. Try using an *untrusted* IP or disable your VPN to ensure it is blocked.

4. **Verify logs**: Inspect log data to confirm that connections are permitted or rejected as intended. In **Logging** | **Logs Explorer**, check firewall or compute logs to confirm blocked or allowed connections.

Turning on Security Command Center

Leverage Google's built-in SCC to gain visibility into assets, detect threats, and remediate risks. The following are the steps for the basic configuration:

1. **Beginning**: Enabling SCC and assigning roles to relevant team members for foundational security coverage.

2. **Enable SCC:** Activate SCC organization-wide or at the project level to start continuous asset discovery and security scans:

    a. Navigate to **Security Command Center** in the Console.

    b. Click **Enable** at the **Organization** or project level (choose org-level for broader coverage).

    c. Wait for asset discovery and initial scans to complete.

5. **Assign security roles:** Provide the right permissions to users who will oversee findings and address vulnerabilities:

    a. Go to **IAM & Admin | IAM**.

    b. Grant **roles/securitycenter.admin** or **roles/securitycenter.findingseditor** to your security team or DevOps leads who will manage findings and scans.

The following are the steps to review findings:

1. **Regularly examine SCC:** Findings to address high-risk exposures and maintain a hardened environment promptly.

2. **Check the security dashboard**. Inspect the central view for flagged issues like open ports or excessive IAM grants:

    a. After SCC scans, view flagged issues (for example, open firewall ports, overly permissive IAM).

    b. Prioritise fixes based on severity.

3. **Remediate quickly**: To minimize potential breaches, prioritize critical vulnerabilities for immediate resolution. For critical issues, immediately update firewall rules or remove excessive IAM privileges.

4. **Continuous improvement:** Use SCC insights to refine policies, adopt better security measures, and enhance overall posture. Use ongoing SCC scans to plan future enhancements (for example, VPC Service Controls and restricted service accounts).

The following are the steps to expand threat detection:

1. **Scale your security:** Operations with advanced features and integrations for comprehensive threat management.

2. **Consider SCC Premium**: Upgrade for real-time threat analytics and deeper visibility into potential attacks. If you need real-time threat detection and advanced insights, opt for SCC Premium. Upgrade to the Premium tier if you need real-time threat detection and advanced insights.

3. **Integrate with external tools**: Streamline your incident response workflow by sending SCC findings to third-party platforms. Send SCC findings to Jira, PagerDuty, or SIEM/SOAR solutions for automated tracking and incident response workflows.

Compliance overview in Google Cloud Platform

Establishing a strong compliance foundation in GCP ensures that your organization meets all legal and regulatory obligations, fosters customer trust, and mitigates risk:

- **Regulatory requirements and enforcement:** The healthcare, finance, and government sectors demand rigorous compliance controls to safeguard sensitive data and maintain licensure. Failure to meet these standards can result in hefty penalties, legal actions, or loss of customer confidence:

  o Industries such as healthcare, finance, and the government enforce stringent data protection and privacy regulations. Failure to comply with these standards can result in significant fines, legal consequences, or the revocation of business licenses.

  o Non-compliance also undermines trust with customers and partners, which is particularly harmful in highly regulated sectors.

- **Risk management:** Aligning early with established compliance frameworks helps identify potential security gaps before they become major incidents:

  o Aligning with compliance frameworks proactively enables anticipation and mitigation of security and privacy risks.

  o Ongoing compliance can also serve as a competitive differentiator, reassuring customers and stakeholders that their data is handled responsibly.

- **Integrating compliance from the start:** Adding compliance late in a project often leads to expensive rework and potential service interruptions:

  o Retroactive or *bolt-on* compliance initiatives frequently result in expensive rework and possible service interruptions.

  o Considering compliance in initial architecture design allows organisations to streamline ongoing audits, cut implementation costs, and prevent last-minute surprises.

Major compliance standards

Different frameworks address specific security and privacy risks; understanding each is key to building a holistic compliance strategy:

- **HIPAA**: The focus and key requirements for HIPAA are as follows:

  - **Focus**: Protecting **Electronic Protected Health Information** (**ePHI**) in the U.S. healthcare system.

  - **Key requirements**: Access controls, audit trails, secure data transmission, and breach notifications.

- **PCI DSS**: The focus and key requirements for PCI-DSS are as follows:

  - **Focus**: Safeguarding cardholder data (credit or debit card information).

  - **Key requirements:** It includes firm access control, rest and transit, vulnerability scans, and regular penetration testing.

- **GDPR**: The focus and key requirements for GDPR are as follows:

  - **Focus**: EU personal data protection, dictating how organisations collect, store, and process **Personally Identifiable Information** (**PII**).

  - **Key requirements:** These include data minimisation, user consent, explicit disclosure of data usage, breach notifications within 72 hours, and the right to be forgotten.

- **ISO 27001 / SOC / FedRAMP:** The focus and key requirements for ISO 27001/SOC/ FedRAMP are as follows:

  - **ISO 27001**: International standard for **information security management systems** (**ISMS**).

  - **Service Organization Control** (**SOC**): Independent audits (SOC 1, 2, 3) validating controls over data processing and security.

  - **FedRAMP**: U.S. federal program ensuring cloud providers meet strict government security standards.

Each standard addresses specific risks, so an organisation could simultaneously be subject to multiple frameworks (for example, HIPAA and PCI-DSS for a healthcare provider accepting card payments).

Addressing compliance in GCP

Google Cloud offers specialized resources and tools to help businesses meet compliance requirements without hindering innovation. The following explains how GCP manages compliance:

- **Cloud compliance resource center:** GCP provides a centralised portal (Google Cloud Compliance) to access certification reports (SOC, ISO, PCI-DSS AOC), regulatory mappings, and other compliance documentation. This resource helps streamline audits by clearly showing how GCP meets various controls.

- **Data residency and resource management:** GCP can help with data residency with regional location and organizational policy management:

    o **Region selection**: GCP offers data centers in many regions, allowing you to store and process data where local regulations require.

    o **Organisational policies**: You can enforce rules that restrict where new projects or resources can be created (for example, only in europe-west1 for GDPR compliance).

- **GCP tools for compliance:** The following tools and services in GCP help attain compliance requirements at breadth:

    o **Cloud KMS/CMEK:** Manage encryption keys and enforce key rotation policies, which are essential for meeting strict encryption requirements.

    o **Access Transparency**: This feature provides near-real-time logs when Google support and engineering teams access your systems under specific conditions, addressing privacy and data sovereignty concerns.

    o **DLP**: Identifies, classifies, and optionally masks sensitive data (e.g., credit card numbers, PHI) to meet compliance mandates.

    o **Security Health Analytics:** Continuously assesses your GCP environment against security and compliance best practices, identifying misconfigurations and vulnerabilities while providing actionable remediation recommendations to strengthen compliance posture.

    o **SCC Premium:** Offers advanced threat detection, vulnerability scanning, and compliance posture management in one dashboard.

Building compliance into your architecture

Designing your cloud environment with compliance considerations from the outset prevents costly rework and security oversights:

- **Zero trust and least privilege:**

    o **Identity-based micro-segmentation**: Instead of relying solely on perimeter security, treat every interaction within your network as potentially risky. Enforce granular IAM policies, limiting access based on identity and context (for example, Access Context Manager).

- o **Service accounts**: To reduce the risk of unauthorized access to protected data, use short-lived tokens and avoid distributing static credentials.

- **Logging and monitoring:** Aggregating logs in BigQuery or secure buckets improves visibility and audit readiness. Proactive notifications and third-party tool integrations accelerate incident detection and response:

  - o **Centralize logs**: Export Cloud Logging data (Admin Activity, Data Access logs) to a secure bucket or BigQuery dataset. This approach simplifies audit trails and compliance reporting.

  - o **Alerts and SIEM Integration**: Set up Cloud Monitoring alerts for suspicious activity or anomalies and integrate with a SIEM solution if needed. This can expedite incident detection and response.

- **Network isolation and encryption:** *To isolate mission-critical data from less secure environments,* use separate VPCs and stringent firewall rules. Rely on default GCP encryption, with options like CMEK for stricter compliance mandates and mutual TLS for internal traffic:

  - o **Segmentation**: Place sensitive workloads in dedicated VPCs or subnets, using firewall rules to enforce the principle of least privilege at the network layer.

  - o **Encryption**: Rely on GCP's default encryption at rest and in transit. For sensitive data that must adhere to stricter policies, enable CMEK in Cloud KMS. Consider mTLS for internal service-to-service encryption.

Next steps for security and compliance

Ongoing vigilance is essential to remain compliant as threats evolve and regulatory landscapes change:

- **Periodic audits and assessments:** Schedule regular internal audits to ensure continuous alignment with compliance frameworks. Alternatively, bring in third-party auditors or partners to validate your security controls and identify blind spots.

- **Incident preparedness:** Have a detailed incident response plan, including breach notifications:

  - o **IR plan**: Develop a formal incident response plan detailing roles, communication channels, escalation paths, and containment steps.

  - o **Breach notifications**: Understand your legal obligations to notify customers or regulators about data breaches (for example, the GDPR's 72-hour rule).

- **Continuous compliance:** Prioritise creating compliance checks in the build pipeline to avoid any misses during the development or build stage of the software development or release lifecycle.

- o **Policy as code**: Use tools like Terraform or Cloud Deployment Manager to define and enforce infrastructure and policy configurations. This ensures changes are automatically tested and reviewed for compliance.

- o **Frequent checks**: To detect drift from approved configurations, implement automated scans and policy evaluations (via the SCC, third-party scanners, or custom scripts).

Final thoughts and next steps

Continuous improvement and strategic automation will keep your cloud environment secure, scalable, and compliant as your business evolves:

- **Implementation and automation**: Consider automating these best practices using IaC (Terraform, Deployment Manager) to ensure new projects inherit the same secure, compliant baseline.

- **Ongoing learning**: Stay updated with changes in GCP's services, new compliance offerings, and industry security trends.

- **Scaling your security posture**: As your organisation grows or new regulations emerge, plan to adopt advanced features like VPC Service Controls, BeyondCorp Enterprise, and custom threat intelligence integrations in SCC Premium.

Following the guidance outlined in these sections, which cover security fundamentals, compliance requirements, and GCP's specialised tools, you will be well-positioned to deploy and operate workloads securely while meeting your industry's stringent regulatory standards.

Complex made simple

The following anecdote illustrates a complex theme simply:

- **Landlord (Google Cloud):** Handles building structure, physical security, data center hardware, hypervisors, and global network redundancy.

- **Tenant (You)**: Lock your doors (configure IAM, firewall, encryption), secure personal items (data, applications), and maintain best practices (least privilege, rotating keys).

- **Key takeaway**: While the landlord ensures the building's infrastructure is safe, you are responsible for managing and protecting what is inside. In GCP, that means effectively leveraging built-in security features while carefully handling your configurations and data safeguards.

Conclusion

By exploring the significance of GCP security, comparing it with other cloud providers, understanding Google's shared responsibility model, and getting hands-on with core security features, you now have a solid understanding of how to establish a secure environment on Google Cloud. You have also reviewed the importance of meeting compliance requirements and how GCP's integrated tools can streamline that process. This knowledge lays the foundation for confidently securing workloads in the cloud, mitigating risks, and maintaining regulatory alignment.

In the next chapter, you will learn more about configuring IAM in Google Cloud.

Exercise

1. Create a new GCP project and assign a service account with minimal permissions to practice the principle of least privilege.

   Begin by logging into the Google Cloud console, selecting *New Project*, and providing a name. Next, navigate to **IAM & Admin | Service Accounts** to create a new service account (for example, **my-basic-service-account**). Assign it a minimal role, such as **Viewer**, which grants read-only access. Optionally, verify its limited scope by checking IAM and Admin | IAM to confirm the service account's Viewer role, or use Cloud Shell to test that only read operations are allowed.

   This hands-on activity demonstrates how to securely set up and control access in GCP, reinforcing best practices around least privilege.

Key takeaways

Summarizing best practices and GCP's distinct advantages helps solidify your path to robust, compliant cloud operations:

- **Security is foundational:** GCP's approach (zero trust, advanced threat detection) provides robust tools, but *your configurations* matter most. Continuously monitor and refine your security posture to guard against evolving threats.

- **GCP versus other providers:** All major clouds operate under a *shared responsibility* model; misconfigurations remain a top-risk user drive. GCP stands out with a *private global network, SCC, Titan hardware* (secure root of trust), and integrated zero trust concepts (BeyondCorp/BeyondProd).

- **Shared responsibility model:** Google secures the physical infrastructure and core services; **you** configure services, data, and code. A clear division of duties and responsibilities helps avoid compliance gaps and reduces operational overhead.

- **Key security features (IAM, VPC, Default Encryption, SCC):** They are as follows:

  o **IAM** enforces granular access control.

  o **VPC** isolates resources via software-defined networking and firewall rules.

  o **Default encryption** at rest, with options like CMEK for increased control.

  o **SCC** unifies asset discovery, vulnerability scanning, and threat detection.

- **Setting up your first secure GCP project:** In a nutshell, one should:

  o Remove broad default roles (Owner/Editor), configure audit logs, adopt OS Login, and enable SCC for continuous visibility.

  o Establish a strong baseline to minimise errors, ensuring smoother expansions into additional services or environments.

- **Compliance overview:** The following summarizes the overall GCP compliance posture:

  o GCP meets various regulations (HIPAA, PCI-DSS, GDPR, FedRAMP), but **you** must configure services correctly to maintain compliance.

  o **Cloud KMS**, **Access Transparency**, and **DLP** support data protection and auditing needs.

  o **Continuous compliance** (policy as code, regular assessments) adapts to evolving regulatory demands and keeps your environment secure.

References

1. https://www.accenture.com/us-en/services/cloud

2. https://services.google.com/fh/files/misc/google_security_wp.pdf

3. https://cloud.google.com/docs/security/infrastructure/design/resources/google_infrastructure_whitepaper_fa.pdf

4. https://services.google.com/fh/files/misc/072022_google_cloud_trust_whitepaper.pdf

5. https://cloud.google.com/docs/security/encryption-in-transit

6. https://cloud.google.com/blog/products/identity-security/titan-in-depth-security-in-plaintext

7. https://cloud.google.com/architecture/framework/security/shared-responsibility-shared-fate

Join our Discord space

Join our Discord workspace for latest updates, offers, tech happenings around the world, new releases, and sessions with the authors:

https://discord.bpbonline.com

CHAPTER 2

IAM and Access Control

Introduction

Identity and Access Management (**IAM**) is the foundation for all other security measures in the cloud. Whether you are running a small startup or overseeing a global enterprise, well-structured IAM policies dictate who can launch virtual machines, modify critical data, and manage sensitive resources.

This chapter examines the processes of creating and managing **Google Cloud Platform** (**GCP**) accounts, encompassing user and service accounts, groups, and external **identity providers** (**IdPs**). You will learn how roles and policies work together to ensure the specific permissions required by everyone or service, thereby reducing the risk of accidental or malicious misuse.

Beyond simply setting up accounts and roles, we will discuss how IAM integrates with GCP's hierarchical resource model, which includes the organization node, folders, and projects. Applying least privilege principles at each layer of the hierarchy ensures that security scales as your environment grows, automatic inheritance and structured policy enforcement maintain consistent yet adaptable permissions. We will also address auditing techniques using Cloud Audit Logs, best practices for managing and rotating service account keys, and the importance of aligning identity policies with compliance obligations such as HIPAA or PCI-DSS.

Structure

- Introduction to GCP IAM
- Importance of Identity and Access Management
- Identity and Access Management building blocks
- High-level use cases
- Core concepts of accounts, roles, and policies
- Cloud Identity vs. external identity providers
- Organizational policies and folder hierarchies
- Auditing and logging IAM changes
- Service accounts
- Case study to design least privilege role
- Complex made simple

Objectives

This chapter offers a comprehensive guide to managing identities, permissions, and organizational structures within the GCP. By mastering these IAM concepts, you will learn how to securely control access by assigning and auditing permissions to minimize the risk of unauthorized use, align your configurations with various regulatory and governance standards, and optimize operational efficiency by streamlining the interactions among teams, apps, and services.

By the end of this chapter, you will know how to quickly identify misconfigurations, such as overly broad role assignments or unmonitored service accounts and resolve them before they escalate. You will also understand how IAM connects with broader GCP security practices, including data security, network security, and monitoring through the Security Command Center, ensuring you maintain a comprehensive defence-in-depth strategy. Whether you aim to prevent unauthorized data access or to set up granular permissions for a global development team, mastering IAM is crucial for a robust and scalable security posture in Google Cloud.

Introduction to GCP IAM

Google Cloud IAM defines who can perform specific actions with your GCP resources. Assigning clearly defined roles (e.g., viewer, editor, custom roles) to the appropriate identities, whether human users or service accounts, ensures precise control over permissions and actions. This foundational approach helps organizations achieve least privilege, minimize misconfigurations, and comply with standards like GDPR, PCI-DSS, and HIPAA.

A well-designed IAM strategy streamlines operations by simplifying the process of granting, auditing, and revoking access. With GCP's resource hierarchy (organizations, folders, projects), you can inherit policies across multiple environments, maintain consistent security, and minimize risk. In short, effective IAM is the key to a robust, scalable, and compliant cloud deployment, empowering teams to innovate while safeguarding sensitive workloads.

Importance of Identity and Access Management

In any cloud environment, the ability to effectively manage who can do what serves as the first line of defense against data breaches, unauthorized resource usage, and compliance failures. In GCP, IAM defines which users, groups, or service accounts have specific roles and, thus, permissions across a tiered hierarchy of resources (organization nodes, folders, projects, and individual services). Properly configuring IAM is essential because even minor oversights can expose critical assets. Conversely, applying the principle of least privilege and enforcing consistent IAM policies at every level significantly improves your overall security posture. The following features in GCP specifically address IAM posture in the cloud:

- **Fine-grained control**: Instead of providing blanket permissions, IAM allows you to customize access so that each principal (user, group, or service account) has only the privileges essential to their role. This granular approach aligns seamlessly with the **zero trust** model, which maintains that no user or system can be fully trusted without explicit authorization.

- **Scalability and automation**: Centralized IAM policies ensure that your cloud environment remains manageable as projects increase and teams grow. Inheritance allows higher-level permissions to automatically apply to child resources, saving time and minimizing the risk of misconfiguration.

- **Integration with other GCP services**: IAM integrates with logging, monitoring, and alerting tools, enabling a unified view of who is doing what. Combine IAM with network controls (for example, VPC firewalls) and data security features (for example, data loss prevention) for a layered, defense-in-depth strategy. IAM also supports integration with external IdPs using **Identity Federation**, allowing users to authenticate with existing credentials (such as those from Azure AD or Okta) while managing authorization policies within GCP.

Tying IAM into broader GCP security model

IAM in GCP is more than just a mechanism to grant or deny resource access. It is a foundational layer that underpins other crucial security measures as follows:

- **Shared responsibility model**: Google secures the underlying infrastructure, but you control who can leverage that infrastructure and how. Misconfigured IAM can bypass even the strongest infrastructure protections.

- **Auditing and incident response**: IAM logs feed directly into Cloud Audit Logs and the Security Command Center, allowing you to track real-time role changes or suspicious actions. This visibility is paramount for quick incident detection and remediation.

- **Compliance-driven architecture**: With the right IAM design, you enforce role separation (for example, developers, testers, auditors) and automatically inherit those controls across projects, crucial for meeting regulatory standards.

When done correctly, IAM policies and roles connect seamlessly with the rest of GCP's security features, ensuring consistent, automated, and traceable enforcement across your entire cloud footprint.

The following figure, on a high level, shows the IAM overview in Google Cloud IAM:

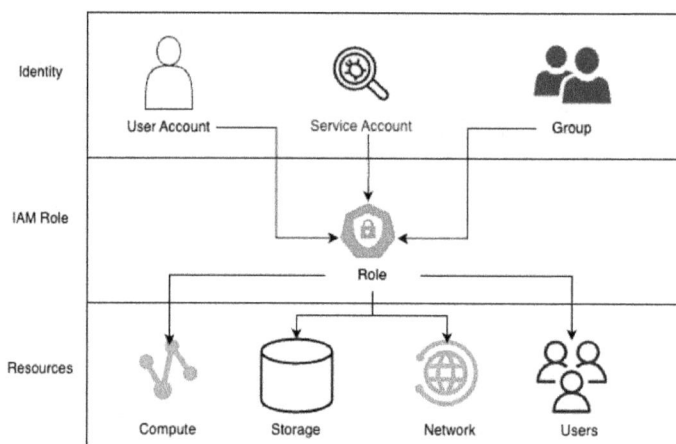

Figure 2.1: IAM overview

The above figure illustrates how IAM functions based on the principle of *who* (identity) has *what* access (role) to *which* resource. The principal entity is typically a user, group, or service account.

Common pitfalls of mismanaged permissions

Despite IAM's robust feature set, errors in design or daily operation can quickly undermine security as follows:

- **Excessive privileges:** Assigning broad roles, such as owner or editor, at the project level grants users near-unfettered control over resources. This can expose sensitive data, allow accidental changes to production settings, or open avenues for malicious activity. Additionally, a lack of **segregation of duties (SoD)**, where the same individual can deploy, modify, and delete critical resources, can increase the risk of insider threats or unintentional disruptions.

- **Lack of visibility:** Without comprehensive logging, it is difficult to pinpoint who performed a critical action, such as deleting a storage bucket or creating an external IP address. Poor visibility hampers both routine troubleshooting and formal incident response.

- **Unclear accountability:** Multiple applications sharing the same service account lead to confusion over which app performed which task. This ambiguity complicates audits and can stall investigations during security incidents.

- **Poorly defined policies:** Inconsistent or unclear IAM policies can lead to confusion among users and administrators, resulting in the misuse of permissions, gaps in enforcement, and non-compliance with security best practices.

Addressing these pitfalls requires regular access reviews, the principle of least privilege, clear SoD, and consistent naming conventions and policies. Tools like **Cloud Audit Logs** and **Policy Troubleshooter** can also help you track permission grants and denials, ensuring clarity in your environment.

Role of IAM in compliance and governance

IAM is central to demonstrating how your organization meets regulatory and governance needs, such as the **Health Insurance Portability and Accountability Act (HIPAA)** for healthcare data or the **Payment Card Industry Data Security Standard (PCI-DSS)** for payment card information. The following are key ways IAM supports compliance:

- **Enforced access controls**: Granular roles ensure only authorized personnel can handle specific data or resources. Role separation (for example, developer versus administrator) aligns with many compliance requirements that dictate the SoD.

- **Auditable trails**: IAM changes and resource accesses are logged in near real-time, creating a trustworthy audit trail. Regulators and internal auditors can verify that your environment enforces policies, captures user actions, and mitigates risks appropriately.

- **Scalable governance**: Implementing IAM policies at the organization or folder level enforces uniform controls across hundreds of projects. This level of centralized management simplifies compliance reporting, as there is no need to check each project individually for misconfigurations.

You decrease the need for manual oversight and simplify compliance by connecting IAM policies to well-defined governance rules while utilizing automated logging. This synergy enables your organization to scale confidently, assured that access controls remain secure, transparent, and compliant with regulatory standards.

Identity and Access Management building blocks

At its core, Google Cloud IAM consists of several essential elements that dictate how permissions are granted and enforced. The first element is *identity*, which can be a user, group, service account, or any other entity requiring access. Next are *roles*, which bundle specific permissions, allowing you to manage capabilities more easily than assigning permissions individually. Finally, *policies* bind these roles to identities at the appropriate resource level (organization, folder, or project), ensuring that only authorized entities can perform specified actions.

By understanding how these components interact, you can implement a least privilege strategy, granting each identity only the permissions required to fulfill its responsibilities and no more. This method not only enhances security but also simplifies audits and compliance checks. Essentially, the building blocks of IAM offer a structured, scalable way to align access controls with your organization's requirements and risk tolerance. The following sections discuss more about identity, resources, policies, and roles, which are the building blocks for IAM.

Identities and resources

In any GCP environment, understanding which identities can act upon which resources is crucial for establishing secure and organized access controls. In the following points, we will go through the key attributes of identities, resources and IAM policies:

- **Identities:** Identities in GCP define the *actors* that interact with your cloud resources: human users, automated services, or groups, collectively influencing how access is granted or restricted:

  - **User accounts**: Individuals signing in with a Google or Google Workspace account. It is commonly used for human users (employees, contractors) who interact with GCP via the console, **command-line interface (CLI)**, or **application programming interfaces (APIs)**.

  - **Service accounts**: Applications, workloads, and automation scripts use non-human identities. Service accounts help grant specific services the permissions they need, such as a **continuous integration/continuous deployment (CI/CD)** pipeline that needs to deploy new application versions.

  - **Groups**: Aggregate multiple user accounts (and possibly other groups). By assigning IAM roles to a group, you control all members' access in one step, reducing administrative overhead when members join or leave.

The following figure describes the fundamental relationship between an Identity, an IAM Role, and Resources from a User/Service account perspective:

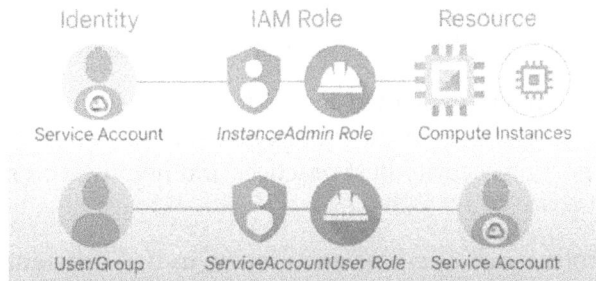

Figure 2.2: *Service account and resource in GCP*

- **Resources:** Resources encompass every object or service within GCP, from top-level organization structures to the most granular elements like storage buckets or Pub/Sub topics. Service accounts serve as non-human identities, enabling applications, services, or automation scripts to perform tasks without relying on human credentials:

  o **Organization node**: Represents your entire enterprise under one domain. You can apply organization-wide policies, such as requiring **multi-factor authentication** (**MFA**) or restricting which services can be used.

  o **Folders**: Logical containers for projects, often aligned to departments, teams, or environments (for example, dev, prod). Help you manage inheritance policies set at the folder level and apply to all projects within that folder.

  o **Projects**: The core entity in GCP groups resources such as compute engine instances, Cloud Storage buckets, and BigQuery datasets. It is typically used to isolate workloads, environments, or billing structures.

  o **Sub-resources**: More granular elements within a project, for example, specific buckets, individual Pub/Sub topics, or BigQuery tables. When you need fine-grained control, IAM roles can be assigned at this level (though it can become complex if overused).

- **IAM policy**: A document binding one or more *roles* to one or more *identities* on a specific resource:

  o **Core purpose**: This specifies who can do what on which resource. For example, *the DevOps group can view logs in this project*.

  o **Structure**: Generally, includes bindings (role | identity mappings) plus any conditions (optional) that must be met for the role to apply.

Policies specific to bindings of roles to identities

Policies (bindings of roles to identities) provide a structured way to define who can do what within your GCP environment. By selecting the right role type, such as *primitive, predefined, or custom*, and binding it to the correct identity, you ensure each user or service has the permissions required to perform their tasks securely and efficiently.

By thoughtfully choosing roles (explained in the following section), whether starting with predefined sets or designing custom ones, your policies will effectively bind these roles to the relevant identities, supporting security best practices and helping you meet organizational or regulatory requirements.

This policy file grants roles, such as editor and viewer, to two different members on a single project. The following sample code explains the creation of a policy file:

```
{
  "bindings": [
    {
      "role": "roles/editor",
      "members": [
        "user:alice@example.com"
      ]
    },
    {
      "role": "roles/viewer",
      "members": [
        "group:dev-team@example.com"
      ]
    }
  ],
  "etag": "BwWWja0Xkic="
}
```

In the code above:

- The user *alice@example.com* has the roles or editor role, granting broad permissions to create, update, or delete resources in the project.

- The dev-team group receives roles or viewers, allowing them read-only access to resources.

- The **etag** field is a concurrency control token automatically maintained by GCP (include it if you retrieved the policy from the project beforehand).

Roles

Roles help you define and manage the exact actions (permissions) that identities can perform on Google Cloud resources. By choosing the right role type, such as *primitive, predefined, or custom*, you can align permissions with specific job functions while minimizing unnecessary access:

- **Primitive roles:** These roles, such as owner, editor, and viewer, provide broad, project-wide permissions that often exceed the needs of most users:

  o **Types**: Owner, editor, and viewer.

  o **Scope**: Project-wide, offering very broad privileges.

    The downside is that you should grant far more permissions than most users need. The Editor alone can create, delete, or reconfigure almost anything in a project.

  o **Recommendation**: Avoid using primitive roles in production. Instead, use predefined or custom roles for more precise control and enhanced security.

- **Predefined roles**: Roles curated by Google that bundle permissions specific to particular services or functions (for example, *Storage Admin*, *Compute Viewer*, *BigQuery DataEditor*). In general, below are the benefits and some use cases of leveraging pre-defined roles:

  o **Benefits:** The key benefits of leveraging pre-defined roles are as follows:

    ▪ **Granularity**: More refined than primitive roles, limiting the *blast radius* if credentials are compromised.

    ▪ **Maintained by Google**: Automatically updated to include new permissions or services as GCP evolves.

  o **Use cases**: This is ideal for everyday tasks. For example, you could assign *Storage Object Admin* to a developer responsible for managing buckets or *Compute Admin* to someone spinning up VMs.

- **Custom roles:** Grant the permissions necessary for unique or specialized job functions. Utilizing Custom Roles offers its own distinct set of advantages and disadvantages:

  o **Advantages**: GCP custom roles offer a clear method for managing access by:

    ▪ **Least privilege alignment**: Include only necessary permissions; no more, no less.

    ▪ **Fine-grained control**: Perfect for internal tools or specialized tasks that do not fit Google's predefined roles.

  o **Disadvantages**: GCP custom roles also have certain downsides, such as:

    ▪ **Ongoing maintenance**: To remain relevant, manually update the custom role as services evolve or new permissions become available.

    ▪ **Requires detailed knowledge**: Creating effective custom roles demands understanding the specific permissions each resource or API requires.

By adequately structuring identities, resources, and roles and binding them through thoughtfully managed IAM policies, you ensure that users and services operate securely within GCP. Implementing the least privilege across this model is a powerful way to reduce risk, maintain compliance, and confidently scale your cloud environment. The following figure shows how an allow policy is structured:

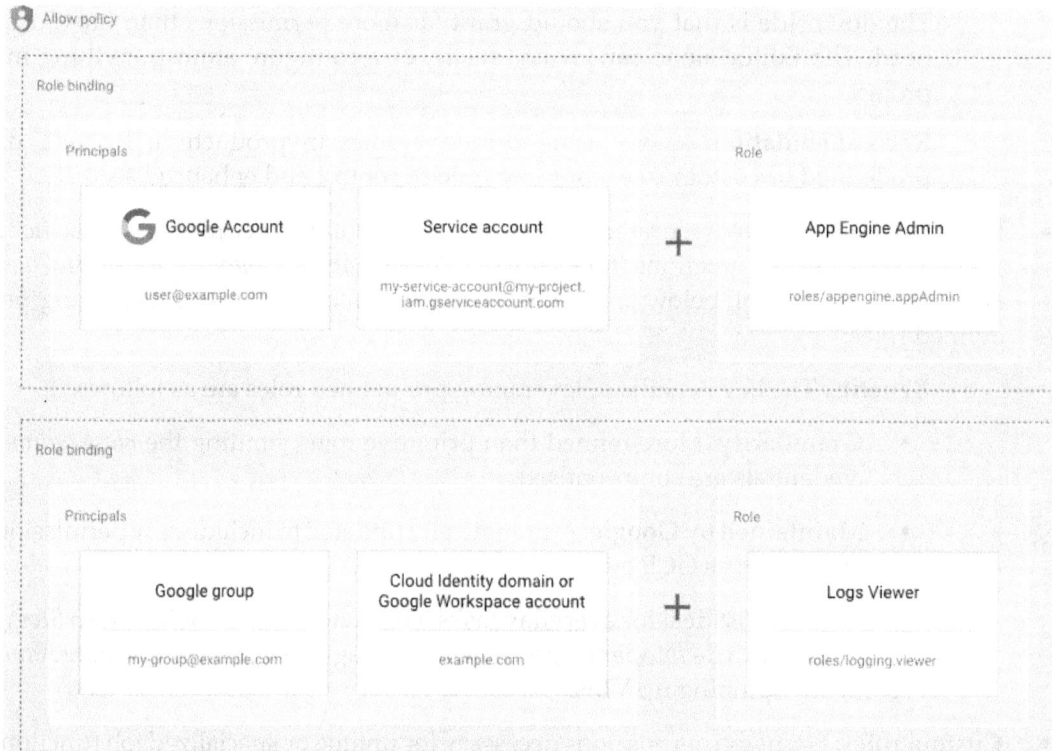

Figure 2.3: Standard role binding to role and users

High-level use cases

These examples illustrate common IAM scenarios, showcasing how roles and permissions can be adapted to various stages and responsibilities within a GCP environment. Some use cases for leveraging GCP IAM include the following:

- **Granting developer access**: Custom roles with just enough privilege to view logs, deploy code, and configure specific services.

- **Restricting production access**: In production environments, minimal or read-only access is available for developers or testers.

- **Delegating admin tasks**: Operations manages VM instances, analytics manages BigQuery, and security manages logs. This is a structured separation of duties.

Core concepts of accounts, roles, and policies

In Google Cloud IAM, *accounts* define the identities that interact with resources. These can be user accounts for real individuals, service accounts for applications or automation scripts, and even group accounts that bundle multiple users. Each account requires the appropriate level of access to perform tasks safely, whether it is spinning up new instances, reading data from Cloud Storage, or deploying applications.

Roles act as a packaging mechanism for permissions, grouping related capabilities (e.g., viewing logs, writing to databases) into manageable sets. Instead of assigning discrete permissions to each account, which can be error-prone and hard to scale, GCP IAM links these roles to identities through *policies*. A policy connects the role(s) to a specific account on a particular resource (like an organization, folder, or project). This structured approach helps ensure clarity and consistency, allowing you to apply least privilege principles, simplify audits, and quickly adapt to changes in team structures or security needs.

Types of Google Cloud Platform accounts

When managing identities in GCP, understanding the types of accounts available is essential for building a secure, efficient, and compliant environment. Each account type, whether a user account, a service account, or a group, serves a unique purpose, aligning different identities with the specific permissions they require. By choosing the right account type for each use case, you can maintain a clear separation of duties, minimize the blast radius of potential breaches, and streamline daily operations ranging from collaboration to automation. The following are the different types of platform accounts in use:

- **Google accounts are owned** by real individuals who authenticate with their Google sign-in credentials. The following describes their usage, characteristics, and best practices:
  - **Usage**: Tied to individual users, typically with personal Gmail or email address tied to a Google Workspace.
  - **Characteristics**: Specific traits of such Google accounts include:
    - It is ideal for human operators interacting with GCP through the console, APIs, or CLI.
    - Often implemented with MFA to enhance security (Recommended).
    - It can be managed centrally within an organization using Google Workspace or Cloud Identity.
  - **Best practices:** From a usability standpoint, one should follow established best practices, such as:
    - Promote robust password policies and implement MFA for all administrative roles.

- Assign precise IAM roles suited to each user's responsibilities instead of relying on broad privileges.

- **Service accounts, or** non-human credentials, are utilized by applications, **virtual machines (VMs)**, or automated scripts. The following outlines their usage, characteristics, and best practices:

  - **Usage**: Non-human identities used by applications, microservices, or automation scripts (for example, CI/CD pipelines).

  - **Characteristics**: Specific traits of these service accounts include:

    - They hold their credentials, often in JSON key files, though the best practice is to avoid static keys and instead use Workload Identity Federation or IAM-based keyless authentication.

    - They are crucial for enabling automated tasks that require GCP API access without tying the process to a human account.

  - **Best practices:** From a usability standpoint, one should follow established best practices such as:

    - Apply for *least privilege* roles, grant only the permissions the application needs.

    - Rotate keys regularly if you must use key-based authentication or prefer short-lived tokens with Workload Identity for better security.

    - Use separate service accounts for each application or environment to simplify auditing and limit the blast radius of potential compromises.

- **Cloud Identity or Google Workspace accounts:** Logical collections of users that enable you to assign roles in a single step and manage access at scale. The following outlines their usage, characteristics, and best practices:

  - **Usage**: A centralized directory solution providing an organization with user, group, and device management.

  - **Characteristics**: The specific traits of these workspace accounts include:

    - Ideal for syncing with on-prem **Active Directory (AD)** or other IdPs, ensuring one authoritative source for user info.

    - Integrates seamlessly with GCP to unify identity management across all Google services and beyond.

  - **Best practice**: Use groups wherever possible instead of assigning roles directly to individual users. This simplifies lifecycle management for users, groups and roles (for example, when employees join or leave).

Identity and Access Management roles and policies

Roles and policies in Google Cloud IAM act as the driving force behind secure, least privilege configurations. By consolidating permissions into logically defined roles and binding them to specific identities through policies, you can effectively enforce who is authorized to perform critical operations, and just as importantly, who is not. This structured approach simplifies ongoing maintenance, promotes compliance, and ensures that only the appropriate entities can access or modify your cloud resources. The following are the various types of roles supported by GCP:

- **Primitive roles** in Google Cloud are general, project-level permissions that represent some of the earliest types of IAM roles. Details of these roles are as follows:

    o **Types**: Owner, editor, and viewer.

    o **Scope**: Extensive privileges at the project level.

    o **Downside**: There are certain disadvantages of such roles, such as:

        ▪ Elevated risk if these roles are compromised.

        ▪ It is hard to enforce the principle of least privilege.

    o **Recommendation**: Avoid them in production; use them only for quick testing in non-critical environments or small proof-of-concepts.

- **Predefined roles** in Google Cloud consist of curated sets of permissions designed for specific services or job functions. They provide a more granular alternative to the older, broader primitive roles (owner, editor, viewer). The details of these roles are as follows:

    o **Definition**: Roles curated by Google to match common use cases or services (for example, *Storage Admin, BigQuery Admin*).

    o **Benefits**: These roles offer benefits such as:

        ▪ More granular than primitive roles, reducing the scope of potential damage if compromised.

        ▪ Automatically updated by Google to include new service features.

    o **Use cases**:

        ▪ Assign *Compute Admin* to DevOps teams managing VM lifecycles.

        ▪ Give data scientists *BigQuery DataEditor* for queries and dataset updates without oversharing other project resources.

- **Custom roles** in Google Cloud enable you to define a specific set of permissions tailored to unique job functions or advanced security needs. Unlike predefined roles, which are created and updated by Google, custom roles are entirely managed by you. This provides fine-grained control, as you can incorporate only the permissions that your team or application requires (for instance, granting just enough access to a CI/CD system). However, this flexibility also brings added maintenance: you must update custom roles as services evolve to ensure compatibility with new or modified permissions. Details of these roles are as follows:

- o **Definition**: Build your role by selecting only the necessary permissions from a list of APIs and services.

- o **Advantages**: These roles offer benefits such as:

  - ▪ Maximally precise permissions, firmly aligning with least privilege principles.

  - ▪ Perfect for specialised tasks that do not fit a predefined role.

- o **Maintenance:** Conversely, these roles necessitate extra maintenance tasks such as:

  - ▪ Requires occasional updates as GCP adds or changes permissions.

  - ▪ Demands more profound familiarity with specific APIs and services.

The following are the policies:

- **Binding**: A policy document assigns *roles* to one or more *identities* (users, service accounts, or groups) at the chosen resource level (org, folder, project, or sub-resource). This process allows you to determine how to assign roles to principals so they can act on resources. The binding can exist at the resource level (though not all resources may support this), the project level, the folder level, or the organization node level. Understanding the appropriate binding level is crucial for achieving the least privileged access while meeting business goals. The higher in the Google Cloud resource hierarchy the binding is established, the greater its impact on downstream resources such as folders, projects, and actual workloads.

- **Inheritance**: Policies set at higher levels (organization or folders) automatically apply to child projects and resources unless explicitly overridden. This can significantly reduce repeated work, but a single misconfiguration at the organization level can unintentionally grant broad permissions.

Hierarchical resource model

Understanding Google Cloud's hierarchical resource structure is essential for streamlining security, compliance, and cost management. By organizing resources into **organizations**, **folders**, and **projects**, you can consistently apply IAM policies across multiple environments, ensuring that higher-level rules automatically propagate to lower-level assets. This approach not only simplifies governance but also helps maintain clear boundaries between departments, teams, and workloads within the same cloud environment. The different hierarchical models include:

- **Organization node:** As the pinnacle of the GCP resource hierarchy, the organization node provides central oversight of all child resources within your domain (for example, company.com), allowing you to establish overarching policies that cascade down to folders, projects, and ultimately sub-resources. The following section explains the purpose, control, and benefits of utilizing an organization node:

  o **Purpose**: The top of the hierarchy represents your domain (for example, company.com).

  o **Control**: This lets you enforce org-wide policies, such as mandatory 2FA or limiting which APIs can be enabled.

  o **Benefit**: Centralized oversight of all child resources.

- **Folders:** Under the organization node, folders serve as logical containers, frequently aligned with departments, cost centers, or environments, that systematically group projects, inheriting or overriding policies to align with operational needs. The usage and inheritance in folders:

  o **Usage**: Logical structure beneath the organization node, commonly matched to departments, cost centers, or production stages (dev, staging, prod).

  o **Inheritance**: IAM policies set on a folder apply automatically to all projects within it unless overridden at a lower level.

- **Projects** are the foundational boundary for GCP resources, such as Compute Engine VMs, Cloud Storage buckets, and BigQuery datasets, serving as self-contained environments with distinct billing and unique permissions. The purpose, separation, and billing for projects are outlined in the following:

  o **Purpose**: Containers for all GCP resources (for example, Compute Engine VMs, Cloud Storage buckets, BigQuery datasets).

  o **Separation**: Projects often correspond to different apps, microservices, or environment tiers.

  o **Billing**: Each project has its billing settings, simplifying cost tracking and chargeback.

- **Sub-resources:** At the most granular level, **sub-resources**, such as individual BigQuery tables, Pub/Sub topics, or specific Cloud Storage objects, allow for fine-tuned access controls, although excessive granularity can complicate management. Some examples and specifics of fine-grained permissions are as follows:

  o **Examples**: Individual BigQuery tables, specific Pub/Sub topics, or single GCS buckets.

  o **Fine-grained permissions**: Apply custom roles or specific predefined roles at this level only when necessary.

○ **Caution**: Overly granular assignments can become cumbersome to manage. Aim for a balance between security needs and manageability.

The following figure is an example of a Google Cloud resource hierarchy:

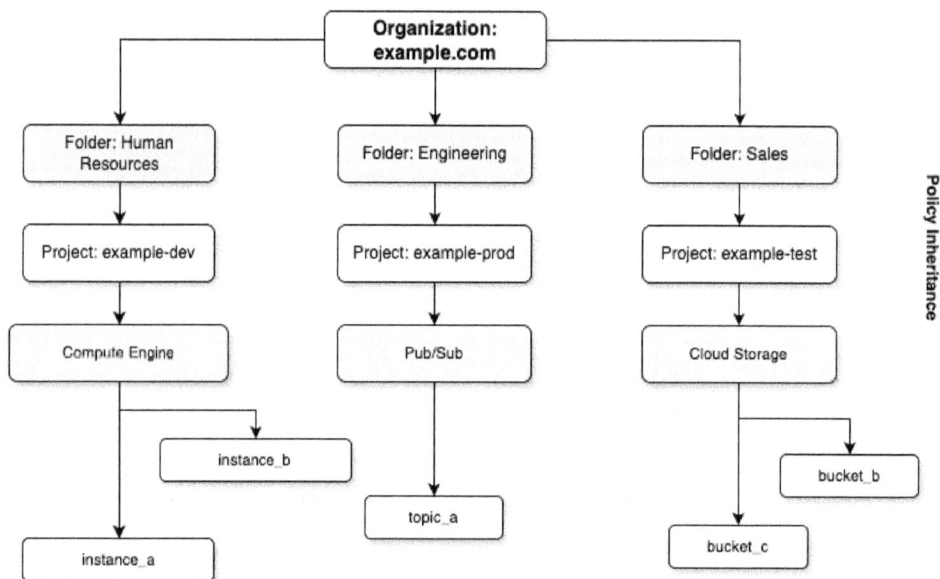

Figure 2.4: Policy inheritance

Policy evaluation

This section explores how GCP IAM processes requests, determining whether an action is allowed or denied based on hierarchical rules. By understanding policy evaluation, you will clearly see how permissions flow from the organization node down to individual resources. These are implemented as follows:

- **Allow-versus-deny:** In GCP, the default stance is *deny unless explicitly allowed*. This heading highlights the implications of that default deny posture, explaining why any request without a matching allow policy is blocked. These serve as:

    ○ **Default deny**: If no policy explicitly *allows* an action, it is blocked.

    ○ **Evaluation order**: GCP checks are performed from the organization to the resource level. The request proceeds when an ALLOW is found for the action; otherwise, it is denied.

- **Policy Troubleshooter:** When **Permission Denied** errors occur, GCP's Policy Troubleshooter identifies missing roles or conflicting settings. Learning to use this built-in tool saves time, eliminates guesswork, and ensures your IAM setup aligns with least privilege principles. Below is a high-level explanation of the troubleshooter:

o **Purpose**: A built-in tool for diagnosing Permission Denied errors.

o **Functionality:** The standard set of features built around the Policy Troubleshooter:

- Explains which permissions or roles are missing.

- Verifies that policies are correctly assigning (or restricting) access.

o **Value**: It saves time and reduces guesswork, ensuring your IAM setup supports the least privilege while granting the required permissions.

Cloud Identity versus external identity providers

When selecting an identity platform for your Google Cloud environment, you are essentially choosing the system that manages *authentication* (who you are) and *authorization* (what you can do). **Cloud Identity** - Google's native identity management service, enables you to create and manage users, groups, and service accounts without depending on external solutions. It provides support for **single sign-on** (**SSO**), MFA, and user lifecycle management (e.g., Provisioning and Deprovisioning), all within the Google ecosystem. This is often ideal for organizations looking for a comprehensive approach to directory services and Google Cloud IAM, especially if they do not already have a complex on-premises identity infrastructure.

On the other hand, many enterprises already utilize **external IdPs** such as Okta, Azure AD, or other SAML/OIDC-based solutions. By federating these providers with Google Cloud, you centralize credentials and policies in a single, trusted directory, allowing users to access GCP resources seamlessly with their existing corporate logins. This integration ensures that accounts, passwords, and security policies remain consistent across on-prem and cloud systems, enhancing security and reducing administrative overhead. Whether you choose Cloud Identity alone or federate with an external IdP, the goal remains the same: to enforce unified authentication standards, minimize credential sprawl, and streamline how both human and machine identities authenticate to your GCP environment.

Cloud Identity fundamentals

When setting up user directories and identity management for Google Cloud, Cloud Identity provides a native approach that can function in standalone mode or integrate seamlessly with Google Workspace. Understanding both deployment models, along with the additional security layers available. This helps you customize access control precisely to your organization's needs. Below is a detailed overview of these:

- **Standalone or integrated:** Whether you require a simple user directory or desire an all-in-one platform that includes email and collaboration tools, Cloud Identity can be deployed in two main ways:

- o **Standalone (Essential directory):** A streamlined option for organizations that require an essential user directory without the complete Google Workspace apps (Gmail, Docs, etc.). The following are the generic features, along with the pros and cons of utilizing the standalone option:

  - **Features**: It provides core identity services, such as managing users, groups, and security settings, and it integrates directly with GCP IAM policies.

  - **Pros and cons**: It has a simple setup but fewer collaboration tools than Google Workspace.

- o **Integrated with Google Workspace (Advanced security features):** If your organization already uses Google Workspace (email, Drive, etc.), Cloud Identity can be enabled seamlessly. Below are the features, pros, and cons:

  - **Features**: Advanced device management, context-aware access, and robust security configurations.

  - **Pros and cons**: Tighter integration with GCP and Google Workspace, but requires additional licensing or subscriptions for some features.

- **Enabling MFA and device policies:** Beyond basic account creation, Cloud Identity supports additional protective measures, like MFA and device posture checks, to reduce unauthorized access and align with a zero trust posture:

  - o **MFA:** Enforce MFA (such as Google Prompt, security keys, or time-based one-time passwords) for high-privilege accounts. MFA significantly reduces the risk of account takeovers.

  - o **Device posture checks:** Integrate device checks (such as OS versions, encryption status, etc.) with MFA to ensure that only secure, corporate-approved devices can access GCP resources. This supports context-aware access by blocking sign-ins from devices that do not meet security criteria.

Federating identities

Integrating an external IdP with Google Cloud allows your organization to unify authentication and user management, whether you utilize on-premises directories or SaaS-based identity solutions such as Okta, Azure AD, or Ping. This method centralizes credentials, decreases administrative overhead, and simplifies multi-cloud or hybrid access. Below are the various types of identities supported:

- **External IdPs:** By linking GCP to providers that manage SAML or OIDC tokens, you can offload sign-in flows while still trusting the resulting tokens in GCP. The following explains various IdPs and their use cases:

- o **SAML or OIDC integration:** With services like Okta or Azure AD, the login experience takes place externally, while GCP verifies the provided SAML or OIDC assertion. The various advantages include:

  - Services like Okta, Azure AD, Ping, and Auth0 can handle authentication, while GCP trusts the resulting **security assertion markup language (SAML)** or **OpenID Connect (OIDC)** tokens.

  - Simplifies user provisioning across multiple cloud platforms, such as Google, AWS, Azure, etc.

  - Reduces the need to recreate user accounts in multiple systems.

- o **Use cases:** Large enterprises that have already invested in a corporate directory benefit from a unified user repository that spans AWS, Azure, GCP, and on-prem systems, preventing duplicate accounts. Some of these use cases include:

  - Large enterprises already invested in a corporate IdP.

  - Companies are aiming for a single directory that spans cloud and on-prem resources.

- **Single sign-on (SSO):** By enabling SSO, users authenticate through the external IdP once and then access GCP resources seamlessly without extra prompts. The advantages include:

  - o **Streamlined user experience:** Users log in once through the IdP and can then access GCP resources without needing to enter an additional password. This reduces support overhead for password resets and lockouts.

  - o **Multi-cloud or hybrid setups:** Ensure consistent authentication across **Amazon Web Services (AWS)**, Azure, GCP, and SaaS applications. Enforce centralized security policies (such as MFA and password rotation) without duplicating effort.

- **Benefits and pitfalls:** While federating identities simplifies administration and improves security coherence, it also introduces new considerations around availability, mapping correctness, and overall complexity. The following concepts explain the different benefits and pitfalls of this model:

  - o **Benefits:** By consolidating user lifecycle management and enforcing consistent MFA, external IdPs lower overhead and facilitate the onboarding or offboarding of users at scale. The various benefits include:

    - **Reduced overhead**: One place to manage passwords, MFA, and user lifecycle changes.

    - **Consistent security**: Uniform enforcement of security requirements across platforms.

    - **Scalable**: Easily onboard or offboard users in a single directory.

o **Pitfalls:** A poorly configured SAML assertion can lead to unintentional over-privileging, and if your IdP goes offline, users may entirely lose access to GCP. Additionally, ensuring that advanced or custom policies consistently sync with GCP's IAM can be intricate. The various pitfalls include:

- **Misconfiguration risks**: Incorrectly configured SAML assertions or group mappings can grant or deny unexpected access levels.

- **Dependency on IdP availability**: Outages in your IdP can block all access to GCP.

- **Complex policies**: Ensuring advanced or custom policies sync correctly with GCP's IAM framework can be intricate.

Hybrid Identity and Access Management scenarios

Many organizations maintain on-premises identity systems, such as Microsoft AD, while also leveraging Google Cloud services. Hybrid setups allow synchronization of credentials and policies across both environments, reducing duplicate accounts and administrative overhead. Understanding the methods for syncing users, groups, and permissions ensures consistency and security, whether your resources reside on-prem or in the cloud. Some approaches include:

- **On-prem AD + Cloud Identity synchronisation:** By linking AD with Google Cloud using tools like **Google Cloud Directory Sync** (**GCDS**), you can replicate user and group data into Cloud Identity or Google Workspace without manual provisioning. A reference is as follows:

  o **Google Cloud Directory Sync (GCDS):** By connecting AD with Google Cloud through tools such as GCDS, you can mirror user and group data into Cloud Identity or Google Workspace without manual provisioning. Some of these also include:

  - Automate importing users and groups from AD into Cloud Identity or Google Workspace.

  - Maps attributes (username, email, department) to corresponding fields in Google.

  o **Use cases:** Organizations with a longstanding AD environment can avoid re-creating accounts in GCP, instead regularly syncing changes to maintain a single source of truth:

  - Organizations with an established AD environment need cloud-based services.

  - Avoid duplication and manual account setup in GCP by regularly syncing with AD.

- **Group synchronization and role mapping:** In addition to individual user accounts, syncing groups allows for centralized management of permissions; when someone joins or leaves a group on-prem, that change automatically applies in Google Cloud IAM. This streamlines the overall process by:

  o **Single source of truth**: Users join or leave an on-prem group, and the exact change reflects automatically in Cloud Identity, no extra overhead.

  o **Seamless IAM role inheritance:**

    ▪ When a GCP role is assigned to the synced group, all members gain (or lose) that role in one step.

    ▪ Prevents inconsistent permissions across on-prem and cloud environments.

- **Ensuring consistent policies:** While syncing identities is crucial, aligning security policies, like password rules or access revocation timelines, between on-prem and GCP helps maintain a unified governance posture. These can be accomplished by:

  o **Aligning GCP IAM with on-prem GPOs:** Match the security posture on-premises (for example, password rotation rules and account lockouts) with your GCP approach. Review your GCP IAM policies to confirm they do not conflict with on-prem governance.

  o **Avoid policy overlaps:** Overlapping or contradictory rules in AD and Cloud IAM can cause confusion. Conduct periodic reviews to align password complexity, MFA requirements, and access revocation timelines across both environments.

Organizational policies and folder hierarchies

Properly structuring your GCP organization node, folders, and projects is crucial for robust governance, cost management, and consistent security. The organization node serves as your top-most control plane, folders help you group and inherit policies across multiple projects, and the Organization Policy Service enforces fine-grained constraints that span your entire domain. This layered approach ensures that security and compliance rules are consistently enforced without requiring repetitive configuration at the project level.

Organization node

The organization node is where you set the tone for security, compliance, and project governance across your domain:

- **Setting up the organization node:** Connecting your root domain to GCP ensures that all newly created projects automatically fall under your organizational umbrella, providing a clear path for visibility and policy enforcement. This is achieved by:

  o **Domain association**: Your organization node is tied to your company's primary domain (for example, company.com), making it the root of all GCP resources.

o **Automatic project ownership**: Whenever someone in your domain creates a project, it is automatically placed under the organization, ensuring you maintain visibility and control.

o **Initial configuration**: Specify super admins or org admins who can create folders, set overarching policies, and manage access at the highest level.

- **Locking down the organization:** Restricting project creation, enforcing data-sharing rules, and adhering to compliance guidelines at the organizational level ensures that cloud usage remains secure and aligned with established standards. This is accomplished by:

o **Restrict new project creation**: Limit who can create projects to prevent shadow IT and uncontrolled spending.

o **Control external sharing**: To comply with data protection rules (e.g., HIPAA, GDPR), set constraints on sharing data outside your domain.

o **Meet compliance constraints**: At the organizational level, you can enforce security policies, such as mandatory **2nd factor authentication** (**2FA**) and restricted API usage, or domain-wide SSO, which will be implemented in every project.

Folders and projects

The following are the folders and projects that are the layers of the organization node. They provide a logical grouping mechanism and a container for GCP resources:

- **Structuring folders:** Folders serve as organizational units within your domain, reflecting functional, departmental, or regional divisions, enabling the enforcement of targeted policies. This is achieved through references such as:

o **Alignment approaches**: Organize folders by department (Finance, Engineering), environment (Dev, Staging, Prod), or region (US, EU, APAC).

o **Policy inheritance**: IAM policies or organization constraints set on a folder automatically apply to all child projects, reducing repetitive configuration.

o **Easier access control**: Grant or revoke a folder-level role once, and the changes propagate to every project within that folder.

- **Applying IAM at the folder level** means setting roles and policies that centralize permissions for teams across multiple projects, while still allowing for fine-tuning at lower tiers if necessary. This is achieved by:

o **Centralized permissions**: If a team manages multiple projects, assign roles at the folder level instead of repeating them for each project.

- o **Granularity when needed**: You can override folder-level permissions at individual projects if you need more fine-grained control.

- o **Audit and visibility**: Logs for folder-level changes help you track *who* configured *what* at scale, simplifying compliance reporting.

- **Projects as resource containers:** Projects define independent resource boundaries, providing each workload (for example, an app or microservice) with its own billing, IAM policies, and data isolation. This is achieved through:

  - o **Isolation**: Each project is a sandboxed environment with its own resources, billing, and IAM policies.

  - o **Lifecycle management**: When a project is no longer needed (for example, after a development sprint or proof-of-concept), it can be archived or deleted without affecting resources in other projects.

  - o **Fine-grained access**: If necessary, you can assign roles at the project level or even to individual resources (such as a bucket or dataset).

Organization Policy Service

The Organization Policy Service enables you to define and enforce global constraints throughout your organization, ensuring consistent security and compliance. These constraints are structured as follows:

- **Defining constraints:** These include disabling external IP addresses on VMs, restricting VM machine families (for example, no GPU usage outside production), and mandating **customer-managed encryption keys (CMEK)**. These also include basic conditions such as:

  - o **Mandatory policy enforcement**: Once set, these constraints override any lower-level configurations, and project admins cannot bypass them.

  - o **Customizing policy scope**: Depending on your governance needs, you can apply constraints at the org, folder, or project level.

- **Real-world constraints:**

  - o **Finance and healthcare:** They often require encryption controls, CMEK for sensitive data in Cloud Storage or BigQuery to comply with PCI-DSS or HIPAA rules.

  - o **Production hardening**: To reduce the attack surface, external IPs should be in deny-all mode on production resources, minimal VM images should be enforced, and certain API services should be limited to authorized teams.

Practical governance tips

Establishing best practices around labelling, naming conventions, billing, and resource management helps keep your GCP environment orderly and secure:

- **Using labels and naming conventions:** By applying meaningful labels and naming patterns, teams can quickly identify the purposes of resources, track costs, and maintain clarity of ownership. These can be accomplished through the following approaches:

  - **Resource identification**: Attach labels (for example, env=production, team=analytics, cost_center=finance) to resources.

  - **Consistent naming**: Use an explicit prefix or suffix (for example, prod-api-vm, dev-backend-gcs) so teams can easily spot the resource purpose and ownership.

  - **Search and filter**: Labels allow you to filter resources in the console or via CLI, streamlining management and reporting.

- **Billing alerts, budgets, and resource monitoring:** Keeping expenses in check is essential. Alerts, budgets, and proactive cleanups help prevent unexpected bills and reveal potential security anomalies, such as unauthorized mining. In general, the methodologies below help:

  - **Avoid sprawl**: Set up alerts for unusual spending patterns. This can signal misconfiguration or a security breach (for example, crypto mining leading to a sudden spike in billing, compute consumption).

  - **Budgets**: Create budgets for folders or projects. You will receive notifications when costs approach thresholds.

  - **Active cleanup**: Regularly review unused VMs, storage buckets, or other idle resources. Removing them cuts costs and reduces the attack surface.

By combining a well-structured hierarchy (org node, folders, projects) with strict organization-wide policies and good governance practices (labels, budgets, audits), you build a cloud environment that is easier to manage, less prone to security gaps, and more transparent from both an operational and compliance standpoint.

Auditing and logging IAM changes

Keeping track of who is doing what with your Google Cloud resources is critical for security, compliance, and operational sanity. By leveraging GCP's built-in audit logs and monitoring tools, you can spot misconfigurations, track role changes, and maintain a detailed history of activities for incident investigations and regulatory audits. In the following sections, we will summarize the core logging features and outline best practices for monitoring and auditing IAM events.

Audit logs overview

GCP automatically records audit logs to capture different interactions within your cloud environment. Each category of logs provides unique visibility into resource and policy modifications:

- **Admin Activity Logs:** Any administrative changes to GCP resources, including updates to IAM policies, project settings, and resource configurations (such as enabling an API or modifying firewall rules). The usage and availability of these logs are defined as follows:

    - **Usage:** These are essential for tracing who altered permissions, added or removed roles, and updated configurations, which is key information for security investigations.

    - **Availability:** All GCP services have Default Availability enabled. No manual setup is required, though you should confirm that retention settings meet your needs.

- **Data access logs:** They read, write, and perform various operations on data stored in GCP services such as Cloud Storage and BigQuery. These have multiple use cases and enablement requirements:

    - **Use cases**: It helps you pinpoint unauthorized data access or exfiltration attempts and supports compliance checks regarding who is viewing sensitive datasets.

    - **Enablement**: Due to the higher volume and cost, data access logs are often disabled by default. You must explicitly enable them for relevant services or projects.

- **System event logs:** These capture System-level actions Google performs on your behalf, such as automatic scaling of managed services, live migrations of VM instances, or software patching events.

    Its importance is that, while not strictly IAM-related, these logs provide context around operational changes that may intersect with security or resource utilization concerns.

Monitoring Identity and Access Management events

Once you have your audit logs, the next step is to monitor them effectively, either within GCP or by exporting them to external platforms:

- **Using Cloud Logging and Monitoring:** Utilize GCP's native logging and alerting services to track and visualize IAM-related events and create custom views or real-time notifications. These include items such as:

- o **Dashboards**: Cloud Logging allows you to create custom views or filters for IAM-related events, while Cloud Monitoring can alert you if, for example, a new owner role is suddenly granted.

- o **Alerts**: Configure alerts to notify security or DevOps teams about high-impact changes (e.g., broad role assignments and service account key creations).

- o **Detection of suspicious activity**: Look for patterns like repeated failed login attempts, rapid role elevations, or unexpected resource creation in sensitive projects.

- **Exporting logs to BigQuery or a SIEM:** External analysis platforms can integrate IAM data with other logs, providing deeper forensics, historical trend analyses, and automation triggers. For example:

- o **Long-term analysis**: BigQuery provides powerful querying capabilities for large volumes of logs, essential for forensics or historical compliance checks.

- o **Integration with SIEM**: Tools like Splunk, IBM QRadar, or Elastic can pull logs from GCP and correlate IAM events with other security data (for example, network intrusion attempts and endpoint logs).

- o **Automation triggers**: Real-time streaming of logs to Pub/Sub can drive security automation, such as automatically disabling a user if suspicious activity is detected.

Least privilege auditing

Regularly reviewing IAM roles is critical for maintaining the principle of least privilege, which ensures that each user or service has only the necessary permissions:

- **Identifying over-privileged accounts:** A simple yet effective approach involves listing IAM roles across your organization, folders, and projects, searching for **editor** or **owner** roles in production environments as red flags. You can achieve this using either of the approaches given in the following:

- o **Manual checks**: Use the GCP Console or gcloud CLI to list roles assigned at the org, folder, and project levels. Look for *editor* or *owner* roles in production projects; these are red flags.

- o **Role-based analysis**: Focus on critical services like BigQuery, Cloud Storage, or Compute Engine.

- **Automated scanning tools:** By using open-source or commercial Policy Analyzers, you can systematically identify misconfigurations, policy drift, or unused roles. Some examples include:

o   **Forseti Security**: An open-source tool by Google Cloud that audits IAM policies, highlights excessive permissions, and checks for policy drift over time.

o   **Policy Analyzer**: Scripts or third-party tools that systematically scan your environment, identifying misconfigurations or roles that have not been used recently.

o   **Continuous Monitoring**: Integrate scanning into your CI/CD pipeline or periodic jobs, ensuring any new policy changes are quickly flagged if they violate best practices.

Compliance driven audits

Many organizations must demonstrate secure access control for various regulatory frameworks, such as **Service Organization Control 2 (SOC 2)**, PCI-DSS, HIPAA, and ISO 27001:

- **Gathering evidence for SOC 2, PCI-DSS, and HIPAA:**

  o   **Required artifacts**: IAM access logs, audit logs of key administrative activities, proof of MFA enforcement, and details on any third-party access.

  o   **Retention policies**: Ensure you store your logs for as long as the regulation requires (for example, PCI-DSS may demand one year of security log retention).

- **Integrating audit logs into compliance dashboards:** Transform raw IAM logs into actionable insights by compiling them in real-time dashboards that simplify regulatory checks and streamline audits. This is done with the objective to:

  o   **Real-time visibility**: Create dashboards (in Data Studio, Looker, or another BI tool) that compile IAM events and highlight anomalies, such as unauthorized role assignments.

  o   **Simplified external audits**: Providing auditors with a consolidated view of your IAM changes and policy enforcement streamlines the audit process.

  o   **Mapping to controls**: Relate each IAM log entry to the specific regulatory control it satisfies. For example, Admin Activity Logs showing that MFA was enabled organization-wide can back up all production users with MFA configured.

Service accounts

Service accounts are essential for secure automation in Google Cloud. They allow non-human processes, such as applications, VMs, and CI/CD pipelines, to interact with GCP resources. However, mismanaging service accounts can create security blind spots if they are granted excessive permissions or use unsecured credentials. In the following section, we discuss best practices for creating, managing, and restricting service accounts to adhere to a least privilege approach.

Service accounts explained

Service accounts replace human credentials with machine-oriented access, providing a more flexible and controlled method to authorize compute resources or CI/CD pipelines. They are typically utilized for:

- **Machine or applications:**

  o **Non-human actors**: Service accounts are identities used by compute resources (for example, VMs, Cloud Functions, App Engine) or automation tasks (for example, CI/CD pipelines).

  o **Fine-grained scopes**: Rather than tying GCP API calls to a human user, service accounts let you assign roles precisely matching the application's operational needs- no more, no less.

- **Minimizing broad permissions:** When provisioning new services or resources in GCP, be aware of default service accounts that may have overly permissive roles. Specific issues related to accounts can be addressed individually, such as:

  o **Default service accounts**: When you create services like Compute Engine or App Engine, GCP can generate default service accounts with broad permissions (for example, editor). This can unintentionally grant full project access.

  o **Specialised accounts**: Instead, create dedicated service accounts for each application or workload, granting only the permissions essential to that task.

  o **Granular roles**: Replace roles like *editor* with narrower predefined or custom roles, for instance, granting a cloud build pipeline the ability to deploy to a single GKE cluster but *not* to manage other resources.

Key management for service accounts

Effective key management ensures that your service accounts do not become attack vectors. By limiting or rotating keys, adopting short-lived credentials, and leveraging tools such as **Workload Identity Federation** (WIF), you minimize the risk of unauthorized access. As a rule of thumb, one should focus on the following principles:

- Ask yourself if you need a service account key or if the application can use a secure method like WIF.

- Cross-development access should be restricted.

- Avoiding long-lived credentials, such as:

  o **JSON key risks**: Storing JSON keys on disk or in repositories can lead to leaks if the storage location is compromised.

- Security best practice: Avoid static service account keys. If you must use them, rotate them frequently. Prefer **Workload Identity** or **impersonation** so that no persistent key is ever stored.

- Short-lived tokens with IAM credentials API, such as:

  - **Ephemeral credentials**: Service accounts can generate short-lived tokens (often valid for minutes to hours) via the IAM Credentials API, ensuring that any compromised token quickly expires.

  - **Use cases**: This is particularly useful in CI/CD pipelines, where each build generates fresh credentials that vanish once the pipeline completes.

Impersonation flows

Impersonation allows a user or service account to *step into the shoes* of another service account temporarily, eliminating the need to distribute or store long-lived credentials while still providing the necessary permissions. Some examples of such flows include:

- **Securely delegating tasks:** A user or service account can temporarily impersonate another service account to perform specific tasks:

  - **Advantage**: No static key exchange, reducing the risk of credential leakage. The impersonating entity gets just enough permission to carry out its operation.

  - **Audit trail**: Cloud Audit Logs still capture who performed the impersonation and which underlying service account was used.

- **CI/CD example**: An example can be where a Jenkins pipeline or Cloud Build job needs to deploy code to **Google Kubernetes Engine** (**GKE**).

  - **Flow**: The pipeline impersonates a service account with a `container.admin` privileges only. The token expires once the deployment is complete; no persistent credentials remain.

  - **Security posture**: If attackers compromise the pipeline environment, they can only use the short-lived token until it becomes invalid.

Case study to design least privilege role

By creating a minimal role specifically designed for a particular application or pipeline, you uphold the principle of least privilege, ensuring that users and automation can only perform necessary tasks, even if credentials are compromised. The following is the step-by-step role creation process:

1. **Step-by-step role creation:** Follow these core steps to define the precise permissions your workload requires, avoiding unnecessary or excessively broad capabilities:

a. **Identify required permissions**: Start by listing the minimal API calls the application needs, such as GKE deployments, reading logs, or writing build artifacts to a specific bucket.

b. **Build a custom role**: In IAM and Admin | Roles, create a new custom role and add only the permissions you have identified.

c. **Test in staging**: Deploy your application or pipeline in a non-production environment. Ensure all necessary actions succeed and any unnecessary actions are blocked.

The Following are DevOps roles:

- **Permissions:** Provide read-write access for Cloud Build and GKE deployments, read-only access for logs, and deny all other requests.

  o **Read-write**: Cloud Build (for triggers, builds), GKE (for deployments, cluster read or write).

  o **Read-only**: Logs (able to view but not delete log entries).

  o **Denied**: Any action outside these areas, no direct Cloud Storage Admin, IAM role modifications, or database migrations.

2. **Implementation**: Assign this custom DevOps role to a dedicated service account. In your CI/CD pipeline, impersonate this account using short-lived tokens to deploy changes.

3. **Outcome**: Even if the pipeline environment is compromised, the attacker's reach is limited to GKE deployments only for the specific cluster or project where the role is valid.

Complex made simple

Imagine your GCP IAM like an office building's access control:

- **Roles:**

  o Each job title (role) dictates what an employee can do (editors, viewers, owners).

  o GCP's primitive roles are equivalent to broad job titles; predefined or custom roles are specialized, such as *IT Manager, Finance Intern, or HR Coordinator*.

- **Policies:**

  o A policy describes which job titles can enter which floors or rooms (resources).

  o By binding a role (job title) to a user or group, you decide who can open doors (perform specific actions).

- **Hierarchy**:
  - The organization node might be the leading corporate campus, with folders akin to building wings, projects akin to floors, and sub-resources as individual rooms.
  - A policy set at the campus (org) or wing (folder) level trickles down unless specifically overridden on floors or rooms (projects, sub-resources).

The key takeaways: Like a well-defined office access system, **GCP IAM** ensures that everyone or service has just enough privileges: no more, no less. By thoughtfully designing job titles (roles) and applying them at the correct levels, you keep your environment *secure* and *easy to manage*.

Conclusion

By exploring the fundamental aspects of Google Cloud IAM, from the broad significance of identity governance and resource hierarchies to more intricate subjects like least privilege best practices and policy evaluation, you are establishing a strong foundation for securing your GCP environment. This chapter demonstrates that IAM goes beyond mere permission assignments. It is a crucial element that aligns cloud use with regulatory standards, operational efficiencies, and robust security measures. *By strategically adopting* IAM roles, policies, and auditing, organizations can reduce risks, prevent misconfigurations, and effectively manage their cloud resources. As you apply these concepts to real-world situations, *remember* that continuous monitoring, ongoing policy refinement, and persistent education are essential for maintaining compliance and ensuring security at scale.

In the following chapter, you will learn about data security and encryption methods applicable to the GCP.

Exercise

1. In a new or existing GCP project, create a service account with minimal read permissions (for example, the *viewer* role). Then, audit your IAM console to verify which users, groups, and service accounts have permissions that are broader than necessary.

   Note any necessary adjustments to align with the principle of least privilege. This hands-on activity underscores the importance of continuously reviewing and refining IAM configurations in a real-world setting.

Key takeaways

Summarizing the key lessons from this chapter, these points emphasize how effective IAM design and governance can protect cloud resources while enhancing operational efficiency:

- **IAM introduction and building blocks:** Misconfigurations are among the leading causes of cloud breaches, and understanding fundamental IAM structures, such as resource inheritance and custom role precision, can help prevent them.

- o   Misconfigured IAM is a top cause of cloud breaches.
- o   Policies can be inherited across the organization/folders/projects.
- o   Custom roles precisely limit privileges.

- **Core concepts of accounts, roles, and policies:** Various account types and roles cater to different use cases, human users, service accounts, or groups, while policies bind them together to manage resource access:
    - o   Different account types (human, service accounts), each best suited for specific use cases.
    - o   Primitive roles are too broad for production; go with predefined or custom roles.
    - o   The hierarchical resource model ensures consistent policy application.

- **Cloud Identity versus external IdPs:** Whether using Cloud Identity independently or integrating an external IdP, the key is to create a unified, secure authentication framework that satisfies compliance and operational requirements:
    - o   Cloud Identity can unify and simplify identity management within GCP.
    - o   Federation (SAML/OIDC) supports SSO for hybrid or multi-cloud setups.
    - o   Syncing on-prem AD with Cloud Identity helps maintain consistent access policies.

- **Organizational policies and folder hierarchies:** By leveraging folders and organizational policies, you can establish consistent, top-down rules across projects, enforcing constraints such as disallowing external IPs, mandating CMEK usage, or restricting resource creation to specific regions:
    - o   Folders enable broad, inherited controls for consistent policy across projects.
    - o   Organization Policy Service sets constraints (for example, no external IPs, forced CMEK usage) to enforce compliance.
    - o   Proper governance includes using labels, naming conventions, and monitoring resource usage.

- **Auditing and logging IAM changes:** Monitoring user activities in your Google Cloud environment is essential for security and compliance. By capturing IAM-related events, such as configuration changes, data access, or unusual role grants, you can swiftly identify misconfigurations or potential breaches:
    - o   Admin Activity Logs capture configuration changes, and Data Access Logs track read or write events.
    - o   Cloud Logging, Monitoring, and SIEM exports reveal suspicious or excessive role grants.
    - o   Tools like Forseti or Policy Analyzer can detect drift and over-privileged roles.

- **Service accounts and least privilege best practices:** Service accounts serve as non-human identities for GCP workloads (such as VMs or CI/CD pipelines). Carefully restricting their permissions is crucial for preventing unauthorized or accidental escalations:

  o Use short-lived credentials or impersonation flows; avoid distributing JSON keys.

  o Default service accounts often have editor-level privileges; replace or restrict them.

  o A well-scoped custom role ensures that service accounts can perform tasks without broad permission creep.

References

1. https://cloud.google.com/iam/docs/overview

2. https://cloud.google.com/iam/docs/best-practices-for-enterprise-organizations

3. https://cloud.google.com/iam/docs/understanding-roles

4. https://cloud.google.com/iam/docs/creating-custom-roles

5. https://cloud.google.com/iam/docs/understanding-service-accounts

6. https://cloud.google.com/iam/docs/workload-identity-federation

7. https://cloud.google.com/iam/docs/managing-service-account-keys

8. https://cloud.google.com/secret-manager/docs

9. https://cloud.google.com/iam/docs/conditions-overview

10. https://cloud.google.com/iam/docs/conditions-attribute-reference

11. https://cloud.google.com/iam/docs/tags-access-control

12. https://cloud.google.com/iam/docs/audit-logging

13. https://cloud.google.com/iam/docs/troubleshooting-access

14. https://cloud.google.com/policy-intelligence/docs/policy-analyzer

15. https://cloud.google.com/resource-manager/docs/organization-policy/overview

16. https://cloud.google.com/resource-manager/docs/cloud-platform-resource-hierarchy

17. https://cloud.google.com/vpc-service-controls/docs/overview

18. https://cloud.google.com/security-command-center/docs/quickstart-security-command-center

19. https://cloud.google.com/storage/docs/access-control/lists

20. https://cloud.google.com/storage/docs/access-control/iam

Join our Discord space

Join our Discord workspace for latest updates, offers, tech happenings around the world, new releases, and sessions with the authors:

https://discord.bpbonline.com

CHAPTER 3

Data Security and Encryption

Introduction

Adequate data protection is paramount for any organization running workloads in the cloud. This chapter explores how **Google Cloud Platform (GCP)** ensures data security at rest, in transit, and even in use. You will learn about *GCP's native encryption defaults*, advanced key management strategies (CMEK, CSEK, Cloud HSM), and how **Cloud Data Loss Prevention (DLP)** automatically detects and masks sensitive information.

We establish the *fundamentals of GCP's encryption*, discussing how data is secured at the hardware, platform, and service layers. You will discuss **Cloud KMS** to create, rotate, and audit encryption keys, including more stringent requirements like **CSEK** and hardware-backed **Cloud HSM**. Next, we examine **Cloud DLP** to discover and transform sensitive data across storage and analytics pipelines, prevent inadvertent leaks, and support compliance. By the end, you can design robust encryption architectures across BigQuery, Cloud Storage, and more, mapping these features to regulations like: **General Data Protection Regulation (GDPR)**, **Health Insurance Portability and Accountability Act (HIPAA)**, and **Payment Card Industry Data Security Standard (PCI-DSS)**, seamlessly integrating encryption best practices into your broader security framework.

Structure

This chapter is organised into the following key sections:

- Fundamentals of data encryption in GCP
- Key management with Cloud KMS
- CSEK and Cloud HSM
- Cloud Data Loss Prevention
- Encryptions for GCP Storage service
- Compliance alignment for regulations
- Complex made simple

Objectives

By the end of this chapter, you will understand how to protect data throughout its lifecycle in GCP. You will learn about encryption at rest, in transit, and in use; explore key management strategies with Cloud KMS; and discover how to integrate these security controls into real-world applications. Additionally, you will gain insights into meeting industry compliance requirements (for example, GDPR and HIPAA) and learn best practices for architecting regulated solutions that align with your organization's security posture.

Fundamentals of data encryption in GCP

GCP data encryption is designed to protect information throughout its lifecycle, whether stored on disk, transmitted over the network, or processed in memory. By combining various layers of encryption technologies, GCP ensures strong confidentiality and integrity for customer and internal data. This comprehensive approach supports compliance with stringent industry regulations and helps organizations maintain trust as they migrate critical workloads to the cloud.

Encryption at-rest and in-transit

Google's encryption strategy secures data when it resides on persistent storage, such as disks, databases, or object stores, and travels across internal or external networks. This twofold model integrates seamless protection into the platform, minimizing gaps where data could be intercepted or modified. GCP offers default encryption for resources like Cloud Storage buckets and Compute Engine disks while enforcing **Transport Layer Security** (**TLS**) or **Secure Sockets Layer** (**SSL**) for data exchange. This is especially important for hybrid setups where data moves between on-premises and GCP services.

The following sections explains how GCP manages default and in-transit encryption.

Default encryption

GCP automatically encrypts data at rest across core services, including **Cloud Storage**, **BigQuery**, and **Compute Engine disks**. This seamless security minimizes misconfiguration risks and streamlines default key management, as GCP regularly rotates and maintains these keys on your behalf.

The following figure shows the different layers of encryption that Google creates and their sources:

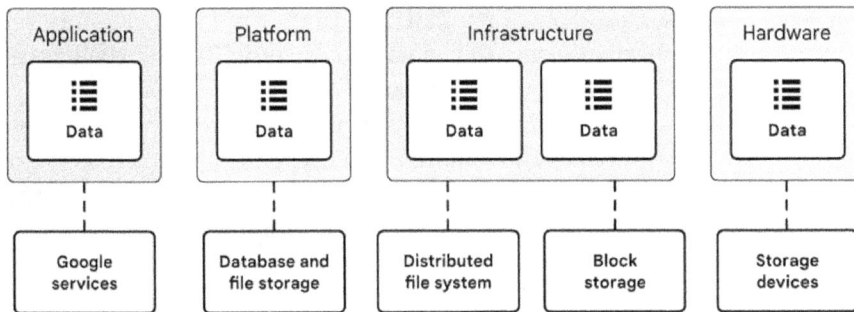

Figure 3.1: GCP's layers of encryption

In transit encryption

Data traversing GCP's network utilises TLS or SSL to ensure confidentiality and integrity. This includes traffic to GCP APIs, load balancers, and internal communication within Google's backbone.

In addition to TLS/SSL, **Secure Shell (SSH)** is widely used for encrypted administrative access to virtual machines, ensuring that credentials and session data remain protected during remote management tasks. Similarly, **virtual private networks (VPNs)** provide secure tunnels for connecting on-premises environments to GCP, encrypting all traffic in transit between your data center and Google Cloud.

This end-to-end encryption approach helps protect against eavesdropping or tampering, meets numerous compliance requirements, and ensures your workloads maintain confidentiality across hybrid and multi-cloud environments.

Shared responsibility model for data

In the cloud, security is a shared endeavor between the provider and the customer. Google Cloud establishes a foundation by protecting physical and virtual infrastructure, data centers, hardware, hypervisors, and automatically applying default encryption mechanisms. At the same time, you, as the customer, maintain *complete* control over your specific data. This *control* includes configuring encryption keys (CMEK, CSEK), granting or restricting IAM permissions, and determining how information is accessed, stored, and protected. By clarifying the distinction between platform-level responsibilities and user-specific obligations, the shared responsibility model ensures that Google Cloud handles the heavy lifting of fundamental security, eliminating the need for manual intervention in areas such as hardware encryption. Meanwhile, you can customize higher-level controls to align with internal policies, compliance standards, and application requirements.

GCP's security responsibilities

Under this model, Google Cloud ensures that the platform is secure and reliable. This includes everything from physically securing data centers with 24/7 surveillance to keeping hypervisor patches for virtual machines up to date. *Default encryption processes* protect your data by automatically encrypting it at rest across services like Cloud Storage, BigQuery, and Compute Engine disks. This reduces the chances of a breach due to misconfiguration at the infrastructure layer. With these built-in protections, you can be confident that the foundational environment remains secure without requiring significant day-to-day oversight from you.

Your responsibilities

While Google provides a strong baseline, you retain full ownership of how your data is encrypted, accessed, and utilized. This includes selecting and configuring CMEK or **customer-supplied encryption keys (CSEK)** if you require additional control over key lifecycle or storage locations. It also involves setting appropriate IAM policies to ensure that only authorized users and service accounts can interact with sensitive information and conducting regular *audits* to confirm that permissions, logs, and key rotation schedules are current. Applying *least-privilege IAM reduces* the attack surface, preventing accidental or malicious misuse. Additionally, auditing enables you to detect unusual activity, verify compliance with relevant regulations (for example, HIPAA, PCI-DSS, GDPR), and maintain a resilient environment capable of adapting to evolving security threats.

Encryption-in-use confidential computing

Encryption traditionally protects data *at rest* (stored on disk) and *in transit* (moving over a network). However, when applications or analytics engines actively process data, it must be decrypted, leaving it momentarily vulnerable to insider threats, compromised kernels, or shared tenancy risks. Confidential computing solves this problem by keeping data *encrypted even during processing*, using specialized hardware.

Google Cloud's confidential computing framework utilizes confidential VMs and confidential GKE Nodes, powered by **Trusted Execution Environments (TEEs)** such as **Secure Encrypted Virtualization (AMD SEV)**. These environments isolate sensitive workloads, ensuring that no other process, hypervisor, or Google administrator can access the data in cleartext, even during runtime.

Introduction to confidential computing

Encryption-in-use ensures data confidentiality during processing, in addition to encryption at rest and in transit. GCP's confidential VMs utilize hardware-based TEEs to protect data in memory, mitigating insider threats and advanced attacks. This approach ensures that sensitive workloads remain encrypted during storage, transmission, and active processing, thereby reducing the risk of data exposure.

Implementing confidential computing

Enabling confidential VMs involves selecting the option when creating new VM instances and deploying sensitive workloads within those TEEs. Integrations with **Identity and Access Management (IAM)** and organizational policies ensure that only authorized users can provision or manage these secure VMs, safeguarding data even during execution. By controlling access and leveraging TEEs, organizations can meet stringent compliance demands, strengthen their security posture, and maintain the confidence that their most sensitive data is protected end-to-end.

Key management with Cloud KMS

Implementing robust cryptographic controls is essential for protecting sensitive data throughout its entire lifecycle, whether at rest, in transit, or in use. **Google Cloud Key Management Service (Cloud KMS)** provides a *centralised, scalable, and flexible* platform for creating, managing, and controlling access to *cryptographic keys*, enabling organisations to easily meet their *security* and *compliance* obligations.

Cloud KMS serves as the backbone for *encryption management* within Google Cloud, providing users *with fine-grained control* over keys used to encrypt resources such as Cloud Storage, BigQuery datasets, Compute Engine disks, and more. Whether your organization prefers *Google-managed keys*, seeks to enforce stricter policies with **customer-managed encryption keys (CMEK)**, or requires hardware-backed keys through Cloud HSM, Cloud KMS enables you to define how keys are created, stored, rotated, and utilized.

Overview of Cloud key management service

Google Cloud KMS centralizes the creation, storage, and lifecycle management of cryptographic keys for your GCP workloads. By organizing keys into rings and versions, Cloud KMS provides a scalable and flexible framework tailored to various use cases, from encrypting individual files to securing entire storage systems. This service significantly simplifies key management while allowing you to set detailed permissions and policies, ensuring alignment with your security needs.

The following sections focus on the foundational architecture for Cloud KMS and the various key types supported by Google.

Architecture of Cloud KMS

Google Cloud's KMS is built on a *highly available, regionally distributed,* and *scalable* infrastructure that provides strong, reliable cryptographic key management without the operational overhead associated with traditional key storage systems.

At the core of Cloud KMS's architecture is the concept of *hierarchical organization* and *versioned key management,* which together provide flexibility and control for organizations of all sizes and compliance requirements.

Core components

The following components form the core Cloud KMS Architecture:

- **Key rings**:
    - A *key ring* serves as a logical container for related cryptographic keys, enabling you to organize keys by application, department, or project.
    - Keys within a ring occupy the same geographical location (region), helping to address data residency concerns.
    - Key rings simplify access control. IAM permissions can be applied at the ring level to govern access to all contained keys.

- **CryptoKeys**:
    - A **CryptoKey** is the key entity for performing cryptographic operations such as encryption, decryption, signing, and verification.
    - Each CryptoKey supports multiple versions that are rotated over time to enhance security while maintaining backward compatibility for data previously encrypted with older versions.

- **Key versions**:
    - Each time a key is rotated, a new version is generated.
    - Cloud KMS provides fine-grained control over the lifecycle states of key versions:
        - **Enabled**: Usable for operations.
        - **Disabled**: Temporarily turned off but can be re-enabled.
        - **Destroyed**: Permanently deleted after a seven-day scheduled destruction period.

Different Key types

Google-Managed Encryption Keys (**GMEK**) meet standard encryption needs with minimal overhead. CMEK provides users with complete control over creation, rotation, and storage, which is essential for strict compliance or adherence to internal policies.

CMEK references are generally straightforward and require users to link the reference to the resource, as shown in the following code snippet:

```
# Enable a bucket to use a specified key for default encryption
gsutil bucketpolicyonly set on gs://my-secure-bucket

gsutil kms encryption set \
    projects/PROJECT_ID/locations/global/keyRings/demo-keyring/cryptoKeys/
demo-key \
    gs://my-secure-bucket
```

Creating and managing keys

Efficient key management is central to any robust encryption strategy. In GCP, you can easily set up new key rings, define cryptographic keys, and add new key versions for regular rotation. This structured approach helps maintain backward compatibility for older data while continuously strengthening your security posture. Tools like the Cloud Console and gcloud CLI provide user-friendly interfaces for provisioning and updating keys.

Steps to creating key rings, keys, and versions

Users create key rings in the GCP console, define cryptographic keys (for example, AES256 for encryption/decryption), and periodically add new key versions to facilitate rotation while ensuring backward compatibility.

The following code block serves as a reference for creating and managing keys in Cloud KMS (gcloud **Command Line Interface (CLI)**):

```
# Create a Key Ring
gcloud kms keyrings create demo-keyring \
    --location=global

# Create a Symmetric Encryption Key
gcloud kms keys create demo-key \
    --location=global \
    --keyring=demo-keyring \
    --purpose=encryption

# Add a new Key Version (for rotation or backup)
gcloud kms keys versions create demo-key \
    --location=global \
    --keyring=demo-keyring
```

Key management best practices

Effective key management is not just a technical safeguard but a compliance imperative for organizations operating in regulated environments. Implementing best practices ensures operational security and alignment with frameworks like PCI-DSS, HIPAA, and GDPR.

The following are the key rotation best practices:

- **Frequent rotation**:
  - Rotate symmetric keys every 90 days or more frequently in sensitive environments.
  - Asymmetric keys, used for signing, may rotate less frequently but should still adhere to a defined policy.
  - Automated rotation in Cloud KMS enables seamless transitions without service disruptions.

- **Versioning strategy**:
  - Maintain multiple key versions to enable decryption of older data encrypted with previous keys.
  - Gradually re-encrypt data with newer keys during routine processing to avoid large re-encryption tasks.

- **Access control**:
  - Follow the principles of least privilege, grant only the CryptoKey Encrypter/Decrypter roles where necessary.
  - Implement separation of duties, with different teams handling key creation, usage, and audits.

- **Logging and monitoring**:
  - Enable Cloud Audit Logs for key access, usage, and policy modifications.
  - Integrate logs with SIEM tools for real-time alerts on suspicious activities.

- **Regular security assessments:**
  - Conduct periodic *key management and encryption policy reviews* to identify gaps and verify compliance with internal standards and regulations.
  - Perform *penetration testing and risk assessments* to evaluate potential weaknesses in key storage and rotation processes.

- **User training and awareness:**
  - Train staff on *secure key management practices, handling of encryption materials,* and the importance of regular key rotation.

○ Reinforce *awareness of phishing risks and credential misuse* that could impact key security.

The following are the compliance-driven requirements:

- **Payment Card Industry Data Security Standard (PCI-DSS)**:

  ○ **Requirement 3.6**: Secure cryptographic key management, including storage, access control, and rotation.

  ○ **Rotation mandate**: Keys must be changed *at least annually* or upon suspicion of compromise.

  ○ **Use Cloud KMS** to enforce automatic rotation policies and log access.

- **HIPAA**:

  ○ Requires *regular review* and *update* of encryption policies and key management processes.

  ○ Keys protecting **Electronic Protected Health Information (ePHI)** must be stored securely, with *access logged*.

  ○ Though no strict rotation frequency, *quarterly or semi-annual* reviews are considered best practice.

- **GDPR**:

  ○ Emphasizes *data minimization* and *protection by design*, encryption and key management are central to this.

  ○ Personal data must be *rendered unintelligible* in case of a breach, achievable through strong key management.

  ○ Keys must be protected with *technical and organizational measures*, and rotation supports data integrity.

- **ISO/IEC 27001**:

  ○ Mandates controls for the *cryptographic key lifecycle*: generation, distribution, storage, rotation, and destruction.

  ○ It requires *documented procedures* for key management that are aligned with risk assessments.

Access controls for KMS

Cloud KMS integrates seamlessly with Google Cloud IAM, enabling you to assign specific roles to different user groups or service accounts. By following least-privilege principles, you can separate key administration tasks, such as creation and rotation, from directly using the keys in encryption or decryption. Additionally, audit logs capture every key-related event, providing invaluable traceability and supporting regulatory compliance requirements.

IAM roles specific to KMS

Cloud KMS integrates deeply with Google Cloud IAM, enabling precise control over who can manage and utilize encryption keys. This integration ensures *least-privilege access* by distinguishing between administrative and operational roles:

- **Cloud KMS admin**:
  - Full control over KMS resources, able to create, delete, and configure key rings and keys.
  - Ideal for trusted security administrators responsible for key lifecycle policies.
  - Should not be assigned to general developers or system users.

- **Cloud KMS CryptoKey Encrypter/Decrypter**:
  - Permits actions for encryption and decryption using keys, but disallows managing the keys themselves.
  - Ideal for applications, services, or users needing to use keys without altering their configuration.

- **Cloud KMS viewer**:
  - Read-only access to critical metadata without the ability to encrypt, decrypt, or modify configurations.
  - Useful for auditors or monitoring tools that need visibility into the key setup.

- **Separation of duties**:
  - Assign encryption and decryption roles to application owners.
  - Assign admin roles strictly to the infrastructure or security teams.

Performing a segregation of roles reduces the risk of an account being compromised, aligning with compliance mandates (e.g., PCI-DSS).

Logging key usage and restricting key access

Understanding how encryption keys are used is essential for both *security* and *compliance*. GCP offers comprehensive logging and monitoring tools:

- **Cloud Audit logs**:
  - Track all key operations, such as creation, destruction, encryption, decryption, and access changes.
  - Log entries include the identity of the key holder, *the time of access*, and *the action* taken.

- **SIEM integration**:
  - Logs can be exported to **security information and event management (SIEM)** systems like Splunk, QRadar, or Chronicle.
  - Real-time alerts can be generated for unusual patterns, such as repeated decryption attempts.

- **Organizational policies**:
  - Enforce policies ensuring keys are only used within *authorised projects* or by *authorised teams*.
  - Example: Restrict specific CMEK keys to be usable only in production environments, disallowing their use in test or development environments.

- **Best practice**: Set up *alerts* for high-risk actions, such as key deletion or changes to IAM roles on keys.

Encrypting GCP Storage and Compute

Google Cloud enables the binding of CMEK to Storage and Compute resources for enhanced control.

- **Compute Engine disks**:
  - CMEK encrypts persistent disks.
  - Only users or services with the proper IAM permissions on the key can boot or attach disks.
  - **Example**: Protect sensitive workloads, ensuring that data is inaccessible if the key is revoked.

- **Cloud Storage buckets**:
  - Configure buckets to use CMEK, enabling control over object-level encryption.
  - Prevents Google from accessing objects unless keys are explicitly permitted.

- **BigQuery datasets**:
  - CMEK ensures datasets are encrypted using customer-controlled keys.
  - Useful for industries needing auditable encryption for analytical workloads.

- **Fine-grained IAM control**:
  - Assign key access per project, team, or workload, ensuring only authorized entities can decrypt data.

Interplay between KMS and other GCP security services

KMS does not operate in isolation; it works seamlessly with other GCP security services to provide *end-to-end protection*:

- **Security Command Center (SCC)**:
    - Provides a centralized dashboard for key insights:
    - Alerts on over-permissive keys.
    - Identifies unused or orphaned keys.
    - Highlights misconfigured resources relying on unprotected keys.
- **Access Transparency**: View logs of *when and why Google staff* accessed your CMEK (if ever), useful for *trust and compliance reporting*.
- **Cloud Armor and VPC service controls**:
    - Combine with KMS to restrict key usage to trusted network zones.
    - Prevent data exfiltration by enforcing service perimeters.
- **Cloud DLP integration**: Identify sensitive data and apply tokenization/encryption using KMS-generated keys.

CSEK and Cloud HSM

Managing encryption keys *externally* offers organizations a *greater degree of control* over their data security posture, which is often required for compliance with strict regulatory frameworks or internal governance policies. While CSEK allows organizations to retain full custody of their keys, Cloud HSM provides hardware-backed security with high assurance, leveraging GCP's infrastructure while maintaining customer-controlled access.

The following sections explores these two methods, highlighting their *advantages, complexities*, and *appropriate use cases* to help you decide when deeper control is worth the operational investment.

Customer-supplied encryption keys

Organizations needing *complete control* over their cryptographic keys, either due to *data residency laws, contractual obligations*, or *risk tolerance*, can use CSEK to ensure that *GCP does not generate or store keys* on their behalf.

Rationale to consider CSEK

CSEK is particularly relevant when:

- *Compliance mandates* specify that encryption keys must be stored *on-premises* or in a *country-specific data center*.

- Internal policies require *complete visibility and control* over the key lifecycle, including generation, rotation, and destruction.

- A *trusted third-party HSM* or key store is already in use, and cloud key management must align with existing security infrastructure.

For example, financial institutions governed by *Basel III* or *local central banks* may need to demonstrate that key custody remains entirely in their control.

Managing your keys on-premises

Implementing CSEK involves the following process:

- **Key generation:** You create the keys using secure tools or hardware, ensuring compliance with *industry cryptographic standards* (for example, AES-256).

- **Secure upload:** Keys are encrypted and securely uploaded to GCP using API calls or the console when creating resources like Compute Engine disks or Cloud Storage buckets.

- **Lifecycle management:**

    o **Rotation:** Periodically update the keys and re-upload them to ensure continued compliance and reduced risk of key exhaustion.

    o **Backup:** Maintain secure, redundant backups of all keys.

    o **Recovery:** Implement documented procedures for key retrieval in case of infrastructure failures.

Potential challenges with CSEK

While CSEK offers maximum control, it introduces significant operational overhead:

- **Responsibility for loss:** If a key is lost or corrupted, GCP cannot recover encrypted data, and the loss is permanent.

- **Security risks:** Keys must be transmitted securely. Poorly handled uploads can lead to interception or leakage.

- **Complexity:** Requires dedicated key management infrastructure (HSMs, key vaults) and trained staff to operate securely.

- **No GCP-managed features:** Features like automatic key rotation or fine-grained access logging available in Cloud KMS are not applicable.

The following are the mitigation strategies:

- Use HSM-backed on-prem key management for higher assurance.

- Employ automated scripts for periodic rotation and secure re-upload.

- Integrate monitoring and alerting for unauthorized access attempts on your internal key systems.

Cloud hardware security module

For organizations requiring *hardware-based assurance*, Cloud HSM provides *FIPS 140-2 Level 3 compliant* hardware for *key generation, storage, and use*, while still leveraging the scalability of GCP.

The following are the importance of Cloud HSM:

- Provides *tamper-resistant hardware* for *cryptographic operations*.

- Ensures that *keys never leave* the hardware boundary.

- Is fully *integrated with Cloud KMS*, offering the same API surface but with *HSM-backed keys*.

The following are the key use cases for Cloud HSM:

- **Regulated industries**: Healthcare, finance, and government sectors requiring *certified hardware* for compliance with HIPAA, PCI-DSS, or FedRAMP.

- **High-value applications**: Encrypting highly sensitive data like *financial transactions, government records*, or *intellectual property*.

- **Hybrid cloud scenarios**: Where *on-prem HSMs* are mirrored in the cloud for disaster recovery or cloud migration strategies.

The following are the benefits of using of a Cloud HSM:

- **High assurance security**: Physical tamper resistance, with hardware-managed lifecycle.

- **Integration with IAM**: Leverage GCP IAM for granular access control.

- **Operational simplicity**: Compared to CSEK, Cloud HSM reduces some overhead by being *fully managed*, though hardware-backed.

The following are the key considerations for implementing a Cloud HSM:

- **Cost**: Cloud HSM services are *more expensive* than standard KMS due to the hardware assurance.

- **Latency**: Slight increase in response time for key operations, although negligible for most workloads.

- **Availability**: Limited to *specific regions*, requiring planning for multi-region redundancy.

The following table shows a summary comparison:

Feature	CSEK	Cloud HSM
Key control	Fully on-prem	Customer-controlled, hardware-backed
Compliance level	High, manual	FIPS 140-2 Level 3
Operational complexity	High (manual rotation, storage)	Medium (GCP-managed, customer-bound)
Risk if the key is lost	Complete data loss	Minimal if IAM controlled
Cost	Low (self-managed infra)	Higher (GCP-managed HSM resources)
Integration with GCP services	Limited	Seamless via Cloud KMS

Table 3.1: Comparative analysis of CSEK and Cloud HSM

Both CSEK and Cloud HSM cater to *advanced encryption needs,* but they serve different security postures:

- CSEK is ideal when *absolute custody* of the key is mandatory.
- Cloud HSM is better when *hardware-backed assurance* is needed without the full burden of on-premises management.

Introducing Cloud HSM

By generating and storing keys in tamper-resistant hardware (FIPS 140-2 Level 3), Cloud HSM enhances security against external attackers and insider threats. This elevated level of assurance makes Cloud HSM an ideal choice for organizations seeking to comply with stringent regulations or formal industry requirements.

The following figure shows a standard Cloud HSM architecture:

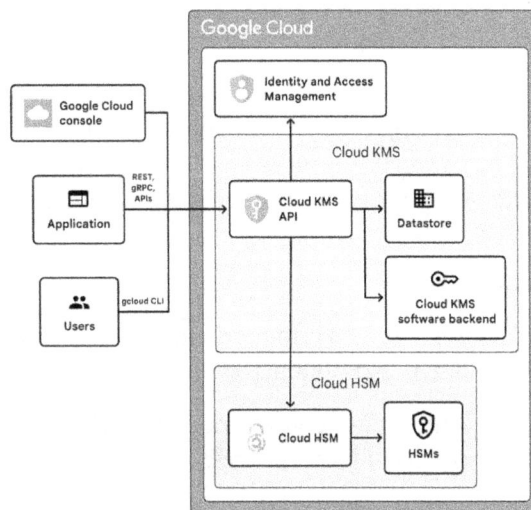

Figure 3.2: Cloud HSM architecture (Isolated by geography)

Generating cryptographic keys within Cloud HSM

Cloud HSM utilizes **FIPS 140-2 Level 3 certified** hardware security modules to *generate, store,* and manage *cryptographic keys* within a *tamper-evident* boundary. When generating keys within Cloud HSM:

- The key *never leaves* the HSM boundary, ensuring *zero exposure* to software-level threats.

- Keys are created using hardware **random number generators** (**RNGs**), adhering to NIST-approved algorithms, including AES-256, RSA-2048/4096, and ECDSA curves.

- Administrators can *define key policies* at creation, controlling key purposes (encryption, signing), and whether keys are *exportable* (by default, keys are non-exportable for maximum security).

GCP *automates redundancy* across multiple HSM appliances, ensuring *high availability* and *low-latency* cryptographic operations, even under heavy workloads. This approach facilitates *cryptographic key lifecycle management* (creation, rotation, and disabling) while meeting *regulatory mandates* for hardware-based encryption, often required in the *finance, government,* and *healthcare sectors.*

Integration with Cloud KMS

Once provisioned, Cloud HSM keys integrate seamlessly with **Cloud KMS**, allowing you to:

- Manage HSM-backed and *software-backed* keys from a *unified interface* (Cloud Console, gcloud CLI, REST API).

- Apply *fine-grained IAM policies,* ensuring *least-privilege access* for both key administrators and service users.

- Use Organizational Policy Constraints to *enforce* HSM-backed key usage across *projects, folders,* or the *entire organization.*

Key operations such as encryption, decryption, and signing are transparently managed through Cloud KMS APIs, whether the underlying key is *software-managed* or *HSM-backed.* This *reduces complexity* for developers while ensuring high-security guarantees for sensitive workloads.

Additional integration benefits include:

- **Audit logging**: All HSM key access is logged via Cloud Audit logs, providing visibility into *who accessed* which keys and when.

- **Compliance tracking**: Automated compliance monitoring via SCC, highlighting any deviations from *key management best practices.*

- **Multi-region support**: Cloud HSM supports *global workloads* by distributing key infrastructure across *GCP regions.*

Latency considerations and cost implications

The hardware-based operations of Cloud HSM offer excellent protection against tampering, however, each interaction with the hardware security module can introduce a slight amount of latency. While many applications may not perceive this difference during normal operations, high-performance environments, such as real-time analytics or ultra-low-latency transaction systems, might need to account for these additional milliseconds. From a budget perspective, the use of Cloud HSM generally appears as a separate cost line item on your monthly invoices, covering both the hardware's maintenance and any associated usage fees.

Meanwhile, implementing CSEK requires additional overhead for secure key generation, protected storage, and orchestrated transfers to GCP. You may need specialized hardware, dedicated software, or third-party key management solutions to maintain and protect your encryption keys. Each of these components contributes to your total cost of ownership. As you consider the financial investment, remember the broader benefits that either approach can offer, ranging from granular compliance controls and data sovereignty to demonstrated alignment with industry regulations. Ultimately, your decision depends on determining which encryption model provides the greatest overall security value in relation to the operational complexity and associated costs.

Cloud Data Loss Prevention

In addition to encryption, protecting data often requires robust detection and masking capabilities. Google Cloud DLP meets these needs by scanning and classifying data in BigQuery, Cloud Storage, and other locations, automating tasks such as tokenizing **personally identifiable information** (**PII**) and generating alerts when sensitive content is detected or identified.

Google Cloud DLP is a powerful service designed to automatically identify, classify, and protect sensitive data across GCP environments. It proactively searches for personal identifiers such as names, addresses, and credit card numbers, allowing organizations to apply customizable policies to mask, tokenize, or encrypt that data. Cloud DLP ensures compliance with privacy regulations like GDPR, HIPAA, and PCI-DSS by reducing the exposure of sensitive fields.

The following are the key features:

- Detects over 150 predefined sensitive data types, including PII, financial, health, and credentials (and this is an evolving data set).
- Supports custom detectors, enabling domain-specific data discovery.
- Integrates with Cloud Storage, BigQuery, Datastore, and Firestore, among others.
- Offers streaming content inspection via REST APIs for real-time data protection.

Core capabilities

Cloud DLP provides a range of capabilities beyond basic scanning:

- **Classification:** Automatically tags data as Sensitive, Quasi-Identifiable, or Non-Sensitive.

- **Risk analysis:** Offers risk scoring for datasets based on detected sensitivity levels.

- **Data redaction:** Removes sensitive data from text or files entirely if necessary.

- **Contextual awareness:** Utilizes **Natural Language Processing** (**NLP**) to understand context, reducing false positives.

This enables organizations to maintain the utility of datasets for business processes or analytics while enforcing privacy-by-design principles.

Supported data sources

Cloud DLP can scan and secure sensitive data across various GCP data repositories:

- **Cloud Storage**: Scans objects in *buckets*, supporting both *structured* (CSV, JSON) and unstructured formats (images, PDFs).

- **BigQuery**: Inspects *tables, views*, or *datasets*, applying transformations inline without disrupting workflows.

- **Datastore and Firestore**: Protects application-level *NoSQL data* by identifying sensitive fields in document structures.

- **Streaming inspection**: Real-time protection for data in transit using *Pub/Sub integration* or *REST API* inspection.

- **Hybrid workloads**: Supports *on-premise* or *multi-cloud environments* through API-driven inspection.

This flexibility makes Cloud DLP effective in hybrid or cloud-native architectures.

DLP inspection and masking techniques

Google Cloud DLP supports *comprehensive inspection* capabilities to identify sensitive data based on *regex, contextual rules*, and *ML models*:

- **Predefined detectors**: Social Security Numbers, credit card numbers, National IDs.

- **Custom detectors**: Build pattern matchers for organization-specific data (e.g., Employee IDs).

- **Likelihood scoring**: Classify matches based on certainty levels (very likely, possible, etc.).

- **Masking techniques:**
    - ○ **Partial masking:** Replace all but the last few characters (e.g., --****-1234).
    - ○ **Character substitution:** Replace sensitive data with a placeholder character.
- **Tokenization:**
    - ○ **Format-preserving tokenization:** Retains structure for compatibility with legacy systems.
- **Encryption:** Field-level encryption for *reversible* data transformation.

Configuring DLP jobs to find patterns

Configuring Cloud DLP jobs often involves *using regex to define custom InfoType detectors* to identify sensitive data patterns beyond built-in detectors. This allows for precise matching of organizational data structures (e.g., internal IDs, customer references) while minimizing false positives:

- **Specifying target data sources:** Define Cloud Storage buckets, BigQuery tables, etc.
- **Creating custom InfoType detectors using regex:** Write regex patterns to match specific data formats your organization considers sensitive (e.g., employee IDs, internal reference numbers).
- **Selecting InfoTypes:** Combine custom regex-based InfoTypes with built-in detectors (e.g., EMAIL_ADDRESS, PHONE_NUMBER) to broaden coverage.
- **Defining inspection rules:**
    - ○ Set thresholds for *match likelihood*.
    - ○ Adjust *confidence levels* to fine-tune detection sensitivity and reduce false positives.
    - ○ Use *sampling* for large datasets to optimize cost during scans.
- **Setting actions:**
    - ○ Log findings for auditing and compliance tracking.
    - ○ Automatically *mask or tokenize* identified fields to protect data at rest.
- **Scheduling:** Set recurring scans or on-demand inspections via UI, CLI, or API.
- **Test and optimize:**
    - ○ Run *sample scans* on representative datasets to validate and refine your regular expression (regex) rules.
    - ○ Continuously monitor findings and adjust regular expression (regex) patterns and thresholds to improve accuracy.

For example, CLI command to launch a DLP job:

```
gcloud dlp jobs create --storage-config=bq://mydataset --inspect-
config=infoTypes=EMAIL_ADDRESS
```

This approach enables *fine-grained, organization-specific data discovery* while maintaining scalability and compliance within GCP environments.

Masking, tokenization, and encryption transformations

DLP supports *granular data transformation* options to protect sensitive information:

- **Simple masking**: Obscure parts of data fields (e.g., John Doe | J*** D**).

- **Deterministic encryption**: Encrypts data such that the same input produces the same encrypted output, useful for *join operations*.

- **Format-preserving encryption**: Keeps data structure intact (e.g., 123-45-6789 remains ###-##-####).

- **Date shifting**: Useful for *healthcare data*, shifts dates by a random range to protect patient privacy.

These transformations are essential for:

- *Anonymizing analytics datasets.*

- Meeting *regulatory compliance.*

- Protecting data while maintaining *business utility.*

The following figure shows a reference architecture for using Google Cloud products to add a layer of security to sensitive datasets by using de-identification techniques:

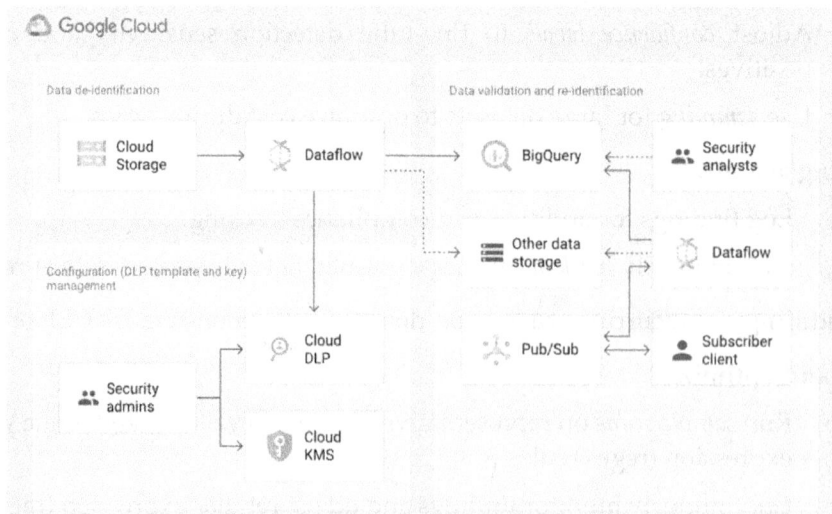

Figure 3.3: Reference design for de-identification and re-identification of sensitive data

Automated versus on-demand scanning

Automated scans periodically review data repositories or incoming streams, flagging sensitive information as it appears. In contrast, on-demand scanning enables you to conduct targeted assessments as needed, providing greater control for one-time checks. Combining both methods strikes a balance between continuous protection and flexibility in responding to emerging threats.

Setting up scheduled scans or real-time scans via Pub/Sub

Automating DLP scanning workflows is crucial to ensure that *newly ingested or modified data* is not overlooked during inspection. Google Cloud DLP offers two primary mechanisms for *automated, continuous protection*:

- **Scheduled scans**:
    - **Purpose**: Ideal for *batch-processing environments* or *static datasets* where new data arrives at predictable intervals (e.g., daily logs, weekly report uploads).
    - **Frequency options**: *Hourly, Daily, Weekly, or Custom Cron Expressions.*
    - **Supported data repositories**:
        - Cloud Storage buckets
        - BigQuery tables or views
        - Datastore/Firestore documents
    - **Configuration**:
        - Use **Google Cloud Console, gcloud CLI**, or **DLP API** to create and manage *recurring DLP jobs.*
        - Optionally enable *email notifications* or *log export* when sensitive data is detected.
    - **Example CLI command**:
      ```
      gcloud dlp jobs create --display-name="Weekly-Bucket-Scan" \
          --schedule="0 0 * * 0" \
          --storage-config=bucket=gs://my-secure-bucket \
          --inspect-config=infoTypes=EMAIL_ADDRESS,PHONE_NUMBER
      ```

- **Real-time scans via Pub/Sub**:
    - **Purpose**: Pub/Sub enables event-driven scanning in environments with *streaming data*, such as *file uploads, API-based ingestion*, or *real-time analytics.*
    - **Functionality**:
        - A *Pub/Sub topic* receives messages when new data arrives (e.g., file upload event in Cloud Storage).

- A Cloud Function or Cloud Run service triggers a *DLP inspection job* automatically.
- Results are logged or processed further for alerting or remediation.

o **Architecture overview**:

- Event (e.g., object created in Cloud Storage)
- Pub/Sub topic
- Cloud Function triggers DLP API
- Inspection job runs
- Results stored in Cloud Logging or sent to the SCC

- **Benefits of automation**:

o **Zero manual intervention**: Ensures *always-on data protection* for sensitive information.

o **Scalability**: Adapts to both *high-throughput streaming pipelines* and *large static datasets*.

o **Policy enforcement**: Automatically enforce redaction or transformation policies as soon as data is ingested.

- **Best practices**:

o Use *different Pub/Sub topics* for *different datasets* to tailor inspection configurations.

o Combine *DLP scan results with SIEM tools* (e.g., Splunk) for centralized incident response.

o Implement *retry logic* in Cloud Functions to handle inspection failures due to transient issues.

By leveraging scheduled scans for *batch data* and Pub/Sub for *real-time pipelines*, organizations can attain *comprehensive, automated data protection* across their cloud environments, *fulfilling compliance requirements* while preserving operational agility.

Integrating DLP findings into dashboards or alerting systems

DLP findings can inform the SCC or third-party SIEM solutions, configure alerts for newly discovered PII or changes in data classification, and prompt immediate remediation or further inspection.

Use cases

Cloud DLP supports various practical scenarios to ensure *data privacy, regulatory compliance, and risk mitigation*. These use cases illustrate how organizations can adapt DLP to their unique workflows, ensuring that sensitive information remains protected while still enabling operational efficiency.

Redacting PII before storing logs

Cloud environments often generate *large volumes of logs* that can unintentionally capture *PII,* such as email addresses, IPs, or user IDs. Before storing logs long-term in Cloud Storage, BigQuery, or logging sinks:

- *DLP can inspect logs* for sensitive content like names, phone numbers, or credit card numbers.

- Fields can be *masked, redacted, or tokenized* before archiving, ensuring that *log data remains useful for troubleshooting* without risking a data breach.

The following are a few examples:

- Mask all detected credit card numbers: `XXXX-XXXX-XXXX-1234`

- Redact email addresses: `[EMAIL_REDACTED]`

The benefit is that it reduces *breach notification obligations* under GDPR or HIPAA in case of a log compromise.

Masking sensitive data in BigQuery analytics pipelines

BigQuery is often used for large-scale *data analytics*, including sensitive user information datasets. With Cloud DLP:

- Specific columns (e.g., name, SSN, date of birth) can be tokenized or encrypted during ETL processes.

- Sensitive data is obfuscated while analytical value is retained, allowing data scientists to query and analyze without direct exposure to PII.

- The advanced use, tokenize PII with reversible tokens, allowing re-identification only under strict access controls.

- The benefit ensures analytics teams can work on rich datasets without violating *privacy.*

Data Erasure Compliance in GCP

Under regulations like **GDPR** and **CCPA**, users have the right to:

- *Access, correct,* or *erase* their personal data.

- Submit **data subject access requests** (**DSARs**) requiring organizations to locate and manage personal data.

Cloud DLP helps by:

- Scanning across Cloud Storage, BigQuery, and other repositories to *identify all occurrences* of an individual's data.

- *De-identifying, masking, or deleting* personal records as per regulatory mandates.

- The automation utilises DLP APIs to automate workflows for responding to DSARS at scale.

- The benefit is to achieve and demonstrate compliance with privacy laws while reducing *manual effort*.

Encryption for GCP Storage Services

Protecting data in analytics platforms and object storage is essential for maintaining privacy, operational resilience, and compliance. In BigQuery, features such as partitioned tables and CMEK enhance security for large-scale queries without sacrificing performance. Meanwhile, Cloud Storage provides encryption configurations that range from GMEK to fully CSEK. By selecting the appropriate encryption model, regularly rotating keys, and integrating with IAM policies, you can create a robust and scalable strategy that prevents data leaks and unauthorized access.

Encrypting data in BigQuery

Encrypting your data in BigQuery is essential for maintaining confidentiality, integrity, and compliance throughout the *data analytics lifecycle*. While Google Cloud offers *default encryption* for all data at rest, more regulated or security-sensitive environments may require CMEK for enhanced control.

Key drivers for choosing advanced encryption in BigQuery include:

- Regulatory compliance (e.g., GDPR, HIPAA, PCI-DSS)
- Internal risk policies requiring more granular key management
- Key lifecycle management, such as periodic rotation and restricted usage
- Data sovereignty and audit requirements for who can access or manage keys

Additionally, understanding how encryption interacts with *table structures*, especially partitioned tables, helps maintain performance while ensuring robust security.

Default encryption vs. CMEK approach for tables

GMEK is sufficient for general encryption. For stricter control, CMEK in BigQuery ensures you have your key rotation and distribution, meeting advanced compliance or internal policy demands:

- **GMEK:** Automatically used by BigQuery for all datasets. Google rotates these keys regularly and meets baseline compliance standards:
  - ○ **Use case:** Suitable for general workloads without strict regulatory demands.
  - ○ **Advantages:** Minimal configuration, automatic protection, no key management overhead.

- **CMEK:**
  - ○ Gives you *control over the encryption keys* used for your BigQuery tables.
  - ○ Allows *key rotation, revocation, and audit logging* for access events.
  - ○ Enforces *data residency* by tying encryption keys to specific geographic regions.

- **When to use CMEK:**
  - ○ Your organization mandates *strict control* over encryption key policies.
  - ○ You need to ensure *key lifecycle compliance* (e.g., monitoring usage logs and rotating keys every 90 days).
  - ○ You want *visibility* into when and how your encryption keys are accessed.

Partitioned tables and encryption interaction

Partitioned tables in BigQuery:

- Divide large datasets into segments (e.g., by date or other columns), improving query efficiency and reducing *costs*.

- Encryption applies *uniformly* to all partitions, whether using GMEK or CMEK.

The following are the key considerations for the implementation of Partitioned tables:

- *Partition-specific access controls* can work in conjunction with encryption, ensuring only authorized users query sensitive partitions.

- Ensure *CMEK policies* align across all partitions to prevent *security gaps*.

- When *rotating CMEK*, verify that all associated partitions are consistently updated to *maintain encryption continuity*.

The following are some additional considerations:

- Monitor *key access logs* through Cloud Audit logs to track who accesses or manages your CMEK.

- Automate key *rotation policies* using Cloud KMS.

- Ensure that any *BI tools or workflows* interacting with encrypted data are configured to handle CMEK-secured datasets properly.

By aligning encryption strategies with *partitioning schemes* and *key management policies*, BigQuery users can maintain high levels of *data protection* without sacrificing *performance* or *operational flexibility*.

CMEK performance in heavy workloads

Encryption overhead may introduce minimal latency or cost. Assess the performance tolerance of your data pipeline. Rotations or frequent key changes can disrupt workflows if not meticulously planned.

Encrypting data in Cloud Storage

Cloud Storage helps you maintain end-to-end data confidentiality for file-based workloads by applying encryption at the bucket or object level. Depending on your desired level of operational oversight, you can choose between Google-managed keys and customer-managed keys (CMEK or CSEK). Proper versioning management, integrated IAM policies, and well-planned key rotation all contribute to a robust encryption model for Cloud Storage.

Per-object vs. bucket-level encryption

Encryption in Google Cloud Storage supports both *per-object* and *bucket-level* encryption, each suited for different security and operational needs:

- **Per-object encryption**:
    - Allows for *granular key management* where each file (object) can be encrypted with a unique CMEK or CSEK.
    - Useful in scenarios where different data owners or departments require *separate key control*.
    - Supports fine-tuned auditing, each key's access is logged individually, making it easier to monitor *specific file access*.

- **Bucket-level encryption**:
    - Simplifies management by applying the *same encryption key* to all objects within a bucket.
    - Reduces *administrative overhead*, especially in environments with thousands or millions of objects.
    - Ideal for *uniform data sets* where applying consistent key policies simplifies *compliance reporting*.

Transitioning from GMEK to CMEK or CSEK

Shifting from GMEK, CMEK, or CSEK involves critical planning to prevent data loss or compliance gaps:

- **Pre-migration steps**:
  - o **Inventory existing data**: Identify resources encrypted with GMEK (e.g., buckets, disks, tables).
  - o **Backup and test**: Before applying new keys, backup critical datasets and validate re-encryption on test workloads.

- **Migration process**:
  - o Re-encrypt data by rewriting it with the new CMEK or CSEK assigned.
  - o Use tools like gsutil rewrite or BigQuery table copy to trigger re-encryption at rest.

- **Post-migration validation**:
  - o Ensure *audit logs* confirm usage of new keys.
  - o Validate that *access controls* linked to CMEK/CSEK are correctly enforced and *no GMEK keys remain active*.

Handling versioned objects under encryption changes

Object versioning enables the *retention of previous file versions* in Cloud Storage, but ensuring encryption consistency across these versions is critical:

- **Encryption alignment**:
  - o When a bucket switches from GMEK to CMEK, all future versions will use the new CMEK, but *older versions* may still be under GMEK.
  - o Perform *version-aware re-encryption* if historical data also requires migration under new keys.

- **Access and lifecycle management**:
  - o IAM policies must ensure that only authorized users can access both current and past versions.
  - o Implement *lifecycle rules* to automatically delete or archive older versions after a compliance-defined period while retaining *encryption integrity*.

Cross-service use cases

In complex cloud environments, data often flows across multiple services, necessitating *end-to-end encryption* consistency:

- **Multi-service pipelines**:
  - o Workflows involving Cloud Storage, Dataflow, BigQuery, and Pub/Sub must apply the same CMEK throughout all stages.

- o This guarantees *data-in-transit* and *data-at-rest* security and streamlines *auditing*.
- **Key policy uniformity**: Ensure that each component of the pipeline respects IAM roles linked to the CMEK, avoiding weak links in encryption enforcement.

Encryption in multi-region storage

GCP offers multi-region and dual-region storage for high availability and disaster recovery:

- **Key accessibility:**
  - o CMEKs tied to multi-region data must be accessible in *all regions* involved.
  - o Set *CMEK locations* strategically to meet *data residency and latency* needs.
- **Compliance considerations:**
  - o Ensure CMEKs comply *with local data laws* (e.g., GDPR for Europe, HIPAA in the US).
  - o *Replicated data* must maintain the *same encryption level* across all regions.
- **Operational continuity:**
  - o **Plan for key redundancy**: if a CMEK becomes unavailable in one region, ensure it can still decrypt data in another without service interruption.

By implementing consistent encryption controls across *objects, services, and regions*, organizations can *enhance their security policies*, ensure *compliance*, and minimize the risk of *data exposure* in hybrid and multi-cloud environments.

Compliance alignment for regulations

Strong encryption policies are essential for regulatory compliance, whether you are handling personal data under the GDPR, protecting health information under HIPAA, or meeting various other industry mandates. Google Cloud's flexible encryption framework, along with thorough auditing and key management, provides the tools necessary to address these obligations. Ensuring that data is properly masked, anonymized, or deleted when required not only fulfills legal standards but also fosters trust with users and stakeholders.

Regulatory landscape

The global regulatory environment encompasses various data protection standards, each with specific requirements for storing, transmitting, and processing information. From well-known frameworks like PCI-DSS, HIPAA, and GDPR to emerging regional laws, maintaining compliance can be challenging for organizations with dynamic cloud workloads. In Google Cloud, features such as Cloud KMS, Cloud DLP, and advanced IAM controls aid in navigating this complex terrain, empowering you to address each regulation's nuanced demands.

Overview of major regulations

Google Cloud's encryption and key management tools are designed to meet the *stringent requirements* of global regulatory standards, supporting organizations across various industries:

- **Health Insurance Portability and Accountability Act (HIPAA):**
    - Requires protection of ePHI.
    - GCP ensures compliance through encryption at rest or in transit, audit logging, and access controls.
    - Covered services are listed in GCP's *HIPAA Implementation Guide*, with signed **business associate agreements** (**BAAs**) available.

- **Payment Card Industry Data Security Standard (PCI-DSS):**
    - Mandates *encryption of cardholder data*, strict *key management policies*, and *access monitoring*.
    - GCP is certified as *PCI-DSS compliant*, and customers can use CMEK to enforce key control for systems handling payment data.

- **GDPR or California Consumer Privacy Act (CCPA):**
    - Focuses on *personal data protection, right to access, right to be forgotten, and data residency*.
    - GCP offers tools like Cloud DLP for data classification and *region-specific key management* to ensure compliance.

- **Federal Risk and Authorization Management Program (FedRAMP):**
    - U.S. government standard for *cloud service security*.
    - GCP offers *FedRAMP Moderate-certified* services, meeting strict *encryption, identity management, and logging* requirements.

- **ISO/IEC 27001, 27017, 27018:**
    - International standards for *information security management and privacy in cloud services*.
    - GCP's global infrastructure meets *ISO certification standards*, assuring customers of robust *risk management and data protection*.

Common encryption requirements

Across regulatory frameworks, *encryption and data protection* principles exhibit *consistent themes* that are well-supported by Google Cloud's security capabilities:

- **Data encryption at-rest and in-transit:**
  - All sensitive data must be *encrypted during storage* (at-rest) and transmission across networks (in-transit).
  - GCP automatically provides *default encryption*, with CMEK/CSEK available for *enhanced control*.

- **Key management and rotation:**
  - Keys must be *securely generated, stored, and rotated* periodically (e.g., annually for PCI-DSS, reviewed regularly for HIPAA).
  - GCP's Cloud KMS and Cloud HSM support *automated and manual key rotation policies*.

- **Access Control and Privilege Management:**
  - Only authorised users/systems can access sensitive data or manage keys.
  - *IAM roles, least-privilege principles, and auditing* are critical.
  - Workload Identity ensures *short-lived credentials* instead of long-term keys.

- **Logging and monitoring:**
  - Detailed *audit trails* are required for tracking *data access, key usage, and security events*.
  - Logs should be *centralised* (e.g., via **Cloud Logging** or the **Security Command Centre**) and retained according to compliance rules.

- **Incident response and breach notification:**
  - Regulations like GDPR require *notification within 72 hours* of detecting a breach.
  - GCP offers tools for *security incident detection, alerting, and automated workflows* to facilitate response.

These unified requirements reflect a *defense-in-depth* approach, ensuring that *data confidentiality, integrity, and availability* are maintained across all cloud environment layers. GCP provides the infrastructure and tools for enterprises to *align with these global standards effectively*.

Google Cloud Platform compliance resources

Google Cloud offers various resources, including its compliance resource center, third-party audit reports, and documentation that maps GCP controls to industry requirements, to support your efforts in demonstrating adherence to privacy and security frameworks. These resources clarify how GCP services align with certifications such as ISO 27001 and SOC 2, helping you reduce the time and effort needed for compliance validation. By leveraging these materials, you can streamline audit processes and confidently showcase a strong security posture.

Compliance resource center

Google Cloud's compliance resource center serves as a comprehensive hub for all certifications, regulatory frameworks, and compliance-related documentation that GCP follows. It is especially beneficial for customers operating in *regulated industries* or preparing for *third-party audits*.

The following are the key features:

- **Audit artifacts**: This provides access to *attestation reports, certifications, and audit documentation* for standards such as ISO 27001, SOC 1/2/3, PCI-DSS, FedRAMP, and more.

- **Mapping guides**: Detailed mappings of GCP services against specific regulations (e.g., GDPR, HIPAA, CCPA) allow you to *align your cloud environment* with compliance mandates.

- **Policy templates**: Pre-built resources that help teams *design policies, risk assessments, and compliance checklists* based on GCP's architecture.

- **Customer responsibility matrix**: This matrix outlines *shared responsibility* across compliance domains, helping clarify *what GCP covers* and *what you must secure*.

The following are the usage scenarios:

- Preparing for *external audits* by providing third-party validated *proof of compliance*.

- Designing *regulated solutions* with confidence, leveraging *certified infrastructure*.

- Benchmarking internal policies against *industry standards*.

Region and residency considerations for GDPR

Under the GDPR, organizations that process the personal data of EU residents must ensure compliance with data residency, localization, and cross-border transfer regulations.

The following are the key considerations:

- **Data localization:**
  - GCP allows data to be *stored and processed in EU-specific regions* such as *europe-west1 (Belgium), europe-west4 (Netherlands), or europe-north1 (Finland)*.
  - These regions ensure *compliance with EU residency laws*, reducing risks associated with data leaving the **European Economic Area (EEA)**.

- **Cross-border data transfers:**
  - If data must be accessed outside the EEA, organizations must use SCCs or rely on *approved frameworks* (e.g., *EU-US Data Privacy Framework, where applicable*).
  - GCP's *Access Transparency* provides visibility into *Google staff access* and *data handling locations*.

- **Multi-regional support:**
  - GCP's *multi-regional configurations* (e.g., *Europe and the US*) allow for *high availability*, but *key usage or CMEK controls* must be restricted to specific *regional endpoints*.
  - Encryption keys can be *regionally scoped,* ensuring data protection aligns with GDPR's *territorial scope*.

- **Key usage compliance:**
  - Using CMEK in *EU regions* guarantees that only *authorized personnel* and *automated systems* can access encrypted data, aiding *cross-border compliance*.
  - GCP logs help *track access,* ensuring *compliance reporting* is possible during audits or breach notifications.

The following are the additional tools:

- **Organization Policy Service:** Enforce region-specific *resource deployment restrictions*.
- **Data residency reports:** Monitor where your data is stored and ensure *geographic* constraints are honoured.

Designing regulated solutions

Building cloud architectures that comply with strict regulatory requirements demands careful planning and robust security measures. With Google Cloud's encryption services, DLP tools, and IAM frameworks, you can establish end-to-end workflows that meet high standards for data minimization, pseudonymization, and auditability. Integrating these capabilities at every layer, from key rotation policies to automated remediation, lays the foundation for reliable, compliant solutions that can withstand both internal and external challenges and scrutiny.

Using CMEK with specific rotation policies

To comply with PCI-DSS, HIPAA, or similar regulatory frameworks, CMEK in Cloud KMS provides granular control over key lifecycle events:

- **Rotation policies:**
  - Rotate keys on a *predefined schedule* (e.g., every 90 days or annually), or immediately following a *security incident*.
  - Automate rotations via Cloud Scheduler or use Cloud KMS API to rotate keys with minimal disruption.
  - *Split key versions* allow old data to remain decryptable while new data uses rotated keys.

- **Access control:**

  - Apply *IAM roles* (e.g., roles/cloudkms.cryptoKeyEncrypterDecrypter) only to authorized users or services.

  - Enforce *IAM conditions* to restrict key usage by *location, time, or specific identities.*

- **Auditability:**

  - Enable *Cloud Audit logs* for detailed tracking of key access, rotations, and usage events.

  - Create *alerts* for anomalous access patterns, e.g., unexpected key use outside approved hours.

By implementing structured rotation policies, you *mitigate key compromise risks*, ensure *cryptographic agility,* and stay compliant with *auditable proof* of security controls.

DLP-driven data classification

Cloud DLP plays a crucial role in ensuring *privacy compliance* by identifying and *managing PII*:

- **Classification workflow:**

  - Run *DLP scans* on *BigQuery datasets, Cloud Storage buckets, or Datastore* to detect sensitive fields like *credit card numbers, SSNs, or email addresses.*

  - Configure *DLP templates* to automatically classify *custom data types* specific to your business.

- **Transformation actions:**

  - Apply *masking* (e.g., partial redaction) *to log data* before storage.

  - Use *pseudonymization or tokenization for analytics* workflows—preserving data utility without exposing identities.

  - Apply *encryption* on sensitive fields if long-term storage with potential re-identification is required.

- **Compliance alignment:**

  - Aligns with GDPR's Article 25 (data protection by design and default) and HIPAA's *privacy rule.*

  - Supports data minimization, limiting exposure by handling only what is necessary.

The key benefit is that it proactively manages sensitive data exposure risks, ensuring regulatory data subject rights and minimizing breach impact.

Documentation and audit readiness

For a secure and compliant cloud environment, *continuous documentation* and *audit preparation* are essential:

- **Logging requirements**:
    - Log all key activities, such as *key creation, rotation, access, IAM role assignments, and DLP transformations*.
    - Export logs to Cloud Logging, BigQuery, or SIEM tools for long-term retention and correlation.

- **Compliance artifacts**:
    - Maintain evidence of security controls, such as:
    - CMEK usage policies.
    - *DLP job configurations* and *execution results*.
    - *IAM audit reports* showing least-privilege enforcement.
    - Generate *automated compliance reports for internal or external audits*.

- **Readiness testing**:
    - Conduct *mock audits* to verify that all *documentation and log data* align with regulatory requirements.
    - Regularly test *data recovery procedures* to ensure key availability during incidents.
    - Use *GCP's compliance resource center* to cross-check your posture against evolving regulatory benchmarks.

Proper documentation ensures *transparency*, supports *incident response*, and *demonstrates due diligence* during compliance reviews.

HIPAA-compliant architecture for healthcare startup

For startups managing ePHI, compliance with HIPAA necessitates comprehensive data security:

- **Data encryption**:
    - Store ePHI in BigQuery, encrypted using CMEK for strict key control.
    - Enable Cloud KMS key rotation regularly (e.g., every 90 days).

- **Access control**:
    - Apply least-privilege IAM roles (e.g., `roles/bigquery.dataViewer`) to restrict who can access patient data.
    - Use IAM conditions to limit access to specific *IP ranges or times*.

- **Data Loss Prevention**:
    - Run Cloud DLP scans on datasets to detect and classify sensitive fields (e.g., names, SSNs, medical records).
    - Mask or tokenize fields where full identifiers are not needed for analytics.
- **Logging and monitoring**:
    - Use Cloud Audit logs to track all access to CMEK keys and ePHI datasets.
    - Logs should be integrated into the Security Command Centre for centralized monitoring and alerts on unauthorised access.
- **Backup and recovery**: Enforce encrypted backups, ensuring disaster recovery meets HIPAA's *availability and integrity* standards.

The outcome is that the startup achieves *regulatory compliance*, maintains *patient privacy*, and scales securely within the cloud.

GDPR compliant workflow for EU-based retailer

Retailers serving *EU customers* must comply with GDPR, emphasizing *data sovereignty, user rights, and secure processing*:

- **Data residency and encryption:**
    - Store personal data in EU multi-region GCP Storage.
    - Apply CMEK for all data, ensuring encryption keys remain under company control.
- **Right to be forgotten:**
    - Use Cloud DLP to identify personal data across Cloud Storage and BigQuery.
    - Implement automated deletion workflows or pseudonymization for data subjects requesting erasure.
- **Cross-border control:**
    - Restrict key operations to EU-only regions, avoiding transfers outside the EEA.
    - Use organization policies to enforce residency constraints on resources.
- **Audit and transparency:**
    - Log all key usage, data access, and DLP actions.
    - Provide audit trails to **Data Protection Authorities (DPAs)** upon request.
- **Consent management:**
    - Maintain logs of user consent for data processing.
    - Align BigQuery analytics pipelines to process only consented data, using partitioned tables for easier management.

The outcome is that the retailer aligns with GDPR mandates, offers customers transparency and control over their data, and avoids penalties from non-compliance.

Complex made simple

Data in GCP is like valuables in a fortress. Multiple layers, including IAM (the gatekeepers), encryption (the strongholds), key management (the master keys), and DLP (the surveillance system), ensure that only authorized individuals can access and handle sensitive information. Regulations serve as legal and safety standards for fortress security, requiring consistent audits, transformations (masking, tokenization), and well-documented defenses. This fortress analogy highlights how each tool and best practice safeguards your *treasure* from internal errors or external threats.

By solidifying strategies such as CMEK vs. GMEK, Cloud HSM for hardware-level security, Cloud DLP scanning, and automated encryption enforcement, you can secure data from end-to-end. With this encryption, key management, and DLP insights, you can confidently extend robust data security across GCP's entire ecosystem, preparing for advanced zero-trust setups, multi-cloud governance, and beyond.

Conclusion

Data security and encryption in GCP go beyond simply activating built-in features; they require a comprehensive understanding of encryption types (at rest, in transit, and in use), key management practices, and compliance factors. By examining Cloud KMS, DLP, and advanced options such as CSEK or Cloud HSM, you can tailor your encryption strategy to meet your operational needs and regulatory requirements. In addition to monitoring, auditing, and adhering to best practices for BigQuery and Cloud Storage, these approaches help maintain data confidentiality and integrity throughout the entire cloud journey.

The next chapter will review network security on the GCP.

Exercise

1. Enable CMEK in a Cloud Storage bucket to gain hands-on experience with GCP's data encryption features.

    a. First, create a new key ring and a symmetric key in Cloud KMS, for example, *demo-keyring and demo-key*.

    b. Then, navigate to Cloud Storage, select an existing or newly created bucket, and under Bucket Settings, enable Default Encryption using the key you just created.

    c. Finally, upload a test file, such as `sample.txt`, to confirm that it is encrypted with your custom key and verify the encryption details either in the Cloud Console or through the gcloud command-line interface.

Key takeaways

- **Encryption fundamentals:**

  o **Encryption at rest and in transit**: GCP automatically encrypts data at rest with Google-managed keys. In transit encryption (TLS/SSL) secures data movements between GCP services and clients.

  o **Encryption-in-use (confidential computing)**: Confidential VMs protect data in memory using hardware-based TEEs, which are ideal for highly sensitive workloads.

- **Key management with Cloud KMS:**

  o **Cloud KMS architecture**: Key rings group cryptographic keys, each with multiple versions for rotation.

  o **CMEK vs. Google-managed keys**: CMEK offers granular control, meeting stricter compliance needs.

  o **Access controls and logging**: IAM roles (for example, CryptoKeyEncrypterDecrypter) restrict usage, while audit logs track key creation, rotation, and usage.

- **CSEK and Cloud HSM:**

  o **CSEK**: Maximum ownership of keys, but adds management complexity (key generation, rotation, backups).

  o **Cloud HSM**: Hardware-backed security at FIPS 140-2 Level 3, integrated with Cloud KMS for tamper-resistant key storage.

  o **Pros or cons**: Deeper compliance vs. operational overhead; evaluate latency, cost implications, and risk appetite.

- **Cloud DLP for sensitive data:**

  o **Discover and classify**: Cloud DLP automatically identifies PII, PCI, and HIPAA data across GCP.

  o **Data transformations**: Masking, tokenisation, and encryption to secure sensitive fields without losing data utility.

  o **Real-time or scheduled scanning**: Integrate via Pub/Sub or scheduled jobs, feeding results into SCC or SIEM for continuous protection.

- **Best practices for BigQuery and Cloud Storage encryption:**

  o **BigQuery**: GMEK for simplicity, CMEK for compliance; partitioned tables remain encrypted seamlessly.

- o **Cloud Storage**: Per-object encryption for fine-grained control vs. bucket-level for uniform policies; handle versioning carefully.

- o **Operational considerations**: Monitor encryption status with logs, automate policy enforcement (for example, Org Policy), and rotate keys without disrupting queries.

- **Compliance alignment:**

  - o **Regulations**: These include HIPAA, PCI-DSS, GDPR, and FedRAMP, which all emphasize encryption at rest and in transit, key management, access control, and logging.

  - o **GCP resources**: Compliance resource center, region-specific data residency, CMEK usage for advanced control.

  - o **Designing regulated solutions**: Combine encryption with Cloud DLP classification or masking, robust documentation, auditable logs, and frequent key rotations.

References

1. https://cloud.google.com/kms/docs/cmek

2. https://cloud.google.com/security

3. https://cloud.google.com/security/encryption-at-rest

4. https://cloud.google.com/kms/docs

5. https://cloud.google.com/hsm/docs

6. https://cloud.google.com/dlp/docs

7. https://cloud.google.com/security/compliance/resource-center

8. https://cloud.google.com/iam/docs

9. https://cloud.google.com/security-command-center/docs

10. https://cloud.google.com/logging/docs

11. https://cloud.google.com/monitoring/docs

12. https://cloud.google.com/identity/docs

13. https://csrc.nist.gov/publications/detail/sp/800-57-part-1/rev-5/final

14. https://cheatsheetseries.owasp.org/cheatsheets/Cryptographic_Storage_Cheat_Sheet.html

CHAPTER 4

Network Security in GCP

Introduction

Network security is a cornerstone of a robust **Google Cloud Platform** (**GCP**) architecture as organizations migrate critical applications and workloads to the cloud. A secure network environment ensures the confidentiality and integrity of data both *in transit and at rest*, while guaranteeing the uninterrupted availability of services to legitimate users. While GCP provides *built-in encryption* for data at rest and in transit, this chapter focuses on *additional controls to strengthen your cloud security posture*.

In an era of increasingly sophisticated cyber threats, a well-designed and well-managed network infrastructure can be decisive in preventing data breaches, service disruptions, and reputational damage. For example, many organizations face **distributed denial-of-service** (**DDoS**) attacks that can overwhelm services and disrupt business operations. GCP mitigates these risks using Cloud Armor, which automatically blocks malicious traffic patterns while maintaining service availability, illustrating how cloud-native tools can proactively defend against real-world threats.

In this chapter, you will establish a foundational understanding of **Virtual Private Cloud** (**VPCs**) in GCP. You will learn how to configure subnets, routes, and firewalls, elements that form the backbone of any secure, scalable cloud network. Building on these fundamentals, the chapter explores advanced features such as Shared VPCs and VPC Service Controls, which enable centralized governance and finely tuned perimeter defenses across multiple projects and teams.

To protect external-facing services and manage outbound connectivity, you will explore tools like Cloud Armor for DDoS protection and Cloud NAT, which enables internet access without exposing private resources. The discussion then transitions to *network segmentation and micro-segmentation*, illustrating strategies for isolating critical workloads and containing lateral movement, thereby reducing an attacker's potential impact.

Lastly, this chapter addresses *hybrid networking solutions* that connect your on-premises data centers to GCP via VPN, Direct Interconnect, or Partner Interconnect. These options combine secure communication with scalable performance, facilitating seamless workload migration and integrated management across hybrid or multi-cloud deployments.

By following the concepts and best practices outlined here, you can build network architectures that meet modern security standards, *adapt quickly to evolving business needs*, and stay resilient against emerging threats, fundamental necessities in today's cloud-centric world.

Structure

In this chapter, we will be discussing the following topics:

- Virtual Private Cloud foundations
- Shared VPC security control
- Securing ingress and egress traffic
- Network segmentation strategies
- Implementing firewall strategies and use cases
- Hybrid connectivity solutions in Google Cloud
- Complex made simple

Objectives

By the end of this chapter, you will have developed a comprehensive understanding of how to design and secure network architectures within GCP. You will explore the fundamentals of VPCs, including how they are organized, governed, and structured through subnetting, routing, and basic firewall configurations. Emphasis will be placed on centralizing network administration by utilizing tools such as Shared VPC and VPC Service Controls, which are essential for strengthening perimeter security across multiple projects.

You will learn how to secure traffic flow by protecting public-facing endpoints using Cloud Armour and managing outbound traffic through Cloud NAT to minimise exposure to external threats. Techniques for isolating and segmenting workloads will also be covered, highlighting the importance of micro-segmentation in reducing attack surfaces and containing potential breaches within the environment. Furthermore, the chapter will explore advanced firewall practices, enabling you to tailor firewall rules to suit specific workload requirements for a robust defense strategy.

Finally, you will understand how to enable hybrid connectivity, integrating on-premises infrastructure with GCP through VPN, Direct Interconnect, or Partner Interconnect solutions to maintain secure, consistent, high-performance connections in hybrid cloud environments. Mastering these skills will prepare you to align cloud deployments with your organization's security priorities and operational demands.

Virtual Private Cloud foundations

A VPC is the cornerstone of network architecture in Google Cloud, enabling secure and scalable connectivity for resources. It provides an isolated environment for deploying, managing, and controlling compute resources, databases, and services, while supporting customizable IP ranges and subnetworks. Organizations can implement VPCs to replicate traditional on-premises networks with added flexibility while benefiting from cloud-native scalability.

Mastering VPC design, including effective subnet structuring, route configuration, and firewall rule management, is critical for establishing secure communication paths and enforcing access controls within the cloud. A well-designed VPC foundation ensures that workloads operate in a controlled and governed environment, supporting internal processes and secure external integrations without unnecessary complexity or redundancy.

Introduction to Virtual Private Cloud

A VPC in Google Cloud offers a flexible, software-defined network for your applications and services. By logically isolating resources, a VPC ensures that traffic remains confined within specific boundaries, providing fine-grained control over how workloads communicate internally and externally. Whether deploying a simple web application or orchestrating a multi-tier architecture across multiple regions, VPCs enable you to design secure, high-performance networks that meet your operational needs.

The following figure reflects how a globally distributed network can be configured across regions, leveraging VPCs:

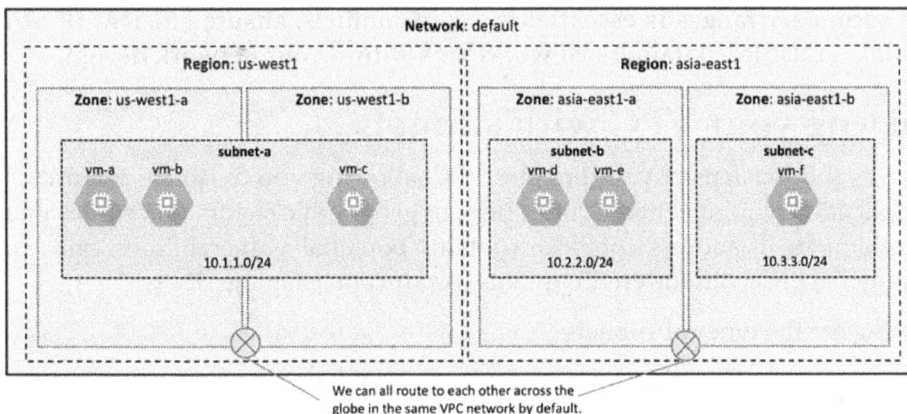

Figure 4.1: A globally distributed virtual network spanning all regions

Understanding the building blocks of GCP networking

GCP networking is anchored by three key components: *subnets, routes,* and *firewall rules.* Together, they establish the foundation of a secure and well-structured cloud environment. Subnets segment your IP address space and organize resources, while routes determine how packets navigate through your networks, and firewall rules control traffic flow in and out. Mastering these elements will prepare you to build robust network topologies that balance security, scalability, and maintainability.

The following are the key components of GCP networking:

- **Subnets:** They divide your VPC into smaller segments within specified regions, enabling you to organize and secure resources logically.

- **Routes:** Create pathways for network traffic to reach its destination, ensuring efficient packet delivery within and outside the VPC.

- **Firewall rules:** Manage inbound and outbound traffic based on IP addresses, ports, protocols, and other attributes.

Subnet configuration for network design

Subnets are the fundamental building blocks of network segmentation within a VPC. By dividing a VPC into subnets, you can control how resources are allocated and accessed across regions and availability zones. Each subnet defines an IP address range and is a logical boundary for deploying virtual machines and other services. Proper subnet design is essential for organizing workloads, implementing security zones, and optimizing network traffic. Through careful planning, you can ensure that subnets align with your organizational structure, regional compliance needs, and scalability requirements while simplifying routing and firewall management.

Note: **Subnets in GCP can also be configured with secondary IP address ranges, which are often used for Google Kubernetes Engine (GKE) pod and service IP allocations. Planning for these secondary ranges is essential to avoid conflicts, ensure efficient IP utilisation, and maintain scalable, containerised workloads within your network design.**

Organizing your VPC with subnets

Subnets act as subdivisions of your broader VPC, allowing you to isolate resources based on specific application requirements, security tiers, or geographic factors. A well-designed subnet strategy minimizes IP address conflicts, contains potential vulnerabilities, and streamlines traffic routing between various environments (production, staging, dev).

The following are the types of subnets:

- **Regional subnets** extend across multiple regional zones, ensuring automatic high availability. If one zone experiences an outage, resources in the other zones within the same subnet can continue to operate without significant configuration changes.

- **Custom subnets** allow you to define specific IP ranges and subnet sizes, providing detailed control over your network design. This approach is particularly advantageous for large deployments or connecting with on-premises networks that need specific address spaces.

To help you decide, which subnet to use, the following table summarizes the key differences between regional and custom subnets:

Feature	Regional Subnets	Custom Subnets
Use case	High availability across zones within a region	Fine-tuning IP ranges for large or complex deployments
Availability	Automatic failover within the region	Depends on the defined IP ranges and configuration
Pros	Simplifies HA setup, resilient to zone outages	Detailed control supports specific addressing needs
Cons	Less granular control over IP allocation	Requires careful planning, potential for complexity
Best for	Standard workloads needing HA	On-prem connectivity, complex network segmentation

Table 4.1: Comparison of regional vs. custom subnets in GCP

The following are the best practices:

- **Plan IP addressing:** Allocate IP ranges that support future growth to avoid tedious renumbering in the future.

- **Utilize private and public subnets:** Isolate resources requiring public internet access (for example, web front-ends) from those that must remain private (for example, databases).

- **Avoid overlapping IPs:** If you have a hybrid setup, ensure your VPC's IP ranges do not conflict with your on-premises networks to prevent routing issues or connectivity problems.

Configuring routes for efficient network traffic

Routing in Google Cloud's VPC determines how traffic moves between subnets, external networks, and the internet. By configuring custom routes, you define the paths packets take, which enables precise control over internal communications and external connectivity. Effective routing ensures optimal traffic flow, reduces latency, and supports secure data transfer across your cloud infrastructure. Understanding how to use system-generated routes and create custom routes tailored to specific workloads or security requirements is essential for maintaining performance and compliance in a cloud environment.

Managing network traffic with routes

Routes define the paths data packets take within your VPC and how they exit external networks. In GCP, each VPC automatically includes a set of routes for internal communication. In contrast, custom routes allow for specialized traffic flows, such as directing requests to a specific security appliance or enabling access to partner services.

The following are the types of routes:

- Default routes are automatically created to facilitate essential communication within the VPC and among subnets. When no more specific route is defined, a default Internet gateway route typically directs traffic to the public Internet.

- Administrators create *custom routes* to tailor routing behaviors. For instance, you can establish a custom route that directs traffic for a specific IP range through a VPN tunnel or firewall appliance.

The following sample code snippet can be used as a reference to create a *subnet, route, and firewall rule* in your VPC:

```
# 1. Create a new custom-mode VPC network named 'my-secure-network'
# Custom mode allows you to define your own subnets rather than auto-created
ones.
gcloud compute networks create my-secure-network \
    --subnet-mode=custom

# 2. Add a custom subnet in the 'us-central1' region with the IP range
10.0.1.0/24
# This subnet will be used to deploy resources within the specified IP range.
gcloud compute networks subnets create my-subnet-us-central \
    --network=my-secure-network \
    --region=us-central1 \
    --range=10.0.1.0/24

# 3. Create a custom route for traffic destined to 10.0.2.0/24 to go via the
default internet gateway
# Useful for defining specific routing behavior for outgoing or inter-subnet
traffic.
gcloud compute routes create my-custom-route \
    --network=my-secure-network \
    --destination-range=10.0.2.0/24 \
    --next-hop-gateway=default-internet-gateway

# 4. Create a firewall rule to allow SSH (TCP port 22) only from a trusted IP
range
# This enhances security by restricting SSH access to known IP addresses.
gcloud compute firewall-rules create allow-ssh-trusted \
    --network=my-secure-network \
    --allow=tcp:22 \
```

```
--source-ranges=198.51.100.0/24 \
--description="Allow SSH only from trusted IP"
```

In the above code:

- The VPC is created in custom subnet mode.
- A custom subnet is added in us-central1 with IP range 10.0.1.0/24.
- A custom route sends traffic destined for 10.0.2.0/24 to the default internet gateway.
- A firewall rule only allows SSH (tcp:22) from the 198.51.100.0/24 IP range.

The following are the best practices to manage network traffic with routes:

- **Simplify route tables** by organizing them to prevent confusion and minimize the risk of conflicting rules.
- **Assign priorities appropriately:** Focus on more specific routes to ensure traffic follows the most accurate path.
- **Review routes regularly:** Conduct regular audits to ensure current routes align with existing architecture and security policies. Retire outdated routes to maintain clarity and compliance.

Firewall configuration for network security

Firewall rules in Google Cloud VPC serve as the first line of defense for controlling network access to and from your resources. These rules define which traffic is allowed or denied based on factors such as IP ranges, protocols, and ports. By strategically implementing firewall configurations, you can protect your virtual machines, services, and data from unauthorized access while permitting legitimate communication for your applications. Understanding and applying firewall policies ensures that your cloud network remains secure, compliant, and resilient against evolving threats.

Implementing firewall rules for traffic control

Firewall rules in GCP act as your first line of defense for managing inbound and outbound traffic. By examining packet attributes such as source IP, destination IP, port, and protocol, you can allow or deny requests based on your application's security requirements. These rules can be configured to apply broadly (across subnets) or narrowly (to specific tagged resources or service accounts).

The following are the different types of firewall rules:

- **Ingress rules:** Manage incoming connections to resources within your VPC. For instance, you can allow HTTPS traffic from the public internet to web servers while restricting SSH access to a trusted IP range only.
- **Egress rules** regulate outbound connections made by instances and services. For example, an egress rule may restrict servers from making outbound calls to unapproved domains, preventing data exfiltration.

The following are the best practices to implement firewall rules for traffic control:

- **Adopt a least privilege approach:** Allow only the necessary traffic for your application. By default, block or deny all other traffic.

- **Use network tags and service accounts:** Instead of relying only on IP addresses, utilize tags or service accounts to target specific groups of instances or microservices with detailed rules.

- **Regularly update rules:** As your workloads evolve, revisit firewall policies to block newly identified attack vectors or accommodate legitimate changes in traffic patterns.

Shared VPC security controls

Shared VPC and VPC Service Controls in Google Cloud enable centralized network and security management across multiple projects within an organization. Shared VPC allows administrators to define and control networking resources from a host project while enabling service projects to utilize those resources securely. VPC Service Controls, on the other hand, add a layer of protection by establishing a security perimeter around services to prevent data exfiltration and enforce strong service-to-service communication boundaries.

For example, an organization can set up VPC Service Controls to create a security perimeter around Cloud Storage buckets containing sensitive customer data, ensuring that only traffic from approved VPC networks or service accounts can access the data while blocking access from unauthorized networks or identities.

Together, Shared VPC and VPC Service Controls streamline network governance, improve isolation, and ensure consistent application of security policies across complex environments.

Centralized network management with Shared VPC

Shared VPC enables multiple projects within your organization to connect to a centrally managed VPC network. Instead of creating and configuring separate networks in each project, you designate one project as the *host*, which owns the VPC infrastructure. Other *service* projects use these shared subnets, firewall rules, and routes. This approach simplifies administration and helps maintain consistent security policies across teams and departments.

The following are the key components of a Shared VPC:

- **Host project:** The central hub for all VPC network resources, including subnets, routes, and firewall rules. This project exclusively owns and manages the underlying network.

- **Service projects:** Connect to the host project network to access its subnets and resources. Each service project retains its IAM settings, budgets, and other configurations.

- **Resource sharing:** It ensures that firewall policies, routing rules, and subnet definitions are managed centrally, which minimizes the risk of conflicting settings across various projects.

The following are the benefits of leveraging Shared VPCs:

- **Centralized control:** A single team can define and enforce network standards, preventing unintentional misconfigurations or overlapping IP ranges.

- **Reduced duplication:** Administrators prevent replicating VPCs across multiple projects, streamlining the addition of new services or teams.

- **Uniform security:** Shared VPCs ensure all service projects inherit the same firewall rules and network routes, simplifying compliance efforts.

The following are the best practices while implementing Shared VPCs:

- **Designate a dedicated host project:** Isolate the core network components within a specialized *infrastructure* or *network* project to separate them from application deployments, ensuring clearer accountability.

- **Implement stringent IAM permissions:** Limit modifications to Shared VPC resources. Clearly defined IAM roles avert unauthorized alterations to firewall policies, subnets, or routes.

- **Utilize network tags and service accounts:** Employ network tags to apply context-specific firewall rules, permit SSH access only from known IP addresses, or utilize service accounts to grant minimal privileges for automated tasks.

- **Monitor shared resources:** Perform regular audits of subnets, routes, and firewall settings to ensure compliance with current organizational requirements and security standards. Dashboards or SIEM solutions can provide real-time visibility into changes or anomalies.

The following figure from Google represents VPC Service Controls to secure cloud resources:

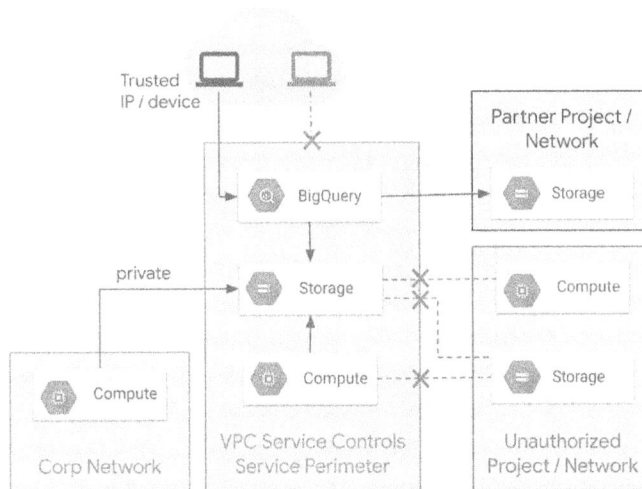

Figure 4.2: VPC Service Controls the security perimeter, protecting cloud resources

Enhancing perimeter security with VPC Service Controls

While Shared VPCs help unify network management, VPC Service Controls add an extra layer of security by defining service perimeters around your Google Cloud resources, such as Cloud Storage buckets, BigQuery datasets, or Cloud Pub/Sub topics. By limiting data movement to only approved networks, identities, or devices, you can lessen the risk of data exfiltration and better protect sensitive information.

The following are the key components of VPC Service Controls:

- **Service perimeters:** Clearly defined boundaries around specific services to limit data access within trusted zones.

- **Access levels** are criteria based on user attributes such as identity, device security posture, and geographic location that determine whether a request is permitted through the perimeter.

- **Data exfiltration protections** ensure data remains within authorized regions or networks, preventing unauthorized copying or export.

The following are the benefits of implementing VPC Service Controls:

- **Stronger data security:** By preventing unauthorized networks or endpoints from accessing sensitive data, you safeguard against unintended leaks.

- **Regulatory compliance:** Industries subject to stringent data handling laws, such as finance and healthcare, often demonstrate improved perimeter control while fulfilling various regulatory obligations.

- **Centralized enforcement:** Configuring service perimeters at the organizational level guarantees extensive coverage and uniform protection across projects.

The following are the best practices while implementing VPC service controls:

- **Identify sensitive resources**: Conduct a thorough inventory of data and services (for example, Cloud Storage buckets containing personally identifiable information). Prioritize applying service perimeters to those high-risk assets.

- **Define clear access levels**: To customize data access, use identity and context-based parameters such as user roles, device security posture, or IP address location.

- **Regularly review perimeters**: As teams develop new services or compliance requirements change, consistently update your perimeters to reflect changes in data flow, project expansions, or more stringent security policies.

- **Integrate with IAM**: Combine VPC Service Controls with IAM roles to enhance layered security. For instance, utilize IAM to enforce the principle of least privilege and further restrict data movement through service perimeter policies.

Securing ingress and egress traffic

Managing data flow in and out of your environment is crucial for network security and application reliability. In Google Cloud, this is accomplished using two key tools: *Cloud Armor* and *Cloud NAT*.

Cloud Armor helps secure externally exposed applications by filtering traffic based on IP, geography, or layer 7 rules, effectively protecting against common threats such as DDoS attacks and unauthorized access. This is especially useful for safeguarding web front ends and APIs accessible over the internet.

Cloud **Network Address Translation (NAT)** complements this by enabling outbound internet access for private Google Cloud VMs that lack external IP addresses. It masks the internal network, preventing unsolicited inbound traffic while allowing for necessary software updates or external API calls.

These services offer a balanced security posture, combining defense from external threats with operational flexibility. For added control, organizations can configure Cloud Logging and alerting policies to monitor traffic patterns, detect anomalies, and enforce compliance with internal or regulatory security standards.

Cloud Armor threat protection

Cloud Armor is a security service that protects your GCP-hosted applications from web-based threats such as DDoS attacks, **structured query language (SQL)** injection, and **Cross-Site Scripting (XSS)**. As a **Web Application Firewall (WAF)**, it offers advanced filtering and monitoring capabilities to identify suspicious patterns, prevent volumetric attacks, and manage excessive requests.

The following are the key features:

- **Layer 7 protection:** This type of firewall uses WAF rules to analyze and filter HTTP/HTTPS traffic at the application layer, detecting more sophisticated threats than traditional layer 3/4 firewalls.

- **DDoS mitigation:** Automatically scales to handle large-scale attacks while preserving performance for legitimate traffic.

- **Rate limiting:** Restricts the number of requests permitted from a specific IP address or CIDR range within a defined timeframe to prevent abuse or brute-force attacks.

Creating and applying Cloud Armor security policies

Cloud Armor provides a robust framework for protecting applications hosted on GCP against various threats, including malicious IP traffic, web-based vulnerabilities, and volumetric attacks. Organizations can enforce perimeter defenses at the network edge by defining security policies that encompass both custom rules and managed rule sets. Cloud Armor policies are particularly effective at preventing common exploits and ensuring that only legitimate traffic reaches your applications.

To illustrate how Cloud Armor can be configured and applied, consider the following example that outlines establishing a security policy, defining access control rules, and attaching the policy to a backend service:

```
# 1. Create a Cloud Armor security policy
gcloud compute security-policies create my-waf-policy \
    --description="WAF rules for blocking malicious traffic"

# 2. Add a rule to block traffic from a specific IP range
gcloud compute security-policies rules create 1000 \
    --security-policy=my-waf-policy \
    --src-ip-ranges=203.0.113.0/24 \
    --action=deny-403 \
    --description="Deny requests from known malicious range" \
    --expression="true"

# 3. Attach the policy to a backend service
gcloud compute backend-services update my-backend-service \
    --security-policy=my-waf-policy \
    --global
```

The following is the explanation of the code:

- **Create**: A new Cloud Armor policy is defined with a descriptive label to manage WAF rules.

- **Add**: A specific rule with priority 1000 denies requests from a known malicious IP range, returning a 403 Forbidden response.

- **Attach**: The defined policy is linked to a backend service that hosts your web application, ensuring the policy takes effect for incoming traffic.

Note: To monitor and analyze blocked and allowed traffic effectively, integrate Cloud Armor with Cloud Logging. This enables you to capture detailed logs of requests evaluated against your security policies, aiding in incident investigation, monitoring attack patterns, and tuning your rules for a better security posture.

The following are the best practices for implementing Cloud Armor security policies:

- **Use managed rules**: Google's predefined WAF rules cover common web vulnerabilities (for example, the Open Worldwide Application Security Project, OWASP Top 10). This saves time and ensures you start with a solid security baseline.

- **Enable logging and monitoring**: Track all requests through Cloud Armor to identify malicious traffic trends and refine your rule sets. Integrating Cloud Logging or SIEM can trigger alerts for abnormal traffic spikes.

- **Combine with IAM**: Limit which individuals or service accounts can modify Cloud Armor policies. Enforcing least privilege IAM helps prevent accidental misconfigurations that may expose your application to attacks.

The following figure depicts the deployment of Cloud Armor at the network edge:

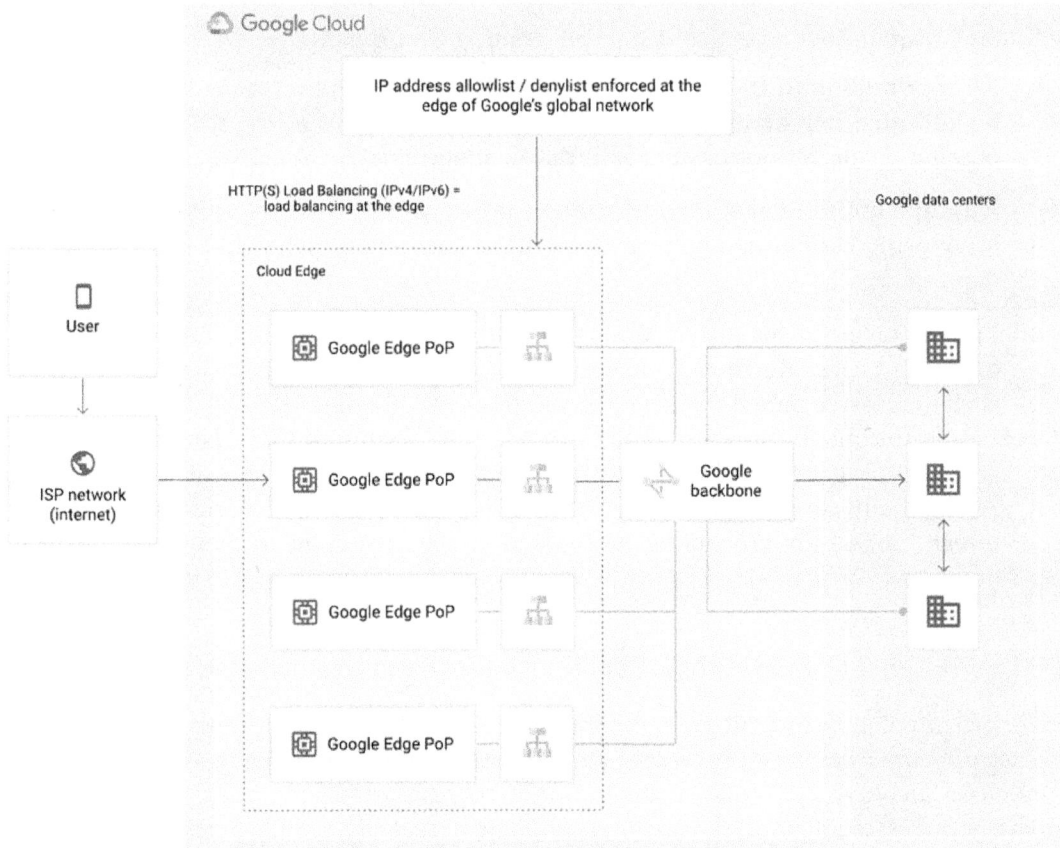

Figure 4.3: Google Cloud Armor deployed at the network edge

Securing outbound access with Cloud NAT

Cloud NAT manages outbound internet access for GCP resources in private subnets. Instead of assigning external IP addresses to individual instances, Cloud NAT centralizes traffic management, ensuring that internal resources remain inaccessible to inbound traffic. This architecture is especially beneficial for instances that require downloading packages, backing up data, or securely calling external APIs.

The following are the key features of Cloud NAT:

- **Private outbound connectivity:** Preserves private instance IPs while allowing them to send requests to the public internet.

- **Scalability:** Adjusts to different traffic levels, ensuring stable performance even during high outbound workloads.

- **High availability:** Prevents single points of failure by enabling automatic failover and load balancing, ensuring continuous connectivity.

The following are the best practices for implementing Cloud NAT:

- **Restrict outbound traffic:** Pair Cloud NAT with egress firewall rules to permit only the essential ports and external addresses. This diminishes the risk of unauthorized outbound connections or data exfiltration attempts.

- **Allocate sufficient IPs:** Plan IP address pools based on your environment's growth. Monitoring NAT usage helps prevent IP exhaustion, which could disrupt outbound requests.

- **Enable logging:** Set up NAT logging to capture the source and destination of outgoing traffic. Reviewing these logs enables you to identify suspicious patterns, such as massive data transfers or connections to unfamiliar IP addresses, and respond swiftly to contain threats. To enhance detection, configure *Cloud Logging filters* to flag anomalies (e.g., unusual volume spikes, repeated connections to untrusted IP ranges). Additionally, consider *pairing NAT logs with Cloud IDS* to detect and alert on potential threats in real-time, enabling automated or rapid manual responses to suspicious outbound activity.

Network segmentation strategies

Network segmentation and micro-segmentation are potent tools for limiting potential damage from security breaches and preventing unauthorized lateral movement when designing a secure cloud architecture. While segmentation involves partitioning your VPC into broader domains (such as subnets and zones) with distinct security profiles, micro-segmentation applies granular, zero-trust rules at the individual workload or application level.

Enhancing security through network segmentation

Network segmentation organizes your GCP environment into distinct sections, each with firewall rules, IAM policies, and resource access boundaries. By isolating resources based on their function, environment, or security risk, you ensure that a breach in one segment does not automatically compromise the remainder of your infrastructure.

The following are the key strategies for implementing network segmentation:

- **Functional segmentation** involves organizing related services (for instance, web front end and database back end) into distinct subnets or zones. This allows for more precise tailoring of access controls; only the web subnet can communicate with the database subnet on specific ports, for example.

- **Environment segmentation:** Separate development, testing, and production environments into subnets or projects. This prevents accidental or malicious cross-contamination of data and configurations.

- **Policy-driven access:** Utilize firewall rules, **Identity and Access Management (IAM)** roles, tags, and organizational policies to define which subnets can communicate with one another. This context-based approach ensures that each segment only permits the traffic necessary for its function.

The following figure explains the standard hub-n-spoke model used for segmentation:

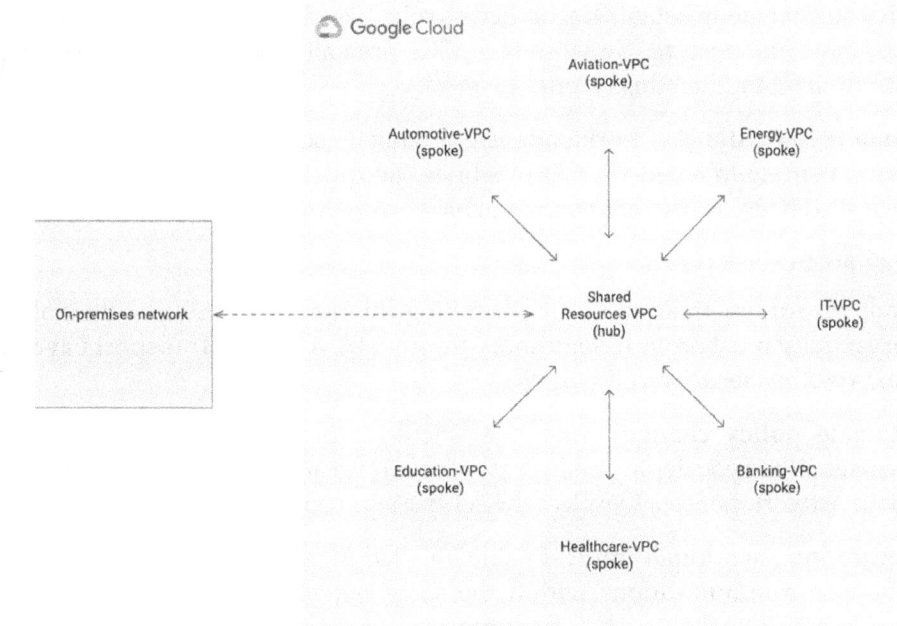

Figure 4.4: A hub-and-spoke network topology is used for segmentation

The following are the benefits of implementing network segmentation:

- **Reduced attack surface:** A compromise in one segment does not expose everything else. Attackers encounter additional hurdles when attempting to move laterally.

- **Easier compliance:** Sensitive data, subject to standards like PCI-DSS or HIPAA, can be contained in highly secure segments, simplifying audits and enforcing strict access controls.

- **Streamlined troubleshooting:** When a network issue occurs, isolating the affected subnet makes root-cause analysis and recovery procedures.

Micro-segmentation controls

Whereas segmentation addresses broad divisions in your VPC, *micro-segmentation* enforces security at the individual workload or application level. By employing zero-trust principles, this approach assumes that no traffic is implicitly trusted and requires each communication path to be explicitly authorized. Micro-segmentation is particularly valuable in dynamic, containerized, or microservices-heavy environments.

The following are the key components:

- **Service accounts or tags:** Identify each service or workload with detailed metadata. This context helps enforce rules, such as *Workload A can only communicate with Workload B on port 443*.

- **Policy enforcement:** Establish strict access rules based on workload identities, adopting a *deny-by-default* posture. Network tags, GCP firewall rules, and service-specific access controls all strengthen this layered defense.

- **Dynamic security:** As workloads are updated, scaled, or migrated within your environment, automated CI/CD pipelines can quickly update the relevant network policies to ensure consistent enforcement.

The following are the best practices.

- **Adopt zero-trust:** Treat all traffic, including internal requests, as potentially hostile. Every request must prove its legitimacy through IAM checks, **Transport Layer Security (TLS)**, or other security validations.

- **Automate policy changes**: Integrate micro-segmentation rules into your CI/CD processes. When you deploy a new service version or add a new workload, automatically update network policies to reflect the service's purpose and communication patterns.

- **Monitor inter-workload traffic**: Enable detailed logging and monitoring for *east-west* traffic and communications within the same network environment. This visibility helps detect anomalies, such as unauthorized internal scans or exfiltration attempts.

You achieve a robust and layered security model by combining network segmentation to divide your environment into high-level zones with micro-segmentation at the application or workload layer. This strategy reduces your overall attack surface, simplifies compliance, and enhances incident response capabilities, thus enabling a controlled and well-organized environment for modern cloud workloads.

Implementing firewall strategies and use cases

Firewalls are a cornerstone of network security, managing both inbound and outbound traffic to ensure only legitimate connections access your GCP resources. By combining clear configuration principles with regular reviews and testing, you can reduce vulnerabilities and establish a strong defensive posture. GCP firewalls operate at the network level, allowing you to set up fine-grained rules that determine which traffic is allowed or denied based on IP ranges, protocols, ports, and target instances or tags. A well-planned firewall strategy ensures resources are protected from unauthorized access while still enabling the necessary functionality for applications to operate smoothly.

Firewall rules can be tailored to meet specific needs, ranging from securing web applications to isolating sensitive database servers. By applying the principle of least privilege, firewalls should permit only the traffic that is essential for your services. Regular audits and log reviews help refine the rules and adapt to evolving security demands.

Strategic approaches for configuring firewall rules

Firewalls in Google Cloud act as gatekeepers for traffic flowing into and out of your virtual networks. A strong firewall strategy begins with the principle of least privilege, allowing only the traffic that is strictly necessary while denying everything else. From this point, you can refine and layer rules to address specific workloads, segments, and threat vectors.

The following are the key methods:

- **Default deny stance:** Start with a policy that blocks all inbound traffic. Then, explicitly open the necessary ports (for example, HTTP or HTTPS for a web app). This strategy significantly reduces the risk of overlooked vulnerabilities.

- **Layered rules:** Instead of relying on a single, all-encompassing firewall rule, implement multiple, more specific rules to manage various types of traffic. This granular approach enhances security and simplifies maintenance.

- **Stateful inspection:** Monitor active connections, ensuring that any traffic not matching an expected connection state is automatically dropped (for example, blocking unsolicited inbound packets). Note that *GCP firewall rules are always stateful by default*, tracking connection states to allow return traffic for permitted outbound connections. This differs from some on-premises firewalls, where statefulness is configurable.

The following figure is an example firewall policy inside a VPC for a workload project:

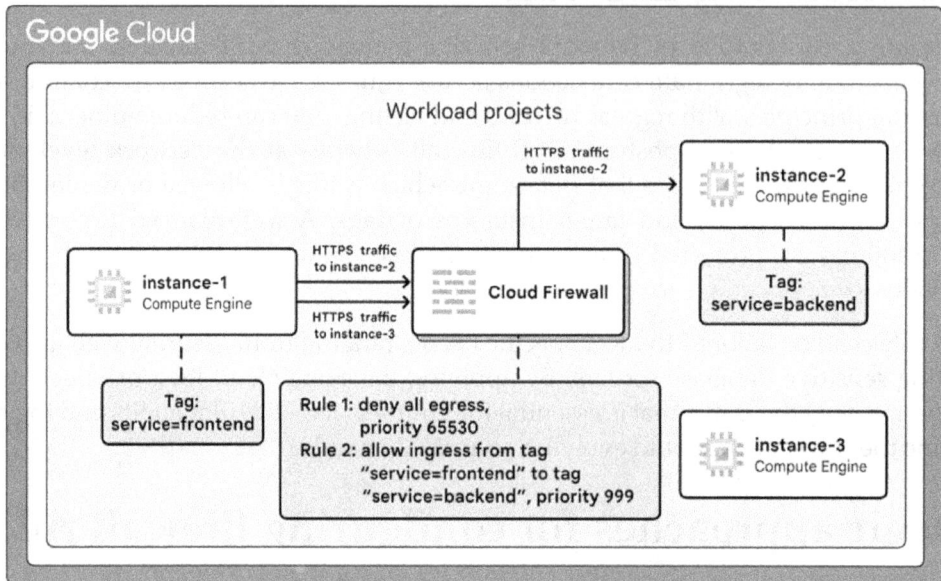

Figure 4.5: An example of firewall policy for micro-segmentation inside a VPC

The following are the best practices:

- **Reduce complexity**: Fewer, more precise firewall rules decrease the likelihood of errors and simplify the identification of potential misconfigurations. Whenever possible, group resources or services with similar access requirements.

- **Regular review**: Monitor firewall logs regularly to identify which rules are most and least frequently used and potential anomalies. Update or remove any rules that have become obsolete or pose unnecessary risks.

- **Test changes**: Before widely deploying firewall modifications, deploy them to a dedicated staging environment or use canary releases. This practice helps prevent unexpected disruptions and provides a safe space to validate rule correctness.

Firewall configuration use cases

Different applications and workloads require distinct firewall rules. By customizing rules to address each scenario's functional and security needs, you can maintain a safe and adaptable environment:

- **Web Application Protection:**
  - **Allow** HTTP (port 80) and HTTPS (port 443), while blocking all other protocols.
  - **Outbound:** Permit only essential traffic for functions such as API calls or database queries.

- o **Purpose:** Reduce entry points for attackers by closing ports that are not essential for public-facing web services.

- **Database isolation:**

  - o **Accept:** Inbound traffic only from the application subnet or authorized service accounts.

  - o **Outbound:** Limit connections to public internet access unless necessary for updates or backups.

  - o **Purpose:** Limit potential damage and ensure that sensitive data, such as user credentials or financial records, remains inaccessible to unauthorized entities.

- **Remote admin access:**

  - o **Restrict:** SSH or RDP access to a specific range of IP addresses or secure it behind a VPN tunnel.

  - o **Identity management:** Regularly rotate credentials or temporary access tokens to prevent outdated or compromised credentials from persisting.

  - o **Purpose:** Reduce the risk of brute-force attacks and restrict administrative access to authorized users and devices.

    The following figure displays a sample VPC firewall rule for a dummy ACME VPC illustrating a multi-tier application:

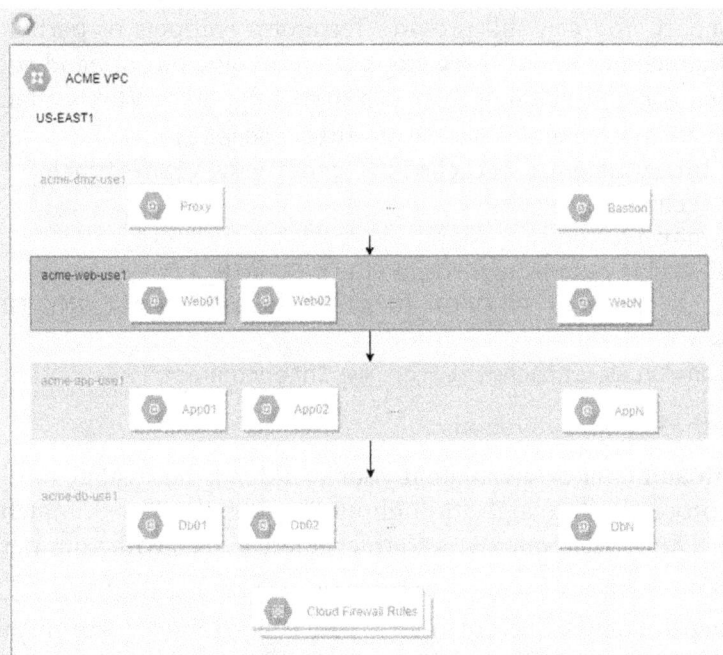

Figure 4.6: A multi-tier application scenario protected by VPC firewall rules

Combining these firewall strategies and use cases enables you to fine-tune network access across different environments, ensuring that each application, database, or administrative interface remains accessible and well-defended. A consistent cycle of planning, monitoring, and testing allows you to keep pace with evolving threats and organizational needs, ultimately safeguarding your GCP workloads over the long term.

Hybrid connectivity solutions in Google Cloud

As organizations expand their cloud presence, connecting on-premises data centers with GCP is often essential. Hybrid networking solutions enable seamless communication across environments and employ a unified security model to protect data in transit. Depending on factors such as available infrastructure, performance requirements, and cost constraints, you can choose among VPN, Direct Interconnect, or Partner Interconnect, or even combine them for optimal connectivity.

Secure hybrid connectivity

Hybrid networking allows you to connect your private data center(s) directly to GCP, creating a unified network. This approach extends your internal IP addressing scheme and security controls to the cloud, making resource sharing and management easier. Integrating both environments enables you to deploy applications across on-premises and cloud resources, gradually migrate workloads, and maintain consistent governance policies. Code snippets for Interconnect are generally more limited in the gcloud CLI because direct lines require a physical cross-connect. You can still provide Terraform snippets or partial CLI commands to request VLAN attachments, but these steps often involve out-of-band processes with the colocation provider. For completeness, here is a short snippet for VLAN attachment creation:

```
# 1. Create a VLAN attachment (aka VLAN interconnect)
gcloud compute interconnects attachments create my-vlan-attach \
    --region=us-central1 \
    --router=my-nat-router \
    --edge-availability-domain=AVAILABILITY_DOMAIN_1 \
    --interconnect=projects/PROJECT_ID/global/interconnects/MY_INTERCONNECT \
    --vlan=1234 \
    --description="VLAN attachment for my Interconnect"
```

The following are the key considerations:

- **Bandwidth and latency:** Evaluate if your workloads necessitate minimal latency (for real-time processing) or high throughput (for data backups). Match the connection type: VPN, Direct Interconnect, or Partner Interconnect, with your performance needs and budget.

- **Security requirements:** Encrypt internet connections and enforce proper IAM practices. Dedicated lines, such as Direct Interconnect or Partner Interconnect, typically provide enhanced security assurance for highly regulated industries.

- **Redundancy:** Critical workloads necessitate multiple connections or failover paths. Addressing outages might include redundant VPN tunnels, dual Direct Interconnects, or a backup Partner Interconnect.

The following figure explains how a highly available hybrid connectivity setup can be achieved in a dedicated interconnect:

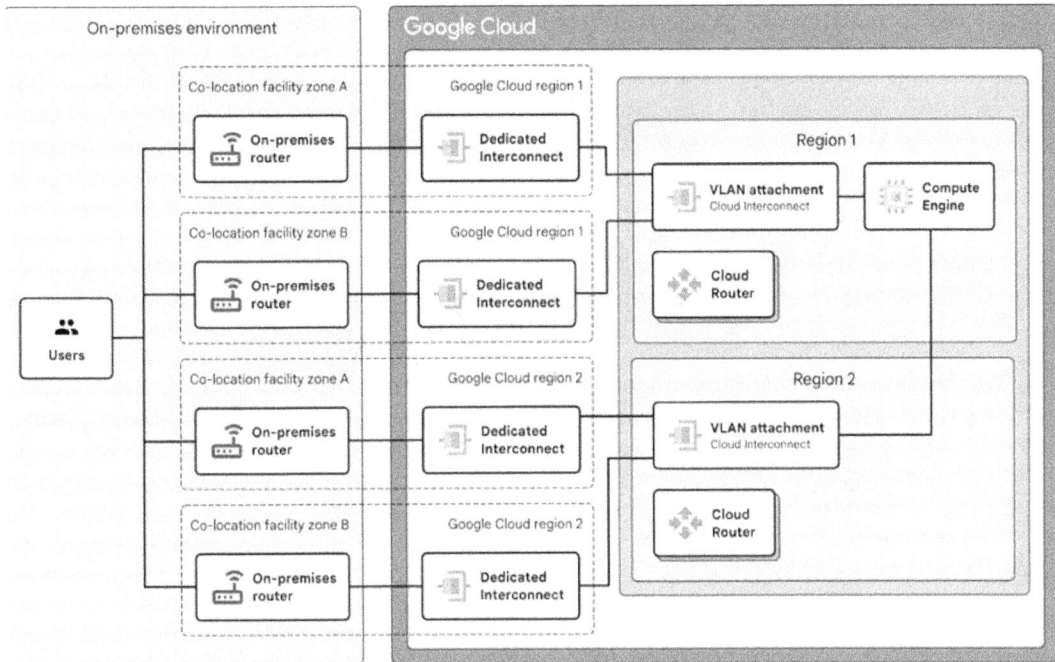

Figure 4.7: *Highly available hybrid connectivity design using dedicated interconnect*

VPN for secure encrypted connectivity

A **virtual private network** (**VPN**) enables secure communication between your on-premises infrastructure and Google Cloud by creating encrypted tunnels over the public internet. This approach allows organizations to extend their private networks into GCP, ensuring that data in transit remains confidential and protected from interception. VPN is particularly suited for scenarios requiring cost-effective, quick-to-deploy solutions for hybrid networking while still maintaining strict security standards through IPsec encryption protocols. With flexible configurations supporting dynamic or static routing, VPN connections provide a reliable method for securely bridging environments, especially in the early stages of cloud adoption or for disaster recovery purposes.

The following are the use cases:

- **Small to medium data transfer:** It is ideal for organizations seeking quick, cost-effective connectivity without the burden of dedicated circuits.

- **Protect administrative access:** VPN tunnels can protect remote management or administrative tasks from exposure to the public internet.

- **Bursting workloads:** Enterprises can dynamically shift fluctuating demands to GCP, preserving on-premises capacity for baseline operations while the cloud manages surges.

The following are the best practices:

- **Choose strong encryption**: Use IPsec-based VPNs with robust ciphers (e.g., AES-256) and secure key exchange methods (IKEv2). *Cloud VPN uses IKEv2 by default, supporting strong encryption, but users should verify the configuration to ensure it aligns with compliance and organizational security requirements.* Regularly review and update these settings to stay current with evolving security standards.

- **Configure redundancy**: Establish multiple VPN tunnels in active/passive or active/active configurations to prevent single points of failure. Ensure that routing automatically fails over when one tunnel fails.

- **Integrate with routing**: Implement dynamic routing protocols e.g., **Border Gateway Protocol (BGP)**, to streamline updates and facilitate failovers. This enables new routes or subnet changes in your on-premises environment to propagate to GCP without manual intervention.

Direct Interconnect connectivity

Direct Interconnect provides a dedicated, private connection between your on-premises data center and Google Cloud, offering high bandwidth and low latency for demanding workloads. Unlike a VPN, which routes traffic over the public internet, Direct Interconnect ensures greater reliability and performance by establishing a physical link to Google's network infrastructure. This option is ideal for enterprises requiring consistent network throughput, minimal latency, and enhanced security for large-scale data transfers or mission-critical applications. By leveraging Direct Interconnect, organizations can optimize hybrid cloud architectures, reduce network costs over time, and meet stringent application performance requirements such as real-time analytics, backup, and disaster recovery.

The following are the use cases:

- **Large-scale workloads:** When transferring terabytes or petabytes of data, particularly for analytics, backups, or media pipelines, Direct Interconnect provides reliable, high-throughput connectivity.

- **Latency-sensitive apps:** Real-time services, such as trading platforms or live streaming, benefit from the ultra-low latency provided by direct, private links.

- **Secure private connections:** Direct Interconnect completely bypasses the public internet, providing predictable performance and strong security assurances for mission-critical operations.

The following are the best practices.

- **Plan for scalability**: Choose an initial bandwidth tier that meets current requirements while allowing flexibility for future growth. Consider the likelihood that your enterprise may soon double or triple its data transfers.

- **Establish redundant links**: Create connections between geographically distinct facilities or various availability zones. This redundancy protects against regional outages, ensuring continuous connectivity. To align redundancy with reliability goals, review the GCP SLA tiers (**https://cloud.google.com/network-connectivity/docs/interconnect/sla?hl=en**) for Interconnect and VPN, as higher tiers offer stronger availability guarantees essential for production workloads.

- **Thoroughly monitor**: Utilize Cloud Monitoring or third-party network management solutions to track link usage, throughput, and latency. Early detection of capacity constraints or performance issues allows you to address problems before they impact business operations.

Partner Interconnect for scalable cloud connectivity

Partner Interconnect enables organizations to connect to Google Cloud through a supported service provider, offering flexibility without needing dedicated physical infrastructure. This option is particularly suitable for businesses that require high-performance connections but lack a presence in Google's Interconnect locations. Partner Interconnect provides scalable bandwidth options and simplifies hybrid networking by utilizing existing service provider facilities. It delivers secure, private connectivity for workloads that require more reliability than public internet connections, while allowing for rapid provisioning and cost-effective scaling. Organizations can choose bandwidth tiers based on their needs, making it an accessible and adaptable solution for expanding cloud adoption.

The following are the use cases:

- **Unavailable Direct Interconnect:** A Partner Interconnect can bridge the gap in regions or facilities where a direct GCP interconnect is not feasible.

- **Scalable mid-range bandwidth:** Suitable for scenarios where traffic surpasses typical VPN capabilities but does not warrant a full Direct Interconnect in terms of cost or volume.

- **Partner solutions:** Some providers manage provisioning, maintenance, and security compliance, allowing you to outsource connectivity complexities.

The following are the best practices:

- **Choose reliable partners**: Evaluate a provider's SLAs, performance history, and security certifications. Look for those with robust data management policies and, if needed, encryption options.

- **Match speeds to needs**: Select an interconnect tier that matches your busiest workloads. This will ensure you do not overpay for unused capacity or run out of bandwidth during peak times.

- **Ensure compliance**: If subject to industry regulations such as HIPAA or PCI-DSS, confirm that the partner's environment and processes align with your legal requirements. This may include data residency constraints and audit capabilities.

Combining these hybrid networking options, such as VPN for cost-effective tunneling, Direct Interconnect for high throughput and low latency connections, and Partner Interconnect for flexible mid-range solutions, enables you to customize connectivity to meet your business's unique demands. Whether you prioritize quick setup, maximum throughput, or fully managed services, GCP provides a pathway for securely extending your infrastructure to the cloud.

To assist in choosing the right connectivity option, the following table summarizes *VPN, Direct Interconnect, and Partner Interconnect* based on *bandwidth, latency, and cost considerations*:

Option	Bandwidth	Latency	Cost	Best For
VPN	Up to ~3 Gbps per tunnel	Higher latency (internet-based)	Lowest (uses public internet)	Quick setup, small/medium workloads, dev/test environments
Direct Interconnect	10 Gbps or 100 Gbps	Lowest (private fiber)	High (dedicated circuit)	High throughput, latency-sensitive prod workloads
Partner Interconnect	50 Mbps to 50 Gbps	Low to moderate (partner dependent)	Medium (shared link)	Flexible bandwidth, balanced cost, prod workloads

Table 4.2: Choosing the right hybrid connectivity option on GCP based on bandwidth, latency, and cost

Complex made simple

Imagine your GCP network as a vast office building, where each floor symbolizes a distinct environment or department, and each office on that floor represents an individual workload or application:

- **Network segmentation (Floors in the building):**
  - Just as you might dedicate one floor to the engineering team, another to finance, and another to HR, segmentation divides your network into subnets or zones.
  - This way, if someone gains unauthorized access to one floor (segment), they cannot automatically roam the entire building (network).

- **Micro-segmentation (Individual offices):**
  - Each office on each floor is locked and only accessible to specific occupants or visitors with the right keys. This corresponds to micro-segmentation, which applies rules per application or workload in your network.

o Even if someone sneaks onto a particular floor, they cannot necessarily open every office door or rummage through every room, so the damage from a security breach is drastically limited.

The key takeaway is that adopting *network segmentation* (separating your networks by floors) and micro-segmentation (locking each office) ensures that unauthorized users cannot freely move around, even if one part of your environment is compromised. This approach minimizes the potential breach's blast radius and *strengthens compliance* by confining sensitive data or workloads to specifically secured spaces.

Conclusion

In this chapter, you have explored various methods and best practices for establishing and maintaining secure network environments in GCP. Each strategy contributes to a comprehensive security posture, from fundamental concepts like VPC design, including subnets, routes, and firewall configurations, to more advanced techniques such as Shared VPC, VPC Service Controls, and micro-segmentation. You have also learned how to securely manage inbound and outbound traffic using Cloud Armor and Cloud NAT, followed by hybrid networking solutions including VPN, Dedicated Interconnect, and Partner Interconnect for connecting on-premises infrastructure to GCP. By integrating these tools, you can design and operate scalable, compliant, and resilient network architectures tailored to your organization's security and performance needs.

In the next chapter, we will shift focus from network architecture to securing your development workflows. You will explore Automating Security in DevOps Pipelines, exploring how to implement DevSecOps practices within GCP environments. Key topics include using **Infrastructure as Code** (**IaC**) with Terraform for security resources, embedding security checks into CI/CD pipelines, automated misconfiguration scanning, managing secrets securely during deployments, and strategies for modernizing legacy pipelines. Real-world examples will highlight how automation enhances security without sacrificing development speed, along with practical mitigations for common DevSecOps challenges.

Exercise

1. **Segment your existing network:**

   a. **Objective:** Apply best practices for network segmentation to your current GCP environment.

   b. **Steps:**

      i. Identify at least two workloads (for example, a database and a web service).

      ii. Create separate subnets or VPCs for each workload. - **https://cloud.google.com/vpc/docs/vpc**

      iii. Configure firewall rules to allow only necessary ports and protocols between them. - **https://cloud.google.com/vpc/docs/using-firewalls**

      iv. Validate that the database is inaccessible from other subnets or the public internet.

2. **Simulate a hybrid setup:**

    a. **Objective:** Practice configuring a simple VPN to link a local environment (or simulated on-prem VM) with a GCP VPC.

    b. **Steps:**

      i. Enable Google Cloud VPN. - **https://cloud.google.com/network-connectivity/docs/vpn/how-to/creating-ha-vpn**

      ii. Create an IPsec tunnel using strong ciphers.

      iii. Verify connectivity by pinging a private instance in GCP from your local or simulated on-prem setup.

3. **Create a custom firewall rule for Ingress:**

    a. **Objective:** Reinforce least privilege principles by only permitting SSH from a specific IP range.

    b. **Steps:**

      i. Navigate to the **VPC networks** | **Firewall** page in the GCP console.

      ii. Create a new firewall rule with *target tags* assigned to your instance.

      iii. Allow **tcp:22** only from your authorized IP or CIDR block.

      iv. Confirm that attempts from outside this range are blocked.

Key takeaways

Consolidating your knowledge of network security in GCP:

- **VPC fundamentals**: Subnets, routes, and firewall rules establish the foundation of a secure, well-structured GCP network.

- **Shared VPCs and VPC Service Controls**: Centralized network management ensures consistency and establishes strong perimeters to protect sensitive data from exfiltration.

- **Cloud Armor and Cloud NAT**: Defensive solutions for managing both inbound and outbound traffic while enabling advanced threat detection and granular traffic control.

    o **Cloud Armor** offers WAF capabilities and DDoS protection for managing inbound traffic.

- o **Cloud NAT** securely manages outbound connections for instances without public IP addresses.

- o **Cloud IDS** offers deep packet inspection to detect threats, including malware and command-and-control attacks, enabling the identification and blocking of sophisticated threats in real-time.

- o **Cloud firewall** offers granular control with hierarchical firewall policies, enabling consistent enforcement of security controls across your organization's networks while providing logging and monitoring for visibility.

- **Network segmentation and micro-segmentation** limit lateral movement by isolating subnets and applying workload-specific security policies.

- **Firewall strategies and use cases**: A systematic approach to creating, maintaining, and auditing firewall rules for robust network defenses.

- **Hybrid networking** combines on-premises resources with GCP using VPN, Direct Interconnect, or Partner Interconnect for a unified and secure infrastructure.

References

1. https://cloud.google.com/vpc/docs

2. https://cloud.google.com/vpc/docs/shared-vpc

3. https://cloud.google.com/vpc-service-controls/docs

4. https://cloud.google.com/armor/docs

5. https://cloud.google.com/nat/docs/overview

6. https://cloud.google.com/vpn/docs

7. https://cloud.google.com/interconnect/docs

8. https://cloud.google.com/interconnect/docs/partner

9. https://cloud.google.com/security/whitepapers

Join our Discord space

Join our Discord workspace for latest updates, offers, tech happenings around the world, new releases, and sessions with the authors:

https://discord.bpbonline.com

CHAPTER 5

Automating Security in DevOps Pipelines

Introduction

Automating security in a DevOps pipeline requires embedding checks and controls at every stage, from the initial commit to the final deployment, ensuring that vulnerabilities never reach production. Instead of treating security as a separate gating function, it is woven into the pipeline itself, utilizing **Infrastructure as Code** (**IaC**) and policy as code to ensure that each environment is built and tested consistently. For example, you can create a Terraform module that establishes a **Virtual Private Cloud** (**VPC**) with restricted inbound rules and enforced encryption, then rely on Cloud Build triggers to lint, scan, and apply that module whenever developers push a change. This strategy eliminates inconsistent *click operations*, making it significantly easier to maintain a secure baseline as the project scales or new team members join the team.

Critically, you do not rely solely on humans to remember best practices; you encode them into the pipeline. Perhaps you have a step that runs tfsec to detect common Terraform misconfigurations (such as accidentally opening ports to the entire internet) following every code merge. Another step might involve fetching credentials from SecretManager at build time, ensuring that no passwords or keys are ever stored in plain text. By unifying these checks, firewall rules, **Identity and Access Management** (**IAM**) roles, vulnerability scans, and secrets management, you create a consistent security posture across development, staging, and production. The result is fewer breaches or compliance headaches and a more agile workflow: developers receive security feedback immediately in their **continuous integration** (**CI**) logs or pull request comments, fix issues on the spot, and move on, confident that each new commit has passed its security gate. This chapter will demonstrate how to integrate policy as code into your pipelines, trigger automated misconfiguration scans, and protect secrets so that each commit successfully passes a security gate before it reaches users.

The following figure illustrates DevSecOps, emphasizing the development stages (plan, code, build, test) and operations stages (release, deploy, operate, monitor), with *security* integrated at the center. It highlights the importance of continuous feedback, such as threat modeling early in the planning and ongoing monitoring with rapid remediation, to shift security left within the SDLC:

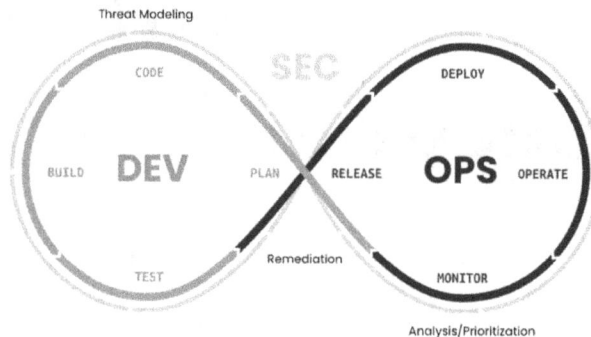

Figure 5.1: A high-level overview of how security intertwines with DevOps lifecycle stages

Structure

This chapter is organized into the following key sections:

- Introduction to DevSecOps and GCP
- IaC with Terraform for GCP security resources
- Integrating security checks into CI/CD pipelines
- Automated scanning for configuration errors
- Secure secrets handling in automated pipelines
- Best practices for DevSecOps implementations
- Securing legacy pipelines
- Compliance enforcement in practice
- Complex made simple

Objectives

By the end of this chapter, you will be equipped to codify security controls using Terraform modules that consistently deploy VPCs, IAM roles, and Cloud KMS keys in a predictable and auditable manner. You will be able to embed security gates directly into CI/CD pipelines, ensuring that every code merge triggers automated vulnerability scans, policy validations, and unit tests, providing immediate feedback when issues arise. You will also gain the ability to protect secrets comprehensively by eliminating hard-coded credentials and replacing them with secure references through Secret Manager and Workload Identity Federation. Moreover, you will understand how to incrementally upgrade legacy pipelines by introducing linting, scanning, and policy as code methods without disrupting existing deployments. Lastly, you will be able to automate compliance readiness by generating audit evidence, such as logs, scan results, and policy files that confirm each deployment aligns with both organisational and regulatory security standards.

With these skills, you will have a robust toolkit for shifting security left. You will be able to create compliant infrastructure using a single Terraform command, embed security checks into every pull request, and ensure secrets are never exposed in code. Most importantly, you will leave with a clear strategy for modernizing older development pipelines, providing assurance to both auditors and engineering teams that every phase of deployment, from code inception to production, adheres to stringent and consistent security practices.

Introduction to DevSecOps and GCP

DevSecOps combines development, operations, and security into a single continuous workflow, treating security controls as code that accompanies each commit. In Google Cloud, native services like Cloud Build, Artifact Registry, and Secret Manager integrate seamlessly with popular open-source tools (Terraform, tfsec, Trivy), making it easy to incorporate vulnerability scanning, policy enforcement, and secret management into every stage of the CI/CD pipeline. By codifying guardrails instead of adding them at the end, teams benefit from real-time feedback, faster remediation, and a unified source of truth for infrastructure and security requirements.

Shifting left on security

Traditional release cycles often positioned penetration tests and compliance reviews after development, which was too late to address issues without substantial rework. Shift-left reverses that order: security checks occur as early as the **integrated development environment** (**IDE**) or the first pull request, preventing risky code from reaching production. In **Google Cloud Platform** (**GCP**), you can trigger image scans during every build, validate Terraform plans against organizational policies, and automatically fail a deployment if it attempts to open an unrestricted firewall rule. The result is a lower cost of fixing bugs, fewer last-minute surprises, and a culture where developers take ownership of security outcomes.

Instead of targeting the deployment pipeline, a malicious actor might try to compromise or replace pipeline input, including source code, libraries, or container images, as illustrated in the following figure:

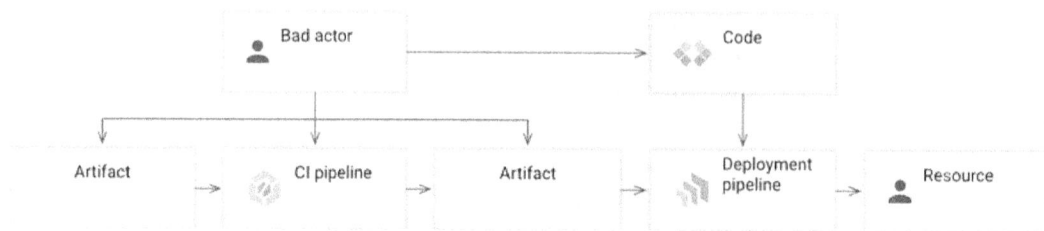

Figure 5.2: Bad actor compromising the supply chain

Key motivations for DevSecOps

By integrating security into the development workflow, organizations achieve tangible benefits beyond mere vulnerability reduction:

- **Reduced human error**: Automated linting, static analysis, and policy as code eliminate manual misconfigurations, such as open buckets or broad IAM roles, frequently leading to breaches.

- **Consistent compliance**: Ongoing assessments against CIS Benchmarks, PCI-DSS controls, or internal standards guarantee that every merge adheres to the same policy standards, automatically generating audit evidence.

- **Faster remediation**: Issues arise in the pull request or build log, enabling developers to resolve them promptly. At the same time, the context is fresh, reducing **mean time to resolution (MTTR)** from days to minutes.

- **Scalability and governance**: As microservices and teams grow, centrally managed policies and automated gates ensure consistent security across hundreds of repositories and projects without hindering delivery.

IaC with Terraform for GCP security resources

Terraform transforms your Google Cloud security posture from a **set-it-and-hope** approach to a *defined and proven strategy*. By expressing every firewall rule, IAM binding, and KMS key in declarative **.tf** files, you create a single, auditable source of truth that the pipeline can test, review, and enforce. When a developer proposes a change, such as opening port 443 or adding a service account role, Terraform shows precisely what will change, and policy as code gates can block the merge if it violates security standards.

This is because Terraform is cloud-agnostic yet deeply integrated with GCP; the same modules can create compliant VPCs in development, staging, and production, each parameterized with environment-specific variables. State files stored in an encrypted Cloud Storage bucket track real-world resources, allowing Terraform to reconcile drift automatically. If someone manually adds a broad firewall rule, the next pipeline run will detect and remove it. In short, Terraform transforms security controls into reusable, version-controlled building blocks, ensuring that every deployment consistently meets the same baseline.

Automating resource creation and configuration

Terraform allows you to manage every Google Cloud component, including VPCs, IAM roles, and firewall rules, as version-controlled code. Instead of navigating through the console, you declare your desired state once and let Terraform build (or update) the environment for you, ensuring that each environment is identical and that security baselines are maintained:

- **Terraform overview:** Three core concepts make Terraform perfect for repeatable, secure deployments in GCP:

    o **Declarative syntax**: Infrastructure is defined in `.tf` files, which specify resources (VMS, subnets, and firewall rules) and their dependencies.

    o **State management**: Terraform maintains a state file to track the real-time status of resources, reconciling changes on each run.

    o **Modular configurations**: Break down infrastructure into reusable modules, simplifying large-scale deployments.

- **Applying Terraform for security:** Security controls become first-class resources in code, enforced uniformly across development, staging, and production environments.

    o **Resource definitions**: Codify firewall rules, IAM policies, and network configurations as Terraform resources.

    o **Automated security baselines**: Ensure that mandatory settings (for example, no external IPs, forced SSL, or Secure Sockets Layer usage) are consistently enforced.

    o **Environment-specific variables**: Differentiate dev, staging, and prod security configurations through variable files.

- **Advanced techniques:** Beyond basic resource creation, the policy as code and secure state handling elevate Terraform from *useful* to *enterprise-grade*:

    o **Policy as code tools**: Combine Terraform with **Open Policy Agent** (**OPA**) or HashiCorp Sentinel to evaluate security compliance before applying.

    o **Terraform cloud or enterprise**: Centralize security checks, team collaboration, and policy enforcement.

    o **State locking and encryption**: Secure Terraform state in Cloud Storage with encryption, restricting access to authorized roles only.

- **Best practices:** A few habits keep your IaC secure, auditable, and easy to maintain:

    o **Version control**: Store Terraform code in Git, enabling code reviews for security changes.

- ○ **Isolate state**: Keep Terraform in a locked, encrypted, and versioned location, such as a GCS bucket with SSE.

- ○ **Modular approaches**: Create separate modules for IAM, VPC, and GCP security policies, enforcing clarity and reusability.

Integrating security checks into CI/CD pipelines

A modern pipeline should ideally do more than compile code and run unit tests; it should function as an automated security gate. By embedding static code analysis, secret detection, and IaC linting into every commit, you transform your CI/CD system into a first-line defender that blocks risky changes before they reach production. Whether you utilize Jenkins, GitLab CI, or Cloud Build, the pattern remains the same: *pull, scan, test, and enforce*. Each stage produces machine-readable results that can fail a build, trigger a Slack alert, or open a Jira ticket, providing developers with instant feedback and reducing the window between vulnerability introduction and remediation.

On Google Cloud, native services like Cloud Build triggers, Container Analysis, and Binary Authorization integrate seamlessly with open-source scanners, such as Trivy, Checkov, and OPA Gatekeeper. A single YAML file can orchestrate the entire flow: checkout | SAST | IaC scan | image build | vulnerability scan | policy check | deploy. If any step returns a high-severity finding, the pipeline halts automatically, protecting downstream environments and, in short, integrating security checks directly into CI/CD shifts risk detection to the earliest possible moment, right where code changes happen, while maintaining the rapid delivery cadence that DevOps demands.

Embedding security from commit to deployment

A secure pipeline treats every code change, application code, Dockerfile, or Terraform plan as a potential security event. When a developer pushes to the main branch, your CI/CD system should initiate a series of automated checks: static code analysis, secrets detection, IaC linting, and policy evaluation. If any stage fails, the build stops, and the developer receives immediate feedback. When all gates pass, the same pipeline promotes artifacts through staging and into production, tagging them with immutable build metadata for traceability. Whether you run Jenkins on-premises, GitLab in SaaS, or Cloud Build natively in GCP, the pattern remains the same: test early, fail fast, and deploy only what meets the security bar:

- **Jenkins, GitLab, and Cloud Build:** Different CI engines provide native or plug-in support for security tasks, allowing you to integrate scans without re-architecting the pipeline:

  - ○ **Jenkins**: Install plugins for static code analysis, secrets scanning, and policy checks (for example, Jenkins Security plugin).

- o **GitLab**: Integrate SAST, DAST, and container scans natively in GitLab CI/CD.

- o **Cloud Build**: Leverage Cloud Build triggers to automate scans and deployments in response to code changes. The following code snippet is a reference example of how to trigger a Cloud Build step running Trivy:

```
steps:
- name: aquasec/trivy
  entrypoint: trivy
  args: ["--exit-code", "1", "--severity", "HIGH,CRITICAL", "gcr.
io/$PROJECT_ID/app:${SHORT_SHA}"]
```

- **Security pipeline stages:** A layered set of scans catches different risk categories before code leaves the repo:

  - o **Static analysis (SAST)**: Lint code for insecure patterns or exposed secrets.

  - o **IaC scans**: Check Terraform or YAML definitions for misconfigurations (for example, open ports, world-readable Storage buckets).

  - o **Policy enforcement**: Evaluate each commit or merge request against compliance baselines (CIS, internal standards) using tools like OPA.

- **Approval workflows:** Not every change should be shipped automatically; critical modifications may need human oversight or automated safety nets:

  - o **Manual gates**: Require two reviewers when a merger request alters iam.tf or adds a firewall rule wider than /24.

  - o **Automated rollbacks**: If post-deploy tests fail or a runtime scan detects a critical CVE, the pipeline triggers a kubectl rollout undo or Cloud Deploy rollback to the last healthy release.

- **Notifications and visibility:** Real-time alerts and dashboards keep developers and security teams in the loop:

  - o **Slack or email alerts**: Notify dev and security teams of pipeline failures or suspicious findings.

  - o **Dashboard monitoring**: Real-time CI/CD status in dashboards (Grafana, Kibana), highlighting security pass/fail metrics.

Key tools and integrations

Modern DevSecOps pipelines rely on a variety of tools to automate, monitor, and enforce security throughout the software development lifecycle. The following table highlights essential categories of tools, their typical examples, and why they are critical to building secure and efficient pipelines:

Category	Examples	Importance
Build engines	Jenkins, GitLab CI, Cloud Build	Orchestrates multi-stage security pipelines.
Scanning	Snyk, Trivy, SonarQube, Checkov	Detect code, image, and IaC vulnerabilities early.
Policy as code	OPA, HashiCorp Sentinel	Enforce complianc e gates automatically.
Notifications	Slack, Teams, PagerDuty	Surface failures instantly to the right people.

Table 5.1: Essential tools for automating security in DevOps pipelines

A Google Cloud CI/CD pipeline architecture shows Cloud Build at its core. The flow includes code pushed to a GitHub repository *triggering Cloud Build, which then builds a Docker image, scans it for vulnerabilities, pushes it to the Artefact Registry, and applies a Binary Authorisation* policy before deployment.

The following figure highlights automated security checks (vulnerability scanning and image policy enforcement) early in the pipeline:

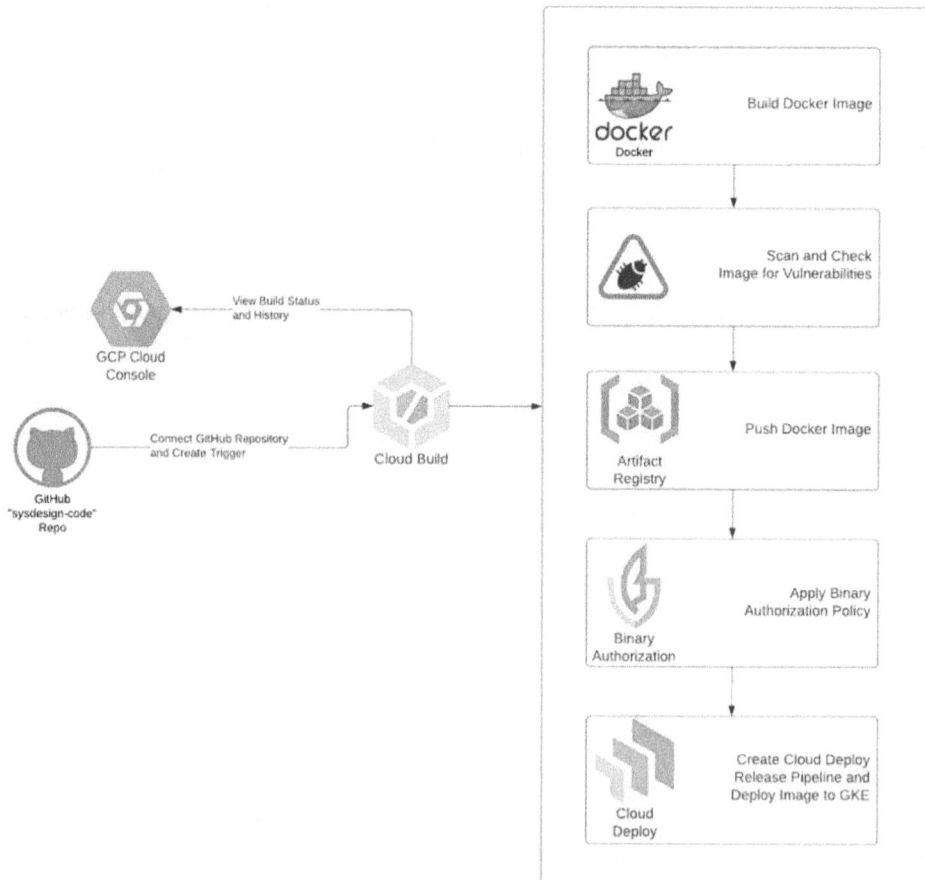

Figure 5.3: Integrating security scanning (SAST/Container scans) and binary authorization into build steps

Automated scanning for configuration errors

Misconfigurations, such as an open firewall rule, a public bucket, or an over-privileged service account, cause more cloud breaches than zero-day exploits. When committed to source control or deployed in an environment, automated scanners catch these mistakes. By combining lightweight linters (which flag obvious issues in Terraform, Kubernetes YAML, or Dockerfiles) with deeper policy as code engines (which evaluate changes against CIS Benchmarks or your guardrails), you ensure that every layer of your stack is scrutinized. The result is a *trust-but-verify* pipeline where risky configurations never pass the build stage, and production drift is detected before it becomes a security incident.

Consistency and early detection

Automated scanning tools serve as a second pair of eyes on every commit, identifying subtle misconfigurations, open firewalls, public buckets, and wildcard IAM that attackers love to exploit. By integrating linting and policy checks into both your CI pipeline and your runtime environment, you ensure that infrastructure definitions remain compliant from the first pull request through day two operations. The following concepts facilitate early detection and maintain consistency across the platform:

- **Misconfiguration risks***:* Even well-intentioned engineers can introduce dangerous settings when deadlines loom; these scans flag the most common slip-ups before they hit production.

    o **Open firewall:** These rules allow `0.0.0.0/0` or overly broad port ranges to expose private services to the internet.

    o **Exposed buckets:** A single misset **access control lists** (**ACL**) can make Cloud Storage objects publicly readable, or worse, writable.

    o **Legacy IAM:** Stale roles or service accounts with Editor privileges create massive lateralmovement potential.

- **Linting tools***:* Linting focuses on static code quality and apparent misconfigurations, providing quick feedback in seconds:

    o `terraform validate / terraform fmt`: Checks syntax, variable types, and enforces style so that plans are readable and consistent.

    o **Checkov** : Scans Terraform for hundreds of known issues (for example, unencrypted disks, unrestricted ingress).

    o **kubeval / conftest** : Validate Kubernetes YAML against the API schema and custom OPA policies before pushing to GKE.

    o Add a Cloud Build step that runs `Checkov` and fails on high-severity findings. The following code demonstrates the same:

```yaml
yaml
CopyEdit
- name: bridgecrew/checkov
  entrypoint: checkov
  args: ["--directory", ".", "--soft-fail", "false", "--quiet"]
```

- **Policy checks:** Policy as code tools go beyond linting, evaluating whether a change aligns with organizational or regulatory standards:

  o **OPA Gatekeeper:** Applies constraints, such as *no external IP on GCE* at admission controller time and in CI.

  o **HashiCorp Sentinel:** It runs inside Terraform Cloud, blocking plans that violate rules such as *subnet CIDR must be /24 or smaller.*

  o **Security baseline modules**: Reusable Terraform or DeploymentManager modules that encode CIS Benchmarks, making compliance the default, not an afterthought.

The following figure, policy as code in CI/CD from open policy agent docs:

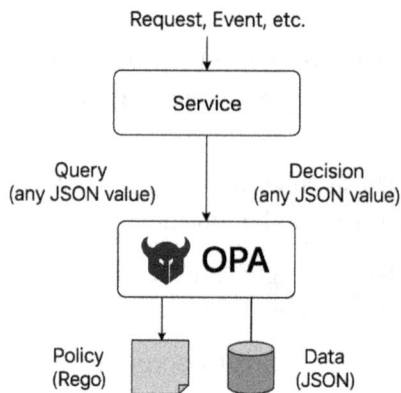

Figure 5.4: Creating policy as code in CI/CD pipelines

- **Integration checks:** Embedding these scans throughout the **software development life cycle (SDLC)** ensures that issues are caught early and production syncs with code:

  o **Continuous integration:** Every commit triggers lint and policy checks; the build fails quickly if critical findings are detected.

  o **Pull request reviews:** Scan results surface inline, giving reviewers context to approve or request fixes.

  o **Production drift detection:** Nightly jobs compare live GCP resources to Terraform state, alerting if someone manually opens a port or changes IAM outside of code.

Secure secrets handling in automated pipelines

Modern pipelines operate swiftly and interact with every environment, making credentials a crucial consideration. With Google Cloud Secret Manager, you treat a password or token like any other versioned artifact: you create it once, tag it, and let the platform manage encryption and access control. A build step that requires a database password calls the Secret Manager API, retrieves the latest version, uses it for the task at hand, and then discards it when the container exits. *No secret ever appears in source control, no one copies it into Slack, and each access event is logged in Cloud Logging for auditing.* Even better, rotating a secret is as simple as adding a new version; pipelines automatically pick it up the next time they run, allowing you to enforce a 90-day rotation without a mass refactor.

Refer to the following example code snippet to see how a build step fetches a secret on the fly:

```
- name: gcr.io/google.com/cloudsdktool/cloud-sdk
  entrypoint: bash
  args:
    - "-c"
    - |
      DB_PASS=$(gcloud secrets versions access latest --secret=db-prod-password)
      export DB_PASS
      ./gradlew test
```

Securing credentials and sensitive data end-to-end

A strong secrets strategy encompasses the entire journey from commitment to deployment and beyond:

- **Before building:** Pre-commit hooks and scanners, such as GitLeaks, prevent developers from pushing secrets into Git.

- **During the build:** The pipelines retrieve credentials from Secret Manager using a short-lived Workload Identity token, inject them as environment variables, and ensure they never appear in stdout.

- **After deployment:** Access logs and alerting policies monitor for unusual secret usage, while scheduled Cloud Functions rotate keys or certificates on a fixed schedule.

By layering IAM least privilege, just-in-time access, automatic rotation, and continuous monitoring, you transform credentials from a liability into a well-governed resource that remains protected whether you have a dozen pipelines or a thousand microservices:

- **GCP Secret Manager:** Secret Manager is a single source of truth for every token, certificate, or connection string your pipeline requires:
  - o **Centralized secret store:** Credentials live in one encrypted location instead of scattered **.env** files.

o **Versioning and rotation:** Update a secret, increment the version, and your pipeline automatically pulls the new value; no code changes are required.

o **IAM-based access:** Grant *read* access to the CI service account and *write* to security engineers; no one else can touch production secrets.

- **Injecting secrets in pipelines:** Fetch secrets only at runtime and scope them to the minimal blast radius:

o **Environment variables:** Cloud Build, GitLab CI, or Jenkins steps call the Secret Manager API, export the value as an env var, and clear it after the step finishes.

o **On-the-fly decryption**: Decrypt secrets within ephemeral containers; never write them to disk or standard output.

o **Short-lived tokens:** Utilize the IAM Credentials API to mint time-boxed tokens, ensuring that credentials expire swiftly even if logs are compromised.

- **Avoid committing secrets:** Prevention is cheaper than incident response; stop secrets before they hit Git:

o **Git hooks:** Local pre-commit scripts scan for AWS keys, JWTs, or Slack tokens and block the push if found.

o **Thirdparty scanners:** GitLeaks or TruffleHog run in CI, searching history for leaked credentials and opening blocking **pull request (PR)** comments.

o **Encrypted commits**: Store only a secret's reference (for example, `projects/123/secrets/db-pass`), never the value itself.

- **Auditing and alerting:** Visibility closes the loop; knowing *who* accessed *what* and *when* helps spot misuse in the pipelines:

o **Access logs:** The Secret Manager writes Admin Activity and Data Access logs to Cloud Logging and forwards them to SIEM for correlation.

o **Alerts:** Create log-based metrics that fire PagerDuty or Slack if a secret is read outside business hours or by an unexpected service account.

Best practices

A few disciplined habits make the difference between a secure pipeline and a headline-worthy breach:

- **Grant minimal access**: The fewer principals who can read a secret, the smaller the blast radius if credentials leak. Create a dedicated service account for each pipeline or runtime, grant it roles/secret manager, and use secretAccessor only for the secrets it needs. Deny access to everyone else, including humans.

- **Rotate regularly**: Even strong secrets can grow stale; people leave, code changes, and threat actors can harvest old credentials. Automate rotation with Cloud Scheduler and Cloud Functions (or utilize Secret Manager's built-in rotation hooks) so that new versions roll out every 90 days or immediately during incident response without requiring code changes.

- **Encrypt by default**: Secret Manager encrypts every value at rest with Google-managed keys, but regulated industries may require **customer-managed encryption keys (CMEK)**. Enabling CMEK provides full control over key rotation schedules, geographic residency, and revocation, satisfying strict compliance requirements without needing to re-architect the pipeline.

- **Avoid hard-coding**: Credentials buried in Git or Terraform become permanent liabilities; anyone who can clone the repository can exfiltrate them. Reference secrets by resource ID (`projects/123/secrets/db-pass`) or inject them as environment variables at runtime, ensuring that no plaintext secret ever touches version control, container images, or Helm charts.

By treating secrets as *first-class resources* that are centrally stored, just-in-time injected, versioned, and audited, you close one of the most straightforward doors for attackers while keeping release velocity high and compliance auditors happy.

Best practices for DevSecOps implementations

DevSecOps thrives when security is integrated into the daily delivery culture, tools, and metrics, not added as an afterthought. The practices outlined in the following sections will assist you in embedding protection without hindering developers. Additionally, embracing these practices transforms security from a last-minute challenge into a continuous, automated defense, ensuring every release aligns with your organization's risk and compliance standards while maintaining delivery speed.

Embedding security throughout SDLC

Building a DevSecOps culture means treating security controls as features that move through the same backlog, sprints, and pull requests as your application code. Each stage: plan, code, build, test, release, and operate, should include an automated gate that enforces policy, captures evidence, and provides feedback for the next sprint. The following aspects help embed security throughout the SDLC phases:

- **Shift security left**: Move vulnerability scanning, secrets detection, and policy checks to the first touchpoint: the developer workstation or pull request. When issues surface in the PR, the same engineer who introduced them can fix them in minutes, not days:

  o **Inline feedback**: Run SAST and IaC linters as precommit hooks (precommit, git-secrets, tfsec).

- o **Fail-fast pipelines**: Configure Cloud Build or GitLab CI to block merges if any high-severity findings are detected.

- o **Developer dashboards**: Expose scan results in the pull request UI so engineers see exactly which line triggered the gate.

Sample Git precommit hook that blocks secrets:

```
#!/usr/bin/env bash
gitleaks protect --staged --exit-code 1
```

- • **Unified logging and monitoring:** A single pane of glass lets security and ops teams correlate build failures with runtime anomalies. Centralizing logs reduces MTTR and gives auditors a complete trail from commit to deploy:

  - o **Log aggregation:** Forward Cloud Build logs, tfsec reports, and runtime events to Cloud Logging | BigQuery (or Splunk or **Elasticsearch, Logstash, and Kibana (ELK)**).

  - o **Real-time alerting:** Create log-based Metrics that display patterns, such as roles, owner-granted, or critical CVES detected in image *gcr.io/app:latest*.

  - o **Visual dashboards:** Grafana panels track build pass or fail rates, scan severities, and timetofix vulnerabilities.

- • **Immutable infrastructure:** Treat every server or container as a resource, not a pet. Rebuilding from code on each deploy eliminates drift and makes rollbacks trivial:

  - o **Ephemeral resources:** Use Terraform and Cloud Build to recreate Cloud Run revisions or GKE pods on every release.

  - o **Golden images:** Bake security updates into a new container image; never patch running nodes.

  - o **Automatic rollbacks:** If postdeploy health checks fail, Cloud Deploy automatically reverts to the previous revision.

- • **Collaboration between Dev and security:** Security champions within development squads bridge the language gap. When developers and security teams share metrics and post-mortems, secure coding becomes a part of the definition of done:

  - o **Shared training:** Monthly lunch-and-learns on the **Open Worldwide Application Security Project (OWASP)** Top 10, tfsec, and Secret Manager usage.

  - o **Joint retros:** After a pipeline incident, development and security collaboratively create action items, such as updating linters, adding tests, or refining policies.

  - o **Threat-modelling workshops:** Conduct brief **Spoofing, Tampering, Repudiation, Information Disclosure (privacy breach or data leak), Denial of Service, Elevation of Privilege (STRIDE)** sessions during sprint planning to ensure security stories are included in the same backlog.

- **Continuous improvement:** Pipelines evolve; so, should your security controls. Quarterly tuneups keep falsepositives low and coverage high:

- **Scanner review:** Retire noisy tools; pilot new ones, such as the **Open Source Vulnerabilities (OSV)** scanner, for open-source **software bill of materials (SBOM)** checks.

- **Policy refinement:** Utilize OPA decision logs to identify which rules are activated most frequently; adjust thresholds accordingly based on the risk appetite:

  o **Metric tracking:** Monitor the MTTR for vulnerabilities and the percentage of builds blocked by security gates, striving for a consistent decline.

A DevSecOps pipeline figure (DoD Enterprise DevSecOps reference) highlights continuous feedback loops and control points. It spans from plan to operate, incorporating automated security scans and tests in each phase, with monitoring feeding back into planning. Diamonds in the timeline represent control gates, such as risk reviews or compliance checks, at key transition points. This emphasizes that security is not a one-time effort; it continuously monitors and integrates findings (vulnerabilities, misconfigurations) back into the development cycle for ongoing improvement. Refer to the following figure:

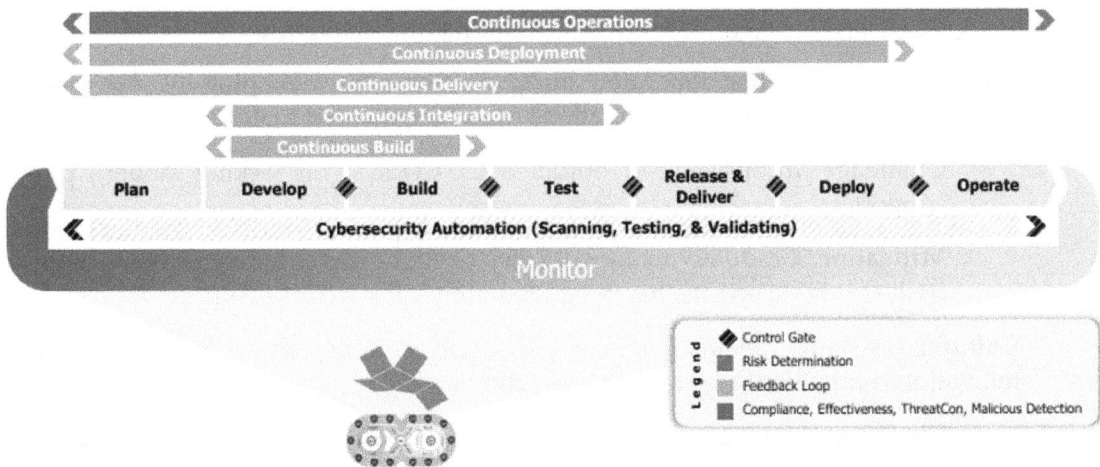

Figure 5.5: Continuous compliance showing how security testing and monitoring provide feedback

Securing legacy pipelines

Legacy pipelines were not designed with continuous security; they often rely on bespoke shell scripts, manual approvals, and credentials stored in plain text. Introducing modern DevSecOps practices into such environments can feel like changing an airplane engine mid-flight. Common hurdles include outdated build servers that cannot support container-based scanners, hard-coded secrets scattered across repositories, and cultural resistance from developers who fear that new gates will slow releases. Visibility presents another challenge: logs are located on individual VMs, making it difficult to correlate a misconfigured firewall in production with the commit that introduced it.

To modernize without disrupting delivery, teams can containerize security tools (for example, Trivy, Checkov), enabling them to operate on any build agent, even those that lack native plug-ins. Secrets should be migrated into Secret Manager and accessed at runtime via short-lived service account tokens, eliminating script passwords. For policy enforcement, start with a *warn-only* OPA step that highlights violations without failing the build; once developers recognize the value and false positives are minimized, switch the gate to *fail*. Streaming legacy build logs to Cloud Logging (or a central SIEM) creates the necessary audit trail for incident response and compliance. Finally, gradually refactor manual infrastructure scripts into Terraform modules, starting with stateless resources like VPCs, to gain drift detection and policy as code benefits for each subsystem as you progress.

Adapting and modernizing old processes

Legacy pipelines often pre-date modern security tooling but ripping them out overnight is not realistic.

A phased approach lets you layer in controls without halting deliveries:

- **Fragmented toolchains:** Outdated build servers may lack plug-ins for modern scanners. The challenges and mitigations to use fragmented toolchains are as follows:

  o **Challenge**: Inconsistent or outdated CI/CD systems lacking modern plugin support.

  o **Mitigation**: Gradually replace old steps with newer scanning or policy tools or create bridging scripts that integrate with GCP's security APIs.

- **Cultural resistance:** Teams fear new gates will slow velocity. The challenges and mitigations for cultural resistance are as follows:

  o **Challenge**: Dev teams may view security checks as slowing deployments.

  o **Mitigation**: Emphasise early detection cost savings and reduced rework. Provide fast, automated scans and minimal false positives.

- **Limited observability:** If logs live on a single VM, you cannot correlate build events with runtime issues. The challenges and mitigations for limited observability are as follows:

  o **Challenge**: Legacy pipelines often lack comprehensive logging and robust monitoring.

  o **Mitigation**: Integrate GCP's monitoring and logging capabilities or connect existing systems to a central aggregator (e.g., Splunk, ELK).

- **Refactoring infrastructure:** Manual scripts cannot be policy-checked. The challenges and mitigations for refactoring infrastructure are as follows:

  o **Challenge**: Complex manual processes are difficult to codify.

  o **Mitigation**: Migrate step-by-step to Terraform or other IaC solutions, rewriting partial configurations for subsystems first and then expanding coverage.

- **Slow security sign-offs:** Human approvals create bottlenecks. The challenges and mitigations for slow-security sign-offs are as follows:

  o **Challenge**: Manual, bureaucratic approvals cause friction and delay.

  o **Mitigation**: Automate policy checks with OPA or Sentinel. Use short-lived *approval gates* only for critical changes.

The following code snippet shows the OPA policy that blocks 0.0.0.0/0 ingress:

```rego
CopyEdit
package gcp.firewall
deny[msg] {
  input.direction == "INGRESS"
  input.source_ranges[_] == "0.0.0.0/0"
  msg := "Ingress rule exposes resource to the internet"
}
```

Compliance enforcement in practice

Integrating security into development pipelines is essential, but absolute confidence comes from seeing how organizations enforce these practices before production deployments. Practical implementations show how automated compliance checks ensure that only secure, policy-compliant code is released, especially in regulated industries.

Organisations operating under stringent compliance standards, such as PCI DSS for payment processing or HIPAA for healthcare data, must integrate robust security controls directly into their CI/CD workflows. For instance, a financial services provider built Terraform-based infrastructure where every deployment was subject to automated policy validation using OPA. Their pipelines were designed to halt any build that did not meet predefined security benchmarks, such as encrypted storage, restricted IAM roles, or verified container images.

In another example, a healthcare startup implemented Cloud Build triggers that automatically scanned each container for vulnerabilities, applied linting rules to IaC files, and enforced encryption policies using Binary Authorization. Their approach ensured that **electronic Protected Health Information (ePHI)** was always handled by HIPAA, with detailed audit logs to demonstrate compliance.

These case studies highlight that achieving regulatory alignment does not mean slowing down. By adopting automated security gates, these teams not only met compliance obligations but also accelerated the safe delivery of features, ensuring that their security measures scaled with their development pace.

Ensuring security at each release

Real-world pipelines prove that automated gates can satisfy stringent regulations without crippling delivery speed. The following pipelines explain different real-life scenarios:

- **PCI-DSS compliant e-commerce:** Cardholder data requires airtight network security and strict data handling protocols. A sample scenario to explain PCI Compliance Issue is as follows:

    o **Scenario**: Code merges must pass Terraform scans, ensuring no open ports beyond 443, no plain-text stored secrets, and only minimal IAM privileges.

    o **Solution**: Integrate Snyk and OPA checks in Jenkins to fail builds if policy violations appear.

    o **Outcome**: The production environment remains continuously compliant, with a near-zero risk of exposing cardholder data.

- **Health Insurance Portability and Accountability Act (HIPAA) pipeline: Protected Health Information (PHI)** must be encrypted and subject to strict access controls. A sample scenario to explain the PHI Compliance Issue is as follows:

    o **Scenario**: GCP resources managing patient data must enforce encryption (CMEK) and have restricted egress from private subnets.

    o **Solution**: Use Terraform modules to define standard HIPAA resources (VPC, subnets, firewall) with policy checks. Automate scanning in GitLab CI for every push.

    o **Outcome**: Each environment adheres to HIPAA's strict security controls, drastically reducing audit overhead.

- **Banking and finance:** Financial regulators mandate dual approvals and zero tolerance for leaked credentials. A sample scenario to explain banking and finance Compliance Issue is as follows:

    o **Scenario**: All code changes require a four-eye principle plus automated static analysis for secrets or keys.

    o **Solution**: Use Secret Manager for ephemeral credentials, scanning with check-in Cloud Build, and gating merges if compliance or secret checks fail.

o **Outcome**: Minimized developer friction while ensuring no unintended secrets or misconfigured network rules slip into production.

Continuation of the GCP pipeline: After a successful build, Cloud Deploy releases the image to GKE in stages (Test, Staging, and Production). Before deploying to production, a manual approval gate is required via Cloud Deploy, Pub/Sub, or Cloud Functions.

Across these examples, the pattern is clear: *policy as code, automated scans, and minimal manual gates* create a release pipeline that meets the toughest compliance bars without slowing teams down.

Complex made simple

Think of your DevSecOps pipeline like a modern assembly line producing automobiles:

- **Terraform (Blueprints and robots)**: Just as an assembly line uses precise, automated robots guided by blueprints, *Terraform* codifies your environment. This ensures each car (environment) is built consistently, minimizing manual errors.

- **CI/CD integration (Quality checks at each station):** Each station on the assembly line checks a component, like a QA station verifying the brakes or electrical wiring. Similarly, your CI/CD pipeline checks code for *security and compliance* at every step, catching issues before they move to the next stage.

- **Policy as code and scanning (Rigorous safety inspections):** The assembly line must comply with safety regulations. Tools like *OPA or Sentinel* act as inspectors, ensuring your car meets all safety standards (for example, no exposed ports, enforced encryption) before it rolls off the line.

- **Secret Manager (Locked toolkit):** Mechanics store special, expensive tools in a locked cabinet. In DevSecOps, sensitive credentials are kept in Secret Manager, preventing them from lying in plain sight or code repositories.

- **DevSecOps best practices (Continuous training and upgrades):** The assembly line constantly improves—technicians learn better methods, adopt new safety standards, and upgrade machinery. Likewise, DevSecOps fosters a continuous learning cycle, refining pipeline checks, adopting new scanning rules, and ensuring faster, safer releases.

The key takeaway is that by treating your DevSecOps pipeline like a secure, automated assembly line, each stage (coding, scanning, deploying) has checks, ensuring the final product meets stringent security criteria. This approach systematically minimizes human error, speeds up feedback, and keeps your GCP environments compliant and robust.

Conclusion

In this chapter, you explored the foundations and practical techniques for automating security within DevOps pipelines. You learned how to use Terraform to create secure and consistent IaC, integrate vulnerability scanning and policy checks at every stage of CI/CD, and securely manage secrets across environments. We also examined how to adapt these practices to legacy systems, ensuring continuous compliance and operational security while maintaining agility.

Security in modern cloud environments is no longer an afterthought or a final checklist item. By embedding controls throughout the development lifecycle, you create a proactive security posture, one where vulnerabilities are identified early, compliance is built-in, and teams can innovate confidently knowing that each deployment meets strict standards.

In the next chapter, we transition from automating pipelines to securing running workloads by focusing on **Google Kubernetes Engine (GKE)**. You will learn how to strengthen clusters, secure workloads through identity and network policies, enforce image integrity with vulnerability scanning and Binary Authorization, and establish secure service-to-service communication. This chapter also includes a comprehensive real-world example that demonstrates how to architect and manage a secure, compliant, multi-tenant GKE cluster. It is your next step in applying defense-in-depth strategies for containerized workloads on Google Cloud.

Exercises

Spin up a *secure end-to-end pipeline* that builds a simple container image, scans it, and deploys only if no critical issues are found:

1. **Repository setup:**
    a. Fork a *Hello World* Go or Python app on GitHub.
    b. Add a Dockerfile and a Terraform folder that creates a Cloud Run service and the IAM roles it needs.

2. **Secret storage:** Store a dummy API key in Secret Manager (demoapikey) and restrict read access to a new Cloud Build service account.

3. **Cloud Build pipeline:** In `cloudbuild.yaml`, add steps to:
    a. Fetch the secret and export it as an env var.
    b. Build the container image.
    c. Run **Trivy** (aquasec/trivy) and **tfsec** (bridgecrew/checkov) fail to build on HIGH or CRITICAL findings.
    d. Deploy to Cloud Run only if both scans pass successfully.

4. **Policy as code gate:**

   a. Add an OPA policy that blocks Terraform plans, creating firewall rules with 0.0.0.0/0 ingress.

   b. Insert an OPA evaluation step before the deployment stage.

5. **Validation**

   a. Push a commit that intentionally violates the OPA rule or introduces an unencrypted bucket.

   b. Confirm that the pipeline fails, and that Slack (or email) receives an alert.

   c. Fix the issue, push again, and verify that the pipeline is complete and the service is live.

Key takeaways

You will have gained practical insights into building secure, automated DevSecOps pipelines on Google Cloud. You now understand how to codify security controls using IaC, embed automated scans and policy checks into every CI/CD stage, and manage secrets securely without manual intervention:

- **Security by default:** You can now shift security left by embedding vulnerability scans, policy validation, and misconfiguration checks early in the development lifecycle, ensuring issues are identified before they reach production.

- **Policy as code:** Compliance gates are no longer manual tasks. With OPA or HashiCorp Sentinel, you can enforce organizational and regulatory standards automatically with every deployment.

- **Secret management:** Sensitive credentials never need to appear in code. By using Secret Manager, you ensure secure, centralized storage with fine-grained access control and automated rotation.

- **Legacy pipeline modernization:** You can incrementally improve outdated pipelines by introducing containerized tools, centralized logging, and phased policy enforcement, enabling secure operations without disrupting delivery.

- **Automated compliance:** From PCI DSS to HIPAA, you can automatically gather audit-ready evidence from logs, scan results, and policy files, demonstrating that each release adheres to both internal and external security requirements.

These takeaways equip you with the knowledge to not only secure new cloud-native environments but also bring legacy systems up to modern DevSecOps standards, ensuring security is consistent, scalable, and resilient across your organization.

References

1. https://cloud.google.com/secret-manager

2. https://cloud.google.com/build

3. https://cloud.google.com/architecture/devsecops

4. https://cloud.google.com/security-command-center

5. https://developer.hashicorp.com/terraform/docs

6. https://github.com/bridgecrewio/checkov

7. https://github.com/aquasecurity/trivy

8. https://www.openpolicyagent.org

9. https://docs.gitlab.com/ee/user/application_security/

10. https://www.jenkins.io/doc/book/pipeline/

11. https://registry.terraform.io/providers/hashicorp/google/latest/docs

12. https://cloud.google.com/container-analysis

Join our Discord space

Join our Discord workspace for latest updates, offers, tech happenings around the world, new releases, and sessions with the authors:

https://discord.bpbonline.com

CHAPTER 6

Securing Containerized Workloads GKE

Introduction

Containers facilitate fast software shipping but also consolidate risk: a single vulnerable image or misconfigured network rule can jeopardize an entire cluster. **Google Kubernetes Engine (GKE)** provides managed control planes, automatic node patching, and deep integrations with Google Cloud's security stack. Yet you can decide how to harden nodes, how workloads authenticate, and how traffic flows between pods. This chapter outlines the end-to-end process of securing a GKE environment, including locking down the cluster, scanning and signing images, enforcing least-privileged identity, and segmenting microservices with network policies. By the end, you will have a blueprint for managing Kubernetes on GCP that meets uptime targets and compliance mandates.

This chapter is intended for *cloud security engineers, platform engineers, and DevOps professionals* responsible for Kubernetes deployments on Google Cloud. It assumes familiarity with *basic Kubernetes concepts (pods, nodes, services)* and *GCP fundamentals*, including IAM, networking, and billing structures. Hands-on experience with **kubectl** and managing container images will help you maximize the benefits of the practical examples provided.

Structure

In this chapter, we will discuss the following topics:

- Introduction to GKE security
- Securing and managing GKE clusters
- Workload Identity vs. service account keys
- Secure Container Builds
- Network policies for microservices isolation
- Securing a multi-tenant GKE cluster in practice
- Complex made simple

Objectives

By the end of this chapter, you will be able to harden GKE clusters using features such as auto-upgrades, Shielded VMs, node isolation, and scoped maintenance windows. You will understand how to implement Workload Identity to eliminate static credentials and enforce least-privilege IAM roles at the pod-level. The chapter will guide you through scanning container images for vulnerabilities and enforcing build security with Binary Authorization.

You will also learn how to segment east-west traffic using Kubernetes Network Policies and apply service mesh capabilities to encrypt communication. Secure pod-to-pod communication using mutual TLS, short-lived credentials, and integration with Secret Manager will be discussed in detail. Additionally, you will gain the skills needed to design and operate a real-world, multi-tenant GKE cluster that adheres to compliance standards like PCI-DSS and HIPAA. Finally, this chapter will help you build confidence in scalable and automated DevSecOps practices that align with modern zero-trust architecture principles.

Introduction to GKE security

GKE provides a managed control plane, automated node upgrades, and seamless integration with the broader Google Cloud security stack, but a secure cluster still requires careful decisions on your part. You determine whether nodes operate Shielded VMs, whether the API server is exposed to the internet, how pods authenticate to Google Cloud APIs, and which workloads can communicate. This chapter aims to offer a blueprint for making those decisions. We will begin by strengthening the cluster foundation, then advance up the stack to Workload Identity, image provenance, and network isolation. Along the way, you will discover how to integrate automated scans and policy checks into your build and deploy pipelines, ensuring that every container and microservice meets the same security standard before it reaches production.

Importance of Google Kubernetes Engine Security

Kubernetes makes it easy to spin up thousands of containers. Still, that same power magnifies risk: a single misconfigured node image or overly permissive service account can expose the entire cluster. GKE removes the burden of running masters and etcd, yet everything above the control plane, such as node hardening, Workload Identity, network segmentation, and image provenance, remains your responsibility. Treating these layers with the same rigor you apply to application code is the difference between a resilient microservices platform and a breach headline.

The following are the key considerations:

- **Shared responsibility:** Google operates the control plane and patches the underlying infrastructure, but you own the security of what runs on top, node OS settings, RBAC rules, and pod-level policies. To meet these responsibilities effectively, you should:

    o Harden nodes with shielded VMs and minimal OS images.

    o Enable private clusters so that traffic never traverses the public internet.

    The following figure references how the Google shared responsibility model is built:

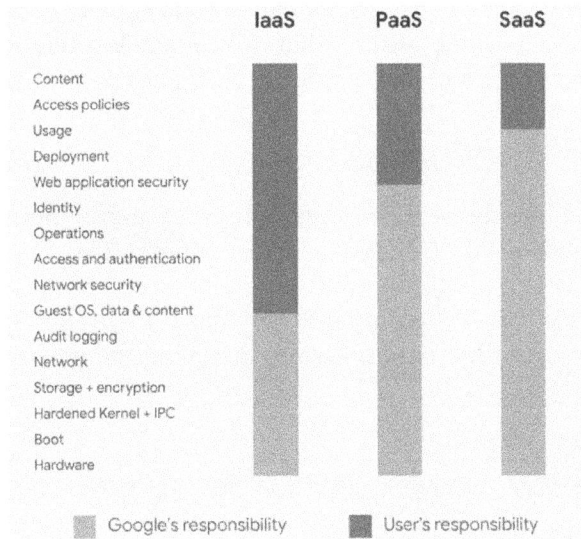

Figure 6.1: Division of responsibilities between Google Cloud and the customer in the shared responsibility model

- **Zero-trust:** Assume every pod could be compromised and design the network so it cannot reach anything unnecessary. This principle can be implemented through the following controls to reduce unnecessary exposure and lateral movement:

    o Use Kubernetes NetworkPolicies to restrict east-west traffic.

- - Map each workload to its own IAM identity with Workload Identity, granting only the GCP APIs it needs.

- **Automation and observability:** Manual checks cannot keep pace with rolling deployments; let pipelines enforce policy and surface issues in real time. The following implementation practices help enforce automated security controls and ensure real-time observability during continuous deployment:

  - - Scan images in Artifact Registry; block unscanned or unsigned images with Binary Authorization.

  - - Forward audit logs, network flows, and container runtime alerts to Cloud Logging or your SIEM for unified visibility.

By anchoring your strategy on these pillars: *clear responsibility lines, zerotrust isolation, and automated, observable controls*, you can build a GKE environment that scales with confidence instead of fear.

Securing and managing GKE clusters

Maintaining a healthy underlying cluster is the first step toward establishing any meaningful security posture. A fully patched control plane, well-designed node pools, and carefully scheduled maintenance windows ensure that **Common Vulnerabilities and Exposures (CVEs)** are addressed promptly and that disruptive upgrades do not impact customers' traffic.

Auto-upgrade and patching

GKE's managed auto-upgrade service automatically patches node pools to the latest Kubernetes version, typically within days of a security release, ensuring continuous alignment with supported and secure images. While auto-upgrades are recommended to maintain a safe posture, it is best practice to test these upgrades in staging environments first to detect any breaking changes or compatibility issues, thereby reducing the risk of unplanned outages in production.

The following are the key actions:

- **Enable auto-upgrade**: Opt in for node pool auto-updates to ensure timely patching of your nodes.

- **Selective upgrade channels**: Based on your risk tolerance and environment criticality, choose a suitable release channel (for example, rapid, regular, stable).

- **Monitor upgrade notifications**: Subscribe to GKE release notes, maintenance event logs, or cloud logs to receive real-time status updates.

Note: **These flags require GKE version 1.15 or later, as CLI flags and behaviors may change over time; always refer to the GKE release notes for compatibility before use.**

The following code snippet demonstrates how to set up an auto-upgrade using gCLI:

```
gcloud container clusters update my-cluster \
  --release-channel=regular \
  --maintenance-window-start=22:00 \
  --maintenance-window-end=02:00
```

This configuration subscribes your cluster to the *regular release channel*, specifying a *maintenance window* for upgrades. This helps you control when updates are applied while benefiting from security patches.

Node pool management

Separate workloads by risk profile, resource need, and OS image. Various node pool strategies can be applied to implement secure and resilient GKE clusters to improve isolation, scalability, and maintenance automation as follows:

Strategy	Importance	Example	Cost implications	Security considerations
Dedicated pools	Limits blast radius; lets you apply taints/labels for high-security pods.	A PCI pool runs payment services only.	May increase cost due to underutilized reserved nodes.	Enables strict isolation of sensitive workloads and application of node-level security policies.
Auto-scaling and auto-upgrade	Nodes scale out under load and patch themselves when traffic is low.	Batch-processing pool with min=0, max=20.	Saves cost during idle periods by scaling down to zero.	Automatic patching reduces the window of exposure to vulnerabilities; ensure upgrades are tested in staging.
OS choice	COS is minimal, read-only, and updated by Google; Ubuntu offers package flexibility.	Use COS for prod, Ubuntu for ML pipelines that need GPU drivers.	COS may reduce operational overhead; Ubuntu may require patch management effort.	COS provides a smaller attack surface; Ubuntu's flexibility may increase risk if unnecessary packages are installed.

Table 6.1: Comparison of node pool strategies in GKE, highlighting benefits and typical use cases

Maintenance windows

Automated upgrades in GKE ensure that security patches and platform updates are applied promptly; however, they can still cause pod rescheduling. To minimize service disruption during these events, it is essential to configure maintenance windows that align with your application's traffic patterns and user activity. GKE provides flexibility in defining when upgrades occur and how node draining is handled. Consider the following best practices while planning your maintenance windows:

- **Define non-critical periods**: If customer activity peaks at 9:00 AM UTC, schedule windows at 3:00 AM UTC.

- **Graceful draining:** GKE cordons and drains nodes during maintenance or scaling, but apps must handle SIGTERM and complete in-flight requests to avoid disruptions. To ensure seamless shutdown:

  o Use preStop hooks to delay pod termination while cleanup tasks complete.

  o Configure readiness probes to signal when a pod is ready to receive traffic and to stop receiving new requests before shutdown.

  o Refer to the Kubernetes best practices for graceful shutdown to implement reliable draining strategies in your workloads.

- **Test in staging first:** Clone production settings in a staging cluster and watch upgrade behaviour before promoting.

The following figure depicts how Google manages pools, private nodes, and maintenance flow:

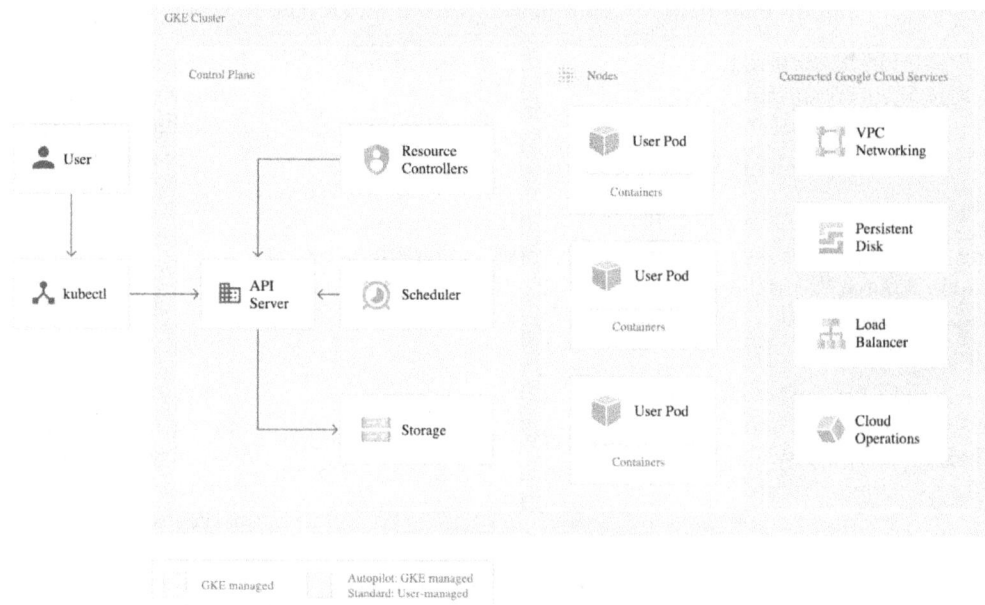

Figure 6.2 *Architecture of a GKE cluster*

This figure shows the following components:

- **Control plane**: Managed by GKE. Runs the Kubernetes API server, workload controllers, scheduler, and cluster state storage.

- **Nodes**: managed by GKE in autopilot mode and managed by customers in standard mode. All your pods run in nodes. Other Google Cloud services are available to integrate with GKE.

Best practices

While GKE offers powerful automation features, operational excellence depends on enforcing best practices in node configuration, workload isolation, and upgrade planning. By following proven practices, you can ensure better uptime, security posture, and workload stability across environments. The following table summarizes key best practices for hardening GKE clusters and their rationale in production environments:

Practice	Quick rationale
Use COS for most nodes	Smaller attack surface, faster security patching.
Alert on node health	Detect upgrade failures or kernel panics early.
Segment workloads	Place high-trust or GPU workloads in isolated pools.
Plan rolling upgrades	Set `maxSurge` and `maxUnavailable` to keep capacity during patching.

Table 6.2: Operational best practices for secure and resilient GKE clusters

With autoupgrade enabled, node pools segmented, and maintenance windows defined, your GKE foundation is resilient against known CVEs and operational surprises, setting the stage for workload-level controls in the following modules.

Workload Identity vs. service account keys

Running pods with long-lived JSON keys is the Kubernetes equivalent of leaving SSH keys on every VM. Workload Identity fixes this by federating **Kubernetes Service Accounts (KSAs)** with **Google Cloud Service Accounts (GSAs)**. Pods request short-lived tokens on the fly, receive only the IAM permissions bound to their mapped GSA, and never touch a static key file.

Warning: **Avoid static credentials in Kubernetes. Storing JSON service account keys in pods or images creates a persistent attack surface. Compromised keys can grant attackers broad, long-term access to cloud resources. Utilize Workload Identity to eliminate static credentials and enforce the use of short-lived, scoped tokens for enhanced security.**

Integrating Workload Identity with Google Cloud IAM

Workload Identity links GKE service accounts (Kubernetes) to GCP service accounts, eliminating the need to manage long-lived JSON keys. This ensures that pods only have the exact IAM permissions they need, following the principle of least-privilege.

A simple three-step mapping replaces JSON key distribution:

- **KSA**: Assigned to pods or deployments.
- **GCP service account**: Mapped 1:1 with the above.

- **Token exchange**: When pods request an identity token, GKE issues short-lived credentials from the mapped GCP account.

The following CLI example demonstrates mapping a KSA to a GSA:

```
# 1. Enable Workload Identity on your GKE cluster
gcloud container clusters update my-cluster \
    --workload-pool=my-project.svc.id.goog

# 2. Allow the KSA to impersonate the GSA
gcloud iam service-accounts add-iam-policy-binding my-gsa@my-project.iam.
gserviceaccount.com \
    --role roles/iam.workloadIdentityUser \
    --member "serviceAccount:my-project.svc.id.goog[my-namespace/my-ksa]"

# 3. Annotate the KSA with the GSA
kubectl annotate serviceaccount \
    --namespace my-namespace my-ksa \
    iam.gke.io/gcp-service-account=my-gsa@my-project.iam.gserviceaccount.com
```

This ensures that pods using **my-ksa** automatically receive short-lived, scoped credentials from **my-gsa**, eliminating the need to distribute or manage static JSON keys within your cluster.

The following are the benefits:

- **No static keys**: Reduces risk of key leakage or rotation overhead.

- **Fine-grained access**: Each workload gets its GCP permissions, ensuring minimal privileges.

- **Easier auditing**: GCP logs show which pod triggered an API call, making for better traceability.

Legacy service account keys and their limitations

The following are the challenges:

- **Key rotation**: Must be rotated regularly to reduce compromise.

- **Key storage**: Risk of exposing or committing JSON keys in repos.

- **Manual management**: Developers can accidentally copy or misuse keys.

The following are the migration considerations:

- **PodSpec changes**: Switch from mounting JSON secrets to referencing a KSA.

- **Re-architect**: Possibly restructure deployments that rely heavily on environment variables or config files containing keys.

- **Security gains**: The transition eliminates static keys, significantly reducing the attack surface.

Strengthening identity and access control for GKE Workloads

Consider the following practices to improve the security posture of GKE workloads that interact with Google Cloud APIs. These recommendations help enforce least-privilege access, minimize key exposure, and enhance auditability:

- **Adopt Workload Identity**: Use Workload Identity as the standard method for assigning IAM roles to Kubernetes pods, eliminating the need for long-lived service account keys.

- **Restrict GCP service account permissions**: Grant only the minimum required roles (e.g., Storage Object Viewer) to avoid overly permissive service accounts.

- **Audit pod IAM access**: Regularly review Cloud Audit Logs to detect unusual or high-privilege access patterns from workloads.

- **Avoid legacy key distribution**: If service account keys must be used, store them securely in Secret Manager. Never embed them in code repositories or expose them via environment variables. Additionally, *enable audit logging* to track all key access events and ensure *regular key rotation* (e.g., every 90 days) to minimize the blast radius if a key is compromised.

Secure Container Builds

Running the *latest* is not a strategy. Every container image you deploy must be scanned, signed, and verified before the pod starts. Google Cloud provides two native controls: *Vulnerability Scanning* (built into Artifact Registry) and *Binary Authorization* (an admission controller that blocks untrusted images). They create a supply-chain shield: scans identify known CVEs in libraries and base layers, while Binary Authorization ensures that only images that pass those scans, and are cryptographically signed, can run on your GKE cluster.

Additionally, *image provenance should be tied to both the source code and trusted base images*, ensuring that what you build is what you deploy and that your builds rely only on verified, secure components.

Container vulnerability scanning

Containers inherit every library, system package, and language runtime that goes into their base image; a single outdated OpenSSL build can compromise dozens of microservices. By wiring vulnerability scans directly into your build pipeline, you turn each Docker build into a security checkpoint that fails the moment a *High or Critical* CVE appears, long before the image lands in a registry or a pod.

The following is how it works (GCP native flow):

- **Build** | `docker push` to **Artifact Registry**.
- **Container analysis API** fires automatically, unpacking the layers and comparing package versions against Google's continuously updated CVE database.
- Findings are written to Cloud Logging and surfaced in the Artifact Registry UI: CVE ID, severity, and available fix.
- *Cloud Build trigger* can fetch the scan result via REST and fail the build if it exceeds a severity threshold.

The following figure illustrates how logs from both GKE and GKE on-prem environments are collected and forwarded to Cloud Logging using common logging agents:

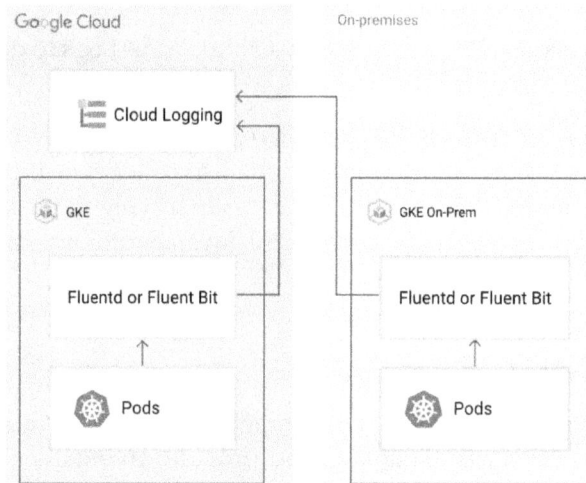

Figure 6.3: Cloud Logging

The pipeline snippet fails the build on `CRITICAL`:

```
id: "Scan image"
name: "gcr.io/cloud-builders/gcloud"
entrypoint: "bash"
args:
  - "-c"
  - |
    IMG="us-docker.pkg.dev/$PROJECT_ID/app:${SHORT_SHA}"
    gcloud artifacts docker images scan $IMG \
        --format=json > scan.json
    JQ_CMD='.[0].vulnerabilityScanSummary.severityCount.CRITICAL'
    CRIT=$(jq -r "$JQ_CMD" scan.json)
    if [[ "$CRIT" != "0" ]]; then
```

```
        echo "CRITICAL vulnerabilities found!"
        exit 1
    fi
```

This pipeline step scans your container image and *fails the build if any CRITICAL vulnerabilities are detected*, enforcing a strict security gate in your CI pipeline.

Note: The jq command is a lightweight, flexible command-line JSON processor used here to extract the number of CRITICAL findings from the scan results. You can learn more about its syntax and filtering capabilities in the jq manual https://jqlang.org/manual/

The following table shows the key tools and when to use them:

Tool	Ideal use-case	Strength
Artifact Registry native scanning	Teams fully on GCP, want zeroconfig scanning	Runs automatically; data lands in Cloud Logging for alerting.
Cloud Build and trivy container	Need custom thresholds or offline scans	Fast, opensource, supports SBOM output.
Snyk container	Commercial orgs needing licence compliance and CVEs	Combines CVE scan with license policy checks.
Clair or Grype in GitLab	Self-hosted registries or airgapped	Works without Google APIs; integrates into GitLab CI.

Table 6.3: Comparison of container vulnerability scanning tools by use case and integration capabilities

CI pipeline security controls

To ensure container scans lead to actionable outcomes, developers must embed scanning checkpoints directly into their CI/CD workflows. The following practices convert passive scans into proactive security enforcement:

- **Integrate scans early**: Run scanners immediately after image builds; surface results in the merge-request interface so issues are resolved before approval.

- **Fail fast on High or Critical**: Use `exit-code 1` in Trivy or the `gcloud` scan JSON to halt pipelines. Automatically generate Slack or Jira tickets to alert responsible teams.

- **Regularly update base images**: Pin images to minimal COS or distroless bases and trigger nightly rebuilds. This often reduces CVE counts without additional patching.

- **Automate re-scans**: Schedule weekly Cloud Scheduler jobs to re-run scans. If new vulnerabilities are found, revoke previous attestations.

- **Store SBOMs**: During the build, generate **Software Bills of Materials** (**SBOMs**); e.g., using `trivy sbom`, and attach them as artifacts for traceable, auditable supply-chain security.

With vulnerability scanning deeply integrated into the build process, security becomes a feedback-driven development habit, rather than a last-minute checkpoint.

Enforcing image trust with Binary Authorization

Running a vulnerability scanner is half the battle; you still need a gate that *refuses to run* anything that fails those checks. Binary Authorization is a gate where an admission controller for GKE looks at every image pull request and asks, *Does a trusted authority sign this image, and does it meet our vulnerability policy?* If the answer is no, the pod never starts.

The following figure depicts how binary authorization integrates with the CI/CD pipeline. It shows steps from source code commit, container image build, signing an attestation (using Cloud KMS), and enforcement in GKE at deploy-time.

This helps illustrate (*Figure 6.4*) how only images that have been signed or attested (trusted) are allowed to run in the cluster:

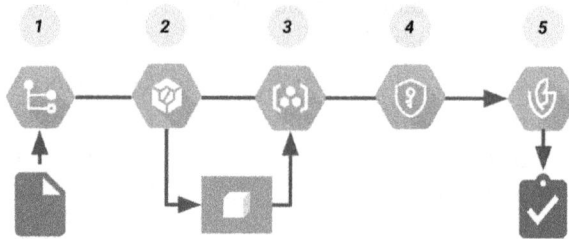

Figure 6.4: Binary authorization in Google

The following is how to set up Binary Authorization:

- **Define attestation authorities**: Decide who (or what) is allowed to bless an image. Common methods for configuring attestation authorities include:

  o Create Cloud KMS keys for each authority: **build-system, security-team, compliance**.

  o Pipeline scanners (for example, Trivy) or human reviewers sign the image digest with those keys.

- **Write policies**: Policies combine signature requirements with CVE thresholds or provenance rules. The following is an example of how to define a production policy in YAML:

```
defaultAdmissionRule:
evaluationMode: REQUIRE_ATTESTATION
requireAttestationsBy:
projects/$PROJECT_ID/attestors/security-team
vulnerabilityBasis:
maximumFixableSeverity: "MEDIUM"
```

Here, `maximumFixableSeverity: "MEDIUM"` means:

o Images with vulnerabilities that have fixes available up to MEDIUM severity will be allowed.

o If an image contains fixable vulnerabilities of HIGH or CRITICAL severity, it will be blocked until those are addressed.

o Vulnerabilities without fixes will not block admission regardless of severity, allowing for practical deployment while still enforcing remediation for fixable issues.

This field ensures your Binary Authorization policies enforce vulnerability gating without halting pipelines unnecessarily while still protecting production environments.

o Dev policy might allow up to HIGH severity or unsigned images for rapid iteration.

- **Enforce at deploytime**: GKE's admission controller checks the policy when a workload deploys. The system responds to image validation as follows:

o The image is pulled if all required attestations are present and the vulnerability scan passes.

o Otherwise, Kubernetes returns a FailedPrecondition error, and the pod stays in Pending.

The following code snippet shows how to sign and create an attestation in Cloud Build:

```
# Sign image with cosign after successful scan
cosign sign \
  --key gcpkms://projects/$PROJECT_ID/locations/global/keyRings/sec/
cryptoKeys/build \
  gcr.io/$PROJECT_ID/app:${SHORT_SHA}

# Create Binary Auth attestation
gcloud container binauthz attestations create \
  --artifact-url=gcr.io/$PROJECT_ID/app@${DIGEST} \
  --attestor=projects/$PROJECT_ID/attestors/build-system \
  --signing-key-version=gcpkms://.../cryptoKeyVersions/1
```

Typical use cases

The following table outlines common scenarios where Binary Authorization delivers tangible security benefits, especially in regulated or multi-tenant environments:

Scenario	Benefit
PCI-DSS / FedRAMP	Proves every prod image passed vulnerability and signature checks.
Multi-tenant GKE	Each tenant's images must be signed by a central security attestor.
DevSecOps pipelines	CI scans, signs, and promotes images automatically; Binary Auth stops anything that misses the signandscan stage.

Table 6.4: Use cases and benefits of enforcing Binary Authorization in GKE Workloads

Binary Authorization signing strategies

To effectively implement Binary Authorization across build and deployment pipelines, consider the following key operational strategies:

- **Automate signing**: CI/CD pipelines should invoke tools like **cosign** or **binauthz attestations create** to and sign artifacts automatically. Manual uploads of signatures should be avoided to reduce risk and ensure consistency.

- **Granular policies**: Enforce strict rules by environment. For example, production may require zero **CRITICAL** vulnerabilities, staging may permit **MEDIUM**, and development may allow any signed image for flexibility.

- **Re-scan and re-sign**: Schedule **cron** jobs to re-scan image digests regularly. If a new vulnerability violates the policy, revoke the previous attestation and trigger a rebuild of the image.

- **Version your policy**: Store attestation policies (JSON or YAML) in version control systems like Git, tag policy changes alongside application releases to track their impact.

- **Alert on denials**: Configure **log-based** metrics on **binauthz.policy_violation** logs to notify DevOps when access to a container image is blocked. This often signals policy misconfigurations or outdated attestations.

When vulnerability scanning is integrated with cryptographic attestations, binary authorization transforms the registry into a secure, policy-driven control point. Only signed and policy-compliant images are allowed to run on production workloads.

Network policies for microservices isolation

Microservices thrive on fast, frequent communication, but that same chatter can become an attacker's express lane if you do not control it. Kubernetes NetworkPolicies lets you draw invisible walls inside the cluster, so each service communicates only with the workloads it truly depends on. Think of them as a *software-defined firewall* residing inside your pods: one YAML manifest can stop a compromised front-end from port-scanning your databases or prevent Tenant A from ever touching Tenant B's API. In this module, you will learn how to design, deploy, and monitor these policies, starting with default-deny isolation and layering in explicit *allow* rules, so lateral movement becomes nearly impossible even if an edge service gets breached.

Securing pod communication

Even if your nodes are patched and your images signed, a single overly chatty pod can undermine the whole cluster. Kubernetes NetworkPolicies act like firewall rules inside the cluster, allowing you to specify precisely which pods, or namespaces, can communicate with one another and on which ports. When used in conjunction with mTLS from Istio or Anthos service mesh, they provide both transport encryption and directional control, achieving true zero-trust security at the micro-service level.

Working of network policies

A **NetworkPolicy** is a YAML manifest that selects which pods can receive traffic and specifies who may connect to them.

The following is a simple example policy:

```
apiVersion: networking.k8s.io/v1
kind: NetworkPolicy
metadata:
  name: allow-api-from-web
  namespace: prod-api
spec:
  podSelector:
    matchLabels:
      app: api
  ingress:
    - from:
        - namespaceSelector:
            matchLabels:
              name: prod-web
      ports:
        - protocol: TCP
          port: 443
  policyTypes:
    - Ingress
```

The following are the explanation for beginners:

- **podSelector**: Selects pods in the **prod-api** namespace with **app: api**.
- **policyTypes: Ingress**: This policy only controls incoming traffic.
- **ports**: Only allows traffic on TCP port 443.

- **namespaceSelector**: Allows connections only from pods in namespaces labelled with `name: prod-web`.

Tip: To use namespaceSelector, you must explicitly label your namespaces (e.g., kubectl label namespace prod-web name=prod-web). This ensures that only traffic from trusted namespaces (like your frontend pods in prod-web) can reach your api pods, enabling namespace-level segmentation and zero-trust enforcement.

To implement effective Kubernetes network policies that align with zero trust principles, consider the following building blocks:

- **Namespace isolation**: Tag each namespace (`team=a, team=b`) and write a defaultdeny policy so pods see only their own namespace by default.

- **Pod selectors**: Use labels like `app=database` or `tier=backend` to target a policy at just those pods.

- **Ingress or egress rules**: List the allowed CIDRs, namespaceSelectors, or podSelectors, plus the port or protocol.

Use cases and patterns

Security policies in Kubernetes environments are seldom one-size-fits-all. Depending on the architecture, whether it is a single-tenant workload, a multi-tenant SaaS environment, or a shared infrastructure, your policy enforcement strategy must align with the underlying use case.

The following table outlines key network policy patterns across different deployment scenarios, highlighting the enforcement strategy and the associated security benefit:

Scenario	Policy pattern	Benefit
Zero trust microservices	Defaultdeny everything, then add allow rules per dependency (web ∣ api, api ∣ db).	Blocks lateral movement from compromised pods.
Multi-tenant SaaS cluster	Each tenant gets a namespace, and denyall ∣ explicit allows the shared auth service.	Tenants cannot sniff or reach one another.
Shared services	Admin namespace exposes metrics on 9090; only the ops namespace can consume it.	Limits sensitive data to operations tooling only.

Table 6.5: Network policy patterns for common Kubernetes use cases

Practical network policy techniques

Effectively deploying Kubernetes network policies requires more than just writing YAML files, it involves strategy, testing, and understanding how policies interact with service mesh and cluster dynamics. The following techniques help operators enforce zero-trust networking principles and ensure strong segmentation across workloads:

- **Start with default-deny**: Create a cluster-wide policy that denies all ingress or egress, then layer explicit allow rules.

- **Use labels, not IPs**: Pods can reschedule at any IP; label-based selectors survive node churn.

- **Version control policies**: Store YAML in Git next to services; changes follow the same PR review process.

- **Test with kubectl exec**: Verify connectivity before and after applying rules; CI can run `netcat` probes in a throw-away job.

- **Combine with mTLS**: NetworkPolicies say *who* can talk; mTLS (e.g., Istio) encrypts *what* they say.

With NetworkPolicies enforcing least-privilege paths and service mesh encrypting traffic, your pod-to-pod communication becomes as tightly controlled as any external firewall. Now it is fully automated and versioned like the rest of your Infrastructure as Code.

Policy enforcement

NetworkPolicies are only YAML until a networking backend enforces them. In GKE, you have two primary engines: GKE Native (built-in VPCnative enforcement) or Calico (Dataplane v2 add-on). Both honor the Kubernetes NetworkPolicy API; the choice comes down to feature depth and observability requirements.

Enabling network policy

Enabling network policies in GKE provides foundational enforcement of east-west traffic restrictions. Depending on your operational complexity and feature requirements, Google Kubernetes Engine offers native options and integrations with advanced policy engines like Calico. The following table compares the options that help you choose the most suitable enforcement layer for your environment:

Option	Enabling	When to choose
GKE Native (Dataplane v2)	gcloud container clusters create secure-cluster --enable-network-policy.	Simpler ops; leverages Google networking stack; good for most production clusters.
Calico on GKE	Enable **Dataplane v2** or install Tigera Calico manifest for enhanced policy types (GlobalNetworkP olicy, egress logging).	Need advanced policy constructs, policy audit logs, or future eBPF features.

Table 6.6: Comparison of GKE-native and Calico-based approaches to enabling network policy enforcement

The following are the differences between the perimeter and East-West:

- *GCP firewall rules* secure traffic *to/from nodes*, think perimeter and North-South.
- NetworkPolicies secure pod-to-pod traffic, your east-west layer, stopping lateral movement.

Network policy operational guidance

As organizations adopt network policies to secure east-west traffic, operational clarity becomes critical. The following recommendations offer tactical guidance to ensure your policies are precise, enforceable, and observable in real time:

- **Granular, predictable labeling**: Select pods using consistent labels; inconsistent tagging can inadvertently expose workloads. Adopt a standard convention such as `app=<service>, tier=frontend|backend|db, env=prod|staging`.

- **Default-deny baseline**: Start with a cluster-wide policy that denies all ingress and egress by default. Then explicitly allow required flows:

```
kind: NetworkPolicy
metadata: { name: default-deny }
spec:
podSelector: {}
policyTypes: ["Ingress", "Egress"]
```

- **Progressive rollout**: Apply policies namespace-by-namespace. Begin in staging environments and monitor metrics for anomalies before extending to production. Use *Calico's* `policyPreview` or deploy policies in audit mode to preview enforcement impact without disrupting traffic.

- **Observability and troubleshooting**: Improve visibility into denied traffic with actionable insights. *Why is my pod stuck?* This becomes a solvable question with visibility tools.

- **Calico flow logs or Dataplane v2 drops**: Use these telemetry sources to detect policy violations and diagnose denied connections. *Create Cloud Logging metrics on* `networkpolicy_blocked` *events to trigger alerts when legitimate traffic is accidentally blocked.*

With enforcement, consistent labelling, and flow visibility in place, network policies act as a dynamic safety net, allowing just enough communication between services without compromising isolation.

Securing pod-to-pod communication

Once your cluster is hardened and workloads are mapped to leastprivilege identities, the final step is protecting the traffic that flows between those workloads. In a zero trust model, every request, East-West or North-South, must be authenticated, authorized, and encrypted. This module shows how to achieve *TLS everywhere*, leverage Workload Identity for runtime IAM, and deploy a service mesh layer (Istio/Anthos) for policy, observability, and finegrained access control.

Enforcing mutual-TLS for pod communication

Encrypting data in transit so even internal traffic cannot be sniffed. The following table outlines the key components involved in implementing **mutual-TLS (mTLS)** within a GKE cluster, including how it is set up and the primary benefits of each layer in securing pod-to-pod communication:

Capability	Implementation	Key benefit
Service mesh mTLS	Enable Istio or Anthos service mesh; sidecar proxies handle certificate issuance and rotation automatically (**istioctl install --set profile=default**). Example: Deploy a sample **httpbin** and **sleep** pod; traffic between them is auto-encrypted with mTLS.	Automatic encryption and mutual authentication for every pod-to-pod call.
Certificates and rotation	Mesh CA issues SPIFFE IDs (**spiffe://cluster.local/ns/prod/sa/api-sa**) and rotates them every 24 h. Example: Use **kubectl get certificates -n istio-system** to confirm auto-issued certificates for workloads.	No manual cert management; compromised certs expire quickly.
Zero-trust handshake	Pod A validates Pod B's SPIFFE ID before accepting a connection. For example, configure Istio **AuthorizationPolicy** to allow only identities with **spiffe://cluster.local/ns/prod/sa/frontend-sa**.	Prevents rogue pods from impersonating trusted services.

Table 6.7: Core capabilities and benefits of enforcing mTLS for intra-cluster communication

The following are the pros:

- Meets PCI-DSS, HIPAA, and FedRAMP encryption in-transit requirements.
- Blocks internal eavesdropping and MITM attacks.
- Identity-aware routing (mTLS and JWT) enables perservice RBAC.

The following are the cons:

- Extra CPU or latency ($\approx$1–2 ms per hop).
- Complexity if you roll your own certificates instead of using a mesh.

Recommendation

Before enforcing strict mutual TLS across your entire GKE cluster, it is important to understand existing traffic behavior to avoid service disruptions:

- **IAM integration at the container runtime:** Give pods the exact Google Cloud API permissions they need, nothing more.

- **Workload Identity mapping**:

```
gcloud container clusters update secure-prod \
    --workload-pool=myproj.svc.id.goog
kubectl annotate serviceaccount api-sa \
    iam.gke.io/gcp-service-account=api-gsa@myproj.iam.gserviceaccount.com
```

  Pods running the **api-sa** now fetch shortlived OAuth2 tokens for **api-gsa**, eliminating JSON keys.

- **IAM least-privilege**: Assign roles like **roles/pubsub.publisher** or **roles/storage.objectViewer**, never broad **roles/editor**.

  Use IAM Conditions if a pod should access an API only from **namespace=prod**.

Note: Start with permissive mTLS mode (STRICT off) to observe traffic patterns, then flip to STRICT cluster-wide once you have validated nothing breaks.

Secrets in pods

Managing secrets within Kubernetes requires balancing security, usability, and automation. In GKE, secrets can be managed more securely by avoiding traditional environment variables and relying on GCP-native mechanisms like Secret Manager and IAM credentials. This section outlines best practices for securely managing secrets in your pod workloads.

The following table summarizes strategies for handling secrets securely in pod deployments:

Best practice	Implementation
On-the-fly retrieval	Initcontainer calls Secret Manager API, injects secret via tmpfs volume; container never sees plaintext on disk.
Short-lived tokens	Use IAM credentials API: **generateAccessToken** valid for 30 min, refreshed automatically by sidecar.
No env vars	Store DB passwords in memory, not **env**, to avoid exposure in **kubectl exec env**.

Table 6.8: Secure secrets management practices for GKE workloads

Service mesh approaches

In addition to secrets management, service mesh tools like Istio and Anthos service mesh offer advanced capabilities for enforcing encryption, traffic policy, and observability across microservices. These service meshes integrate seamlessly with GKE, enabling fine-grained control over service-to-service communication.

The following table outlines the key features of service meshes and their implementation benefits:

Feature	Reason	Example
mTLS by default	Clusterwide encryption & identity.	`PeerAuthentication` set to **STRICT**.
AuthorizationPolicies	Layer7 RBAC (*frontend can call* **/** `api/v1/*` *on backend*).	Finegrained allow or deny.
Observability	Builtin Prometheus metrics, Kiali dashboards, and distributed tracing with Zipkin/Jaeger.	SREs pinpoint highlatency hops in minutes.

Table 6.9: Key features of Istio and Anthos service mesh in GKE

The figure shows how Anthos ties together policy management, service mesh, and operations for all clusters, providing a single pane of glass to view and manage workloads:

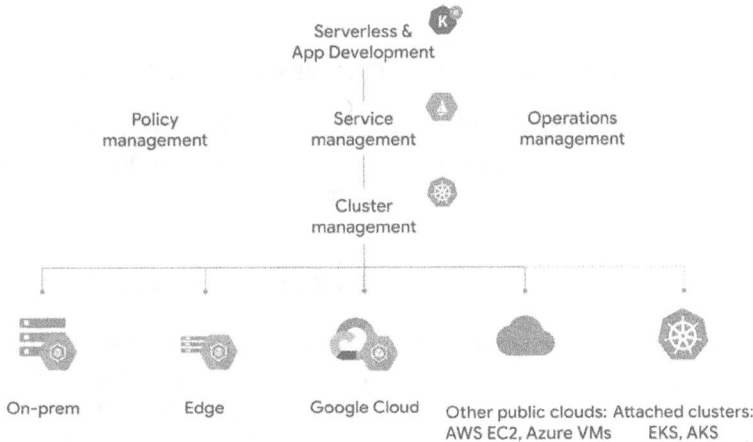

Figure 6.5: Unified cluster management for Google

To implement fine-grained access control in Istio, AuthorizationPolicies can be defined to restrict which services are allowed to communicate with one another.

Performance note

While Istio AuthorizationPolicies with mTLS significantly enhance security by enabling fine-grained, service-to-service encryption and identity-based access control, they can introduce *performance overhead* (typically 5 to 10% CPU and latency impact) due to the encryption and decryption processes and certificate management. It is recommended to benchmark your workloads, especially latency-sensitive applications, and consider *sidecar resource tuning or ambient mesh (if supported)* to mitigate potential performance impacts while retaining security benefits.

The following example demonstrates how to allow only the **payment-service** to call the **orders** service by enforcing a Workload Identity-based policy in the **prod** namespace:

```
apiVersion: security.istio.io/v1beta1
kind: AuthorizationPolicy
metadata:
  name: allow-payment-to-orders
  namespace: prod
spec:
  selector:
    matchLabels:
      app: orders
  rules:
  - from:
    - source:
        principals: ["spiffe://cluster.local/ns/prod/sa/payment-sa"]
```

By combining *mTLS encryption, Workload Identity IAM, secreton-demand retrieval,* and *mesh-level RBAC,* you close the loop on pod-to-pod security: every request is authenticated, authorized, encrypted, and fully observable, delivering true zerotrust inside your GKE cluster.

Securing a multi-tenant GKE cluster in practice

Consider a scenario, a **Software as a Service (SaaS)** provider runs hundreds of tenant applications on a single Google Kubernetes Engine cluster to save costs and streamline operations. Tenants share the control plane and compute nodes, yet strict isolation is mandatory so that an exploit in Tenant A can never touch data or services in Tenant B. The solution layers node-level separation, namespace isolation, Workload Identity, and policyascode gates, proving that multi-tenant efficiency and zero-trust security can coexist.

Cluster setup

Physical and operational boundaries begin at the node pool. To ensure tenant isolation in a shared Kubernetes environment, it is crucial to define both physical and logical boundaries at the node pool level.

The following table outlines the key controls, their implementations, and the resulting benefits in a multi-tenant GKE cluster:

Control	Implementation	Benefit
Tenant-dedicated node pools	`bash gcloud container node-pools create tenant-a-pool \ --cluster=my-cluster \ --node-labels=tenant=a \ --node-taints=tenant=a:NoSchedule \ --num-nodes=3`	Ensures noisy-neighbor bursts or kernel exploits stay within a tenant.
Auto-upgrade and release channel	`bash gcloud container clusters update my-cluster \ --release-channel=regular gcloud container node-pools update tenant-a-pool \ --enable-autoupgrade \ --maintenance-window-start=02:00 \ --maintenance-window-end=04:00 \ --maintenance-window-day=all`	Critical CVEs patched within days, downtime shifted to the tenant's off-hours.
Shielded VM and COS	YAML snippet for node pool: `yaml nodeConfig: shieldedInstanceConfig: enableSecureBoot: true enableVtpm: true imageType: COS_CONTAINERD` CLI: `bash gcloud container node-pools create secure-pool \ --cluster=my-cluster \ --image-type=COS_ CONTAINERD \ --shielded-secure-boot \ --shielded-vtpm`	Minimal OS surface; prevents rootkit persistence.

Table 6.10: Node pool-level isolation and hardening strategies in GKE

Networking and policies

Namespace boundaries and network rules prevent lateral movement:

- **Namespace per tenant: `tenant-a, tenant-b`**. Default NetworkPolicy: deny all ingress or egress.

- **Ingress gateway**: Only a shared Envoy/Istio IngressGateway can reach tenant services.

- **Service mesh mTLS**: Istio in **STRICT** mode encrypts EastWest traffic; AuthzPolicies allow calls only from the gateway.

- **Cloud NAT**: Nodes have no public IPs; outbound HTTPS egress goes through a tenant-tagged NAT, which is logged for audit.

Workload Identity and auth

Each pod gets its own IAM persona, no shared keys, no cross-tenant access. In a secure multi-tenant cluster, each workload must be independently authenticated and authorized. GKE enables through Workload Identity, IAM role scoping, and policy-driven enforcement.

The following table summarizes the core controls and examples for identity isolation and access control:

Control	Example
Tenant GSA	`tenant-a-app@PROJECT.iam.gserviceaccount.com` with `roles/pubsub.publisher` only.
Annotation	`kubectl annotate sa app-sa iam.gke.io/gcp-service-account=tenant-a-app@…`
Binary authorization	Policy: require build-system and security-team signatures AND zero CRITICAL CVEs.
Secret Manager	Secret `projects/…/secrets/tenant-a-db` readable only by `tenant-a-app` GSA.

Table 6.11: Identity isolation and authorization controls for tenant workloads in GKE

Security enforcement pipeline

In a secure GKE environment, enforcement starts early, within the CI/CD pipeline. By integrating automated checks and gates at each stage, organizations can prevent misconfigurations, vulnerabilities, or policy violations from ever reaching the cluster.

The following list highlights the key components of the security enforcement pipeline:

- **Terraform lint and Open Policy Agent (OPA) check**: Blocks any Kubernetes manifest that includes insecure configurations such as **hostPath** usage or **privileged: true**.

- **Build | Artifact Registry scan | cosign sign**: Fails the pipeline for container images with HIGH or CRITICAL CVEs; successful builds are signed using **cosign**.

- **Binary Authorization gate in Google Kubernetes Engine (GKE)**: The admission controller automatically rejects unsigned or non-compliant container images.

- **Post-deployment compliance script**: Uses Google Cloud Functions to query the GKE API and verify that no public IPs or wildcard **role-based access control (RBAC)** permissions exist.

- **Audit trail**: Integrates Cloud Audit Logs and **Security Command Center (SCC)** with Splunk to visualize tenant-specific CVE scores, denied deployments, and **Network Address Translation (NAT)** egress traffic.

With these controls in place, combined with node-level segmentation, namespace-based **NetworkPolicies**, Workload Identity, and Binary Authorization, each tenant achieves isolation comparable to a dedicated cluster. Yet the operations team benefits from centralized, scalable GKE infrastructure management.

Complex made simple

Visualize GKE cluster security like a modern hotel:

- **Cluster hardening (Hotel infrastructure):** The hotel invests in auto-maintained elevators, air conditioning, and key infrastructure updates, like auto-upgraded node pools and patched Kubernetes versions in GKE.

- **Workload Identity vs. service account keys (Room keys vs. physical keys):** Instead of distributing physical keys (service account JSON files) that can be lost or copied, each guest (pod) uses an electronic key card (Workload Identity) that provides only the exact access needed and can be revoked at any time.

- **Container scanning and binary authorization (Security screening):** Like a hotel security scanner verifying guests and baggage, the container vulnerability scan ensures no dangerous items (vulnerabilities) exist. Binary authorization parallels allowing only screened and approved guests (signed images) onto your property.

- **Network policies (Floor restrictions):** Each floor (namespace) might only be accessible to those with the right elevator key card, preventing guests on the *engineering floor* from freely wandering to the *finance floor*. This is akin to micro-segmentation with Network Policies restricting pod-to-pod traffic.

- **Multi-tenant secure hotel (Real-world example):** Multiple businesses can rent different floors in the hotel. Each tenant's data and employees remain separated, with tailored security and zero cross-tenant infiltration, mirroring a secure multi-tenant GKE cluster.

The key takeaway is that like a hotel's intricate security system, which combines automatic infrastructure updates, electronic key cards, screening processes, and floor-specific access, *GKE security* demands layered approaches: *node auto-upgrade, Workload Identity, container scanning, network policies,* and advanced checks. This ensures that every tenant (workload) remains well-guarded in a seamlessly shared environment.

Conclusion

Securing containerized workloads in GKE is not a one-time setup; it is a continuous, layered process that integrates across build pipelines, infrastructure configurations, identity management, and runtime controls. This chapter offered a blueprint to help you move beyond default settings and embrace a security-first mindset in Kubernetes operations.

You learned how to harden the cluster with Shielded VMs, scoped maintenance windows, and node pool isolation from the ground up. You eliminated long-lived credentials with Workload Identity and enforced least-privilege access at the pod-level. Container image provenance was ensured using vulnerability scanning and Binary Authorization, transforming your CI/CD pipeline into a proactive security gate.

At the communication layer, Kubernetes Network Policies and service mesh features like mutual TLS enable microservice segmentation and encryption in transit. These controls prevent lateral movement and ensure that every request, regardless of source, must be authenticated, authorized, and observable.

By combining these security practices, GKE becomes more than a container orchestration platform; it becomes a zero-trust execution environment. Whether you support regulated workloads, operate in multi-tenant architectures, or aim for secure-by-default operations, the practices outlined here will help you ship fast and stay secure.

At scale, security is not a checklist; it is a fundamental architectural principle. When configured correctly, GKE gives you the primitives to build a defensible, compliant, and resilient platform.

As a reminder, GKE security rests on three key pillars: *cluster hardening*, shielded VMs, scoped maintenance windows, and Workload Identity to enforce least-privilege; *secure supply-chain*, vulnerability scanning, binary authorization, and image provenance to ensure trusted workloads; and *network segmentation*, Kubernetes Network Policies, and service mesh mTLS to prevent lateral movement.

As your GKE workloads scale and mature, securing them is only part of the equation. Ensuring those controls remain effective, auditable, and compliant over time requires continuous monitoring and transparent enforcement.

In the next chapter, we shift focus from security controls to compliance assurance, exploring how to track policy violations, generate reliable audit trails, and establish real-time visibility across your Google Cloud environment. Whether you are meeting internal governance goals or external regulatory mandates, the following chapter will help you build a defensible, continuously monitored cloud platform.

Exercise

Spin up a *small, disposable GKE environment* demonstrating every security control covered in this chapter. The goal is to prove, hands-on, that a pod can run only if: its image is scanned and signed, it has the exact IAM role it needs, and it can talk to other pods only through an approved path.

1. **Create a private GKE cluster** (`--release-channel=regular, --enable-private-nodes, --workload-pool=$PROJECT_ID.svc.id.goog`) and a single node pool running Shielded VM + ContainerOptimized OS.

2. **Enable NetworkPolicy** and apply a defaultdeny rule on the **dev** namespace.

3. **Build a tiny "helloapi" container**, push it to Artifact Registry, let the native scan complete, and use *cosign* to sign the digest with a Cloud KMS key.

4. **Configure Binary Authorization**: require the cosign signature *and* zero HIGH/CRITICAL CVEs.

5. **Create a KSA (`api-sa`)** mapped to a new GCP service account (**`api-gsa`**) that has **Storage Object Viewer** rights—nothing else.

6. **Deploy the pod** with **`api-sa`** into the dev namespace and watch it start successfully.

7. **Negative tests**:

   a. Redeploy the same image *without* a cosign signature, verify GKE rejects it (Binary Auth violation).

   b. Try to **`curl`** the pod from another namespace—confirm that NetworkPolicy blocks the request.

   c. Exec into the running pod and list GCP permissions (**`gcloud auth list &&`** **`gcloud storage ls`**) to verify it can read a test bucket but cannot list BigQuery datasets.

8. **Clean up** and record findings: which policy blocked each negative test, and where you saw the denial event in Cloud Logging.

Completing this sandbox proves you can combine private clusters, Workload Identity, vulnerability scanning, Binary Authorization, and NetworkPolicies to achieve endtoend zero-trust for containerized workloads on GKE.

Key takeaways

- **Blueprint-to-production mapping**: Translate GCP security certification domains into deployable architectures, covering IAM hardening, VPC security, encryption, and logging.

- **IR-ready design**: Build architectures with incident response in mind, including conditional IAM policies, forensic isolation, and automated lockdown workflows.

- **Control validation**: Integrate security checks into CI/CD using tools like Binary Authorization, Artifact Analysis, and Terraform Validators for policy enforcement.

- **Identity and access security**: Prefer Workload Identity federation over long-lived service account keys to minimize exposure and enable immediate credential revocation.

- **Data protection**: Enforce CMEK for BigQuery and Cloud Storage, and audit encryption configurations regularly.

- **Workload and container hardening**: Apply GKE baseline security configurations, node OS hardening, network segmentation, and lifecycle patching strategies.

- **Continuous compliance**: Implement Cloud Asset Inventory, Policy Controller, and Security Command Center for proactive drift detection and compliance reporting.

References

1. https://cloud.google.com/kubernetes-engine/docs/how-to/hardening-your-cluster

2. https://cloud.google.com/kubernetes-engine/docs/how-to/private-clusters

3. https://cloud.google.com/kubernetes-engine/docs/concepts/cluster-release-channels

4. https://cloud.google.com/kubernetes-engine/docs/how-to/workload-identity

5. https://cloud.google.com/kubernetes-engine/docs/how-to/network-policy

6. https://cloud.google.com/artifact-registry/docs/container-analysis

7. https://cloud.google.com/binary-authorization/docs

8. https://cloud.google.com/architecture/using-container-analysis-and-binary-authorization-for-governance

9. https://cloud.google.com/istio/docs/concepts/security-overview

10. https://cloud.google.com/anthos/service-mesh/docs/security

11. https://cloud.google.com/secret-manager/docs

12. https://cloud.google.com/kubernetes-engine/docs/how-to/secure-multi-tenant-cluster

Join our Discord space

Join our Discord workspace for latest updates, offers, tech happenings around the world, new releases, and sessions with the authors:

https://discord.bpbonline.com

CHAPTER 7

Compliance, Auditing, and Continuous Monitoring

Introduction

Maintaining compliance in cloud environments is not a one-time activity but a continuous process that requires constant vigilance, monitoring, and adaptation. As regulations evolve and threats become more sophisticated, organizations must move beyond periodic audits and implement systems that provide real-time visibility, control, and assurance. This chapter focuses on building a sustainable, automated compliance and auditing framework within **Google Cloud Platform (GCP)**.

You will explore the essential tools and techniques for continuously monitoring your cloud infrastructure, detecting policy violations, and generating reliable audit trails. Specifically, you will learn how to leverage Cloud Logging and Cloud Monitoring to capture system events and user activities, set up *custom alerts* for real-time anomaly detection, and use Access Transparency and Access Approval to oversee internal access by Google Cloud personnel. Furthermore, you will explore tools like Forseti Security and Policy Analyzer to identify and remediate misconfigurations, ensuring that your environment remains aligned with both internal policies and external regulatory requirements.

By the end of this chapter, you will have a comprehensive understanding of implementing continuous compliance strategies, generating audit-ready logs, and maintaining a secure, policy-driven cloud environment that can withstand evolving compliance demands.

Structure

This chapter is organized into the following key sections:

- Foundations of continuous monitoring
- Centralized logging, monitoring, and alerting
- Administrative access and visibility
- Detecting misconfigurations with policy scanning
- Building a continuous compliance strategy
- Continuous compliance in Google Cloud
- Dashboards and reporting for compliance visibility
- Adapting compliance policies to evolving needs
- Complex made simple

Objectives

By the end of this chapter, you will be able to configure comprehensive logging and monitoring for your GCP environment using Cloud Logging and Cloud Monitoring, ensuring that all activity is captured and anomalies are promptly detected. You will understand how to implement Access Transparency and Access Approval to track and control internal access by cloud provider personnel. You will gain proficiency in using tools like Forseti and Policy Analyzer to detect misconfigurations, enforce policy compliance, and automate corrective actions. Additionally, you will be able to design and maintain a continuous compliance framework that utilizes dashboards, automated alerts, and policy as code to provide real-time visibility and enforcement. Lastly, you will be prepared to generate audit trails and reports that support forensic investigations and meet the demands of external auditors, ensuring that your organization maintains ongoing regulatory compliance.

Foundations of continuous monitoring

As organizations scale their cloud usage, managing compliance and maintaining security posture cannot be treated as periodic check-ins or once-a-year audits. In Google Cloud, where infrastructure is often built and updated through code, and services can be created or deleted in seconds, *continuous monitoring and auditing* are essential to ensure that every change always aligns with security policies and regulatory requirements.

This section lays the groundwork for understanding how and why continuous compliance should be a core part of your cloud operations. You will learn what drives this shift in compliance thinking, what principles underpin an effective monitoring strategy, and how Google Cloud's native capabilities support automated, scalable, and proactive oversight.

Continuous compliance in cloud environments

Traditional security audits focus on verifying whether the infrastructure is secure at a specific point-in-time. However, this approach is ill-suited for cloud-native environments where change is constant. A policy misconfiguration or open firewall rule introduced between audit cycles can expose sensitive systems to risk.

Modern compliance frameworks such as the **Health Insurance Portability and Accountability Act (HIPAA)**, **Payment Card Industry Data Security Standard (PCI-DSS)**, and **System and Organization Controls 2 (SOC 2)** have evolved to demand *ongoing, demonstrable assurance* that systems are configured securely throughout their lifecycle. This includes maintaining secure baselines, continuously monitoring access, and preserving detailed audit trails to support forensic investigations or regulatory inquiries.

To meet these evolving demands, organizations are increasingly adopting *automated compliance validation* through **Infrastructure as Code (IaC)** *scanning, real-time policy enforcement*, and **cloud security posture management (CSPM)** solutions. These tools enable proactive detection of misconfigurations before they are deployed, and in some cases, auto-remediate violations based on predefined guardrails. For example, Terraform validator can assess proposed infrastructure changes against policy constraints before deployment, while CSPM platforms continuously evaluate deployed resources for drift from compliance baselines.

In addition, enabling Cloud Audit Logs ensures that every administrative action, such as modifying **Identity and Access Management (IAM)** policies, changing firewall rules, or launching new compute instances, is recorded and made available for real-time monitoring and historical analysis.

Drivers for continuous monitoring

The following key drivers highlight why continuous monitoring is essential for modern cloud environments:

- **Increasing regulatory pressure**: Global privacy and data protection laws are becoming more stringent. **General Data Protection Regulation (GDPR)**, for example, mandates clear auditability of who accessed what data and when. **PCI-DSS** requires continuous monitoring of access to **cardholder data environments (CDE)**. Cloud-native organizations need to generate *near-real-time compliance evidence* that satisfies auditors and regulators.

- **The speed of cloud-scale threats**: Attackers today exploit cloud misconfigurations at an unprecedented rate. A publicly exposed storage bucket or an over-permissive IAM role can be scanned and exploited in minutes. Continuous monitoring identifies such vulnerabilities before adversaries can take advantage.

  For example, using Security Command Center or Forseti Security, you can detect and alert when a bucket is accidentally made public or when new roles are granted excessive privileges.

- **Operational sprawl and multi-team deployments**: With multiple DevOps, **Site Reliability Engineering (SRE)**, and data teams deploying resources simultaneously, even well-meaning changes can lead to *drift from compliance baselines*. Without centralized visibility and consistent enforcement, security gaps emerge silently.

The following is a code example of Forseti Scanner Alerting on Public Bucket:

```
rule_name: 'Bucket should not be publicly accessible'
resource: 'storage.googleapis.com'
violation: 'Bucket has allUsers or allAuthenticatedUsers permissions'
```

This Forseti policy identifies GCS buckets with public access and can alert or auto-remediate.

Building effective continuous auditing programs

A strong cloud compliance program in GCP rests on four fundamental pillars:

- **Visibility across all resources**: You cannot protect what you cannot see. Enable **Admin Activity logs**, **Data Access logs**, and **System Event logs** across projects, folders, and organizations. Use **Cloud Logging** to centralize this telemetry and export it to **BigQuery** for long-term analytics.

- **Real-time alerting**: Define *custom log-based metrics* that trigger alerts on key security events (e.g., someone assigning an Owner role or creating a new firewall rule that allows 0.0.0.0/0). Route these alerts to *Slack, PagerDuty*, or your SIEM for rapid incident response.

- **Auditable reporting and dashboards**: Set up dashboards in Cloud Monitoring, Looker Studio, or Grafana that track compliance posture over time. Highlight trends like:

  o   IAM roles with admin privileges

  o   Projects missing audit logging

  o   Buckets with public access

  These visualizations make it easier for security and compliance teams to spot issues and report to stakeholders.

- **Automation-first remediation**: Pair continuous detection with continuous correction. Tools like Policy Analyzer, OPA Gatekeeper, and Forseti Enforcer allow you to detect and fix drift before users know the issue.

Centralized logging, monitoring, and alerting

A comprehensive monitoring and logging framework is foundational for continuous compliance in any cloud environment. In GCP, this process begins with robust configurations of Cloud Logging and Cloud Monitoring, as well as the creation of custom alerts. These tools work together to centralize event data, enable real-time security awareness, and generate the visibility essential for compliance audits and incident response.

To build a resilient compliance posture, organizations should architect logging and monitoring as tiered layers:

- **Baseline coverage**: Enable Admin Activity logs, Data Access logs, and System Event logs across all projects to ensure traceability of user actions and resource changes, supporting audit and incident investigation requirements.

- **Proactive monitoring**: Use Cloud Monitoring to visualize resource metrics, uptime checks, and anomaly detection aligned with compliance needs (e.g., spikes in storage API calls may indicate unauthorized data access).

- **Automated enforcement**: Pair logging pipelines with Security Command Center for real-time misconfiguration detection and integrate alert policies that trigger on policy violations or suspicious behavioral patterns.

- **Integration with compliance workflows**: Export logs to BigQuery for long-term querying and compliance reporting, or to Cloud Storage for archival. Use Pub/Sub for streaming logs into SIEM tools to ensure continuous compliance evidence pipelines.

- **Log integrity and tamper-resistance**: To ensure that compliance data remains trustworthy, implement *log immutability* by leveraging Bucket Lock in Cloud Storage or Object Versioning, and use checksum validation or cryptographic signing where applicable. This protects logs from accidental deletion or malicious tampering, critical for meeting regulatory and forensic standards.

Establishing centralized and tamper-resistant logging and monitoring not only enables *policy alignment across teams* and reduces manual audit overhead but also accelerates the detection of misconfigurations or policy drift before they escalate into incidents. Ensuring the *integrity of logs* further strengthens trust in the compliance evidence they provide.

Event logging for compliance and forensics

Cloud Logging is the cornerstone for recording all user activity, API calls, and system behavior across Google Cloud services. It supports built-in logs from GCP resources and allows custom log ingestion from external systems, making it possible to create a unified, auditable event stream across your organization.

The following are the key logging categories for compliance and forensics:

- **Admin Activity logs:** Record administrative operations that modify the configuration or metadata of resources. For example, adding a new IAM member or changing a firewall rule.

- **Data Access logs:** Capture access to user-generated data within services like Cloud Storage or BigQuery. These are critical for demonstrating data privacy compliance.

- **System event logs:** Report infrastructure-level events such as auto-scaling actions or disk health failures.

- **Custom logs:** Allow you to ingest data from on-prem services or third-party systems using the Cloud Logging API or agents.

The following are the implementation best practices:

- **Enable all relevant logs**: Many GCP services do not enable Data Access logs by default. Turn them on explicitly to ensure coverage.

- **Retention management**: Align log retention with the regulatory context. For example, GDPR may require logs to be retained no longer than necessary, while SOX may require up to seven years.

- **Log export pipelines**: Use sinks to route logs to BigQuery for querying, Cloud Storage for archiving, or Pub/Sub for stream-based processing.

- **Label-based filtering**: Apply resource labels and use advanced filters in the Logs Explorer to quickly locate compliance-relevant records.

Visibility and metrics with Cloud Monitoring

Cloud Monitoring transforms operational data into structured, queryable, and visualized insights. It provides continuous health checks, performance baselines, and service-level indicators that enable early detection of configuration drift or policy violations.

The following are the monitoring capabilities:

- **Metrics collection**: Tracks native and custom metrics (CPU, memory, HTTP request counts, etc.).

- **Dashboards**: Build visual representations of key systems, color-coded by severity, tailored to security and compliance stakeholders.

- **Uptime checks**: Monitor availability of critical services, with optional multi-region probes.

- **Alert policies**: Define metric thresholds (e.g., high CPU, network surge) to trigger automated alerts via integrations.

The following are the operational recommendations:

- Define SLIs relevant to regulated workloads (e.g., availability of a healthcare portal).

- Use role-specific dashboards so different teams can focus on compliance-relevant metrics.

- Correlate monitoring and logging data to trace an alert back to the root log event.

Real-time notifications and custom alerts

Custom alerting is essential for proactive compliance enforcement. By defining conditions that identify potential threats or non-compliance events, you can respond before audit failures or security breaches occur.

The following are some examples of proactive alerts:

- **Log pattern matching**: Monitor for frequent failed authentication attempts, abnormal user behavior, or bulk IAM changes.

- **Threshold-based alerts**: Identify anomalies, such as a 200% spike in outbound traffic, which may be possible indicators of data exfiltration.

- **Security event filters**: Create alerts for high-risk actions, such as creating overly permissive roles or disabling audit logging.

All alerts can be forwarded to communication tools such as Slack, PagerDuty, or custom workflows in Cloud Functions or ServiceNow.

The following is the code snippet for creating a log-based alert for repeated permission errors:

```
resource.type = "gce_instance"
logName = "projects/your-project/logs/cloudaudit.googleapis.com%2Factivity"
severity = "ERROR"
protoPayload.methodName = "SetIamPolicy"
```

By combining logging, monitoring, and real-time alerting, GCP enables a comprehensive, automated, and compliance-ready observability strategy that scales with your infrastructure.

Administrative access and visibility

Enforcing administrative access controls and maintaining user visibility are core pillars of continuous compliance in Google Cloud. Controlling who can perform administrative actions and monitoring those actions help prevent privilege misuse, meet regulatory requirements, and strengthen accountability.

Organizations should:

- **Implement least privilege:** Assign roles with the minimum permissions necessary, using predefined or custom IAM roles instead of broad Editor or Owner roles.

- **Enable Access Transparency:** Monitor and review Google personnel's administrative access to your data, ensuring regulatory obligations are met during support activities.

- **Use Access Approval:** Enforce customer-controlled approval workflows before Google support personnel can access your resources, aligning with privacy regulations such as GDPR and HIPAA.

- **Audit admin activities:** Collect Admin Activity logs for all projects to track changes to configurations, IAM policies, and critical resources.

- **Monitor user behavior:** Use Cloud Audit logs with Security Command Center to detect unusual administrative activities, such as sudden privilege escalations or changes to logging policies.

- **Integrate with workflows:** Configure real-time alerts for sensitive actions, sending notifications to security teams via Slack, PagerDuty, or SIEM integrations for immediate response.

By systematically controlling administrative access and maintaining clear visibility, organizations can enforce compliance, reduce insider risks, and maintain operational integrity across their Google Cloud environments.

Monitoring provider access with transparency

Access Transparency delivers near real-time logs when Google Cloud staff access your environment. This is essential for sectors where internal data sovereignty and auditability are non-negotiable.

The following are the key features:

- **Comprehensive logging**: Captures user identity, access method, timestamp, resource targeted, and the reason for access.

- **Service integration**: Includes popular GCP services like Cloud Storage, BigQuery, Compute Engine, and Cloud SQL.

- **Compliance alignment**: Meets audit requirements for HIPAA, PCI-DSS, FedRAMP, and similar frameworks.

The following is the implementation sample:

```
{
  "protoPayload": {
    "authenticationInfo": {
      "principalEmail": "google-admin@google.com"
    },
    "resourceName": "projects/project-id/buckets/bucket-name",
    "serviceName": "storage.googleapis.com",
    "methodName": "storage.objects.get",
    "requestMetadata": {
      "callerIp": "203.0.113.1",
      "regionCode": "US"
    },
    "authorizationInfo": [
      {
```

```
      "resource": "bucket-name",
      "permission": "storage.objects.get",
      "granted": true
    }
  ]
 }
}
```

The following sample illustrates how Access Transparency logs capture and provide visibility into actions performed by Google personnel on your GCP resources:

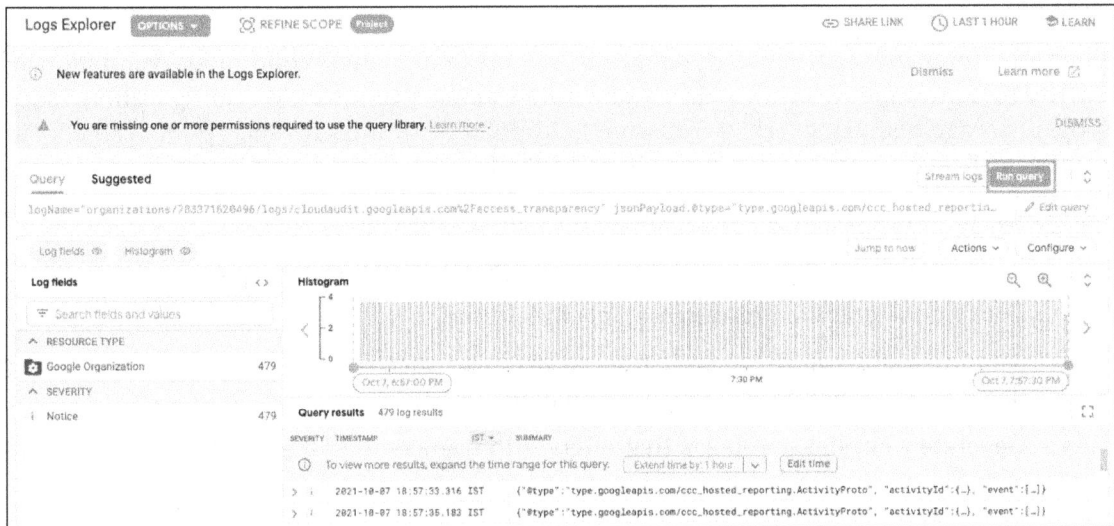

Figure 7.1: Access Transparency logs for Google Workspace

Controlling administrative access with Access Approval

Access Approval adds a layer of human control, enabling you to approve or deny access requests from Google personnel before they are granted.

- **Approval workflow:**
  - **Request issued**: Triggered during support or maintenance activities.
  - **Notification sent**: Delivered via email or integrated channel with full context.
  - **Decision logged**: Approvers grant or deny; decisions are permanently recorded.

- **Best practices:**
  - Assign access approvers from your compliance or security team.
  - Integrate approvals with ServiceNow or Jira for streamlined handling.

- o Set up Slack or email alerts for real-time notifications.

- o Review Access Approval logs quarterly as part of audit readiness.

By integrating Access Transparency with Access Approval, organizations ensure visibility and actual governance over cloud provider administrative activity, closing a critical trust and compliance gap in cloud operations.

Detecting misconfigurations with policy scanning

Cloud environments that scale dynamically require automated, continuous validation of security configurations to prevent drift and reduce human error risks. Misconfigurations, such as open storage buckets, overly permissive IAM policies, or missing encryption, can expose sensitive data even when there is no malicious intent.

Using tools like Forseti Security and Policy Analyzer, teams can:

- Continuously scan cloud resources against policy baselines.

- Detect non-compliant resources in near real-time.

- Automatically trigger remediation workflows, such as updating IAM policies or flagging unencrypted storage for immediate review.

- Generate compliance reports that align with frameworks like PCI DSS, HIPAA, and SOC 2.

- Integrate findings with ticketing systems to ensure accountability and tracking.

By embedding these tools into your operational pipeline, you reduce the chance of drift from compliance baselines while maintaining agility in cloud operations.

Comprehensive infrastructure auditing with Forseti Security

Forseti Security is a powerful open-source toolkit purpose-built for auditing Google Cloud environments. It enables organizations to gain visibility into resource configurations, evaluate compliance posture, and optionally take corrective actions based on customizable policies.

Architecture overview

Forseti's architecture is modular and extensible, making it suitable for both periodic audits and continuous compliance programs. The core modules include:

- **Inventory module**:
  - Gathers real-time metadata from GCP resources such as **IAM policies, firewall rules, GCS buckets, Cloud SQL**, and **BigQuery datasets**.
  - It stores resource metadata snapshots in a Cloud SQL database, allowing point-in-time audits and historical tracking.

- **Scanner module**:
  - Compares collected inventory data against pre-defined policy rules.
  - Supports built-in templates for **CIS Benchmarks, NIST guidelines**, or **custom organization-defined constraints** (e.g., no open firewall rules, restricted regions for resource deployment).
  - Can be extended with custom rule definitions written in YAML.

- **Notifier module**:
  - Sends violations to configured sinks such as **Cloud Pub/Sub, email**, or **Slack**, ensuring actionable visibility.
  - Helps security teams respond rapidly to non-compliant states.

- **Enforcer module**:
  - Optionally applies automated remediations, such as removing public access from GCS buckets or disabling risky firewall rules.
  - Enforcements are highly configurable to suit different environments or enforcement modes (dry-run vs. active remediation).

The following is the deployment and integration example:

```
# Enable necessary APIs and create a dedicated Forseti project
export PROJECT_ID=forseti-security
export REGION=us-central1

gcloud projects create $PROJECT_ID --set-as-default

# Enable services
for SERVICE in compute.googleapis.com cloudresourcemanager.googleapis.com iam.
googleapis.com; do
  gcloud services enable $SERVICE
  done

# Clone Forseti and deploy with Terraform
git clone https://github.com/forseti-security/forseti-security.git
cd forseti-security/terraform
terraform init && terraform apply
```

The following figure presents Forseti Security's architecture, highlighting its core modules and their interactions within GCP:

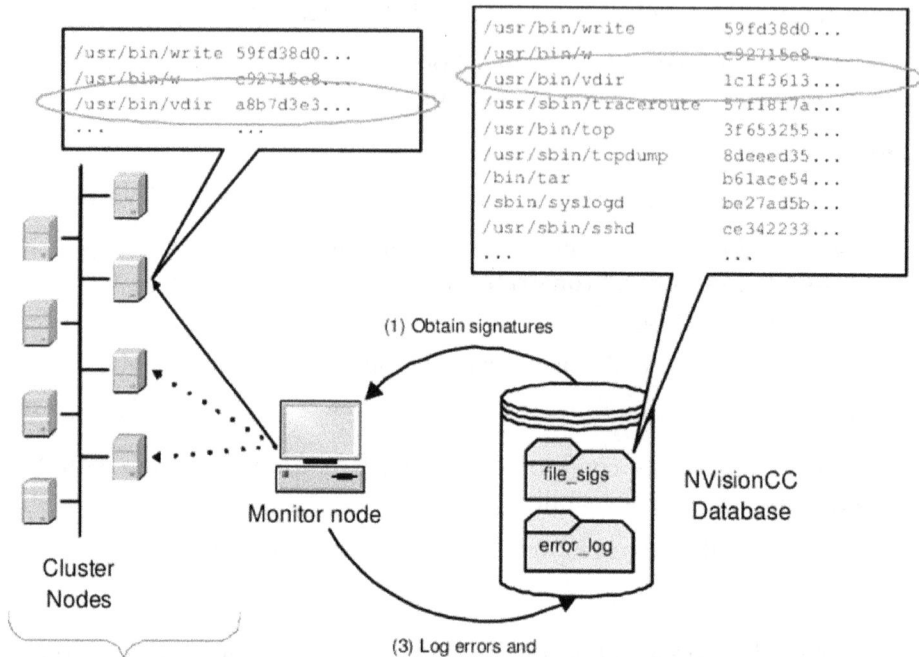

Figure 7.2: Forseti Security architecture

The following are the best practices for Forseti usage:

- Deploy in a *separate audit project* to ensure *isolation and traceability*.

- *Schedule regular scans* via Cloud Scheduler or *integrate with CI/CD pipelines* for enforcement before deployment.

- Use the *Notifier module* to push alerts to ticketing or messaging systems for rapid triage.

- Continuously *update policy rules* as compliance standards (e.g., PCI-DSS, HIPAA, ISO 27001) evolve.

- Leverage *Cloud Storage snapshots* to retain scan results for long-term compliance evidence.

Policy review and risk detection with Policy Analyzer

While Forseti handles broad compliance scans, Policy Analyzer focuses on fine-grained IAM and firewall configuration review. It helps identify roles and bindings that violate the principle of least privilege or expose risky permissions.

Policy Analyzer can *compare current IAM policies against security baselines* to detect excessive grants, wildcard permissions, and inherited roles that may not align with organizational policies. It also highlights public firewall rules and overly broad network access that could increase attack surfaces.

By leveraging *automated analysis and exporting findings to BigQuery*, teams can:

- Track risk trends over time.
- Correlate IAM misconfigurations with audit logs.
- Integrate detections with Slack or ticketing systems for fast remediation.
- Support audit preparation by enforcing least-privilege policies.

Using Policy Analyzer alongside Forseti builds a layered compliance monitoring approach, ensuring both high-level posture and granular IAM enforcement are maintained as your environment scales.

Workflow

The following workflow outlines practical steps to operationalize Policy Analyzer and Forseti findings, enabling teams to identify, analyze, and remediate IAM misconfigurations efficiently:

- **Export IAM policies**:
  ```
  gcloud projects get-iam-policy my-project --format=json > policy.json
  ```
- **Analyze excess permissions**: Use scripts or custom tools to analyze **policy.json** for over-privileged bindings.
- **Correlate with usage logs**: Compare permission usage frequency from Cloud Logging to highlight unused access.
- **Remediation techniques:**
  - Generate reports for manual reviews.
  - Auto-flag sensitive roles like **Owner** or **Service Account Token Creator**.
  - Script auto-removal of unused bindings via pre-approved pipelines.

By integrating Forseti and Policy Analyzer into your continuous compliance framework, you can ensure that both broad infrastructure configurations and fine-grained access policies stay within approved security boundaries. Forseti Visualizer provides an interactive interface to explore GCP resource hierarchies and policy violations, as depicted in the following figure:

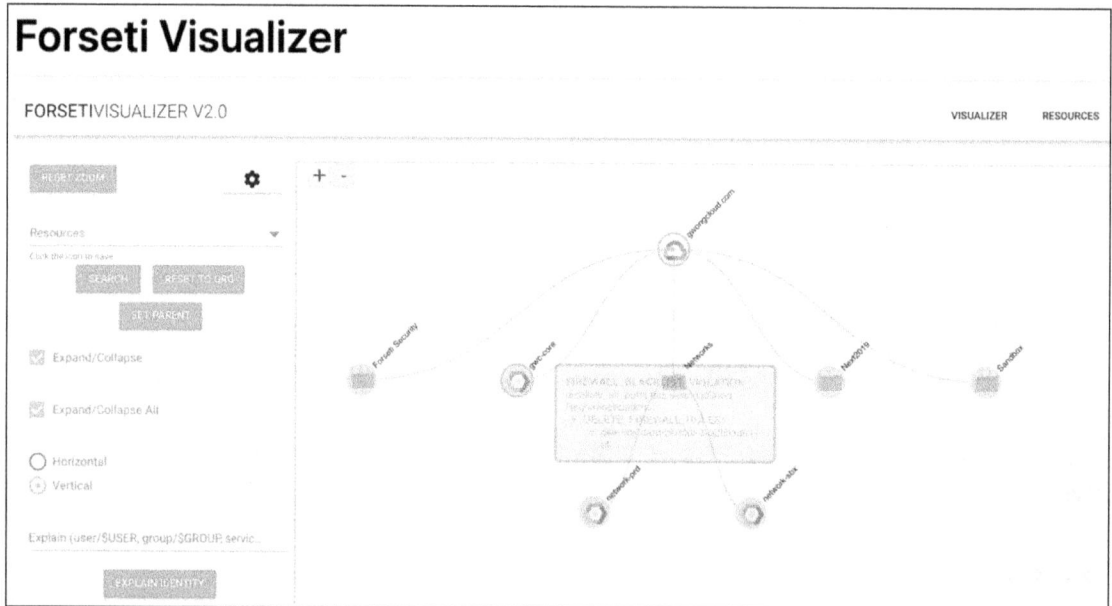

Figure 7.3: Forseti Visualizer

Building a continuous compliance strategy

Establishing a continuous compliance strategy involves aligning your technical enforcement controls with organizational policies and regulatory requirements. This means:

- Using *automated policy checks* during CI/CD to prevent non-compliant resources from deploying.

- Integrating *logging and monitoring* with dashboards that provide clear, actionable compliance visibility for engineering and audit teams.

- Performing *regular policy reviews* to adapt to evolving threats and regulatory changes while maintaining a secure operational baseline.

- Incorporating *incident response playbooks* tied to compliance events, enabling swift remediation when violations are detected.

- Ensuring *cross-functional collaboration* between security, operations, and compliance teams so that compliance is integrated into delivery pipelines, rather than being a bolt-on process.

By embedding these practices, your teams can maintain compliance without slowing down development velocity, ensuring your Google Cloud environment remains secure, resilient, and aligned with zero trust and audit requirements.

Continuous compliance foundations

A strong compliance foundation in GCP involves integrating compliance checks directly into the development and deployment lifecycle. Four key pillars guide this foundation:

- **Policy as code**: Policies such as IAM role restrictions, firewall constraints, and data residency requirements should be version-controlled and deployed using IaC tools. This ensures traceability, reviewability, and rollback capability. Tools like Google's Config Validator and **Open Policy Agent (OPA)** can enforce policies programmatically.

- **Automated checks**: Security controls must be continuously evaluated through automated pipelines. Use scanners like Forseti or OPA integrated with CI/CD workflows to identify misconfigurations before deployment. Scheduled jobs or commit-triggered evaluations enable real-time visibility into compliance drift.

- **Drift detection**: Compare the actual state of cloud resources (as collected via GCP APIs) to the desired configuration state (defined in Terraform or Deployment Manager). When deviations are detected, notify relevant stakeholders or automatically roll back unauthorized changes.

- **Incident response integration**: Tie detection systems with defined incident response workflows. For instance, if a non-compliant firewall rule is created, trigger an alert and optionally initiate rollback or ticket creation in ServiceNow for review.

Dashboards and reporting

Compliance visibility is incomplete without clear, actionable reporting. Dashboards allow organizations to track current posture, identify hotspots of non-compliance, and respond to changes over time:

- **Real-time and historical views:**
  - **Compliance dashboards**: Aggregate and visualize real-time data such as *Excessive IAM Bindings, Unrestricted Firewall Rules, or Unscanned Container Images*. Present this data using Cloud Monitoring or third-party BI platforms. You can see a high-level overview of all your audit logs on the Cloud Console Activity page, as shown in the following figure:

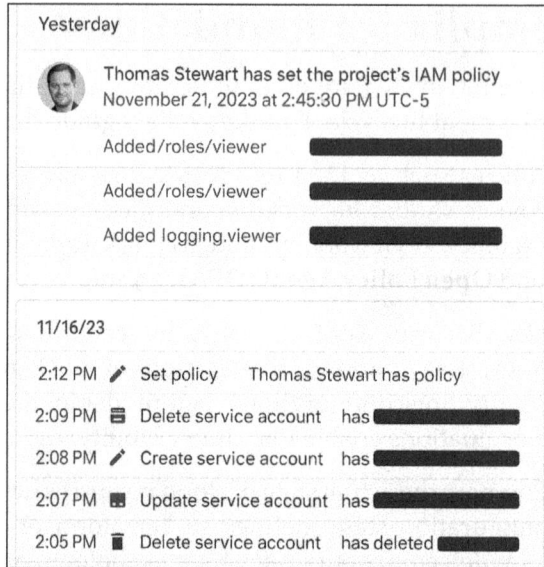

Figure 7.4: *Detailed view of an event under Cloud Console Activity (Masked Sensitive Details, User and Name In Image are fictitious)*

   o **Historical reporting**: Track trends and regression. For example, visualize which teams repeatedly violate a security policy or which policies are most frequently remediated.

- **Implementation guidance:**

   o Use BigQuery to store and query structured audit logs, policy scanner results, and access activity.

   o Leverage *Looker Studio or Data Studio* to create customizable dashboards for compliance, with role-based views for security analysts, auditors, and leadership.

   o Provide *auditor-ready exports* such as PDF reports or frozen BigQuery datasets that preserve historical posture snapshots.

Continual policy evolution

Security and compliance frameworks are not static. GCP regularly adds new services, and standards like CIS or NIST update benchmarks to reflect emerging threats. Therefore, a continuous compliance strategy must evolve in response.

The following are the best practices for continual policy evolution:

- **Review benchmarks regularly**: Schedule quarterly reviews of your enforced rulesets to match the latest industry guidance. Subscribe to release notes from CIS, NIST, and GCP.

- **Collaborate with security teams**: Policy authorship should be a collaborative effort. Security leads, compliance officers, and engineering teams should co-own policy lifecycles to ensure operational feasibility and enforceability.

- **Safe testing and rollout**: Use GCP dry-run or preview modes (where applicable) to validate new policies before enforcing them. Maintain a staging project to test the impact of rules on real workloads.

- **Policy versioning and change history**: Store policies in GitHub/GitLab with change history and peer reviews. Automate pull requests to notify compliance stakeholders about upcoming changes.

- **Feedback loops from incidents**: Every audit finding, incident postmortem, or near-miss should inform future policy evolution. Maintain a living document for policies under review or pending enforcement.

- **Ongoing training and awareness**: Ensure teams are continually educated on new policies, benchmark updates, and tooling changes. Integrate compliance training into the onboarding process, host periodic refresher sessions, and create hands-on labs to simulate real-world misconfigurations. This fosters shared accountability and reduces policy drift resulting from unawareness.

By treating compliance as a code-defined, automation-driven, and feedback-oriented discipline, organizations can confidently meet regulatory obligations and adapt swiftly to security challenges.

Continuous compliance in Google Cloud

Building continuous compliance on Google Cloud requires more than just tools; it also requires *embedding compliance into the engineering culture* and workflows. This includes:

- *Automated guardrails* in CI/CD pipelines to block non-compliant configurations before deployment.

- *Real-time monitoring and alerting* that detect and surface policy violations immediately, enabling rapid response.

- *Policy as code frameworks* for defining, versioning, and evolving compliance policies in line with infrastructure changes.

- *Cross-team ownership* where developers, security, and operations share responsibility for maintaining compliance across services.

- *Continuous audit readiness* through centralized logging and automated reporting, reducing manual audit burdens.

By making compliance an operational habit rather than an afterthought, organizations can reduce risk while maintaining delivery velocity, aligning cloud practices with internal policies and external regulatory standards seamlessly.

Core foundations of continuous compliance

An effective compliance architecture relies on four interlocking pillars, each building toward end-to-end visibility, policy enforcement, and remediation:

- **Policy as code (PaC)**: Codify your compliance controls using declarative definitions that are version-controlled, peer-reviewed, and traceable. Define policies such as:

  - *All Cloud Storage buckets must be encrypted with CMEK*

  - *No firewall rule should allow 0.0.0.0/0 ingress on port 22*

  - *Service accounts must not have roles like* `roles/owner`

  PaC ensures that infrastructure and controls are enforced consistently across projects and environments, utilising tools such as OPA, Config Validator, or Terraform validator.

  The following figure illustrates how policy as code evolves from authoring and version control to automated enforcement and drift correction:

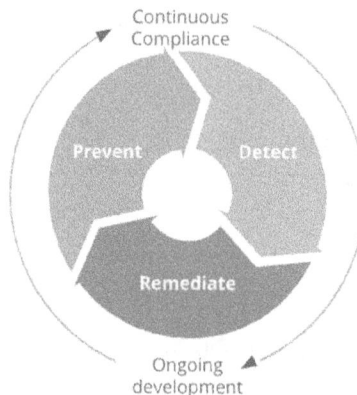

Figure 7.5: Continuous monitoring for security and compliance drift via Security Command Center

- **Automated compliance checks:** Integrate continuous scanning tools like *Forseti, OPA Gatekeeper, or Google Cloud Policy Intelligence* into your CI/CD pipelines and post-deploy monitoring systems. These tools detect misconfigurations as part of your DevSecOps flow and can:

  - Block deployments that violate organizational policies

  - Flag IAM changes granting excessive permissions

  - Detect disabled audit logging on sensitive projects

- **Drift detection and enforcement:** Drift detection compares your desired state (defined in Terraform or Deployment Manager) with the actual GCP environment. Any divergence, such as a firewall rule created manually outside IaC, can be:

  - Logged and alerted

- o Auto-remediated via reapply jobs
- o Routed to a ticketing workflow for manual triage

This closes the gap between design and runtime enforcement, ensuring infrastructure does not silently drift out of compliance.

- **Incident response integration:** Compliance violations should trigger downstream workflows automatically:
  - o *Slack or PagerDuty alerts* for security teams
  - o *Jira tickets* with metadata from logs (e.g., IAM user, timestamp, affected resource)
  - o *Playbooks* for violation triage and escalation

Dashboards and reporting for compliance visibility

Compliance is as much about visibility as enforcement. Without centralized reporting, security teams and auditors cannot track posture or prove adherence to controls:

- **Real-time monitoring and historical trends:** Build compliance dashboards that show:
  - o **Current state**: For example, *15 GCS Buckets without CMEK, Projects without audit logging enabled*
  - o **IAM anomalies**: For example, *five users with Owner roles, Unused Service Accounts with broad permissions*
  - o **Historical view**: Trends over weeks or quarters that highlight whether your organization is improving or regressing

Use *Looker Studio, Grafana (via BigQuery source), or third-party BI* tools to customize views for technical, compliance, and executive teams.

- **Integration with analytics and reporting tools:**
  - o **BigQuery for Data Aggregation**: Export data from
    - Cloud Logging (audit logs, system events)
    - Policy scanner (Forseti, Config Validator)
    - IAM policy diffs

Use **Structured Query Language-based (SQL-based)** queries to define compliance **Key performance indicators (KPIs)** and generate datasets for automated report generation.

The following figure demonstrates a typical compliance data flow: aggregating logs, exporting to BigQuery, and visualizing through BI tools:

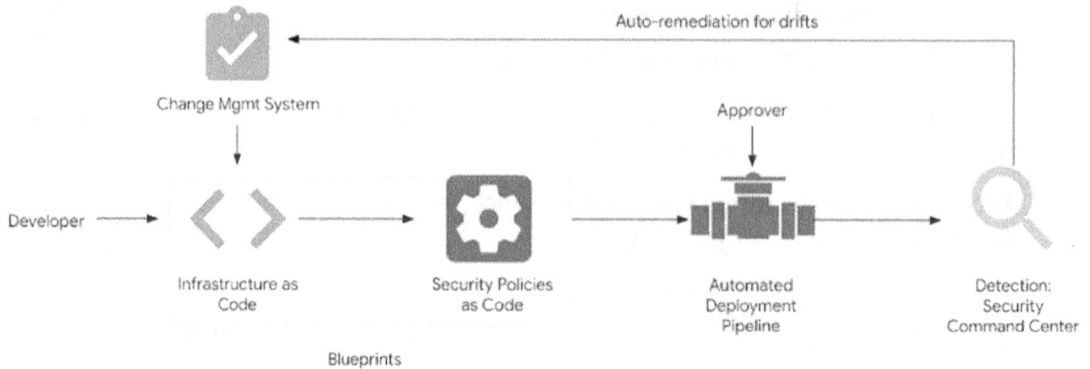

Figure 7.6: *A sample BigQuery for compliance pipeline*

- **Visualization layer**: Build team-specific dashboards:
  - **Compliance team**: Policy violations, audit logs, risk scores
  - **Security Ops**: Real-time alerts, drift reports
  - **Executives**: SLA adherence, compliance KPIs
- **Audit-ready deliverables**: Provide downloadable PDF reports, versioned exports, and locked BigQuery snapshots for audit evidence. Use IAM bindings to restrict edit access and preserve data integrity.

Adapting compliance policies to evolving needs

Compliance is not static. GCP evolves rapidly, new threats emerge, and regulatory bodies revise benchmarks (CIS, PCI-DSS, ISO 27001). Therefore, a compliance strategy must adapt, not only technically but also culturally.

The following are the best practices for policy management and evolution:

- **Benchmark tracking:**
  - Subscribe to updates from CIS, NIST, and GCP security best practices.
  - Maintain a Git-based changelog of benchmark deltas and corresponding internal changes.
- **Cross-functional ownership:**
  - Involve DevOps and security teams in policy writing and enforcement to ensure feasibility.
  - Use structured processes for policy reviews: monthly syncs, quarterly governance boards.

- **Safe testing and rollouts:**
    - o Use *dry-run* or *preview* flags before enforcing policies org-wide.
    - o Maintain a pre-production project for testing new policies without risk.
      ```
      # Sample OPA dry-run evaluation
      opa eval --data policies.rego --input test-resource.json "data.
      gcp.deny"
      ```

The following example shows how to use OPA in a dry-run mode to validate firewall rules before enforcing them:

```
package gcp.security

deny[msg] {
  input.resource.type == "compute.firewall"
  input.resource.properties.sourceRanges[_] == "0.0.0.0/0"
  msg := "Unrestricted ingress detected in firewall rule"
}
# Run policy evaluation in dry-run mode
opa eval --data policy.rego --input test-resource.json "data.gcp.
security.deny"
```

- **Policy change lifecycle:**
    - o Create a GitHub repository dedicated to compliance-as-code.
    - o Use pull requests for reviews, tagging approvers based on policy category (e.g., IAM, networking, encryption).
    - o Annotate each change with links to benchmark references or internal incident reports that triggered the update.

- **Postmortems and feedback loops**: Every audit finding or incident should feed directly into policy evolution. Maintain a backlog of pending policy improvements tied to event root causes.

Complex made simple

Think of compliance, auditing, and continuous monitoring like managing an airport with security checks, logs of passengers, and ongoing flight operations:

- **Logging and monitoring (Airport surveillance and flight control):** Just as an airport has cameras everywhere and an air traffic control tower that monitors flights and ground movements, **Cloud Logging** and **Cloud Monitoring** track your GCP resources and activities in real-time.

- **Access Transparency and approval (Airport ID checks and special clearance):** In an airport, certain restricted areas (control tower, baggage handling) require special clearances, with logs of who entered and why. Similarly, Access Transparency shows you when GCP staff access your resources, and Access Approval demands your go-ahead for any behind-the-scenes involvement.

- **Forseti or Policy Analyzer (Security patrols and inspectors):** Airport security teams do spot checks and routine inspections. Forseti or Policy Analyzers regularly scan your environment, checking that gates, baggage systems, and no-fly zones (misconfigurations) remain secure and meet guidelines.

- **Continuous compliance strategy (Daily airport operations):** Airports do not just check compliance once a year; they maintain daily checks, staff training, runway inspections, and passenger screening. In the same vein, GCP's continuous compliance approach ensures logs, policies, and dashboards are regularly updated, guaranteeing no security drift or overlooked vulnerabilities.

- **Audit trails (Flight logs and incident reports):** An airport retains flight plans, passenger manifests, and security incident reports. GCP's audit logs and compliance dashboards do the same: proving your environment's security stance to regulators (akin to aviation authorities).

The key takeaway is just like an airport relies on constant surveillance, ID checks, security patrols, and thorough flight records to ensure safe, compliant operations, your GCP environment depends on *Cloud Logging, Monitoring, Access Transparency, Forseti,* or *policy checks,* and *automated compliance* to remain secure and compliant. By adopting these measures, you maintain an airtight system that stands up to ongoing regulations and evolving threats.

Conclusion

This chapter establishes the strategic and technical foundation for building a continuous compliance ecosystem in Google Cloud. You explore how to instrument your cloud environment with audit-grade telemetry using Cloud Logging and Monitoring, enforce strict access controls with Access Transparency and Approval, and operationalize security policy through tools like Forseti and Policy Analyzer.

You now understand how to treat compliance-as-code, design for drift detection, and maintain dashboards and alerting systems that reflect your real-time security posture. These systems not only enforce preventive guardrails but also provide actionable insights into violations and risks, bridging the gap between security policy and operational reality.

Importantly, this chapter also reinforced that compliance is not static. Whether it is adapting to updated benchmarks, onboarding new GCP services, or evolving your response processes, your strategy must be dynamic and driven by automation.

In the next chapter, we transition from proactive policy enforcement to real-time threat detection. You will discover how to harness the capabilities of Security Command Center

Premium to identify threats across compute, storage, and network surfaces. You will configure **Event Threat Detection (ETD)** for anomaly detection and inspect threat signatures in real-time.

Additionally, we will discuss Chronicle, Google Cloud's advanced threat detection and SIEM platform. Chronicle offers petabyte-scale log ingestion, accelerated threat hunting through YARA-L rules, and timeline-based investigation across your enterprise assets, laying the foundation for incident response, breach investigation, and strategic threat intelligence.

This next phase will finalize your cloud defense posture, from configuration hygiene to active defense, providing you with a full-stack security architecture on Google Cloud.

Exercise

Objective: Apply the concepts from this chapter by setting up continuous compliance, auditing, and monitoring in a Google Cloud environment.

Tasks:

1. **Enable Cloud Logging and Cloud Monitoring:**

    a. Create a GCP project or use an existing sandbox environment.

    b. Enable Cloud Logging and Cloud Monitoring APIs.

    c. Set up basic dashboards to monitor CPU, memory, and IAM activity across your project.

2. **Configure Data Access logs:**

    a. Enable Data Access logs for Cloud Storage and BigQuery to capture user activity.

    b. Verify logs in Cloud Logging to confirm entries are being recorded.

3. **Create log-based alerting:**

    a. Write a filter to detect SetIamPolicy changes in your project.

    b. Create a log-based alert to notify you via email or Slack when a new IAM role is added.

4. **Test Access Transparency (if available in your org):**

    a. Review Access Transparency logs to identify Google support's access to your environment.

    b. Note how this can support compliance readiness and investigation.

5. **Run Forseti or Policy Analyzer:**

    a. Deploy Policy Analyzer (or Forseti if available) to scan your IAM policies.

    b. Identify overly permissive roles or unused bindings.

6. **Simulate a misconfiguration:**

   a. Intentionally create a public Cloud Storage bucket or add an overly broad IAM policy.

   b. Observe detection through your logging and alerting setup.

   c. Remediate the misconfiguration and record the time it took to detect and resolve the issue.

7. **Document findings:**

   a. Record:

      i. The alerts you created.

      ii. IAM misconfigurations detected.

      iii. Response and remediation workflow.

      iv. Improvements you identified for your compliance posture.

Key takeaways

- **Compliance is continuous**: Achieving compliance in the cloud is not a milestone but an ongoing operational discipline. Regulatory frameworks such as GDPR, HIPAA, and PCI-DSS increasingly demand evidence of real-time governance and policy enforcement. As cloud environments scale and evolve rapidly, continuous compliance becomes the only sustainable model to meet audit and security expectations.

- **Visibility and control**: Cloud Logging and Monitoring form the telemetry backbone of Google Cloud. They provide rich, queryable data sets on user activity, service health, resource state changes, and security events. When combined with Access Transparency and Access Approval, you gain complete visibility, not just into your own operations but also into interactions initiated by the cloud provider, enabling a higher level of trust and audit assurance.

- **Automated policy enforcement**: Manual compliance reviews do not scale. Tools like Forseti Security and Policy Analyser automate the detection and (optionally) remediation of policy violations across your organisation. Whether identifying public access on storage buckets, over-permissioned IAM roles, or configuration drift, these tools maintain your GCP environment's alignment with internal and external security baselines.

- **Real-time alerts and dashboards**: Compliance is not just a backend report; it must be observable. With custom alerting and visual dashboards (built via Cloud Monitoring, Looker, or BigQuery), your teams can track deviations as they occur. Alerts for conditions like *IAM role escalation, network egress spike, or disabled logging* enable proactive investigation and rapid mitigation.

- **Audit-ready at all times:** Automated evidence collection, including log exports, IAM policy snapshots, and violation records, ensures a state of continuous audit readiness. Rather than scrambling to compile compliance reports, organizations can produce point-in-time or rolling compliance artifacts to meet the needs of internal risk teams or external regulatory audits, dramatically reducing operational overhead.

References

1. https://cloud.google.com/logging

2. https://cloud.google.com/monitoring

3. https://cloud.google.com/access-transparency

4. https://cloud.google.com/access-approval

5. https://forsetisecurity.org/

6. https://cloud.google.com/policy-intelligence/analyzer

7. https://cloud.google.com/security/compliance

8. https://cloud.google.com/architecture/continuous-compliance

9. https://cloud.google.com/bigquery

10. https://cloud.google.com/data-studio

Join our Discord space

Join our Discord workspace for latest updates, offers, tech happenings around the world, new releases, and sessions with the authors:

https://discord.bpbonline.com

CHAPTER 8

Threat Detection using SCC and Chronicle

Introduction

Modern cloud environments are dynamic, complex, and constantly evolving, which brings an ever-expanding attack surface. As organizations migrate critical workloads to **Google Cloud Platform (GCP)**, the need for real-time threat detection, historical context, and automated response becomes not just important, but essential.

Traditional security tools often fall short in cloud-native architectures. Static alerting systems can't keep up with ephemeral resources, and manual triage processes introduce unacceptable delays. Google Cloud addresses these gaps through its **Security Command Center (SCC)** Premium and Chronicle platforms. Together, they form a comprehensive threat detection and response ecosystem that combines immediate insights, historical correlation, and automation on a large scale.

This chapter examines how SCC Premium identifies and mitigates misconfigurations, container threats, **Identity and Access Management (IAM)** misuse, and web vulnerabilities in real-time. It also demonstrates how Chronicle empowers teams to uncover threats long after they have occurred, enabling in-depth forensic analysis and pattern detection. Combined with Google Cloud's automation capabilities, organizations can not only detect threats faster but also respond to them consistently, efficiently, and at cloud scale.

Whether you are building a security operations pipeline from scratch or optimizing an existing GCP deployment, this chapter provides the technical guidance and architecture patterns to implement effective, measurable, and scalable threat detection and response workflows.

Structure

In this chapter, we will be covering the following topics:

- Advanced threat detection in GCP
- Criticality of advanced threat detection
- Core capabilities that power detection
- Integrating vulnerability and threat intelligence
- Chronicle for threat hunting
- Automating response and remediation
- Combining SCC with Org alerts
- Complex made simple

Objectives

This chapter aims to equip cloud security architects, engineers, and operations teams with the knowledge and practical strategies necessary to implement scalable, automated threat detection and response workflows on the GCP. By the end of this chapter, you will understand the critical need for both real-time and historical threat detection in cloud-native environments and be able to distinguish between the capabilities of SCC Standard and Premium to determine the best fit for your organization.

You will learn how to configure SCC Premium to monitor IAM abuse, container threats, misconfigurations, and anomalous behaviour across GCP projects. The chapter also covers how to leverage **Event Threat Detection** (**ETD**) and **Container Threat Detection** (**CTD**) for real-time insights into runtime risks, as well as how to utilize Web Security Scanner for integrating application vulnerability detection into **continuous integration/continuous deployment** (**CI/CD**) pipelines.

Additionally, you will explore Chronicle's ability to retain and correlate petabytes of log data for retrospective threat hunting and IOC matching. You will gain hands-on strategies to build automated remediation workflows using Pub/Sub, Cloud Functions, Cloud Run, and SOAR tools. The chapter guides you in normalizing alert severity, unifying escalation paths across SCC, Chronicle, and on-premises SIEMs, and tracking key metrics such as **mean time to detect** (**MTTD**) and **mean time to remediate** (**MTTR**). Ultimately, you will be equipped to integrate these capabilities into a comprehensive security operations strategy that aligns with zero-trust principles, compliance requirements, and audit-readiness goals.

Advanced threat detection in GCP

As enterprises adopt GCP at scale, the attack surface expands across virtual machines, containers, **application programming interfaces (APIs),** and user identities. In this dynamic environment, threats can bypass traditional controls if not addressed proactively. GCP's advanced threat detection capabilities, available through the SCC Premium tier, are designed to deliver deep visibility, rapid detection, and automated response, all natively integrated into the cloud platform.

Advanced threat detection on GCP is not a monolithic engine but a combination of real-time, historical, and behavioural detection mechanisms. These include:

- ETD for immediate log-based detections,
- Chronicle for retrospective threat hunting, and
- CTD for runtime insights into container activity.

Together, they create a layered defence that supports modern security operations. Before discussing configuration and use cases, it is helpful to understand how Google Cloud's native threat detection components, SCC, Chronicle, and ETD, fit together in a layered architecture. Refer to the following figure:

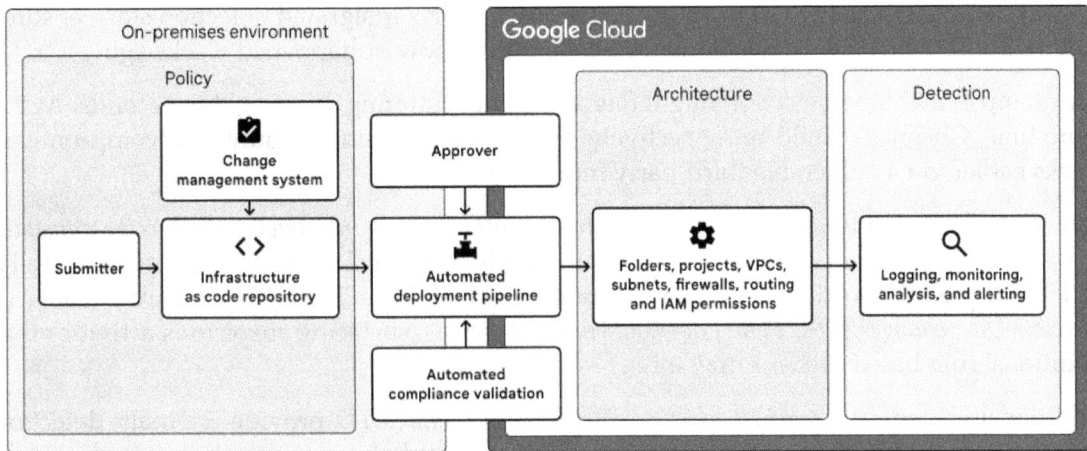

Figure 8.1: High-level architecture of Google Cloud's threat detection and response ecosystem

ETD provides rules for specific attack classes based on audit logs and cloud traces. The following table provides a reference of detection types mapped to log sources and typical alerts:

Detection type	Example alert	Log source
IAM anomaly	Privilege escalation to owner role	Cloud Audit logs
Brute-force detection	Multiple failed login attempts	Cloud IAM, login events
Cryptomining detection	Suspicious CPU usage patterns in ephemeral VMs	Cloud Audit logs, Compute Engine
Lateral movement	Service account impersonation or token misuse	Cloud IAM, token audit logs
Malware command and control	Unusual outbound network traffic	VPC Flow Logs
Kubernetes threats	Exec access into containers, pod privilege misuse	GKE logs, Kubernetes Audit logs

Table 8.1: Detection types supported by ETD, mapped to log sources

Criticality of advanced threat detection

Cloud-native environments introduce both agility and complexity. Every new service, identity, or container introduces potential blind spots. Relying solely on reactive controls often results in delayed detection and high incident response costs. GCP's integrated detection stack ensures that malicious actions are detected whether they occur now or happened weeks ago.

For example, real-time detection might flag a credential stuffing attack within seconds. At the same time, Chronicle could retrospectively reveal that the same account was compromised weeks earlier via a vulnerable third-party integration.

In modern threat landscapes, *dwell time (the time an attacker remains undetected) directly translates to business risk.* Attackers often leverage cloud elasticity to escalate privileges, move laterally, and rapidly exfiltrate data. Advanced threat detection in GCP enables security teams to *correlate IAM changes, VPC Flow Logs, and endpoint signals,* surfacing suspicious activities that traditional rule-based systems may miss.

Additionally, *machine learning-backed detections in SCC and ETD* provide anomaly detection across your environment without requiring you to predefine every possible indicator of compromise. This proactive approach, combined with retrospective threat hunting using Chronicle, ensures your organization is equipped to detect *both real-time attacks and slow, stealthy compromises,* improving your overall incident response readiness while reducing time to contain and remediate threats.

Core capabilities that power detection

Advanced detection on GCP revolves around *visibility, correlation,* and *actionability.* These pillars ensure defenders can observe, investigate, and respond to threats before they escalate.

Here is a breakdown of these core elements:

- **Holistic visibility**: SCC Premium unifies data from assets, vulnerabilities, misconfigurations, and runtime logs, providing a comprehensive view of your environment. It provides a single pane of glass for understanding your GCP security posture, from Compute Engine instances to Cloud Functions and **Google Kubernetes Engine** (**GKE**) nodes.

- **Historical analysis with Chronicle**: Traditional log storage is ephemeral, often expiring within days or weeks. Chronicle retains logs for extended durations (months to years) and applies high-speed correlation algorithms across billions of events. This allows for uncovering dormant threats, such as compromised service accounts that are reused long after initial infiltration.

- **Automated Actions via SIEM or Workflows**: SCC can route high-priority alerts to Pub/Sub, trigger workflows via Cloud Functions, or integrate with SIEMs such as Splunk. This automation offloads manual triage, enabling fast containment.

- **Behavioural detection and UEBA integration**: GCP integrates with **User and Entity Behaviour Analytics** (**UEBA**) tools to enhance behavioural detection. These tools apply baselining and anomaly detection to identify deviations such as unusual login times or geographies, privilege escalations, abnormal API usage patterns, or sudden spikes in data exfiltration activity. When integrated with Chronicle or SCC, UEBA insights can enrich detection rules and trigger high-confidence alerts for insider threats or credential misuse.

For example, here is how you can export SCC findings to Pub/Sub and process them:

```
gcloud scc notifications create my-finding-feed \
  --organization=ORG_ID \
  --pubsub-topic=projects/PROJECT_ID/topics/my-scc-topic \
  --filter="severity=\"HIGH\""
```

Once routed to Pub/Sub, you can connect the topic to a Cloud Function for automatic remediation.

Security Command Center Premium overview

SCC is GCP's centralized security management solution, designed to provide visibility, threat detection, and security posture management across your entire cloud environment. While the Standard tier offers foundational capabilities, SCC Premium significantly expands the platform's detection and automation capabilities, making it a critical tool for organizations with high compliance, threat detection, or zero-trust needs.

Security Command Center Premium vs. Standard

Understanding the differences between the two editions helps determine which suits your operational maturity and threat model:

- **SCC Standard**: Provides essential asset discovery and vulnerability insights. Basic threat detection includes simple misconfiguration checks and exposure alerts, helping organizations get started with cloud security hygiene.

- **SCC Premium**: Builds on the standard offering by introducing advanced threat detection, custom detection logic, and compliance automation. With integrations like ETD, CTD, and Chronicle, it empowers mature teams to scale detection and response.

Key features in Security Command Center Premium

SCC Premium includes several advanced features that enable organisations to move beyond reactive security and into predictive and behavioural detection models. Below are the significant capabilities:

- **ETD**: Continuously scans logs for suspicious patterns, such as brute-force attacks, credential misuse, and privilege escalation. ETD uses built-in rules and Google's threat intel feeds for real-time alerts:

```
# Example: Enable ETD via CLI
gcloud scc settings update \
   --organization=ORG_ID \
   --enable-event-threat-detection
```

- **CTD**: Analyses runtime container activity in GKE clusters to detect threats, such as malicious images, crypto miners, or privilege escalation, within containers:

```
# Enable Container Threat Detection
 gcloud scc container-threat-detection update \
   --organization=ORG_ID \
   --enable
```

- **Security Health Analytics:** Automatically identifies misconfigurations in GCP services. It flags publicly exposed resources, overly permissive IAM roles, disabled logging, and other security drifts.

- **User and Entity Behavior Analytics (UEBA):** Leverages Chronicle to baseline user and service account behavior, detecting anomalies such as lateral movement, exfiltration attempts, or unusual geographic access.

Security Health Analytics mapping to CIS benchmarks

Security Health Analytics (SHA), a core component of SCC Premium, offers proactive detection of misconfigurations across a wide range of GCP services. One of its most powerful use cases is aligning your cloud configuration posture with compliance standards, such as the CIS benchmarks.

Google Cloud's SHA modules are mapped to CIS Google Cloud Foundations Benchmark v1.3, allowing security teams to use out-of-the-box detections as control validation mechanisms.

Here is a brief mapping of SHA modules to relevant CIS controls:

SHA category	Example detection	CIS benchmark mapping
IAM	IAM policy grants overly permissive roles	1.6: Ensure least privilege
Networking	VPC firewall allows 0.0.0.0/0 unrestricted	2.5: Restrict ingress rules
Storage Buckets	Public access enabled	2.8: Ensure buckets aren't public
Logging and monitoring	Audit logging disabled on key services	2.1: Ensure logging is enabled
Encryption	CMEK is not used for sensitive data	2.7: Use customer-managed encryption

Table 9.2: Mapping of SHA detection modules to relevant CIS benchmark controls

These rules not only support audit readiness but also provide continuous validation as configurations change.

Enabling SHA with CIS Benchmark focus:

```
gcloud scc settings update \
  --organization=ORG_ID \
  --enable-security-health-analytics
```

By operationalizing SHA findings, teams can embed compliance enforcement directly into CI/CD pipelines, creating policy as code guardrails that ensure configurations always align with baseline controls.

SCC data schema and custom detectors

Beyond its out-of-the-box detection capabilities, SCC Premium allows organizations to define custom detectors tailored to their cloud environment. These detectors analyze log events using match conditions, allowing teams to track behaviors that may indicate risk or policy violations.

Each custom detector is defined as a SHA module or ETD custom module. These detectors operate by scanning ingested logs for patterns based on attributes such as API method names, resource types, principal emails, or geographic locations.

For example, detect public **Google Cloud Storage (GCS)** bucket creation by a non-admin user:

```
customConfig:
  predicate:
    expression: "resource.type == 'gcs_bucket' && protoPayload.methodName
== 'storage.setIamPermissions' && !protoPayload.authenticationInfo.
principalEmail.endsWith('@admin-domain.com')"
  resourceSelector:
    resourceTypes:
      - "gcs_bucket"
```

This YAML-based policy could be uploaded to SCC using gcloud:

```
gcloud scc custom-modules create \
  --organization=ORG_ID \
  --module-type=SECURITY_HEALTH_ANALYTICS \
  --custom-config-from-file=custom_detector.yaml
```

Once deployed, the custom detector generates findings in the same manner as native SCC detections. These findings can then be routed to Pub/Sub for automated remediation or manually triaged via the SCC dashboard.

Custom detectors are particularly useful in regulated environments, where compliance requirements necessitate controls that exceed the default detection logic. Teams can define modules for:

- Blocking external IP access to BigQuery
- Preventing deletion of production VMs outside maintenance windows
- Flagging storage buckets created without encryption enabled

Use cases for Security Command Center Premium

SCC Premium is especially valuable in high-stakes environments or those with dynamic resource deployment patterns. Its capabilities align well with modern cloud security demands:

- **Regulated industries**: Industries such as finance, government, or healthcare must maintain and inspect detailed logs and adhere to stringent regulatory compliance requirements. SCC Premium offers long-term retention, continuous monitoring, and audit-friendly reporting.

- **Large dynamic environments**: Enterprises running thousands of ephemeral workloads benefit from real-time visibility and fast triage. ETD and CTD help catch threats that manifest in short-lived containers or transient service accounts.

- **Zero-trust architectures**: With identity as the new perimeter, SCC's UEBA and IAM analysis complement zero-trust strategies by surfacing behavior-based anomalies tied to identity misuse.

Enabling and configuring SCC Premium

Setting up SCC Premium effectively involves several critical steps to ensure your coverage is comprehensive and detection capabilities are fully utilized:

- **Activation**: You can enable SCC Premium through the GCP Console or via the **command line interface (CLI)**. Choose whether to apply it at the organization, folder, or project level, depending on your scope of protection:

```
gcloud scc settings update \
  --organization=ORG_ID \
  --enable-premium
```

- **Scope and coverage:** Map out your resource inventory and define which areas SCC should monitor. For example, you may want SCC to initially scan only production projects to minimize costs while maximizing impact.

- **IAM permissions:** Secure configuration begins with assigning the right roles. Grant the Security Center Admin role only to trusted team members and leverage Security Reviewer roles for read-only access.

- **Asset discovery:** Ensure that all resources are being inventoried. SCC can only detect threats within its line of sight. Verify that Compute Engine, GKE, Cloud SQL, and Cloud Storage assets are included:

```
gcloud scc asset-inventory update \
  --organization=ORG_ID \
  --enable
```

Best practices for operationalizing SCC Premium

To maximize the value of SCC Premium, teams should embed it into their incident response and DevSecOps workflows:

- **Configure high-signal alerts**: Set up Pub/Sub notifications for high-severity findings and pipe them into your SIEM or ticketing systems. This ensures that no critical issue goes unnoticed.

- **Review dashboards regularly**: Establish a weekly schedule for reviewing SCC dashboards. Track open findings, verify remediations, and identify recurring patterns.

- **Automate remediation workflows**: Leverage tools such as Cloud Functions, Workflows, or third-party ticketing platforms (e.g., Jira, ServiceNow) to tag, assign, and automatically close remediated issues.

  The following snippet demonstrates how you can use a Cloud Function to automate remediation workflows by triggering actions based on findings ingested from Pub/Sub, enabling scalable, event-driven response pipelines in your GCP environment:

```
# Example Cloud Function trigger
exports.remediateFinding = (pubSubEvent, context) => {
  const finding = JSON.parse(Buffer.from(pubSubEvent.data, 'base64').
toString());
  // Trigger remediation or alerting logic based on finding severity/type
};
```

Integrating vulnerability and threat intelligence

Threat detection is not only about detecting runtime anomalies. GCP strengthens its defense-in-depth strategy by combining log-based detection mechanisms with dynamic application scanning capabilities. Together, ETD and Web Security Scanner provide continuous visibility across infrastructure and application layers.

Beyond surface-level detections, *integrating vulnerability management and threat intelligence* enables teams to prioritize and contextualize alerts. By correlating CVEs identified through Container Scanning and Web Security Scanner with threat indicators in ETD and Chronicle, security teams can:

- Identify exposed vulnerabilities that are actively exploited in the wild.

- Prioritise patching efforts on severity-based risk scoring that accounts for exploitability and asset criticality.

- Track exploit attempts across logs and audit trails, even if runtime anomalies have not yet occurred.

For example, if Web Security Scanner detects an SQL injection vulnerability on a production application and ETD concurrently flags suspicious query patterns in Cloud SQL logs, these signals together indicate active exploitation, warranting immediate containment actions.

Additionally, leveraging *Google Threat Intelligence and VirusTotal integration within SCC* enables teams to enrich findings with external IOCs and malware analysis, further enhancing GCP's detection pipelines and allowing for *faster, more informed response decisions*.

Event Threat Detection

ETD works by analyzing audit logs and correlating them with threat intelligence patterns. It flags activities indicative of account compromise, abnormal access, or abuse of compute resources. This is especially critical in catching attacks that unfold slowly or abuse IAM policies. The following points outline *common detections provided by ETD and the practical configuration steps* to operationalize ETD within your GCP environment for effective, automated threat monitoring:

- **Common detections**:
  - **Brute-force attempts**: Detects repetitive failed logins across services.
  - **IAM escalation**: Flags sudden assignment of high-privilege roles such as `Owner` or `Editor`.
  - **Crypto mining**: Identifies ephemeral resources launching CPU-intensive operations.

- **ETD configuration steps**:
  - ○ **Enable log monitoring**: Activate ETD under SCC Premium and select log sources (IAM, Cloud Audit, VPC).

  - ○ **Apply filters**: Narrow detection scope by applying filters to reduce false positives.

  - ○ **Route alerts**: Utilize Pub/Sub or SCC notification channels to send alerts to your triage stack (e.g., Slack, SIEM):

    ```
    # Enable specific ETD detections
    gcloud scc event-threat-detection-settings update \
      --organization=ORG_ID \
      --detection-category=IAM \
      --enable
    ```

Web Security Scanner

Web Security Scanner offers dynamic application security by crawling and fuzzing web apps deployed on GCP. It detects issues that static analysis or IAM policies might miss. The following points outline *how to configure and operationalize Web Security Scanner* effectively within your GCP environment to enhance application-layer visibility and security:

- **Detection examples**:
  - ○ **Cross-Site Scripting (XSS)**
  - ○ Outdated JavaScript libraries
  - ○ Mixed-content issues (HTTP content over HTTPS pages)

- **Working**:
  - ○ **Define targets**: Specify target URLs or App Engine endpoints.
  - ○ **Schedule scans**: Run them periodically or trigger after deployments.
  - ○ **View reports**: SCC ingests the results and visualizes findings by severity. Use the following command to run a manual Web Security Scanner scan via CLI for targeted application endpoints:

    ```
    # Run a manual scan using CLI
    gcloud web-security-scanner scans start \
      --display-name="weekly-scan" \
      --starting-url=https://myapp.example.com
    ```

- **Best practices**:
  - ○ Run scans weekly to capture new vulnerabilities.
  - ○ Integrate into CI/CD pipelines for automated post-deployment validation.
  - ○ Exclude dev or ephemeral endpoints to avoid noise in findings.

These integrations not only provide threat intelligence but operationalize it within your GCP environment, bridging the gap between detection and response.

Chronicle for threat hunting

Chronicle offers unmatched capabilities for historical threat hunting and deep log analysis. Unlike traditional SIEMs, which struggle with scale or retention, Chronicle is built natively for the cloud and optimized to handle massive data volumes with long-term retention.

Chronicle automatically normalizes, enriches, and correlates data from diverse sources such as VPC Flow Logs, Cloud Audit logs, and endpoint telemetry, making it easier to investigate incidents across your cloud and hybrid environments. Security teams can quickly pivot across IP addresses, domains, and user activities over months or years to uncover stealthy attack patterns and lateral movements that may have been missed by real-time detection alone.

Chronicle's integration with Google's threat intelligence further enhances investigations by correlating internal signals with known **indicators of compromise (IOCs)** and advanced threat actor behaviors. This enables teams to *retrospectively identify compromises, understand attacker dwell times, and enhance detection engineering for future incidents*, thereby strengthening their security posture while leveraging the scalability and cost efficiency of Chronicle.

Chronicle as a cloud-native SIEM

Chronicle ingests data at a petabyte scale, indexing and normalizing logs from GCP, on-premises systems, and third-party cloud platforms. It provides low-latency querying, even across years of data, making it ideal for advanced security operations and retrospective forensics.

The following are the key capabilities:

- **Petabytes-scale data**: Chronicle scales to massive volumes, accommodating high-throughput log sources like VPC Flow Logs, Cloud Audit logs, and firewall logs.

- **Long-term retention**: Chronicle stores and indexes logs for months or years by default, supporting forensic timelines well beyond the typical 30-to-90-day windows.

- **Integrated threat feeds**: Native threat intelligence integration enables the automatic detection of known IOCs, including malicious IP addresses, URLs, and file hashes, against log events.

Retrospective threat hunting

With Chronicle, security teams can revisit older events, trace attack paths, and uncover long-dormant compromises.

The following is the step-by-step workflow:

1. **Centralize logs**: Forward GCP logs and additional third-party or custom logs into Chronicle using Logging export sinks or the BFS agent.

2. **Correlate events**: Query logs by user account, IP address, or domain across arbitrary time spans.

3. **IOC matching**: Chronicle enables the import of threat intelligence feeds **(comma-separated values (CSVs), Structured Threat Information Expression (STIX), Trusted Automated Exchange of Indicator Information (TAXII)** for automated detection and flagging of suspicious artefacts.

4. **Pivot and expand**: From one malicious event, pivot to related user activities, affected services, or correlated sessions across environments.

The following are the best practices:

- Use BigQuery or Chronicle's built-in UDM for multi-dimensional correlation.

- Tag logs by business unit or asset group for faster filtering and access control.

- Build triage workflows that connect Chronicle alerts with ticketing platforms or **Security Orchestration and Automation (SOAR)** tools. Use the following Log Explorer filter example to query and export specific logs from GCP to Chronicle for deeper threat hunting and long-term retention:

```
# Example: Export logs to Chronicle from GCP
resource.type="gce_instance"
logName="projects/PROJECT_ID/logs/cloudaudit.googleapis.com%2Factivity"
```

Chronicle's power lies in its ability to answer the questions: *What happened, when, and who was impacted?*, even if the attack occurred months ago. It is the investigative backbone for teams adopting a proactive security posture.

Automating response and remediation

Automation is a key enabler of modern cloud-native security operations. Google Cloud's SCC and Chronicle are not just designed to detect threats; they also support the automation of real-time responses. These responses range from tagging alerts and notifying stakeholders to full-scale, policy-driven remediation across IAM, compute, networking, and container services.

By linking SCC findings to Pub/Sub messages and utilizing Cloud Functions or SOAR platforms, organizations can create self-healing systems that mitigate threats before human intervention is necessary.

Security Command Center findings lifecycle

SCC generates structured security findings when it detects misconfigurations, vulnerabilities, or active threats. Understanding the lifecycle of a finding is crucial for developing effective triage, remediation, and closure processes.

A finding begins in an *active* state when SCC or Chronicle first detects a relevant security event. Each finding includes metadata such as severity, category, resource affected, source module, and timestamps for creation and last update. Findings can transition to an *inactive* state once resolved or automatically when the condition no longer persists. Finally, findings can be *archived*, either manually or through automation workflows, for audit and compliance purposes.

Example JSON payload excerpt from an SCC finding:

```
{
  "name": "organizations/123/sources/456/findings/abc-def",
  "category": "PUBLIC_BUCKET_ACL",
  "severity": "HIGH",
  "state": "ACTIVE",
  "resourceName": "//storage.googleapis.com/my-bucket",
  "eventTime": "2024-12-10T10:00:00Z"
}
```

Security teams often build automation logic that filters findings based on category, state, or time-to-live windows. For instance, critical findings can be automatically escalated if they remain active for more than 24 hours, whereas low-priority findings may be batched and reviewed on a weekly basis.

Defining response workflows

Real-time detections from SCC and long-term patterns uncovered by Chronicle can both serve as triggers for automated response logic. Security teams can design multi-layered workflows where severity, type, and context determine the depth of response:

- **Detection sources**:
  - ○ **SCC Premium**: Detects IAM misuses, container threats, and misconfigurations.
  - ○ **Chronicle**: Performs historical analysis and identifies anomalies that unfolded over longer timelines.
- **Triggering actions**:
  - ○ On detection of a high-severity issue, SCC publishes findings to Pub/Sub.
  - ○ Cloud Functions or Cloud Run services ingest these events and execute remediations.

o Chronicle detections can be routed to the same workflows using integration bridges or custom alert forwarding logic. Use the following command to create a Pub/Sub notification configuration for routing high-severity SCC findings into automated remediation workflows or SOAR pipelines:

```
# Example: Create a Pub/Sub notification config
gcloud scc notifications create auto-remediation-feed \
  --organization=ORG_ID \
  --pubsub-topic=projects/PROJECT_ID/topics/scc-findings \
  --filter="severity=\"CRITICAL\""
```

SCC supports publishing real-time security findings to Pub/Sub, which can trigger automated responses or alerting pipelines. The following figure represents how SCC findings are routed to Pub/Sub:

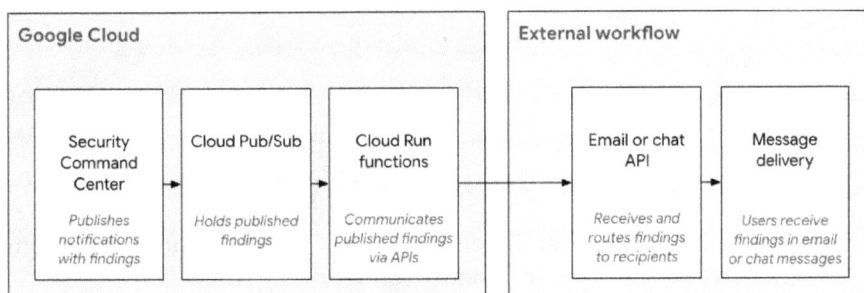

Figure 8.2: *SCC findings routed to Pub/Sub trigger Cloud Functions or SOAR tools for remediation*

Automated remediation tactics

Once SCC or Chronicle has raised a finding, your automated remediation engine can take over. The following are the real-world security events and examples of response actions that can be applied:

- **IAM anomaly**:
  - o Remove newly granted **Owner** or **Editor** roles if the change is not pre-approved.
  - o Lock the affected user or service account via **gcloud iam service-accounts disable**.
  - o Log the event and notify the security team for audit trail purposes.

- **Malicious container activity**:
  - o Quarantine the container by removing it from the deployment pool.
  - o Prevent future deployments by updating Binary Authorization policies to disallow the compromised image digest.
  - o Trigger a rebuild pipeline with known-good images.

- **Data exfiltration attempt**:
    - ○ Add a deny egress rule to the firewall policy for the suspicious IP address.
    - ○ Isolate the affected Compute Engine instance or Cloud Function using VPC **Service Controls (SC)** service perimeters.
    - ○ Rotate credentials if access tokens or service keys were exposed. Use the following command to create a VPC firewall rule that blocks outbound traffic to a suspicious IP address during incident response containment:

        ```
        # Example: Block IP address with VPC firewall
         gcloud compute firewall-rules create deny-suspicious-ip \
           --direction=EGRESS \
           --priority=100 \
           --destination-ranges=203.0.113.42/32 \
           --action=DENY \
           --rules=all \
           --network=default
        ```

Response automation tools and patterns

Choosing the proper response tooling depends on your cloud maturity and team structure. Here's how GCP-native and third-party systems can work together:

- **Cloud Functions / Cloud Run**: Ideal for lightweight, stateless automation based on Pub/Sub triggers from SCC. Use this for precise, atomic actions, such as revoking a role or quarantining an IP.

- **SOAR platforms**: **Security Orchestration, Automation, and Response (SOAR)** platforms, such as Splunk Phantom, Cortex XSOAR, or Swimlane, can chain multiple actions across detection, enrichment, remediation, and documentation. They also support conditional approvals.

- **Slack/PagerDuty Integration**: In some scenarios, a human-in-the-loop is required. Set up notification hooks that enable team members to approve, reject, or escalate automated responses before irreversible actions are taken. Use the following example to send a Slack notification via webhook, enabling human-in-the-loop approval for critical automated actions during incident response workflows:

```
# Slack Notification Example using Webhook
import requests

msg = {
  "text": "SCC detected critical IAM privilege escalation. Approve
automated role revocation?",
  "attachments": [
    {"text": "Approve or escalate via SOAR UI"}
```

```
    ]
}
requests.post('https://hooks.slack.com/services/TOKEN', json=msg)
```

Automated response workflows turn your detection capabilities into an actionable security posture. By combining SCC's real-time analysis with Chronicle's historical depth and routing events into customizable remediation pipelines, your cloud defenses become faster, more consistent, and scalable without sacrificing control.

GCP-native and third-party SOAR tools, such as Cortex XSOAR, can integrate with SCC for orchestrated incident response. The following figure represents the Automated SCC finding response pipeline:

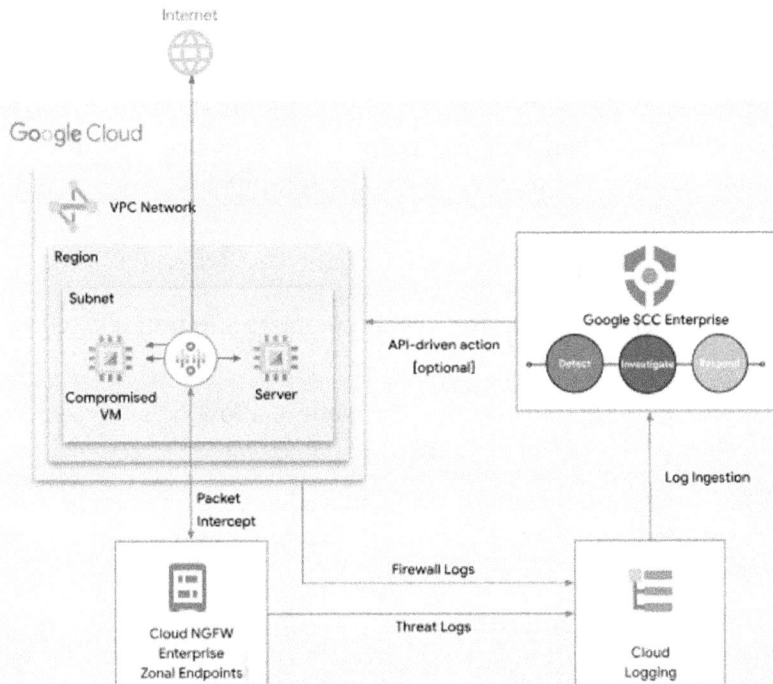

Figure 8.3: *Automated SCC finding response pipeline using SOAR to manage alerts and orchestrate remediation*

Combining SCC with Org alerts

A unified alerting and triage strategy is essential when multiple detection sources operate across your infrastructure. SCC, Chronicle, and legacy systems, such as on-premises SIEMs, must be synchronized into a central pipeline to avoid alert fatigue and reduce time-to-response.

To achieve this, integrate *SCC findings with your organization's alerting systems (Slack, PagerDuty, SIEM)* to ensure that high-severity findings are routed with appropriate context and priority.

Use filters to suppress noisy or low-priority findings while ensuring that critical detections, such as IAM escalations, suspicious network activity, or malware signals, are escalated immediately.

Enrich SCC findings with asset metadata, business context, and vulnerability status before routing them to your triage system, enabling analysts to *make faster, informed decisions without having to switch between consoles*. Additionally, implement *deduplication and correlation logic* to merge related alerts across SCC, Chronicle, and endpoint telemetry, reducing redundant noise during incidents.

Finally, perform *regular playbook testing with your integrated pipeline* to ensure SCC alerts trigger the appropriate workflows, human approvals, and automated remediations aligned with your organization's risk tolerance and cloud governance policies.

Unified alert strategy

Alerts are most actionable when they are normalized, enriched, and routed with context. This section outlines how to build an effective alerting pipeline that spans GCP-native and enterprise-wide sources:

- **Primary detection feeds**:

    o **SCC**: Generates alerts for real-time misconfigurations, vulnerabilities, and security anomalies.

    o **Chronicle**: Adds retrospective correlation, allowing analysts to confirm breach duration or detect stealthy patterns.

    o **SIEM integration**: Ingests alerts and telemetry from endpoint security tools, proxies, and on-premises firewalls for comprehensive visibility across the whole stack.

- **Implementation of best practices**:

    o **Severity standardization**: Unify alert severity definitions (Critical, High, Medium, Low) across Chronicle, SCC, and your SIEM to ensure consistent prioritization.

    o **Single escalation path**: Route alerts, whether from SCC or Chronicle, into a central platform, such as Slack or Jira, for unified triage.

    o **Mixed remediation modes**: Allow automation to handle repeatable threats, while reserving complex cases for manual review and analysis.

    o **Playbook integration**: Link alerts to predefined response playbooks that outline investigation and containment steps. This reduces **mean time to respond (MTTR)**, ensures consistency during incident handling, and allows junior analysts to take immediate action with confidence.

Combining SCC, Chronicle, and SIEM alerts into a single triage pipeline improves signal clarity and speeds decision-making. The following figure shows the centralized alert funnel:

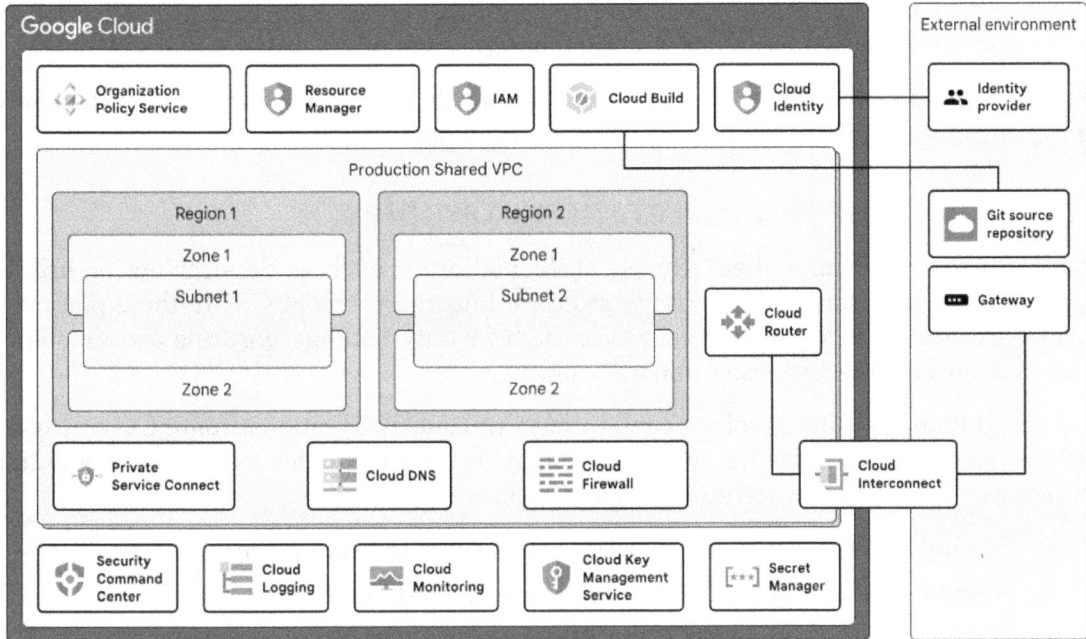

Figure 8.4: Centralized alert funnel combining
GCP-native detections and enterprise logs for unified triage

Tracking and incident response

Tracking the entire lifecycle of a security event, from initial detection to confirmed closure, ensures operational maturity and effectiveness. Here is how to connect SCC findings to broader incident management workflows:

- **From detection to resolution**:
  - **Ticketing integration**: Automatically create incident records in platforms like ServiceNow for every high-severity SCC finding.
  - **Threat pattern matching**: Chronicle can check whether similar alerts occurred in the past or across multiple assets.
  - **Remediation confirmation**: Ensure the patch, configuration fix, or access revocation addressed the underlying issue.
- **Key metrics to track**:
  - **MTTD**: How quickly is the issue discovered post-intrusion?
  - **MTTR**: How fast does your team close the loop once alerted?

- o **False positive rate**: Measure the number of non-actionable alerts that waste triage cycles.

- o **Coverage depth**: Continuously verify that all critical assets (e.g., Cloud Run, GKE, IAM) are under SCC surveillance.

These practices ensure not only that alerts are seen but also that they are acted upon efficiently, paving the way toward a proactive, resilient security operations centre.

ServiceNow or Jira integration example

Enterprise security teams often rely on ITSM platforms, such as ServiceNow or Jira, to track incidents and manage response workflows. Integrating the SCC with these platforms enables the automated creation of tickets for high-severity findings, ensuring accountability, prioritization, and effective resolution tracking.

This integration typically involves configuring Pub/Sub notifications from SCC to trigger a Cloud Function or integration middleware that creates or updates incident tickets within ServiceNow or Jira. Tickets can automatically populate with:

- Finding name, severity, and category (e.g., *Critical IAM Escalation*)
- Affected resources (project ID, instance name, IP addresses)
- Detection timestamp and SCC link for immediate analyst investigation
- Recommended remediation steps or playbook links

By mapping SCC severities to your ITSM priority schemes, your team ensures that critical alerts are triaged quickly while avoiding low-severity noise. You can also add labels for environment (prod/dev), business owner, or impacted services to streamline routing to the appropriate team.

Additionally, these tickets can be automatically updated or closed when the SCC finding is resolved, maintaining synchronization between your detection pipelines and operational workflows. This ensures measurable accountability, improves audit readiness, and reduces manual handoffs during incident response.

Automating ticket creation from SCC findings

When SCC identifies a high-severity issue (e.g., privilege escalation or exposed bucket), the finding can be exported to Pub/Sub. A Cloud Function then consumes this message and calls the ServiceNow or Jira API to open an incident or issue.

Sample pseudo-code to push SCC finding into ServiceNow:

```
import requests

SERVICENOW_URL = "https://instance.service-now.com/api/now/table/incident"
HEADERS = {"Content-Type": "application/json"}
```

```
payload = {
  "short_description": "SCC Finding - IAM Privilege Escalation",
  "description": "Detected an IAM Owner role granted to user@example.com",
  "urgency": "1",
  "impact": "1",
  "category": "Security"
}

requests.post(SERVICENOW_URL, auth=("api_user", "api_password"),
headers=HEADERS, json=payload)
```

The same can be adapted for Jira using their REST API.

The following are its importance:

- Ensures findings are tracked like traditional IT tickets
- Creates centralized audit logs for investigations and compliance
- Enables escalation workflows and ownership assignment

Security teams can also link SCC ticket resolution to remediation validation logic. For example, a ticket is only closed when SCC marks the finding as inactive or resolved.

Chronicle uses a UDM to normalize logs, enabling robust cross-asset threat correlation. The following figure shows an overview of log ingestion, normalisation, threat intel, and retro-search:

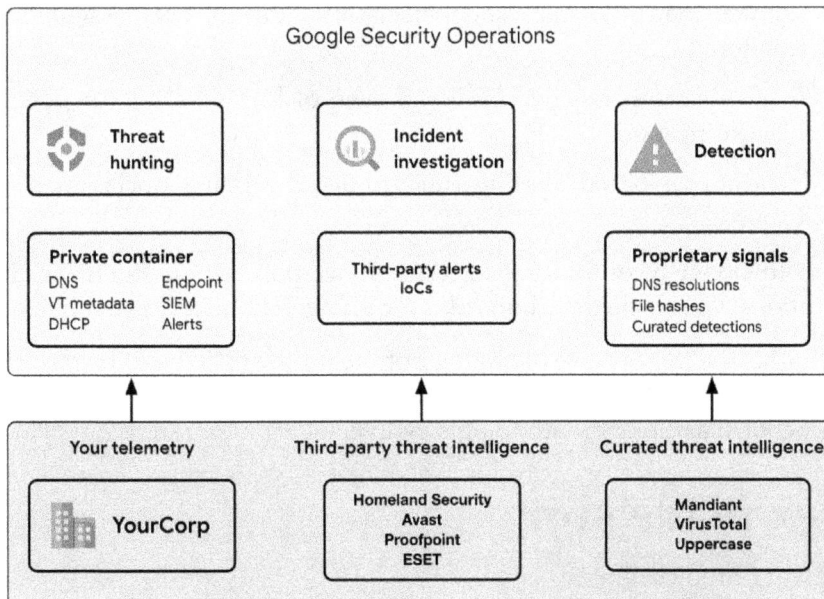

Figure 8.5: Chronicle architecture overview showing log ingestion, normalization, threat intel, and retrospective search

Misconfiguration case study

Even with SCC and Chronicle deployed, security blind spots can emerge from incomplete coverage, misrouted alerts, or poorly enforced workflows. This case study examines a real-world scenario where a misconfiguration went undetected, emphasizing the importance of fine-tuning detection pipelines and validating control efficacy:

- **The incident:** A development team created a new Cloud Storage bucket with default settings. Due to a lapse in the project's organizational policy enforcement, the bucket was inadvertently made public. SHA was configured, but no finding was generated.

  Upon investigation, it was discovered that the SCC scope was not correctly applied to the specific folder where the project was located. Additionally, the IAM reviewer role responsible for triaging findings had changed hands, and no one was actively monitoring low-severity SHA events.

- **How it was caught:** Two weeks later, Chronicle ingested VPC Flow Logs showing exfiltration behavior to a previously unseen IP range. A security engineer ran a retrospective IOC search, which correlated the traffic with an untagged bucket. Manual inspection revealed public read access enabled via `allUsers`.

- **Lessons learned:**
    - Ensure all folders, projects, and assets are explicitly included in SCC's asset inventory scope.
    - Validate that SCC roles and permissions are not only assigned but actively monitored.
    - Routinely audit inactive findings, even of low severity, for potential drift or misclassification.
    - Integrate tag-based alerting rules to avoid missing unclassified or "shadow" resources.

The resolution involved reconfiguring organizational policies, updating SCC filters, and setting up additional Chronicle detection rules for untagged buckets with open access logs.

This case highlights the importance of having both real-time (SCC) and historical (Chronicle) analysis capabilities, as well as the need to validate that security controls remain correctly scoped and functional as cloud environments evolve.

Complex made simple

Think of SCC and Chronicle like:

- **SCC (Real-time observers):**

- o SCC Premium is akin to security guards posted throughout a city, spotting and reporting crimes as they happen, someone breaking a window or suspiciously loitering.

- o ETD and CTD provide immediate alerts, similar to guards calling central dispatch. Meanwhile, vulnerability scans are like routine pat-downs or building checks to ensure no unlocked doors.

- **Chronicle (Ancient historians and archive):**
  - o Chronicle acts as the city's historical archive, with near-infinite memory of every reported incident or suspicious event for years.

  - o Investigators can consult these archives to determine if a burglar's pattern matches that of old unsolved crimes or whether an intrusion method used last year recurs.

  - o This is because logs never truly expire in the city archives; any new clue can spark a re-examination of old evidence.

- **Working together:**
  - o SCC is your on-the-ground force, catching threats in near real-time. At the same time, Chronicle is your comprehensive library of events, enabling you to piece together major conspiracies or overlooked infiltration attempts from months or years ago.

  - o By combining immediate detection with deep retrospective analysis, you maintain not only agile daily security (SCC) but also robust historical insight (Chronicle) to fortify your GCP environment.

Conclusion

Securing a modern cloud environment requires more than just visibility, it demands speed, precision, and the capability to act on intelligence in real-time. Google Cloud's Security Command Centre and Chronicle integrate advanced threat detection, historical context, and scalable automation to assist organizations in staying ahead of evolving threats.

By integrating automated remediation workflows, aligning severity across tools, and centralizing alerts into a unified triage pipeline, teams can significantly reduce response times while enhancing overall coverage. More importantly, these capabilities allow security teams to transition from reactive firefighting to proactive defense, enabling continuous monitoring, guided investigation, and consistent enforcement of cloud security best practices.

As your organization matures, the next step is to embed these capabilities more deeply into CI/CD pipelines, threat intelligence enrichment systems, and organizational playbooks. When executed correctly, GCP-native threat detection transforms from merely a monitoring layer into a critical engine of resilience across your cloud footprint.

Let this serve not only as a reference but also as a blueprint for operationalizing real-time detection and response within your cloud-native infrastructure.

The next chapter explores how to extend these threat detection and response capabilities across distributed environments. You will learn how Anthos enables unified policy enforcement, consistent security controls, and centralized visibility across GCP, on-prem, and third-party clouds. This sets the stage for building secure, scalable, and resilient architectures in hybrid and multi-cloud deployments.

Exercise

Test your understanding of continuous compliance, logging architecture, alert strategy, and automated enforcement on Google Cloud. Complete the following tasks to reinforce learning.

1. Configure Audit logs for centralized visibility

   Objective: Ensure Admin Activity logs and Data Access logs are enabled for all services in a project.

   a. Enable Audit logs for a test project via the GCP Console or `gcloud`.

   b. Verify logs in **Cloud Logging > Logs Explorer**.

   c. Identify whether the following logs appear:

      i. IAM policy changes

      ii. Firewall rule updates

      iii. GCS bucket access

   Reference: **https://cloud.google.com/logging/docs/audit**

2. Simulate policy drift and detect via SCC

   Objective: Observe how SCC identifies policy violations from misconfigurations.

   a. Create a VM instance with an external IP (in violation of org policy).

   b. Set a constraint in organization policy to deny external IPs.

   c. Review SCC findings under Misconfigurations tab.

      Bonus: **Export the finding via Pub/Sub and trigger a dummy Cloud Function.**

      Reference: **https://cloud.google.com/security-command-center/docs/how-to-notifications**

3. Automate compliance checks using Terraform Validator.

   Objective: Detect non-compliant IaC configs before deployment.

   a. Install Terraform Validator

      b.   Write a sample **main.tf** with a public GCS bucket.

      c.   Run **terraform plan** and validate the plan with your org policies.

```
terraform plan -out=tfplan.binary
terraform-validator validate tfplan.binary --policy-path=./org-
policies
```

4.   Design a multi-tier logging strategy

    Objective: Architect a logging setup that enables compliance and long-term analysis.

      a.   Enable log exports from Cloud Logging to BigQuery and Cloud Storage.

      b.   Create a Pub/Sub sink to stream logs to a third-party SIEM.

      c.   Visualize anomalies using Logs Explorer or build a dashboard in Looker Studio.

    Reference: **https://cloud.google.com/logging/docs/export**

5.   Implement a unified alerting pipeline

    Objective: Route and triage alerts from SCC and Chronicle using severity-based playbooks.

      a.   Set up SCC with a custom severity threshold for alerting.

      b.   Route alerts to Pub/Sub.

      c.   Create a Cloud Function that parses findings and creates a Jira ticket.

    Bonus: **Try integrating a security playbook (Google Cloud Functions or SOAR platform).**

Key takeaways

- GCP's SCC Premium and Chronicle enable real-time and retrospective threat detection across your cloud estate.

- ETD, CTD, and Security Health Analytics are essential components of SCC Premium.

- Chronicle offers long-term log retention and correlation, supporting deep forensic analysis and threat hunting.

- SCC integrates with Pub/Sub, Cloud Functions, and SOAR platforms to trigger automated remediation workflows.

- Unifying alert severity and routing across SCC, Chronicle, and SIEM ensures consistent triage and incident management.

- Integrating Web Security Scanner into CI/CD pipelines helps identify vulnerabilities in web apps before production deployment.

- Success metrics such as MTTD, MTTR, false positives, and asset coverage should guide operational improvements.

- Visual workflows, ticketing integration, and Slack/PagerDuty hooks enhance response efficiency and accountability.

References

1. https://cloud.google.com/security-command-center

2. https://cloud.google.com/security-command-center/docs/how-to-notifications

3. https://cloud.google.com/security-command-center/docs/how-to-respond-findings

4. https://cloud.google.com/chronicle/docs/concepts/overview

5. https://cloud.google.com/security-command-center/docs/incident-response-playbook

6. https://cloud.google.com/security-command-center/docs/how-to-remediate-findings

7. https://cloud.google.com/web-security-scanner/docs/quickstart

8. https://cloud.google.com/logging/docs/export/configure_export

9. https://cloud.google.com/security-foundations

10. https://cloud.google.com/security-command-center/docs/how-to-enable

11. https://cloud.google.com/security-command-center/docs/how-to-container-threat-detection

12. https://cloud.google.com/security-command-center/docs/how-to-event-threat-detection

Join our Discord space

Join our Discord workspace for latest updates, offers, tech happenings around the world, new releases, and sessions with the authors:

https://discord.bpbonline.com

CHAPTER 9

Hybrid and Multi-Cloud Security with Anthos

Introduction

As organizations embrace multi-cloud and hybrid architectures to meet business, regulatory, and performance demands, they encounter a new level of operational complexity. Managing diverse infrastructure stacks across Google Cloud, AWS, Azure, and on-premises data centres presents challenges related to policy consistency, service networking, observability, and identity governance. Maintaining security and compliance across these environments becomes increasingly error-prone and fragmented without a unified framework in place.

Anthos is Google Cloud's answer to this complexity. It provides a cohesive application platform designed to unify operations across environments while preserving flexibility and autonomy at the edge. Anthos extends core Google Cloud technologies, including Kubernetes, Istio, policy management, and service networking, into external and on-premises environments. Whether you are managing hundreds of edge clusters in retail stores, maintaining data locality for compliance, or integrating newly acquired cloud environments, Anthos ensures your workloads follow consistent policies and governance models.

This chapter explores Anthos from both architectural and operational perspectives. It covers the foundational components, key use cases, and best practices that help teams build secure, scalable, and consistent cloud application platforms. You will learn how Anthos brings policy as code to Kubernetes clusters using Config Management and Gatekeeper, enables unified service connectivity via Service Mesh, and abstracts the cloud-specific nuances of running GKE on AWS and Azure. Crucially, Anthos acts as a security and governance enabler by enforcing consistent identity, access, policy, and configuration controls across environments, regardless of where workloads run, helping teams reduce risk and respond to compliance requirements more effectively.

Structure

This chapter will cover the following topics:

- Anthos
- Policy consistency with ACM and Gatekeeper
- Managing GKE clusters with Anthos
- Hybrid connectivity and service mesh
- Challenges and mitigation strategies
- Cross-cloud identity and governance
- Complex made simple

Objectives

This chapter is intended to help platform and security teams understand how Anthos simplifies multi-cloud governance, policy enforcement, and service management. It will equip readers with the knowledge to plan, deploy, and operate Anthos across cloud and on-prem clusters.

By the end of this chapter, you will understand the architectural components of Anthos, how they work together across different environments, and how to apply them to real-world hybrid and multi-cloud scenarios. You will also learn the foundational steps to consistently enforce security and compliance using GitOps principles, OPA-based policies, and centralised cluster management.

Anthos

A successful multi-cloud strategy depends on consistently managing workloads, policies, and identities across clouds and on-prem environments. Anthos provides a modular framework for centralising cluster governance, enabling local autonomy and ensuring alignment with compliance. This section breaks down the architecture and components that power Anthos and how they integrate to form a control plane across heterogeneous environments.

Anthos enables organisations to deploy, operate, and secure applications consistently across *GCP, other clouds (such as AWS and Azure), and on-premises data centres*, using Kubernetes as the foundation. Anthos Config Management allows teams to enforce policies and configurations across fleets using GitOps practices, reducing configuration drift and ensuring compliance. Anthos Service Mesh integrates advanced traffic management, observability, and security for microservices, providing consistent visibility and control across environments.

Additionally, Anthos integrates with **Google Kubernetes Engine** (GKE) for managed Kubernetes clusters, allowing workload portability without requiring refactoring and supporting modernisation at your pace. By leveraging Anthos, enterprises can build a unified operational model, enhance governance, and reduce operational overhead while maintaining flexibility across both cloud and on-premises infrastructures.

To better appreciate the unique positioning of Anthos in the hybrid and multi-cloud ecosystem, the following table compares it against native multi-cloud tools such as *AWS EKS Anywhere* and *Azure Arc*, focusing on security, policy enforcement, and operational consistency:

Feature or capability	Anthos (Google Cloud)	EKS anywhere (AWS)	Azure Arc (Microsoft Azure)
Policy as code enforcement	Native support via Config Management and Gatekeeper across GKE, AWS, Azure, and on-prem.	Limited; relies on open-source tools like OPA Gatekeeper.	Available via Azure Policy extensions for Kubernetes.
Unified Service Mesh	Built-in support through Anthos Service Mesh (Istio-based) for traffic security, telemetry, and policy.	No native mesh; requires separate setup of Istio or AWS App Mesh.	Azure Service Mesh is still in early maturity stages.
Multi-cluster security posture	Enforces IAM, network, and workload policies across clusters with GitOps integration.	Requires custom integrations or third-party solutions.	Arc-enabled Kubernetes supports policies but has limited portability.
GKE integration	Deeply integrated with GKE, enabling seamless portability and lifecycle management.	Native integration only with EKS, not GKE.	Limited to AKS clusters; no native GKE support.
Compliance and drift detection	Continuous compliance via Cloud SCC, config sync, and pre-built policy libraries.	Manual or third-party tooling required.	Supports Azure Defender for Kubernetes, but is limited to non-Azure infra.
Cross-cloud portability	Abstracts cloud-specific differences (GCP, AWS, Azure) via unified APIs and tooling.	EKS-focused; portability is limited outside the AWS ecosystem.	Primarily focused on Azure-native services and extensions.

Table 9.1: Anthos vs. Native multi-cloud tools (EKS Anywhere, Azure Arc)

Anthos architecture

Anthos is composed of four primary components, each serving a distinct purpose in establishing consistency and visibility across clouds:

- **Anthos Config Management (ACM)**: A GitOps-driven engine that synchronizes Kubernetes configurations, **role-based access control** (RBAC) policies, and network controls across clusters. This ensures that changes to infrastructure and security are version-controlled and automatically reconciled.

- **Anthos Service Mesh (ASM)**: Built on Istio, ASM enables mutual **Transport Layer Security (TLS)**, traffic control, telemetry collection, and service identity between microservices. It supports cross-cluster routing and enforces zero-trust principles.

- **Anthos multi-cluster management**: This centralized console and API layer enables teams to view, label, and apply policies to Kubernetes clusters running across GCP, AWS, Azure, and on-premises environments. It includes views on health, status, and compliance.

- **Connect agent**: A lightweight binary installed on non-GCP clusters that registers them with the Anthos control plane, allowing them to participate in centralized configuration and policy enforcement.

Figure 9.1 architecture references a standard Anthos control plane:

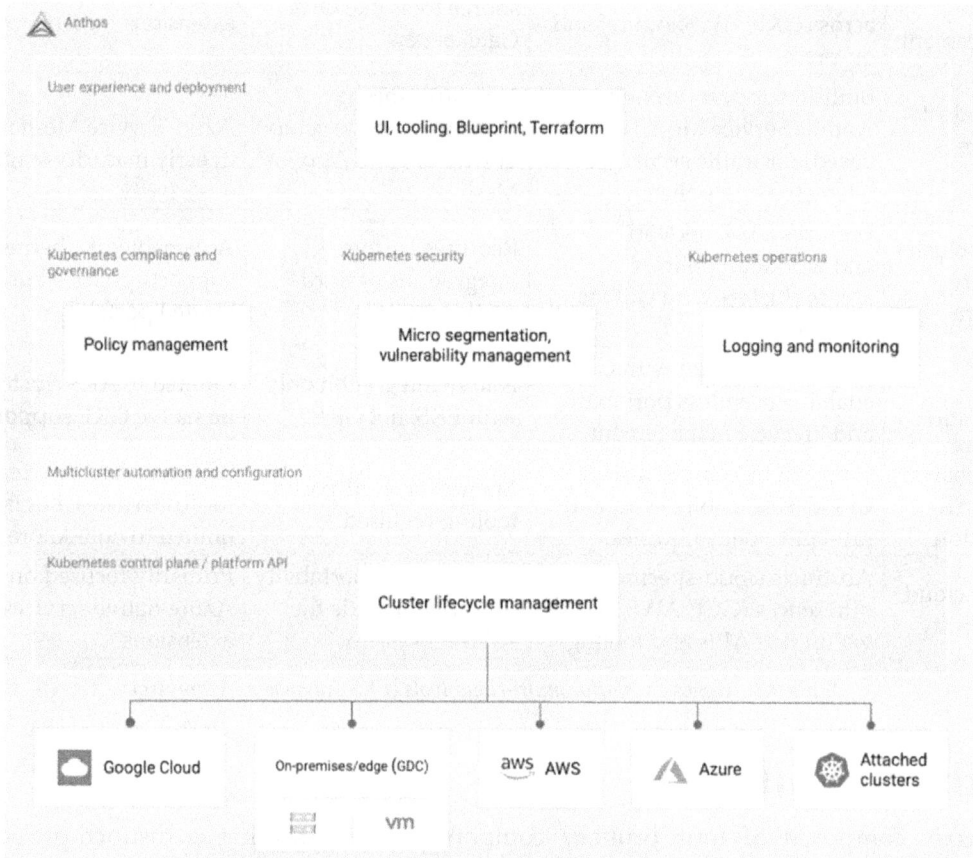

Figure 9.1: *Anthos control plane overview connecting multi-cloud clusters through Connect Agent, ACM, and ASM*

These components work in tandem to build a reliable foundation for consistent governance, whether the cluster resides in a GCP region, on-premises server rack, or in an AWS **Virtual**

Private Cloud (VPC). As we will see in the next section, this architecture enables a predictable flow for workload onboarding and policy propagation across clouds.

Multi-cloud flow

Anthos's operational flow revolves around declarative synchronization and centralized visibility. Each GCP project maintains metadata and control configurations relevant to its registered clusters. External clusters (in AWS, Azure, or on-prem) must install the Connect Agent to establish bidirectional control.

Once connected, configuration and service mesh policies from GCP can be applied consistently to each cluster, including those running on-premises or in other cloud environments. To establish this connection, GCP uses Connect Agent, which securely registers external Kubernetes clusters with the Anthos control plane. This enables central visibility, policy application, and service mesh configuration from the Google Cloud Console.

For example, the following command registers a non-GCP Kubernetes cluster using the Connect Agent CLI:

For example, registering a non-GCP cluster with Connect Agent:

```
connect-register \
  --project=acme-hybrid \
  --location=us-central1 \
  --gke-uri=https://CLUSTER_ENDPOINT \
  --service-account-key-file=connect-agent-key.json
```

This step is critical for onboarding external clusters to Anthos, enabling features such as Config Management, Policy Controller, and Anthos Service Mesh to operate securely and consistently across hybrid environments.

This command registers an on-prem or AWS-hosted GKE cluster, ensuring it appears in the Anthos dashboard and receives ACM and ASM policies.

This unified operational flow becomes essential when scaling across cloud providers or integrating workloads from newly acquired environments. The following section highlights where these capabilities are being used in real-world settings.

Use cases

While Anthos simplifies cross-cloud governance, long-term success depends on aligning architecture decisions with operational, security, and compliance goals. The following best practices are tailored for Anthos-based hybrid and multi-cloud environments:

- **Plan resource naming with Anthos Fleet Identity in mind**: Adopt a structured and hierarchical naming convention across clusters, namespaces, and workloads to ease policy targeting, access reviews, and troubleshooting. Anthos Fleet allows grouping clusters under a logical fleet ID—ensure resource names align with fleet boundaries (e.g., `retail-eu-fleet, store-gke-cluster01, namespace-prod-billing`). This consistency benefits centralized policy deployment via config sync.

- **Federate IAM using Anthos Workload Identity Federation**: Configure federated identity using OIDC or Google's Workload Identity Federation early in the rollout. This avoids IAM sprawl across clouds and enables centralized authentication for workloads running outside GCP (e.g., on EKS or AKS). Proper federation ensures workloads receive the right access without duplicating secrets or long-lived service account keys.

- **Monitor and secure inter-cluster communication using Anthos Service Mesh**: Secure service-to-service communication with mutual TLS and identity-based authorization across environments. Use Anthos Service Mesh to enforce fine-grained access policies between microservices, regardless of their location. Combine this with VPC Peering or Cloud Interconnect for encrypted connectivity and isolate environments using namespace boundaries and mesh policies.

- **Enforce config consistency using ACM**: Leverage GitOps-based workflows to manage policies, RBAC, and network configs as declarative code. This reduces configuration drift and enables secure rollouts through staged Git branches, ensuring a seamless deployment process. Use Policy Controller to enforce admission control on risky configurations, such as overly permissive ingress rules or privilege escalation in pods.

These foundational steps help teams transition from fragmented governance to a *secure, scalable, and audit-friendly multi-cloud architecture,* making Anthos a control plane for consistent policy enforcement and operational governance.

Best practices

While Anthos simplifies cross-cloud governance, success depends on thoughtful architecture. The following practices ensure long-term maintainability:

- **Plan resource naming**: Adopt a structured naming convention across clouds to ease debugging, policy targeting, and automation. Use consistent prefixes for cluster, namespace, and service names (e.g., `retail-eu-cluster1, gke-prod-gcp`).

- **IAM Federation**: Early on, choose a federated identity provider strategy (e.g., Workload Identity Federation or OIDC). This avoids inconsistent access policies and reduces team onboarding friction.

- **Monitor inter-cluster networking**: Utilize tools such as VPC Peering, **virtual private network (VPN)**, or Interconnect to connect clusters securely. Use an overlay service mesh to restrict and observe traffic between services.

These foundational steps prepare teams to build repeatable, secure, and highly scalable multi-cloud environments. The next module will explore how these environments are governed using policy as code and admission controls through ACM and Gatekeeper.

Policy consistency with ACM and Gatekeeper

Consistent policy enforcement across clusters is critical in a hybrid or multi-cloud environment. **ACM** and **Gatekeeper** provide a scalable, declarative approach to enforcing configuration and security policies across Kubernetes clusters, regardless of their location. This module examines how ACM utilises GitOps principles and how Gatekeeper, based on **Open Policy Agent (OPA)**, ensures runtime policy compliance.

ACM enables organizations to store Kubernetes configurations and policies in a *central Git repository*, automatically syncing them to clusters to maintain consistent configurations and reduce drift. Teams can version-control security policies, network configurations, and RBAC rules, ensuring that all clusters adhere to approved standards and *automatically roll back* if unauthorized changes are detected.

Gatekeeper extends this consistency by providing *admission control*, ensuring that any resource deployed into a cluster complies with defined policies before it is created. Using `ConstraintTemplates`, teams can enforce policies such as restricting the use of privileged containers, requiring TLS encryption for services, or enforcing the use of labels for environment segregation.

Together, ACM and Gatekeeper provide a *GitOps-driven, automated, and scalable approach* to policy governance across fleets of Kubernetes clusters, enabling security and platform teams to align operational security with compliance goals across environments seamlessly.

Quick tutorial: Enforcing a no-root container policy with Gatekeeper in 5 Steps

1. **Set up Gatekeeper**: Install Gatekeeper using the official Helm chart or YAML manifests:

   ```
   kubectl apply -f https://raw.githubusercontent.com/open-policy-agent/
   gatekeeper/release-3.11/deploy/gatekeeper.yaml
   ```

2. **Create the `ConstraintTemplate`**: This template defines what *no-root* means:

   ```
   apiVersion: templates.gatekeeper.sh/v1beta1
   kind: ConstraintTemplate
   metadata:
     name: k8srequiredrunasnonroot
   spec:
     crd:
       spec:
         names:
           kind: K8sRequiredRunAsNonRoot
     targets:
       - target: admission.k8s.gatekeeper.sh
         rego: |
           package k8srequiredrunasnonroot
           violation[{"msg": msg}] {
   ```

```
            container := input.review.object.spec.containers[_]
            not container.securityContext.runAsNonRoot
            msg := "Containers must set securityContext.runAsNonRoot to
    true"
            }
```

3. **Apply the template:**

   ```
   kubectl apply -f k8srequiredrunasnonroot_template.yaml
   ```

4. **Define and apply the constraint:** This tells Gatekeeper to enforce it cluster-wide:

   ```
   apiVersion: constraints.gatekeeper.sh/v1beta1
   kind: K8sRequiredRunAsNonRoot
   metadata:
     name: no-root-containers
   spec:
     match:
       kinds:
         - apiGroups: [""]
           kinds: ["Pod"]
   ```

5. **Test with a non-compliant Pod:** Try deploying a pod that lacks the **runAsNonRoot: true flag**. Gatekeeper will block it:

   ```
   apiVersion: v1
   kind: Pod
   metadata:
     name: root-test
   spec:
     containers:
       - name: nginx
         image: nginx
   ```

This quick tutorial allows security engineers to experience firsthand how GitOps and OPA policies in Anthos prevent misconfigurations from ever reaching production.

Anthos Config Management

ACM provides the foundation for centralized Kubernetes configuration, utilizing a GitOps workflow. A designated Git repository, known as the config repo, defines all cluster-level resources, including namespaces, RBAC bindings, network policies, and security controls. Every registered cluster in the Anthos ecosystem monitors this repository and continuously synchronizes its configuration state, eliminating drift and manual errors.

This design ensures IaC is extended to Kubernetes policy. Teams can manage versioned updates, audit changes, and enforce global standards without manually updating individual clusters.

Note: As deployments grow to hundreds of clusters, teams may encounter scaling challenges such as Git repo contention, sync conflicts, and latency in policy propagation. Addressing these requirements involves practices such as sharding configurations by fleet or environment, utilising hierarchical repository structures, and monitoring reconciliation performance through ACM metrics and error reporting dashboards.

Key components

Each cluster that runs ACM contains three core subsystems that drive enforcement:

- **Config sync**: A controller that watches the config repo and reconciles the cluster's live state against its declared configuration. Any drift is automatically corrected.

- **Hierarchy controller**: Enables hierarchical namespace management, allowing parent-child namespace relationships to propagate policies and resources automatically. This supports multitenancy and organizational scoping.

- **Multi-repo support**: ACM supports a flexible repo structure where teams can use a single shared repo or break configurations across environments (e.g., staging, production) using multiple Git repositories.

Gatekeeper

Gatekeeper extends Kubernetes admission control with policy as code enforcement using OPA. It allows you to define custom constraints (e.g., disallowing privileged containers) or utilise built-in ones that map to compliance frameworks and operational best practices.

When a resource (like a Pod or deployment) is submitted to the Kubernetes API, Gatekeeper evaluates it against declared policies. If the resource violates a constraint, Gatekeeper blocks it from being created.

Open Policy Agent integration

Gatekeeper integrates with OPA using constraint templates written in Rego (OPA's policy language). These templates define the validation logic; constraints apply that logic to specific Kubernetes objects. The following Rego policy snippet demonstrates how to create a Gatekeeper constraint template to block Kubernetes pods from running containers as root, enforcing security best practices at deployment. This example also includes a whitelist for trusted namespaces where exceptions are permitted:

```
# Example Rego rule to block containers running as root, with whitelist
support
violation[{
  "msg": sprintf("Privileged container usage is not allowed in namespace: %v",
[input.review.object.metadata.namespace]),
```

```
}] {
  input.review.object.spec.securityContext.runAsNonRoot == false
  not input.review.object.metadata.namespace == whitelist_ns[_]
}

# Define list of whitelisted namespaces
whitelist_ns := ["kube-system", "monitoring"]
```

Rego syntax explained: Rego is a declarative policy language used by OPA and Gatekeeper. Policies are written as rules that evaluate inputs (such as Kubernetes resources) and generate violations when specific conditions are met:

- **violation[{...}]** is a set of results returned when a policy condition fails.

- **input.review.object** refers to the Kubernetes resource being evaluated.

- **runAsNonRoot == false** detects containers configured to run as the root user.

- **not input.review.object.metadata.namespace == whitelist_ns[_]** excludes trusted namespaces defined in **whitelist_ns**.

This logic is embedded in a constraint template and deployed using **kubectl apply** as part of your configuration repository. Templates are reusable and parameterized, allowing teams to define environment-specific policies while accommodating approved exceptions.

Constraint templates

Gatekeeper enforces policies in Kubernetes using *constraint templates*, which define validation logic, and *constraints*, which apply that logic to resources. Key aspects include:

- **Prewritten or custom**: Teams can use Google-provided templates (e.g., Pod Security Standards, naming conventions, encryption policies) or build their own using Rego.

- **Admission Webhooks**: Gatekeeper runs as an admission webhook, enforcing constraints before the resource is persisted. This provides strong prevention over detection-based tools.

Implementation steps

To bring policy as code to life using ACM and Gatekeeper, follow these foundational steps:

1. **Set up Git repos**: Create and version-control a repository (or set of repos) that defines your Kubernetes manifests, policy templates, and constraints.

2. **Enable ACM**: Use the GCP console or CLI to install ACM on each registered cluster:

```
gcloud beta container hub config-management apply \
    --membership=prod-cluster \
    --config=acm-config.yaml
```

3. **Configure Gatekeeper**: Deploy constraint templates and constraint objects from the repo:

```
kubectl apply -f template-no-privileged-containers.yaml
kubectl apply -f constraint-no-privileged-containers.yaml
```

4. **Automated validation**: Set up CI checks to validate that commits to the repo follow policy structure and that test clusters do not reject synced resources.

When implemented correctly, any unauthorized configuration changes are either rejected at admission or automatically reverted via Git synchronization.

Best practices

Adopting ACM and Gatekeeper at scale requires thoughtful repo and environment design. Here are strategies that reduce operational friction:

- **Modular repo structure**: Separate global constraints (applied to all clusters) from environment-specific configurations using folders or separate repos.

- **Stages or branches**: Introduce policies into non-production environments using feature branches and promote them using pull requests with CI checks.

- **Continuous integration**: Use tools like OPA test frameworks or **conftest** to test Rego policies before merging to production:

```
conftest test deployment.yaml --policy ./policy
```

ACM and Gatekeeper offer a declarative, auditable, and automated way to enforce policy across Kubernetes clusters, ensuring that your multi-cloud workloads comply with organizational and regulatory standards.

In the next module, we will examine how Anthos extends these configurations and policies to external clouds like AWS and Azure using GKE-on-External-Cloud capabilities.

Managing GKE clusters with Anthos

Anthos enables organizations to operate Kubernetes clusters across clouds using a consistent interface and policy framework. Through GKE on AWS and GKE on Azure, Anthos brings the familiar GKE experience to external environments, while preserving cloud-native integrations such as VPC networking, IAM, and storage configurations specific to each provider. This allows platform teams to maintain uniformity without sacrificing cloud-specific flexibility.

By treating non-GCP clusters as first-class citizens, Anthos ensures that workloads deployed across AWS, Azure, and GCP benefit from central observability, security enforcement, and policy consistency. The architecture integrates deeply with existing public cloud infrastructure, enabling teams to meet local data residency requirements, business continuity planning, or regional redundancy needs.

That said, it is important to note specific *feature gaps and limitations* when running GKE outside of GCP:

- *Auto-upgrade and autopilot support* are currently exclusive to GKE on GCP. GKE on AWS and Azure require manual version upgrades and lacks native autopilot capabilities.

- *Version parity* may lag slightly on GKE for AWS and Azure, where the available Kubernetes versions are often a few releases behind those on GCP.

- *Node auto-scaling behavior* differs on GCP, Cluster Autoscaler is tightly integrated and highly responsive, while on AWS and Azure, auto-scaling may depend on cloud-native primitives (e.g., EC2 Auto Scaling or VMSS) and may require additional configuration.

- *Load balancing and networking* are implemented using cloud-specific components (e.g., AWS ALB, Azure Load Balancer), which may differ in behavior or feature support from GCP's native options like Cloud Load Balancing.

These nuances require platform engineers to balance abstraction with awareness of cloud-specific behaviors when building portable workloads across GKE environments.

Differences between GKE on GCP vs external clouds

While Anthos GKE aims to replicate the GCP-native Kubernetes experience on AWS and Azure, important operational and financial differences exist.

For example, *auto-upgrades and node auto-provisioning* behave differently depending on the external cloud provider's VM lifecycle APIs and image support. Teams may need to script their own update workflows or adapt Terraform/CloudFormation stacks to maintain parity with GCP's native automation.

Cost considerations are significant when operating GKE externally. Non-GCP clusters do not benefit from Google's native pricing tiers and committed use discounts. Additionally, observability tooling such as Cloud Operations Suite (formerly Stackdriver) often requires *custom exporters or OpenTelemetry sidecars*, increasing per-node overhead and ingest costs on platforms like Cloud Logging, BigQuery, or third-party SIEMs.

Networking configurations also introduce complexity. On GCP, GKE integrates natively with VPC routing, firewall rules, and global load balancing. In contrast, AWS and Azure require manual setup of VPCs/VNets, often lacking native support for features like global DNS, internal LBs, or cross-region peering. This increases operational burden and can lead to *unexpected data egress charges* if traffic routing is not optimized.

Service mesh observability differs as well. On GCP, Anthos Service Mesh integrates tightly with Cloud Monitoring and Cloud Trace. For external clouds, additional setup is required for metrics scraping (Prometheus), tracing (OpenTelemetry and Jaeger), and logging pipelines. You should monitor dashboards that track:

- `istio_requests_total` and `istio_request_duration_milliseconds` for service latency

- `istio_tcp_sent_bytes_total` for abnormal traffic spikes

- TLS coverage across service-to-service communication

- Policy violations or deny metrics from Envoy or OPA integrations

RBAC and IAM are another area of divergence. GCP-native GKE supports Cloud IAM bindings natively, while AWS and Azure clusters require federation using OIDC tokens, Workload Identity Federation, or third-party tools like Dex. This adds setup complexity and can result in inconsistent access controls if not managed uniformly.

These architectural nuances, when unaddressed, can lead to a fragmented security posture, cost overruns, and increased operational burden. Platform teams should proactively budget for additional logging infrastructure, observability tool licenses, and ingress configuration overhead when adopting Anthos GKE on external clouds.

Core features

Anthos GKE on external clouds replicates the complete GKE control and management plane while respecting the target provider's infrastructure primitives:

- **Standard GKE experience**: Use familiar GKE tooling: *kubectl*, node pools, auto-upgrades, and Workload Identity, without changes to your developer or CI/CD workflows.

- **Common Anthos control plane**: Manage and observe all clusters (GCP, AWS, Azure) from the GCP console or CLI, benefiting from shared policies, unified IAM, and visibility.

- **Federated networking**: Integrate seamlessly with each provider's network layer, VPCs in AWS or VNets in Azure, to allocate cluster subnets, configure LBs, and apply firewall rules.

The following figure explains what a unified control plan spanning across multi-clouds would look like:

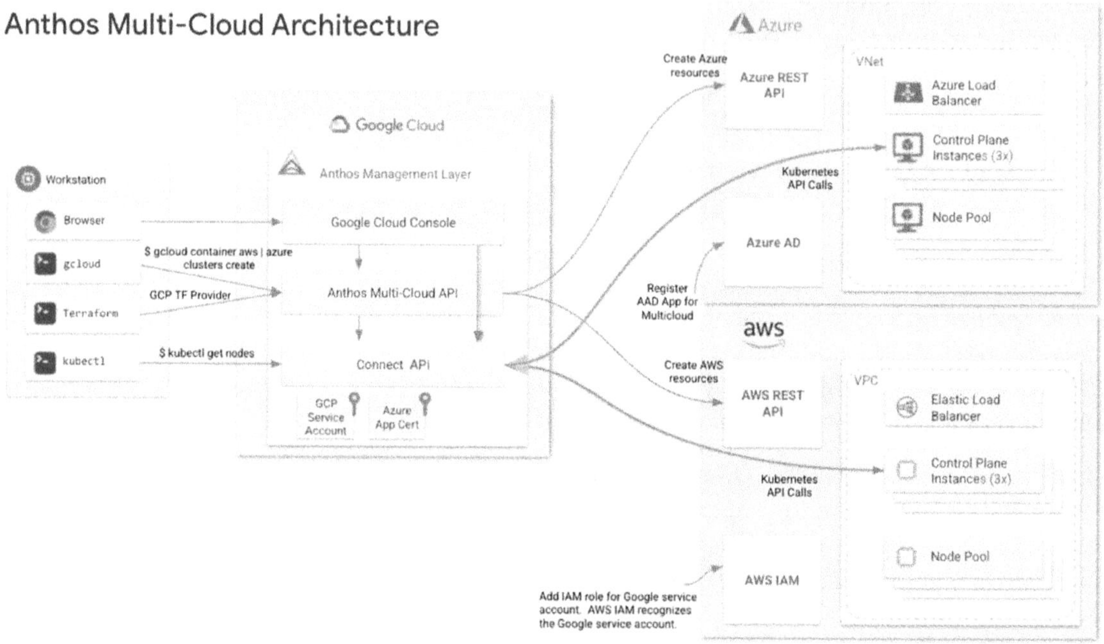

Figure 9.2: *Anthos unified control plane spanning AWS, Azure, and GCP clusters via GKE on external clouds*

This consistency enables policy enforcement through ACM and Gatekeeper even in non-GCP environments.

Setup and configuration

Getting started with GKE on AWS or Azure through Anthos involves configuring access, networking, and registration workflows; follow these steps:

1. **Create a service account**: In your GCP organization, create a service account with the necessary permissions to deploy and manage clusters on external clouds. Attach IAM roles such as `GKE Hub Admin, GKE Multi-Cloud Admin`, and `Service Account Token Creator`.

2. **Connect external cloud**: Use Anthos multi-cloud CLI (`gcloud container aws|azure clusters`) or console to provide credentials for AWS or Azure. Anthos provisions the control plane and worker nodes in that environment:

```
# Example: Provision a GKE cluster on AWS
gcloud container aws clusters create aws-test-cluster \
    --region=us-west-2 \
```

```
  --cluster-version=1.27 \
  --vpc-id=vpc-123456 \
  --subnet-ids=subnet-a,subnet-b \
  --iam-instance-profile=gke-node-role
```

- **Configure networking**: Define subnets, firewall rules, load balancer configs, and CIDR ranges within the external cloud. Anthos uses cloud-native constructs to map Kubernetes resources to underlying infrastructure.

- **Register clusters**: Once the external cluster is running, register it with GKE Hub to bring it under Anthos governance:

```
gcloud container hub memberships register aws-test-cluster \
  --gke-uri=... \
  --enable-workload-identity
```

Once registered, the cluster becomes eligible for ACM sync, Gatekeeper constraints, and mesh injection via Anthos Service Mesh.

Best practices

To ensure consistent operations and security across external clusters:

- **Network topology**: Plan regions and connectivity with care. Use VPNs or Direct Interconnects to minimize latency between clusters. Avoid overlapping CIDRs between cloud VPCs.

- **Identity integration**: Securely manage access using AWS **IAM roles for service accounts** (**IRSA**) or Azure Workload Identity Federation. Keep tokens short-lived and rotate them using CI automation.

- **Hybrid egress**: For scenarios where external clusters must connect to GCP-hosted services or on-prem apps, establish NAT gateways, egress proxies, or service mesh tunnels to enforce encryption and reduce exposure.

Anthos allows for maintaining GKE's opinionated Kubernetes stack in environments beyond Google Cloud, without sacrificing control, compliance, or observability.

Hybrid connectivity and Service Mesh

ASM and hybrid connectivity capabilities together provide a powerful framework for secure, observable, and resilient service-to-service communication across distributed environments. Whether your workloads reside on GCP, AWS, Azure, or on-premises infrastructure, ASM offers unified control over traffic behavior, authentication, and policy enforcement, helping platform teams implement zero-trust architectures and simplify service discovery across clusters.

ASM, built on Istio, enables **mutual TLS (mTLS)** encryption by default between services, ensuring secure communication while reducing developer overhead. Traffic policies, such as retries, circuit breaking, and fault injection, can be configured declaratively, allowing platform teams to manage service reliability without modifying application code.

Hybrid connectivity components such as *Cloud VPN and Cloud Interconnect* integrate with ASM to extend secure, low-latency connectivity across environments, ensuring consistent policy enforcement across on-premises and multi-cloud workloads. With integrated observability, ASM provides telemetry data including *latency metrics, error rates, and request traces*, enabling platform and security teams to monitor microservices effectively and troubleshoot issues quickly.

Together, ASM and hybrid connectivity form a *control plane for service communication*, aligning with zero-trust principles while improving operational efficiency, security posture, and developer productivity in hybrid and multi-cloud Kubernetes environments.

Advanced traffic control in ASM

Anthos Service Mesh provides more than just basic service-to-service encryption and observability. It allows security and platform engineers to control and shape traffic flows between services in a sophisticated manner. Fine-grained policies such as traffic mirroring, circuit breaking, fault injection, and header-based routing offer robust control over microservice communication.

However, *misconfigured traffic policies*, such as overly aggressive rate limits, incorrect destination rules, or unintended traffic splits, can lead to outages, degraded service performance, or broken user experiences. To mitigate these risks, it is essential to test new policies in a *staging or canary environment* before enforcing them in production. ASM supports preview modes and gradual rollouts, enabling the safe validation of traffic control configurations and helping teams strike a balance between agility and reliability.

Key advanced capabilities include:

- **Traffic splitting**: Gradually route a percentage of traffic to a new version of a service using Istio's VirtualService definitions. This is useful for progressive rollouts and A/B testing:

```
apiVersion: networking.istio.io/v1beta1
kind: VirtualService
metadata:
  name: payment-service
spec:
  hosts:
    - payment.example.com
  http:
    - route:
```

```
        - destination:
            host: payment-v1
          weight: 90
        - destination:
            host: payment-v2
          weight: 10
```

- **Fault injection and circuit breaking**: Test system resilience by simulating service latency, failure, or enforcing max concurrent connections per instance. This is valuable for validating reliability and recovery strategies.

- **Rate limiting**: Enforce limits on inbound or outbound requests, optionally using per-user quotas or service-level objectives.

- **Request or response headers manipulation**: Add custom headers for identity propagation, debugging, or observability tagging across services.

These controls enable production-safe experimentation and enforce boundaries between critical services in a controlled, observable manner.

ASM and hybrid connectivity capabilities provide a robust framework for secure, observable, and resilient service-to-service communication across distributed environments. Whether your workloads reside on GCP, AWS, Azure, or on-premises infrastructure, ASM offers unified control over traffic behavior, authentication, and policy enforcement, helping platform teams implement zero-trust architectures and simplify service discovery across clusters.

Anthos Service Mesh

ASM is Google's managed implementation of Istio, tailored to work seamlessly across hybrid and multi-cloud clusters. It supports consistent traffic management rules, telemetry collection, and strong security postures for Kubernetes workloads running anywhere.

Key capabilities include:

- **mTLS**: Encrypts traffic between workloads by default, preventing eavesdropping and spoofing attacks. Certificates are automatically rotated using Istio's built-in CA.

- **RBAC and auth**: Enables fine-grained access control by defining service-to-service communication policies. You can restrict traffic based on namespaces, service accounts, or request attributes.

- **Cross-cluster routing**: Allows services in one cluster to discover and communicate with services in another. This enables global load balancing and high availability across clouds.

- **Observability**: Exposes telemetry to request-level metrics, distributed traces, and service logs using tools like Prometheus, Grafana, and Google Cloud Operations Suite.

With these capabilities, ASM provides the foundation for secure microservice networking in Anthos environments.

Anthos Service Mesh enhances visibility and control of service-to-service traffic across environments; the following figure shows the Cloud Service Mesh components and features for managed Cloud Service Mesh:

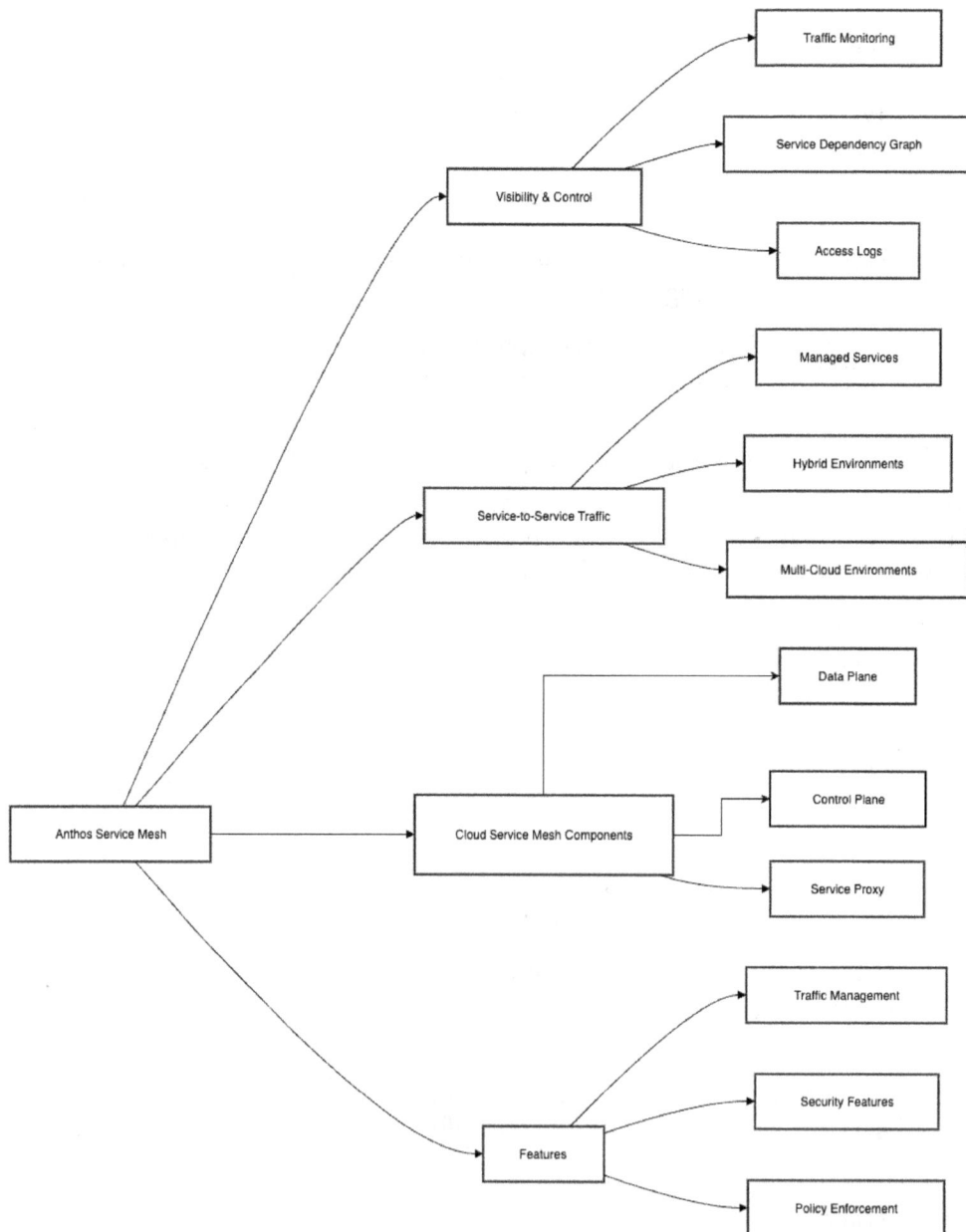

Figure 9.3: Cloud Service Mesh components and features for managed Cloud Service Mesh

Hybrid connectivity

Hybrid connectivity enables secure communication between on-premises environments and GCP-hosted services, bridging traditional infrastructure with modern cloud-native apps.

Key approaches include:

1. **VPN or interconnect**: Establish secure, low-latency connections between your data center and GCP. Cloud VPN is quick to provision, while dedicated or partner interconnect offers higher throughput and SLA-backed connectivity for latency-sensitive services.

2. **Anthos attached clusters**: Attach on-prem clusters to the Anthos control plane. These clusters run Connect Agent and participate in ACM and Service Mesh.

3. **Service discovery**: ASM dynamically resolves services across attached and native clusters. Mesh expansion enables seamless communication by federating service registries across environments.

   For example, A service in a GCP-hosted cluster can call `orderservice.namespace.svc.cluster.local` running on-prem as if it were local.

Hybrid connectivity ensures your services can communicate reliably and securely regardless of physical location, creating a consistent application layer across clouds and data centers.

The following are the best practices:

- **Plan IP overlaps**: Carefully segment IP address ranges to avoid conflicts across environments. If overlapping ranges are unavoidable, use NAT or translation gateways.

- **Zero-trust**: Use Istio's mTLS and PeerAuthentication policies in combination with Gatekeeper constraints to enforce authenticated, encrypted, and authorized traffic.

- **Test failover**: Use cross-cluster failover logic to simulate cluster unavailability and validate whether traffic is properly routed to alternate services or regions.

Anthos Service Mesh and hybrid connectivity unlock true cross-environment resilience, ensuring your services remain secure and discoverable regardless of where they are deployed.

Challenges and mitigation strategies

Operating in a multi-cloud environment offers flexibility and resilience but introduces various security and operational challenges. These challenges are not simply a product of scale; they arise from the fundamental differences in identity systems, networking architectures, policy enforcement models, and deployment practices between cloud providers. Teams risk misconfigurations, policy drift, and siloed observability without a consistent governance strategy.

This module addresses the most common pitfalls encountered in multi-cloud Anthos deployments and outlines clear mitigation strategies to help teams proactively reduce risk.

The following are the common multi-cloud security pitfalls:

- **Inconsistent IAM:** Each cloud platform has its own **Identity and Access Management (IAM)** model, ranging from IAM roles and service accounts in GCP, to IAM users and roles in AWS, and role assignments in Azure. Users may have fragmented identities without federation or bridging, resulting in role sprawl and an increased attack surface.

- **Unaligned network policies:** Networking rules such as security groups, firewall rules, and ingress/egress controls are implemented differently across clouds. This makes it difficult to enforce traffic policies uniformly, which can result in inconsistent behavior or accidental exposure of services.

- **High complexity:** Anthos introduces several new control layers, including GKE, Config Management, Gatekeeper, and Service Mesh. Without structured planning, this stack can be misconfigured, leading to conflicting policies, excessive resource consumption, or poor performance.

To mitigate these risks, teams can leverage automation tools and policy scanners such as:

- `kubeval`, `conftest`, or **OPA Gatekeeper** to validate Kubernetes configurations and custom policies across clusters.

- Google's **Policy Controller** for real-time policy auditing based on predefined ConstraintTemplates.

- IaC testing with `terratest` or `checkov` to ensure declarative GCP/AWS/Azure templates adhere to compliance standards.

- GitOps pipelines integrated with CI tools like Cloud Build or GitHub Actions to trigger automated policy checks on pull requests before deployment.

These pitfalls are common but avoidable. With the right design patterns and tooling, teams can abstract complexity and enforce consistency across cloud boundaries, ensuring secure, compliant multi-cloud operations.

Mitigations

The following strategic practices can mitigate these challenges and enable scalable, secure multi-cloud operations:

- **Federate identity:** Adopt **Security Assertion Markup Language (SAML)** or **OpenID Connect (OIDC)** federation with a central identity provider (e.g., Google Workspace, Okta, Active Directory). Use Workload Identity federation for service-level authentication across GCP, AWS, and Azure. This ensures a consistent and portable identity.

- **Designate a single control repo:** Consolidate all configuration and policy definitions into a single ACM repo. Segment by environment using folder structure or multi-repo support. Enforce code reviews and CI tests before merges.

- **CI/CD and testing**: Replicate your production topology in staging environments to validate config sync, constraint enforcement, and mesh behavior. Use **conftest**, OPA test suites, or **kubectl diff** to catch misconfigurations early.

- **Documentation and governance**: Maintain a central knowledge base for operational procedures, cluster registration steps, and known issues. Define runbooks for adding clusters, applying constraints, or updating policies in controlled phases.

Real-world considerations

In real-world deployments, architectural design is often influenced by external constraints such as regulatory mandates, latency requirements, or financial overhead:

- **Data residency**: Some data and workloads must stay in a specific jurisdiction. Anthos allows teams to enforce policy compliance while maintaining in-region cluster deployments. This is especially critical for financial, healthcare, and public sector workloads.

- **Latency**: Cross-cloud service mesh or long-haul traffic between regions can introduce latency. This affects user-facing apps and real-time processing pipelines. For performance-sensitive use cases, favour region-local routing or geo-aware load balancers.

- **Cost management**: Multi-cloud architectures often involve higher operational costs. Egress traffic, redundant CI pipelines, licensing for service mesh observability tools, and interconnect charges must be considered early in design.

While Anthos brings consistency to a multi-cloud footprint, strategic architecture, testing, and operations discipline are essential to achieving secure, performant, cost-effective outcomes.

Cross-cloud identity and governance

In multi-cloud and hybrid deployments, access control and data governance consistency are critical to ensuring security, compliance, and operational clarity. Anthos, through tools like Gatekeeper and Config Management, provides a strong foundation for unifying IAM models, enforcing encryption standards, and creating auditable environments.

Using Anthos, organizations can *enforce consistent IAM policies* across clusters running on GCP, AWS, and Azure, integrating with identity providers using SAML and OIDC for secure authentication. Gatekeeper can implement granular policies such as mandatory encryption for data in transit and at rest, restricting privileged container usage, and enforcing labeling for data classification.

ACM ensures that *role bindings, network policies, and encryption configurations are version-controlled and automatically synced* across environments, reducing misconfigurations and drift. Additionally, audit logging across clusters and clouds can be aggregated into Chronicle or SCC for centralized monitoring, enabling teams to maintain *clear visibility and compliance reporting across workloads regardless of their location.*

Compliance checklist for identity and governance

To help teams maintain security posture and compliance alignment, consider the following checklist:

- Enforce SSO integration across clouds (SAML or OIDC)
- Enable IAM policy inheritance and least privilege roles
- Ensure encryption at rest and in transit is enabled and enforced via Gatekeeper
- Enforce consistent RBAC policy across environments via ACM
- Configure audit logging and export to Chronicle/SCC or a third-party SIEM
- Periodically validate Git-tracked policy changes for drift detection

Auditing IAM Policies with GCP's Policy Intelligence

GCP's Policy Intelligence provides insights into IAM policies through features like:

- **Policy Analyzer:** Lists all permissions granted to users or service accounts across GCP projects, highlighting excessive access.
- **Policy Troubleshooter:** Simulates permission checks to validate access grants or denials.
- **Access Approval Logs:** Tracks sensitive resource Access Approvals.

To audit IAM across multi-cloud, follow these steps:

1. Use Policy Analyzer to export IAM bindings across GCP projects.
2. Cross-reference with federated identity mappings for AWS and Azure using external IdPs.
3. Ingest results into a central compliance dashboard (e.g., BigQuery or SCC).
4. Set up scheduled scans to detect permission drift or over-privileged accounts.

By leveraging these best practices, enterprises can build a *zero-trust-aligned, scalable identity and data governance model* that supports security, compliance, and operational efficiency across hybrid and multi-cloud infrastructures.

Identity across clouds

Multi-cloud identity management is a cornerstone of operational integrity. Without consistent access control, organizations risk duplicate user identities, mismatched roles, and audit gaps.

To address this, Anthos supports:

- **Workload Identity Federation**: Extend GCP IAM to AWS or Azure workloads, allowing Kubernetes pods or VMs to assume ephemeral Google credentials without storing static keys. This enables unified service-to-service authentication.

- **Single sign-on (SSO) and federation**: Integrate a single **identity provider (IdP)** with all environments. SAML or OIDC-based federation allows identity bridging across cloud-native (GCP IAM, AWS IAM) and enterprise (Active Directory, Okta) domains, reducing redundancy and improving traceability.

- **Anthos and Gatekeeper**: Use Gatekeeper to enforce identity-aware policies (e.g., restrict cluster-admin privileges, deny unauthenticated service accounts) across all clusters. Constraints are applied uniformly, reducing the risk of identity drift across clouds.

Data governance and compliance

Data governance in Anthos environments focuses on uniform policy enforcement across cloud providers, regardless of where workloads or data reside.

Key strategies include:

- **Encryption**: Apply consistent encryption policies using **customer-managed encryption keys (CMEK)** or equivalent across clouds. Enforcing encryption at rest and in transit ensures compliance with frameworks like the **Health Insurance Portability and Accountability Act (HIPAA)**, the **Payment Card Industry Data Security Standard (PCI-DSS)**, or FedRAMP.

- **Labels and tagging**: Use resource labels (e.g., `env=prod, compliance=HIPAA`) to identify regulated data. These metadata markers can trigger automated policy checks via Gatekeeper or external scanning tools.

- **Shared responsibility**: Acknowledge each cloud's native security responsibilities. Use Anthos to apply supplemental controls, like consistent RBAC or network policies, on top of platform defaults.

- **Logging and auditing**: Aggregate logs across all cloud platforms into a unified SIEM or data lake for visibility and compliance audits. Tools like Cloud Audit logs (GCP), AWS CloudTrail, and Azure Monitor can feed into centralized log pipelines.

This layered approach ensures that data governance policies are defined and verifiably enforced.

Governance strategy

Strong governance ensures that policy consistency, access integrity, and compliance objectives are sustainable at scale:

- **Central policy team**: Assign a dedicated team responsible for defining and reviewing multi-cloud policies. This group should monitor changes across GCP IAM, AWS IAM, Azure AD, and Anthos configurations. A quarterly policy review cycle is recommended to evaluate shifts in cloud provider IAM models, service usage patterns, and organizational requirements.

- **Periodic audits**: Establish a monthly cadence for reviewing environmental compliance. Validate policies against recognized benchmarks (e.g., CIS GCP Foundations, NIST 800-53) using tools like Security Health Analytics or OPA-based test suites. These audits should capture drift, expired credentials, and unapproved privilege escalations.

- **Standardized tools**: Prevent drift by using ACM and Gatekeeper to apply reusable, codified policies. Avoid ad-hoc YAML definitions by integrating policy validation into CI pipelines, enforcing structured pull requests, and enabling pre-commit hooks to lint and validate configuration files.

Cross-cloud identity and data governance are not just technical problems but foundational to operational trust and security assurance. Anthos provides the structure to scale these principles across a hybrid or multi-cloud architecture, allowing organizations to meet compliance and operational resilience goals proactively.

Complex made simple

Think of Anthos in a multi-cloud setting like running a global airline alliance:

- **Multiple airlines (Different clouds):**
    - Each airline (AWS, Azure, GCP, on-prem) has its planes and routes, analogous to separate infrastructure.
    - The challenge is that you need consistent boarding procedures, security checks, and flight coordination across them for a seamless passenger experience.

- **Anthos (Alliance HQ and common standards):**
    - Anthos acts as the alliance headquarters, creating universal policies for flight safety, baggage handling, and frequent flyer benefits (Kubernetes, ACM, ASM).
    - Each airline adheres to these standard rules, including how gates are assigned and how tickets are scanned.

- **Policy consistency (Unified rules for all):**
    - ACM is like distributing uniform checklists, protocols, and brand experiences to each airline. Whether you fly *AWS Air* or *Azure Airlines*, the security steps are identical.
    - Gatekeeper ensures no plane can fly without mandatory safety checks (pod policies, container restrictions).

- **Multi-cluster, hybrid connectivity (Global hubs and codeshares):**
  - o Just as alliances share routes (codeshares) or hubs, so do you unify on-prem, GCP, and external clusters via Connect Agents and Service Mesh.
  - o This ensures travellers (data) can move seamlessly between providers (airport gates) and are protected by consistent security screenings.

- **Data governance and identity:**
  - o Passengers' frequent flyer membership (IAM) must be recognized, no matter which airline or flight (cloud) they use. Similarly, Anthos manages cross-cloud identity and governance to ensure travellers cannot bypass security if they switch planes.

The key takeaway from the above is like a global airline alliance providing uniform security protocols, brand experience, and code sharing across different carriers. Anthos establishes consistent policies, identity management, and connectivity among multiple clouds and on-prem environments. This allows your workloads to *travel* seamlessly, securely, and uniformly, whether in AWS, Azure, or GCP.

Conclusion

Securing and operating modern workloads across multiple clouds and hybrid infrastructures is no longer an aspiration but a necessity. Anthos offers the necessary abstractions, tools, and integrations to build cloud-agnostic platforms that are secure, compliant, and manageable. From enabling consistent Kubernetes operations on AWS or Azure to implementing fine-grained access control using Gatekeeper, Anthos equips security, platform, and DevOps teams with a robust governance and enforcement framework.

Organizations can reduce complexity, enforce security posture, and gain operational clarity by adopting a unified configuration model, implementing GitOps-based controls, and leveraging federated service mesh and identity strategies. While Anthos does not remove the inherent differences across cloud providers, it provides the tooling to abstract, align, and control them under a centralized platform governance model.

As infrastructure evolves, Anthos ensures that your security policies and governance mechanisms evolve without compromising flexibility, portability, or speed.

The next chapter focuses on identity-aware access and endpoint security with *BeyondCorp Enterprise*. You will explore how Google's zero-trust model treats all traffic as untrusted and how to implement context-aware access controls, real-time device posture checks, and frictionless user experiences without depending on perimeter-based VPNs. This zero-trust foundation complements Anthos' platform governance with continuous, risk-aware security for users, devices, and apps.

Key takeaways

Anthos enables platform teams to implement a secure, consistent, and observable control plane across hybrid and multi-cloud environments. The following are the key learnings from this chapter:

- Using a unified control plane, Anthos brings consistency to GKE clusters across GCP, AWS, Azure, and on-prem environments.

- Config synchronization via ACM ensures cluster state consistency using GitOps principles.

- Gatekeeper and OPA provide policy as code enforcement for admission control across all clusters.

- GKE on AWS and Azure enables native workloads in other cloud providers to be governed under Anthos with centralized policy and identity.

- Anthos Service Mesh delivers mTLS, cross-cluster routing, and observability for microservice traffic across distributed clusters.

- Hybrid connectivity strategies like VPN and Interconnect securely connect on-prem workloads with cloud-native services.

- Common multi-cloud challenges such as IAM drift, network misalignment, and policy sprawl can be mitigated with federation, unified configuration repos, and strong CI/CD pipelines.

- Identity federation and Workload Identity approaches ensure access control is centralized and ephemeral across clouds.

- Data governance using CMEK, tagging, and centralized logging enforces compliance in diverse cloud environments.

Exercise

Objective

Apply a security policy that *blocks root containers* and enforce it across *multiple clusters*, including a *non-GCP (external)* cluster, using GitOps with Anthos.

Prerequisites:

- GCP project with billing enabled
- At least one GKE cluster (on GCP) and one external Kubernetes cluster (e.g., EKS or AKS)
- `gcloud`, `kubectl`, and `connect-register` CLI tools installed

- ACM enabled
- A Git repository to serve as your ACM config source

Step-by-step walkthrough:

1. **Register the external cluster to GCP:**
```
connect-register \
  --project=acme-hybrid \
  --location=us-central1 \
  --gke-uri=https://CLUSTER_ENDPOINT \
  --service-account-key-file=connect-agent-key.json
```

This connects an external EKS/AKS cluster to the Anthos control plane.

2. **Set up ACM:** Clone your config repo and create a folder structure:
```
config-repo/
├── clusters/
│   ├── gke-cluster/
│   └── eks-cluster/
├── namespaces/
└── policies/
```

3. **Create the Gatekeeper constraint template:** Create **template-no-root.yaml**:
```
apiVersion: templates.gatekeeper.sh/v1beta1
kind: ConstraintTemplate
metadata:
  name: k8snoroot
spec:
  crd:
    spec:
      names:
        kind: K8sNoRoot
  targets:
    - target: admission.k8s.gatekeeper.sh
      rego: |
        package k8snoRoot
        violation[{"msg": msg}] {
          input.review.object.spec.securityContext.runAsNonRoot == false
          msg := "Privileged container usage is not allowed."
        }
```

4. **Apply the constraint policy with exceptions:** Create **constraint-no-root.yaml**:
```
apiVersion: constraints.gatekeeper.sh/v1beta1
kind: K8sNoRoot
metadata:
```

```
    name: block-root-containers
spec:
  match:
    kinds:
      - apiGroups: [""]
        kinds: ["Pod"]
    namespaces:
      - "*"
    excludedNamespaces:
      - "logging"
```

This policy blocks root containers, except in the logging namespace.

5. **Commit and push:**

```
git add .
git commit -m "Add Gatekeeper root-blocking policy"
git push origin main
```

ACM will automatically sync this to all registered clusters.

6. **Validate policy enforcement**: Deploy a non-compliant pod:

```
apiVersion: v1
kind: Pod
metadata:
  name: bad-pod
spec:
  containers:
    - name: insecure
      image: nginx
      securityContext:
        runAsNonRoot: false
```

```
kubectl apply -f bad-pod.yaml
```

Expected result: Rejected with message: *Privileged container usage is not allowed.*

7. **Monitor violations (Optional):** Enable Policy Controller metrics and view violations in **Cloud Console** or use:

```
kubectl get constraintviolations
```

8. **Cleanup:**

```
kubectl delete -f constraint-no-root.yaml
kubectl delete -f template-no-root.yaml
```

References

1. https://cloud.google.com/anthos/docs/overview

2. https://cloud.google.com/anthos-config-management/docs/overview

3. https://cloud.google.com/anthos-policy-controller/docs/overview

4. https://cloud.google.com/kubernetes-engine/docs/how-to/workload-identity

5. https://cloud.google.com/anthos/multicloud/docs

6. https://cloud.google.com/service-mesh/docs/overview

7. https://cloud.google.com/architecture/implement-anthos-service-mesh-securely

8. https://cloud.google.com/anthos/clusters/docs/multi-cloud/aws

9. https://cloud.google.com/anthos/clusters/docs/multi-cloud/azure

10. https://cloud.google.com/solutions/anthos-security-blueprint

11. https://cloud.google.com/kubernetes-engine/enterprise/docs/architecture/anthos-hybrid-environment-reference-architecture-part-1-archived-dec-2023.pdf

Join our Discord space

Join our Discord workspace for latest updates, offers, tech happenings around the world, new releases, and sessions with the authors:

https://discord.bpbonline.com

## CHAPTER 10

Zero Trust and BeyondCorp Enterprise

Introduction

Traditional perimeter-based security models assumed that everything inside the network could be trusted. However, that assumption no longer holds in today's highly distributed, cloud-native, and remote-first environments. Users access enterprise resources from unmanaged devices, across various networks, and often from outside the organization's firewall, creating new blind spots and attack surfaces. In response to this shift, *zero-trust architectures* have emerged as the new foundation for modern security.

A key set of business drivers, *the rapid adoption of cloud services, expansion of remote and hybrid workforces, increased reliance on SaaS applications, and the growing sophistication of targeted attacks*, has accelerated the need to move beyond traditional trust models. These factors demand a model that is resilient, context-aware, and scalable across dynamic and decentralized environments.

At its core, zero trust flips the traditional model: instead of trusting by default, it requires *continuous verification* of every user, device, and access request, regardless of origin. All traffic is considered untrusted until proven otherwise, and every access decision is made dynamically based on identity, device posture, location, risk signals, and more. This approach drastically reduces reliance on legacy tools like **virtual private networks** (**VPNs**) and static IP allowlists, which often fail to adapt to the complexity and speed of cloud-native operations.

In this chapter, we explore Google's **BeyondCorp Enterprise**, a fully managed implementation of the zero trust model built upon the original BeyondCorp principles, which were pioneered within Google. BeyondCorp Enterprise combines secure access to web apps with deep device and user context, allowing organizations to enforce granular policies without introducing user friction.

We will discuss how BeyondCorp integrates with **Google Cloud Identity, Identity-Aware Proxy (IAP), Access Context Manager**, and **Endpoint Verification** to deliver adaptive access controls. You will also learn how to evaluate your environment's readiness for zero trust, migrate from legacy VPN-based models, and implement posture-aware policies that dynamically adjust based on device security signals and user context.

Whether you are just beginning your zero trust journey or looking to mature your existing GCP security posture, this chapter offers a practical blueprint for operationalizing Zero trust with BeyondCorp Enterprise.

Structure

This chapter is organized into the following sections:

- Introduction to Zero trust in GCP
- Zero trust principles
- BeyondCorp Enterprise Context Aware
- Securing internal applications with IAP
- Integrating device signals and posture checks
- Metrics to evaluate zero trust implementations
- Migrating VPN access to zero trust
- Complex made simple

Objectives

This chapter will equip you with a foundational understanding and practical tools needed to implement zero trust architecture on Google Cloud using BeyondCorp Enterprise. It introduces the core principles that define zero trust, including continuous verification, least-privilege enforcement, and device posture validation, and applies them across the identity, application, and infrastructure layers.

Through detailed step-by-step configuration examples, policy design considerations, and real-world migration stories, you will learn to secure internal applications without relying on perimeter-based VPNs, enforce fine-grained access control, and utilize GCP-native tools like IAP, Access Context Manager, and Endpoint Verification to assess context in real-time. By the end of this chapter, you will be equipped to architect and operate a scalable, context aware zero trust model for modern cloud environments.

Introduction to zero trust in GCP

Traditional perimeter-based security models, where trust is granted based on network location, are increasingly ineffective in a world of cloud-first applications, remote work, and sophisticated social engineering threats. These models assume that users inside the corporate network can be trusted by default. Unfortunately, attackers have learned to exploit that trust, often moving laterally within networks undetected.

Zero trust fundamentally reimagines this model. Instead of assuming anything inside the perimeter is safe, it adopts the principle of *never trust, always verify*. Every access request must prove its legitimacy, and access is granted dynamically based on identity, device health, location, time, and behavioral risk. This approach significantly reduces exposure to phishing, lateral movement, and credential-based attacks.

In Google Cloud, zero trust is implemented with BeyondCorp Enterprise, a commercial product based on Google's internal security model that eliminates reliance on VPNs. Instead, access is managed through cloud-native tools that validate both user and device context.

Zero trust access in GCP relies on three foundational pillars:

- **Identity-centric access control**: Cloud Identity and IAM are used to verify and authorize users.

- **Device posture verification**: Evaluates endpoint health using Endpoint Verification, ensuring that only secure devices are granted access.

- **Context-aware policies**: With Access Context Manager, GCP enforces fine-grained controls based on signals like geolocation, time of day, or IP reputation.

The following figure shows how BeyondCorp replaces VPN-based access with context-aware proxy controls for enterprise apps:

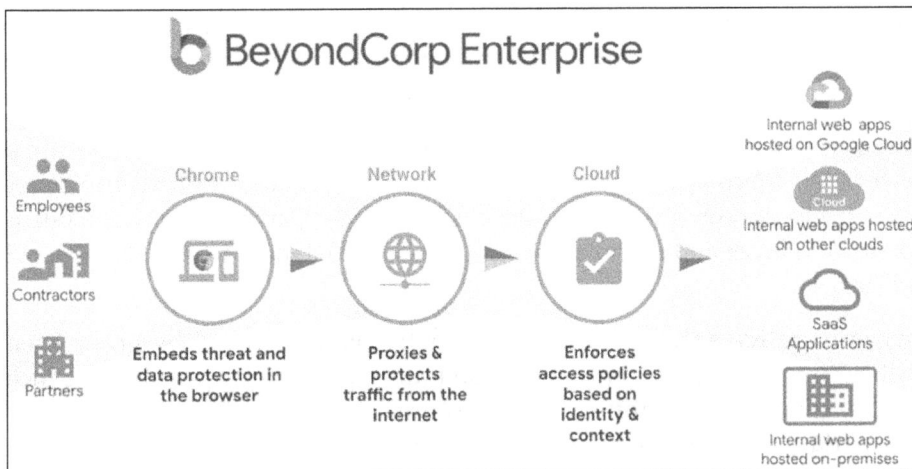

Figure 10.1: BeyondCorp Enterprise enforcing Zero trust with identity and context

Together, these components enable real-time, adaptive access decisions that minimize the impact of compromised credentials and devices. Instead of relying on the network for trust, zero trust in GCP establishes trust with every request, enhancing the safety of your cloud environment by design.

Zero trust principles

Zero trust in Google Cloud is not a single tool or product but an *architectural mindset*. It assumes that threats may originate both outside and inside the network and requires that no request, user, or device be implicitly trusted. Instead of relying on static perimeter controls, zero trust dynamically evaluates context, including user identity, device posture, location, and request time, before granting access to applications or data.

A key tenet of this model is the *principle of least privilege*, which enforces that users and services are granted only the minimum access necessary to perform their tasks. For example, a developer working on backend microservices should not have access to financial reporting tools or billing data. In contrast, a member of the finance team should not have permissions to modify application infrastructure or CI/CD pipelines. By enforcing such role-based segmentation, organizations can significantly reduce the blast radius of compromised credentials or insider threats.

This section will examine the fundamental building blocks that underpin zero trust implementations, including Google's BeyondCorp model. You will learn how modern security principles are applied using native GCP services and how these practices transform everything from authentication and authorisation to network segmentation and real-time enforcement.

Core concepts of zero trust

Zero trust architecture is built on the idea that no user or device, whether inside or outside the network, should be trusted by default. Instead, access decisions must be enforced on a per-request basis, considering as much real-time context as possible. This section outlines the three core concepts that are foundational to zero trust in Google Cloud:

- **Micro-perimeters**: Traditional networks create a single perimeter, typically protected by a VPN. In contrast, zero trust applies fine-grained, context-driven security to each application or service boundary. These micro-perimeters are established at the application layer and enforced using IAP, Load Balancer frontends, or service mesh policies.

- **Dynamic policy enforcement**: Access control is determined by group membership or IP address and is evaluated based on multiple runtime signals. These include user identity (via Cloud Identity), device posture (via Endpoint Verification), geolocation, time of day, login behavior, and risk levels (based on Google's security signals).

- **Least privilege access**: Access should be narrowly scoped to what the user or service needs, no more, no less. This means avoiding blanket roles and ensuring every action is governed by fine-grained IAM or VPC-SC boundaries. Users, workloads, and devices are treated as untrusted by default until verified.

Historical evolution to BeyondCorp

The shift to zero trust has been a gradual evolution. It did not happen overnight; it emerged from the realization that legacy models could not keep up with modern attacker tactics and distributed workforces. Here is a breakdown of how this evolution occurred:

- **VPN-centric beginnings (Pre-2009):** For years, organizations protected internal systems by placing them behind VPNs. Once authenticated, users had extensive access to internal resources. This model relied heavily on the notion that being *inside the network* implied trust.

- **Google's BeyondCorp (2009–2018):** In response to attacks such as Operation Aurora in 2009, Google launched BeyondCorp. It eliminated the notion of *inside vs. outside* the network. Instead, every request was validated using device posture, user identity, and policies enforced at the proxy layer.

- **BeyondCorp Enterprise (2018–present):** Google Cloud's commercial offering, BeyondCorp Enterprise, extends these principles to customers. It integrates directly with GCP workloads, GKE, custom applications, and SaaS platforms, providing posture-based access, threat intelligence integrations, and compliance reporting out of the box.

This transition represents a cultural and architectural pivot, shifting focus from protecting networks to safeguarding users and services through identity and context.

Architectural guidelines

Certain architectural principles must be followed to operationalize zero trust on GCP effectively. These guidelines shape the interaction between identity, policy, and infrastructure to provide secure, adaptive access:

- **Identity-centric access control**: All users must authenticate using strong mechanisms such as **multi-factor authentication (MFA)**, **single sign-on (SSO)**, or Identity Federation (**Security Assertion Markup Language (SAML)** or **OpenID Connect (OIDC)**). Cloud Identity should serve as the authoritative source of truth, supported by enforced password policies and step-up authentication for high-risk actions.

- **Device compliance enforcement**: Zero trust assumes devices can be compromised. Before granting access to applications, tools like Endpoint Verification are used to check OS version, encryption status, and root or jailbreak status. Posture-based conditions can be written in Access Context Manager and enforced at runtime:

```
accessPolicies:
  - name: "require_compliant_device"
    conditions:
      devicePolicy:
        osConstraints:
          - osType: DESKTOP_WINDOWS
            minimumVersion: "10.0.19044"
        encryptionStatuses:
          - ENCRYPTED
```

- **Policy as code**: Access policies should be defined and managed using **Infrastructure-as-Code (IaC)** tools, such as **Terraform** or the **gcloud CLI**, which enable teams to codify access conditions (including identity, device posture, and location) in a repeatable and auditable format. For example, Terraform modules can declare rules in Access Context Manager, while gcloud commands can update them via script. For teams unfamiliar with these tools, it is recommended to start with small, well-documented policy files and utilize version control systems (e.g., Git) for change tracking. All policies should be peer-reviewed, tested in staging, and validated before promotion to production to avoid unintended lockouts or over-permissiveness.

- **Monitoring and anomaly detection**: Logging and telemetry are essential. Stackdriver Logging, Access Transparency, and Event Threat Detection should be enabled to ensure visibility into access events, policy enforcement decisions, and suspicious behavior. This data feeds into SIEMs or alerting systems.

Together, these principles ensure that credentials not only gate access but are also accompanied by active trust signals that are continuously enforced across Google Cloud's control and data planes.

The following table outlines key zero trust architectural components and their functional purposes in GCP:

Component	Description	GCP Service(s) used
Identity verification	Ensure strong user identity via SSO, MFA, and federation.	Cloud Identity, identity platform
Device posture enforcement	Validate OS version, encryption, and **mobile device management** (**MDM**) compliance before access.	Endpoint verification, BeyondCorp
Context-aware access	Grant access based on user role, device, and location.	Access Context Manager, IAP
Granular policy enforcement	Apply fine-grained permissions on a per-app or per-resource basis.	IAM conditions, BeyondCorp policies
Logging and monitoring	Continuously track access patterns and violations.	Cloud Logging, security command centre

Table 10.1: Zero trust architectural components and their functional purposes

BeyondCorp Enterprise Context Aware

Zero trust policies are most effective when enforced with both identity and real-time context awareness. This section introduces Google's BeyondCorp Enterprise framework, which shifts security from the network layer to the application and user layers. BeyondCorp enables organizations to transition away from VPN-based trust models by providing scalable, fine-grained access control based on *user identity, device trustworthiness, and environmental context.*

- **User identity** refers to authenticated attributes tied to the person making the request, such as their email address, group membership (e.g., *engineering@company.com*), or role (e.g., developer vs. finance). For instance, a developer might have access to a code repository, while a finance team member would be restricted to billing systems.

- **Device posture** refers to the security state of the device being used. This includes signals like whether the device is encrypted, running an approved OS version, or enrolled in MDM. For example, even if a developer is authenticated correctly, access can be denied if they are using an outdated laptop lacking disk encryption.

By integrating with GCP IAM, Access Context Manager, and other native services, BeyondCorp enables teams to make dynamic, real-time access decisions, evaluating *who* is accessing *what, from where,* and *under what conditions.* This continuous evaluation ensures that only trusted users on secure, compliant devices can access sensitive workloads.

BeyondCorp Enterprise overview

BeyondCorp Enterprise provides a scalable, fully managed framework for enforcing zero trust in cloud-native environments. Unlike legacy models that assume trust based on network boundaries, BeyondCorp evaluates each request in real-time using rich context, identity, device posture, and environmental signals.

At the heart of BeyondCorp is *context-aware access,* a framework that applies security policies based on user and device attributes:

- **User identity**: Every access attempt is associated with a verified identity, using GCP-native Cloud Identity or federated identities (SAML/OIDC). Requests carry identity tokens encoding user metadata, group memberships, and authentication context.

- **Device posture**: Devices must be enrolled and verified through **Endpoint Verification**. Device signals such as OS version, encryption status, certificate presence, and patch level are evaluated dynamically. Non-compliant or unverified devices may be blocked or experience restricted access.

- **Location and network context**: BeyondCorp can optionally integrate IP reputation, geolocation, and ASN data to assess risk. For example, login attempts from anonymised networks, such as TOR, or unexpected geographies can be flagged or blocked.

- **Granular policies**: Organizations can enforce specific rules—for instance, allowing the finance team to access dashboards only from corporate-managed Windows 11 machines with full disk encryption and up-to-date antivirus protection.

Prerequisites and limitations: Implementing BeyondCorp requires integration with Google Cloud Identity or a federated identity provider, as well as enrollment of devices via Endpoint Verification. Environments lacking centralised device management or with unmanaged endpoints may encounter adoption challenges. Additionally, deploying granular context-aware policies requires a well-maintained IAM and Access Context Manager setup. Legacy applications without proxy compatibility or modern authentication support may require rearchitecture to leverage BeyondCorp's capabilities fully.

The following figure illustrates how BeyondCorp integrates identity, device posture, and location to evaluate access decisions dynamically:

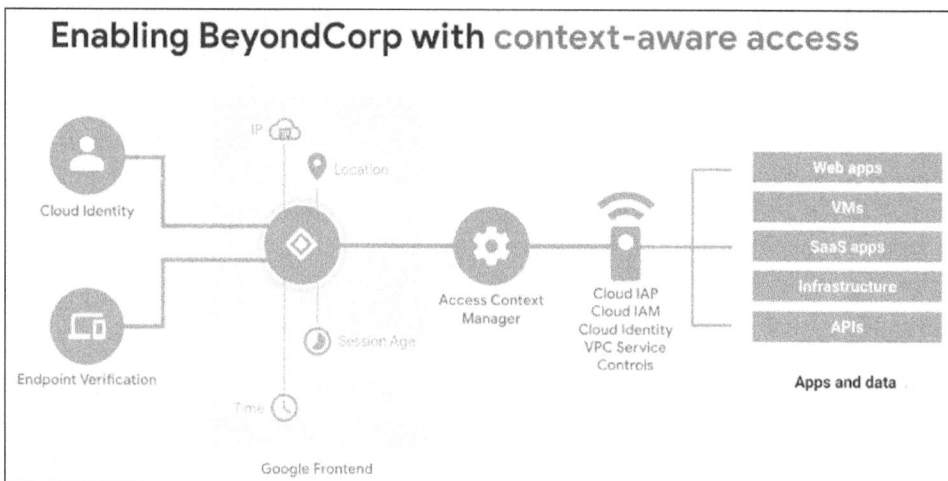

Figure 10.2: High-level flow of context-aware access evaluation in the BeyondCorp Enterprise

BeyondCorp Enterprise includes:

- **Policy console**: A unified control plane for defining, simulating, auditing, and deploying context-aware policies. This integrates with Access Context Manager and supports a staged rollout of policies.

- **IAM integration**: IAM policies now support conditions tied to device compliance and user attributes. For example:

```
condition {
  expression = "device.encryption_status == 'ENCRYPTED' && request.auth.
claims.group == 'finance-team'"
  title       = "Finance Devices Only"
  description = "Access allowed only from encrypted finance laptops."
}
```

- **Real-time enforcement**: If a previously compliant device becomes non-compliant (e.g., loses encryption or changes its antivirus state), access is revoked immediately without requiring a log-out or session reset.

This architectural approach ensures that access enforcement is continuous rather than static, responding to changes in user, device, or environment.

Identity-based policies

BeyondCorp Enterprise integrates with IAM to extend zero trust to identity and role-level granularity. The following capabilities illustrate how BeyondCorp Enterprise leverages IAM to enforce granular, context-aware zero trust policies:

- **IAM conditions**: IAM now supports rich conditions that evaluate identity signals and environmental context. For example, you can enforce that a user's device must be encrypted and up to date if they are in a sensitive role.

- **Service accounts**: For machine-based interactions, policies can evaluate service account trust levels, origin IPs, or Workload Identity bindings. For instance, CI/CD pipeline access might necessitate execution on GKE with Shielded VMs.

- **Group-based access**: Integration with Google Groups or Active Directory enables policies to reference dynamic team memberships. *Example:* Sales engineers can access internal CRM dashboards from unmanaged networks, provided they are using up-to-date laptops registered to the company.

- **Practical tip for communicating policy changes**: Zero trust policy enforcement can impact user workflows. To ease adoption:

  o Proactively notify users before enforcing new conditions (e.g., email or Slack notifications).

  o Use change banners in internal portals to highlight upcoming policy requirements.

  o Provide self-service help (FAQs, step-by-step guides) for users to validate device posture or understand group-based access.

  o Pilot changes with a limited user group and gather feedback before rolling out to the organization.

These measures not only help with transparency but also foster a security-first culture by helping users understand why the policy exists and how to remain compliant.

The following table outlines examples of identity-based policy enforcement across common departments:

Department	Access condition	Enforcement policy example
Finance	Must use a company-managed device with encryption	Allow access to financial tools only on encrypted laptops
Developers	Allow access from any location with device posture verified	Enable staging access with a patched OS and verified user group
Contractors	Permit time-bound access only during working hours from whitelisted IPs	Restrict external access to non-prod apps between 9 AM to 6 PM and enforce automatic revocation after 7 days
Executives	Enforce device attestation and MFA for all access types	Require Titan M-backed devices with biometric auth

Table 10.2: Examples of identity-based policy enforcement

To ensure smooth deployment, BeyondCorp policy adoption is staged in three distinct phases:

- **Pilot**: Start with a non-critical internal application. Implement context-aware policies in audit mode to assess policy performance without hindering users.

- **Expand** by onboarding additional business-critical applications (e.g., admin portals, customer dashboards, or Git repositories).

- **Refine**: Optimize policies by utilizing feedback loops, analytics dashboards, and introducing risk scoring across users and devices.

The following are the best practices:

- **Contextual risk scoring**: Combine various inputs (role sensitivity, device risk, geo anomalies) to calculate a decision confidence score.

- **Audit mode testing**: Always simulate a new policy before enforcing it. Audit mode logs violations while preserving access.

- **Change communication**: Inform users early about new enforcement models. Provide alternative access paths for support and reduce frustration.

These features turn BeyondCorp Enterprise into a practical zero trust engine, enabling secure, seamless access for the workforce and workloads.

Securing internal applications with IAP

As organizations adopt zero trust, securing internal applications becomes a critical aspect of the journey. Traditional access models depend on network perimeter controls, such as VPNs, to regulate entry to applications. However, these models often grant overly broad access once a user is *inside*. IAP reverses this paradigm by enforcing authentication and access policies at the application level, regardless of the user's location. It enables secure, internet-facing access to internal services while continuously evaluating the user's identity, device posture, and contextual signals, such as location or time.

This section will explore how IAP works architecturally and how to configure it to protect your enterprise applications. It also highlights common deployment issues, such as incorrect backend service configurations, missing OAuth client IDs, or misaligned firewall rules, and provides practical troubleshooting tips like checking IAP audit logs, validating HTTPS health checks, and ensuring service accounts have the correct roles (e.g., IAP-secured Web App User) to minimize downtime and provide reliable enforcement.

Identity-Aware Proxy architecture

IAP provides a scalable and modern alternative to VPNs for securing internal applications. It functions as a secure reverse proxy, positioned in front of HTTP(S) workloads deployed on GCP or on-premises environments. Additionally, it brokers access decisions based on verified user identity and rich context.

Instead of granting blanket access to a private network, IAP ensures that each connection is authenticated and authorized individually. This minimizes lateral movement risks typically associated with VPNs.

The following are the core components of the IAP architecture:

- **The IAP web proxy** serves as the entry point for users accessing protected resources. It prompts authentication and functions as the enforcement point for policies.

- **OAuth or OIDC integration**: IAP integrates with Google Sign-In, Workspace, or third-party identity providers via SAML/OIDC.

- **Context-aware IAM policies**: Uses IAM roles like `roles/iap.httpsResourceAccessor` along with Access Context Manager to evaluate device and user context.

- **Backend application**: Can run in App Engine, GKE, Compute Engine, or even on-prem through HTTPS and Cloud Load Balancing.

The following figure shows how IAP enforces per-user, per-device access to protected apps:

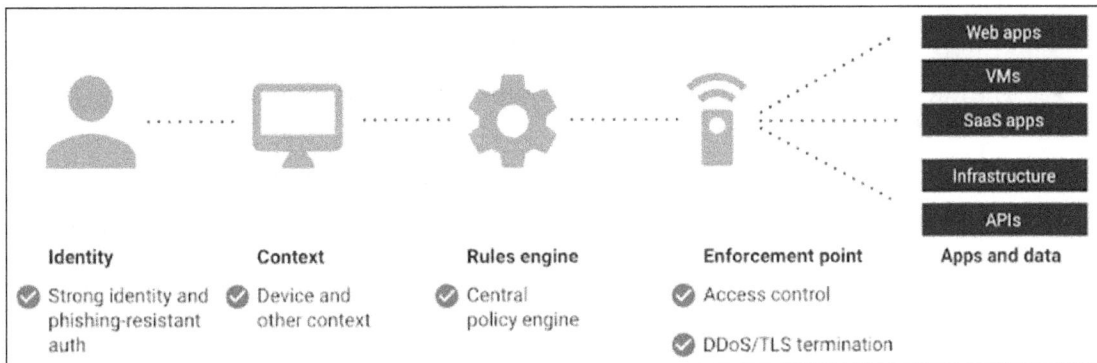

Figure 10.3: IAP secures application access by verifying user identity and device context

Configuring IAP for internal access

Setting up IAP involves enabling the proxy, securing your endpoints, and layering in identity and context-aware logic; follow these steps:

1. **Enable IAP**:

   a. Navigate to the GCP Console.

   b. Locate your App Engine app, HTTPS Load Balancer, or Cloud Run service.

   c. Toggle IAP to *enabled* and ensure you have OAuth consent configured.

2. **Assign IAM roles**:

   a. Grant **roles/iap.httpsResourceAccessor** to users, groups, or service accounts that should have access.

   b. Use IAM conditions to attach device or location-based rules:

   ```
   condition {
       title       = "Device Encryption Requirement"
       expression  = "request.device.encryption_status == 'ENCRYPTED'"
   }
   ```

3. **Integrate context-aware signals:**

   a. Configure Access Context Manager to evaluate posture (OS version, IP range, region).

   b. Set up Endpoint Verification for enrolled device compliance.

4. **Certificates and custom domains:**

   a. Most production workloads use a custom domain fronted by HTTPS load balancing.

   b. Upload SSL certificates or use managed certs for secure access.

The following are examples of deployment:

- The internal admin portal running on Compute Engine is protected behind an HTTPS Load Balancer.

- IAP is enabled with access granted to **admin@example.com** and the *IT Ops* group.

- A condition is added to allow access only from encrypted ChromeOS or Windows devices:

```
accessPolicies:
  - name: "admin-access"
    conditions:
      devicePolicy:
        osConstraints:
```

```
    - osType: DESKTOP_CHROME_OS
    - osType: DESKTOP_WINDOWS
encryptionStatuses:
    - ENCRYPTED
```

The following are the best practices:

- **Replace VPN**: Utilise IAP as a modern alternative to VPNs in internal applications. It minimizes overhead and enhances granularity.

- **Multi-factor enforcement**: Pair IAP with identity providers that support MFA for stronger assurance.

- **Path-specific policies**: Use IAM per URL path if your application supports multiple roles (e.g., `/admin, /billing, /read-only`).

By implementing IAP with context-aware access, organizations can enhance internal app security and provide zero trust access without exposing backends to unnecessary network access.

The following table shows a comparison of IAP vs. traditional VPN models across core access dimensions:

Dimension	IAP (zero trust)	VPN (Traditional)
Access Method	Web-based, IAP	Network tunnel into the internal IP range
Device Validation	Enforced per-request with posture checks	Manual or absent
User Context Awareness	Yes (identity, location, risk score)	Limited or none
Scalability	Fully managed via Google Cloud	Requires client installation and upkeep
Logging & Audit	Detailed logs tied to IAM and device state	IP-level logs, limited user attribution
Operational Costs	Lower overhead due to no client infrastructure and reduced helpdesk load	Higher due to VPN servers, client maintenance, and support

Table 10.3: IAP vs. traditional VPN comparison

Integrating device signals and posture checks

As zero trust matures, device posture becomes as critical as user identity in the access equation. Attackers often exploit weak or unmanaged endpoints, such as unpatched operating systems, unencrypted disks, or jailbroken phones, as entry points. Google Cloud mitigates these risks by continuously assessing the security health of user devices and incorporating this posture data into access decisions.

BeyondCorp Enterprise leverages Endpoint Verification and device inventory to gather real-time signals, including operating system version, encryption status, device management state, and security patch levels. These signals are evaluated during every access request, ensuring that only devices that meet organizational security policies can access sensitive applications and data.

Admins can enforce granular access conditions, for example:

- Allow access only from encrypted and company-managed devices.
- Require devices to have up-to-date security patches before accessing sensitive workloads.
- Block access from devices with known vulnerabilities or non-compliant configurations.

For stronger guarantees, organisations can incorporate hardware-backed attestation using technologies such as Titan M (Android) or **Trusted Platform Module** (**TPM**) on Windows devices. These chips provide cryptographic validation of the device's integrity, ensuring that even low-level components, such as firmware and bootloaders, have not been tampered with. This makes it significantly harder for attackers to spoof device trust or bypass posture checks through firmware-level attacks.

Posture checks can be combined with user identity, location, and application context to enforce adaptive access controls, aligning with zero trust principles while maintaining productivity. This device-aware approach significantly reduces the attack surface by ensuring that compromised, risky, or unmanaged endpoints cannot bypass controls, regardless of network location.

Device identity and posture

Zero trust is not just about authenticating users; it also ensures that the devices used to access resources are trustworthy. Google Cloud offers multiple mechanisms to verify and enforce device posture, ensuring that only healthy, secure endpoints are permitted access to sensitive environments.

The following are enforcing trusted devices:

- **Client certificates**: In high-security environments, certificates may be issued by GCP or an enterprise Certificate Authority and installed on corporate-managed laptops. These certificates enable identity binding at the device layer, ensuring access is granted only to authenticated and provisioned endpoints.
- **Endpoint verification**: A Chrome extension or native system agent is used to report device-level telemetry, including:
    - Operating system and version
    - Patch and update status
    - Disk encryption status
    - Presence of security software (e.g., antivirus)

This data integrates into Access Context Manager to enforce policies based on real-time posture:

- **Hardware-backed attestation**: For environments with elevated security requirements (e.g., finance, healthcare, and regulated workloads), devices can leverage secure cryptographic chips, such as the **Titan M (Android)** or **TPM (Windows/Linux)**. These chips provide tamper-resistant validation of firmware and boot processes, ensuring that devices have not been compromised at a hardware or firmware level. This level of assurance is crucial for protecting against sophisticated threats, such as firmware implants or rootkits.

- **Dynamic risk classification**: Based on posture, devices are automatically scored as compliant, non-compliant, or untrusted. For instance, a device with antivirus disabled or missing OS patches may be downgraded to an unhealthy state, triggering conditional access (e.g., view-only permissions or a whole block).

BeyondCorp Enterprise device security

BeyondCorp Enterprise builds on posture signals with deeper hardware- and platform-level validation.

The following are the device attestation and platform trust mechanisms:

- **Hardware-backed attestation:** Devices equipped with chips such as Titan M (on Pixel) or TPM (on enterprise laptops) are validated for secure boot status, firmware integrity, and verified OS layers, providing strong assurance against firmware-level attacks or tampering.

- **Platform compliance:**
  - **For Windows**: Enforce patch baselines, BitLocker encryption, and Windows Defender status.
  - **For macOS**: Validate FileVault encryption, OS version, and presence of MDM configuration profiles.

- **Mobile devices:**
  - Posture is validated through MDM integrations.
  - Android Enterprise or iOS device compliance includes enforcement of screen lock, encryption, and app-level policy controls.

The following are the everyday use cases:

- **Contractor access**: Contractors are permitted to use their personal devices. Context-aware rules can permit limited access (e.g., dev or staging environments) if the device meets essential posture criteria, such as a supported OS version and active antivirus software.

- **High-security environments**: Industries like healthcare, finance, and government can enforce strict device posture requirements, full-disk encryption, no rooted/jailbroken devices, frequent patching, and session protection through password and biometric enforcement.

The following are the best practices for integrating MDM with BeyondCorp:

- **Utilise MDM for centralised device visibility and control:** Ensure all corporate and BYOD endpoints are enrolled in a supported MDM platform (e.g., Google Endpoint Management, Microsoft Intune, Jamf, or Workspace ONE).

- **Enforce baseline configurations via MDM:** Define posture baselines such as OS version, encryption, password policy, and app control, and sync these with Access Context Manager policies.

- **Leverage API integrations:** Connect MDM signals (device ID, compliance status) to BeyondCorp using context-aware access attributes, ensuring dynamic policy enforcement at runtime.

- **Monitor and remediate drift:** Regularly audit device compliance through MDM dashboards and configure automatic remediation workflows (e.g., quarantine non-compliant devices or block access).

- **Apply conditional access:** Tailor access levels based on the device's risk posture reported by MDM, compliant devices may receive full access. In contrast, partially compliant ones may be restricted to read-only access.

The following are the steps to the implementation workflow:

1. **Enroll devices**:

   a. Distribute the Endpoint Verification agent or enforce MDM profiles.

   b. Register devices via Google Workspace or enterprise tools.

2. **Link devices to users**: Devices appear in the Cloud Identity or Workspace admin console and can be associated with a specific user account or organizational unit.

3. **Create Contextual Access Policies**:

   a. Use Access Context Manager to define posture-dependent access tiers. For example:

   ```
   accessPolicies:
     - name: "restricted-production-access"
       conditions:
         devicePolicy:
           osConstraints:
             - osType: DESKTOP_MAC
               minimumVersion: "13.5"
   ```

```
encryptionStatuses:
  - ENCRYPTED
requireScreenLock: true
```

b. This rule enforces that only encrypted, up-to-date macOS laptops with screen lock enabled may access production.

Posture verification and device context transform zero trust from an identity-only approach to an identity-plus-device approach. BeyondCorp Enterprise ensures that these signals are continuously enforced, making access decisions reactive to real-world changes in device health.

The following architecture figure outlines how device trust and context are incorporated into BeyondCorp access decisions:

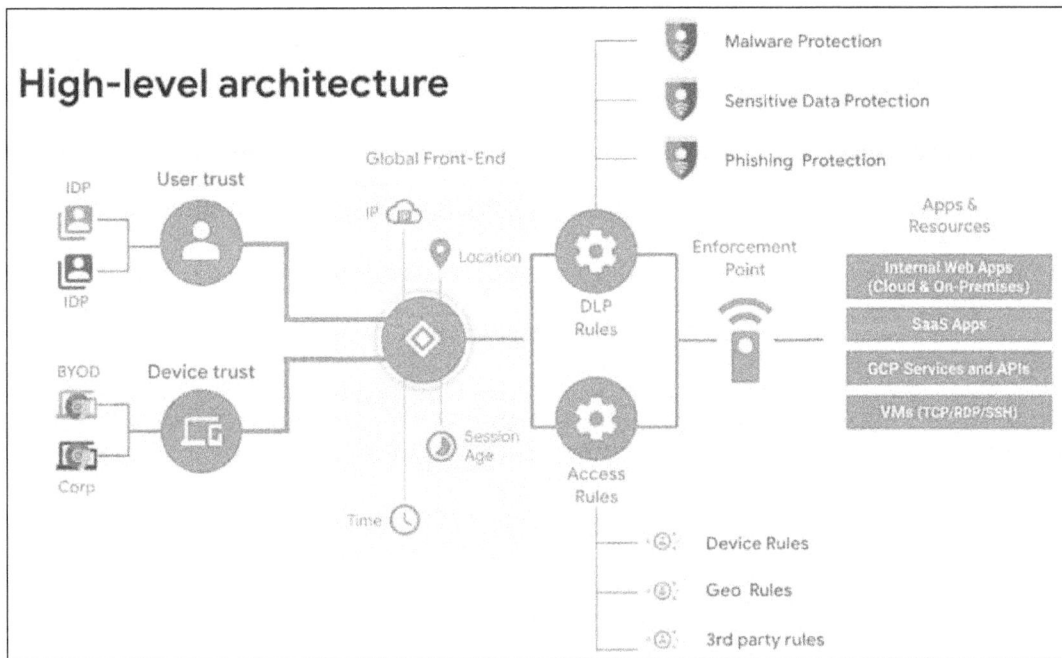

Figure 10.4: Device-based access enforcement via context-aware access and Endpoint Verification

Metrics to evaluate zero trust implementations

Implementing zero trust is only half the battle; measuring its success is just as crucial. Without metrics, it is impossible to determine whether your posture enforcement is effective, user friction is minimized, or policy violations are trending in the right direction. Metrics provide the feedback loop needed to fine-tune controls and justify the investment. This section will explore how to quantify zero trust maturity using actionable KPIs and observability tooling within GCP.

Key metrics for zero trust evaluation include:

- **Policy compliance rate:** Percentage of devices and identities meeting posture and identity requirements during access attempts.

- **Access denial rate:** Tracking how often risky access attempts are denied, segmented by reason (e.g., device non-compliance, location anomalies).

- **User friction indicators:** Login success rates, MFA challenge frequency, and device re-authentication rates, to measure the impact on user experience.

- **Incident reduction:** Number and severity of security incidents attributable to compromised endpoints or identity abuse before and after zero trust enforcement.

- **MTTD and MTTR improvements:** Assessing reductions in mean time to detect and mean time to respond to incidents with zero trust telemetry and observability.

GCP tools such as *Cloud Monitoring, Cloud Logging, Security Command Center dashboards,* and *Chronicle* can collect, visualize, and alert on these metrics. By setting baseline measurements before implementing zero trust, teams can track tangible improvements in their security posture while ensuring operational efficiency and minimal user disruption.

Evaluating these metrics regularly helps organizations identify misconfigurations, detect policy bypass attempts, and adjust thresholds to balance *security, usability, and business continuity* as zero trust evolves.

Key performance indicators

Measuring the effectiveness of a zero trust rollout requires clear, actionable KPIs that assess both technical coverage and user experience. These metrics should track policy effectiveness, system responsiveness, and operational adoption.

The following are the core KPIs to track:

- **Coverage:** It is the percentage of applications transitioning from legacy VPN access to zero trust enforcement using BeyondCorp or IAP. A high coverage percentage indicates broader adoption and better perimeter deconstruction.

- **Time to remediate**: The average time it takes for issues flagged by posture checks (e.g., out-of-date OS or missing antivirus) to be resolved by end users or IT administrators. This can help identify whether policy enforcement creates undue friction or if remediation workflows require improvement.

- **Policy violations**: The frequency and type of access rejections are due to context-aware rules. Examples include access being blocked due to device non-compliance or login attempts from restricted geographic regions. A spike may indicate policy misconfiguration or emerging threats.

- **User experience metrics**:
  - ○ **Authentication latency**: Time taken to complete login and policy evaluation.
  - ○ **Friction scores**: Number of MFA prompts or repeated posture revalidations.
  - ○ **Helpdesk tickets**: Volume of support cases linked to access blocks or device posture errors.

The following table shows the suggested zero trust KPIs, aligned to security, experience, and adoption metrics:

KPI name	Purpose	Example target
% of apps behind IAP	Tracks coverage of apps protected via context-aware access	Less than or equal to 90% for internal-facing services
Mean Time to Remediate	Time to resolve a blocked posture or identity incident	More than 30 minutes average
Policy Violation Count	How often are users or devices blocked due to policy breach	Less than five per week (after tuning)
User Experience Score	Measures perceived friction or latency	Less than or equal to 90% satisfaction post migration

Table 10.4: Suggested zero trust KPIs with purpose
and target benchmarks for monitoring adoption and effectiveness

Observability tools

Implementing observability tools throughout your zero trust stack is crucial for maintaining visibility and swiftly identifying misconfigurations or policy gaps. GCP provides integrated services to help you analyse access flows, evaluate device compliance, and detect anomalies in real-time.

The following tools, integrations, and practices help teams maintain zero trust observability while refining enforcement without degrading user experience:

- **Key tools and integrations**:
  - ○ **Cloud monitoring**: Tracks backend health and latency for IAP-protected applications. For instance, monitor response times from internal dashboards secured by IAP to ensure context-aware checks do not introduce excessive delays.
  - ○ **Cloud Logging and alerts**: Use logs from IAP, Access Context Manager, and Endpoint Verification to:
    - ▪ Flag rejected login attempts due to device non-compliance.
    - ▪ Monitor spikes in posture-related denials.
    - ▪ Alert on unauthorized access attempts or conditional policy mismatches.

- Security Command Center (SCC): SCC Premium can ingest posture and access data to identify insider threats, unauthorized device access attempts, or overly permissive IAM conditions that may be bypassing zero trust controls.

- **Optimizing the implementation:**
  - **Reduce false positives**: Fine-tune context-aware policies to prevent legitimate users from being blocked unnecessarily. For example, allow a short grace period for patching after posture violations.

  - **Continuous user feedback loops**: Actively integrate lightweight prompts or feedback forms when access is denied, collecting insights about user intent and pain points. These insights can drive incremental improvements to policy logic or user messaging.

  - **Regular audits and posture reviews**: Periodically validate IAM roles, group memberships, and device posture baselines to ensure policy rules reflect current organizational reality. Stale entries or dormant users with elevated permissions often introduce blind spots that observability tools can help identify and address.

  - **Iterative refinement**: Combine audit findings and user feedback to continuously evolve your observability strategy, prioritizing policies that balance enforcement rigour with a smooth user experience.

By leveraging these metrics and incorporating regular feedback loops and audits into their operational rhythm, security teams can ensure their zero trust model remains not only enforced but also adaptable, practical, and user-aware.

Migrating VPN access to zero trust

Transitioning from VPN-based access to zero trust is a strategic move that reduces the risks associated with broad network-level permissions while improving user experience. Instead of granting users access to entire network segments, zero trust evaluates each request based on user identity, device posture, and contextual signals, ensuring least privilege is enforced dynamically.

Security considerations during transition, during the migration period, legacy VPN pathways may still expose organizations to risks such as credential theft, lateral movement, and misconfigured split tunnels. It is essential to closely monitor VPN access, enforce strong authentication, and segment critical assets to prevent these vulnerabilities from becoming exploitation points while zero trust enforcement is being phased in.

A successful migration involves:

- **Assessment and inventory**: Identify applications currently accessed via VPN, prioritizing high-impact internal services with sensitive data.

- **Segmenting applications**: Group applications by sensitivity and complexity to plan phased zero trust onboarding.

- **Deploying IAP**: Start with low-risk applications and configure IAP to enforce identity and context-based access without requiring network-level connectivity.

- **User training**: Communicate benefits and changes to end users, emphasizing reduced friction and improved security.

- **Monitoring and tuning**: Track authentication logs, device compliance metrics, and user feedback to fine-tune policies, minimizing disruptions while maintaining posture enforcement.

- **Decommissioning VPN incrementally**: As zero trust coverage expands, scale back VPN dependency for targeted groups and applications, using GCP's insights to validate readiness.

By following these structured steps, organizations can confidently replace legacy VPN models with zero trust, reducing operational bottlenecks, eliminating implicit trust boundaries, and aligning security posture with modern cloud-native principles

Legacy VPN environment

Before adopting zero trust, many organizations relied heavily on VPNs for remote access. While functional, this model introduced significant risks due to overly broad network-level access and minimal context evaluation. Once users connected to the VPN, they often had access to extensive segments of the internal network, regardless of the systems' sensitivity.

The following are the key challenges:

- **Flat network trust**: VPN connections implicitly trust the endpoint and allow lateral movement. No granular access control existed for individual services or user roles.

- **Manual device checks**: Security checks (e.g., antivirus, OS updates) were manually verified or completely bypassed. There was no automated enforcement mechanism for device compliance.

- **Operational burden**: VPN client management across operating systems, certificate distribution, and IP conflict resolution consumed IT resources and slowed productivity.

- **Phased decommissioning strategy**: Organizations transitioning away from VPNs should adopt a structured approach. Start by identifying low-risk apps and pilot zero trust enforcement using IAP. Gradually expand coverage to high-sensitivity workloads while monitoring posture compliance and user impact. Establish clear milestones (e.g., 50% app migration, 90% posture enforcement) and implement rollback plans that allow for the temporary reinstatement of VPNs for critical paths in the event of policy misconfigurations, service disruptions, or unforeseen exceptions.

Phased migration

A real-world implementation of zero trust typically follows a phased approach. This minimizes disruption while enabling security teams to gather insights and optimize gradually.

The following is a step-by-step migration path:

- **Identify key internal apps**: Start with low-risk applications, such as internal dashboards, development tools, or staging environments. These provide a safe space for piloting zero trust enforcement.

- **Enable IAP for app access**: Migrate these apps behind IAP, replacing IP-based access controls with identity- and device-aware checks. Configure HTTPS Load Balancers and Cloud Identity for access control.

- **Roll out BeyondCorp enterprise**: Integrate device signals using Endpoint Verification. Define access tiers based on encryption, OS version, and user role. Deploy audit-mode policies to fine-tune enforcement without user disruption.

  Sample audit-mode policies are as follows:

  o   Log access attempts from unencrypted or unmanaged devices, but allow access.

  o   Flag access outside business hours for sensitive roles without blocking.

  o   Monitor requests from unverified OS versions to identify unsupported devices.

- **Hybrid coexistence**: Continue to support VPN for legacy workloads (e.g., monoliths, mainframes) that cannot yet be integrated. Educate teams on the gradual transition path.

- **Decommission legacy VPN**: As all critical services are migrated to zero trust enforcement, suspend VPN usage, and rotate off privileged network routes. Retire legacy access gradually.

Outcomes and lessons

After transitioning from VPN to zero trust, the following benefits and insights emerged:

- **Reduced attack surface**: With no blanket network access, attackers had fewer options for lateral movement. Every access decision was tied to a strong user and device context.

- **Improved auditability**: Every access event, including device posture and contextual metadata, was logged, enabling detailed forensics and better compliance alignment.

- **User productivity gains**: Users can securely access internal tools without a VPN connection, improving performance and reducing helpdesk friction associated with VPN failures.

- **Organizational learnings**:
  - **Cultural change**: Educating employees and admins about new workflows took effort. Emphasizing security benefits and providing fallback options was essential.

  - **Policy tuning**: The initial posture enforcement rules were too strict, resulting in false blocks. Rolling out audit mode policies first allowed refinement before full enforcement.

  - **Device enrollment**: Registering unmanaged endpoints (e.g., contractor laptops) took time. Automating device verification and integrating with MDM tools accelerated this.

Ultimately, the transition validated zero trust's core promise: security does not need to come at the expense of usability. With the proper tooling and rollout plan, organizations can gain tighter control and improve employee experience simultaneously.

Complex made simple

Imagine a theme park that traditionally had one entrance gate (the VPN). Once inside, visitors roam freely across all rides and areas:

- **Old model (One gate, full access):**
  - The entire park is *trusted* if you pass the main gate. That is the old perimeter approach.

  - The risk is that if a bad actor slips in, they can access any ride or employee-only zones.

- **Zero trust model (Ride-by-ride checks):**
  - Instead, each ride or zone has a checkpoint that verifies your ticket, height requirement, device posture, or membership level.

  - Visitors with insufficient clearance for a certain ride are politely turned away, even if they are inside the park.

  - The benefit is that no single infiltration grants unlimited access. You prove your eligibility at each step.

- **BeyondCorp Enterprise (High-tech turnstiles):**
  - Each ride's turnstile scans your ticket (user identity), checks if your pass is valid for that ride (context-aware policy), and verifies your device is *safe* (no OS vulnerabilities).

  - This system seamlessly updates if your pass is revoked or if you fail a posture check; no manual staff intervention is needed.

- **Migration from one main gate**: Over time, the park has reduced its reliance on that big perimeter fence and gate. Instead, guests approach each ride directly, with no waiting and no bulky overhead. If a ride is off-limits, the turnstile enforces it.

The key takeaway in zero-trust, each resource (or ride) demands verification. BeyondCorp is an advanced system for verifying user tickets and device posture at every step. This eliminates broad trust once inside, ensuring tight security per resource, like a theme park's network of ride-by-ride turnstiles.

Conclusion

Zero trust is more than a security model; it represents a paradigm shift in how organizations view trust, access, and risk. Enterprises can enforce access controls with precision and flexibility by focusing on the identity and posture of users and devices. BeyondCorp Enterprise delivers the capabilities needed to operationalize zero trust across GCP environments, replacing static network controls with dynamic, adaptive policies. While cultural and operational shifts are necessary, the long-term benefits, improved auditability, reduced attack surface, and enhanced user experience make the transition worthwhile.

As we move forward, the next chapter will focus on formulating a response strategy tailored to Google Cloud. You will learn how to use GCP's native logs for forensics, isolate compromised resources, snapshot workloads for evidence, and triage real-time incidents with services like Cloud Logging and SCC. From defining escalation paths to conducting effective post-mortems, this chapter equips you with techniques to transform incidents into lessons that strengthen your GCP security posture over time.

Call to action, begin evaluating your current access architecture, identify low-risk applications as zero trust pilots, and lay the foundation for device-aware access enforcement. Each step you take today accelerates your journey toward a resilient, scalable, and context-aware future of cloud security.

Exercise

Objective

This lab guides you through securing an internal web application using IAP and Endpoint Verification, incorporating key principles of zero trust: identity, device posture, and contextual access control.

Prerequisites

- A GCP project with billing enabled
- Access to Google Cloud Console
- Admin privileges (Owner or IAM Admin)

- A test web application running on GCE, GKE, or App Engine
- Chrome browser with Endpoint Verification extension installed

Lab steps

1. **Enable APIs and set up identity platform:**

    a. Enable IAP, Cloud Identity, and Access Context Manager APIs.

    b. If not already done, enable Cloud Identity Premium (trial is available).

    ```
    gcloud services enable iap.googleapis.com \
      cloudidentity.googleapis.com \
      accesscontextmanager.googleapis.com
    ```

2. **Deploy a test app and enable IAP**

    a. Deploy a sample app on App Engine or behind a HTTPS Load Balancer on GCE/GKE.

    b. Enable IAP on the app via: **Security | Identity-Aware Proxy | Add App | Enable Access**

    c. Grant access to specific users or groups via IAM (IAP-secured Web App User role).

3. **Configure Endpoint Verification**

    a. Install the Endpoint Verification extension on Chrome.

    b. Ensure device reporting is enabled in the Google Admin Console.

4. **Create access levels via Access Context Manager**

    a. Navigate to **IAM & Admin | Context-Aware Access**.

    b. Create an access level based on:

        i. Device encryption

        ii. OS version

        iii. User identity

        iv. Location/IP restrictions

    c. Example condition:

    ```
    "devicePolicy": {
      "osConstraints": [
        { "osType": "DESKTOP_MAC", "minimumVersion": "12.0.0" }
      ],
      "requireScreenlock": true,
      "requireAdminApproval": false,
      "requireCorpOwned": true,
    ```

```
        "requireEncrypted": true
    }
```

5. **Test and validate:**

   a. Attempt access from a compliant device and user.

   b. Attempt access from a non-compliant device (e.g., incognito mode or a different OS version).

   c. Observe access rejections in Cloud Logging and Security Command Center.

6. **Optional bonus tasks:**

   1. Configure audit-mode policy for silent enforcement.

   2. Export logs to BigQuery for posture trend analysis.

   3. Write a policy to block access from non-corporate networks using ipSubnetworks.

7. **Deliverables:**

   1. Screenshot of working app with IAP access.

   2. Access level policy JSON.

   3. Log sample showing posture-based access decision.

Key takeaways

This chapter provided a hands-on blueprint for adopting zero trust in GCP environments using BeyondCorp Enterprise:

- Zero trust eliminates reliance on network location by enforcing identity- and device-based access at every layer of the network.

- BeyondCorp Enterprise allows secure, context-aware access without VPNs, integrating with IAM, IAP, and device posture signals.

- IAP enables per-app access policies that validate device health and user role.

- Device verification, posture evaluation, and hardware-backed attestation help block risky endpoints before they reach sensitive data.

- KPIs such as policy violations, coverage metrics, and user friction should guide iterative improvements.

- Real-world migrations benefit from phased rollouts, hybrid coexistence with VPNs, and careful policy tuning.

References

1. https://cloud.google.com/beyondcorp-enterprise

2. https://cloud.google.com/iap

3. https://cloud.google.com/access-context-manager

4. https://cloud.google.com/endpoint-verification

5. https://cloud.google.com/security-command-center

6. https://cloud.google.com/chronicle

7. https://cloud.google.com/docs/security/zero-trust

8. https://cloud.google.com/beyondcorp/docs/concepts-overview

9. https://cloud.google.com/architecture/zero-trust-overview

10. https://cloud.google.com/beyondcorp-enterprise/docs/policy

11. https://cloud.google.com/iap/docs/concepts-overview

12. https://cloud.google.com/beyondcorp-enterprise/docs/device-trust

13. https://cloud.google.com/logging/docs

14. https://cloud.google.com/monitoring

15. https://cloud.google.com/iam/docs/conditions-overview

16. https://cloud.google.com/identity/docs/federating-gcp-with-azure-ad

17. https://cloud.google.com/architecture/developing-zero-trust-strategy

Join our Discord space

Join our Discord workspace for latest updates, offers, tech happenings around the world, new releases, and sessions with the authors:

https://discord.bpbonline.com

CHAPTER 11
Incident Response and Forensics in GCP

Introduction

Incident response and forensics are essential for any security practitioner working in **Google Cloud Platform** (**GCP**), where the speed, scale, and dynamic nature of cloud-native workloads demand modern, automated approaches to detection, containment, and remediation.

In GCP, incident response operates under a shared responsibility model. While Google secures the infrastructure and core services, customers are accountable for their configurations, IAM policies, and data. This requires a clear understanding of detection and response boundaries, as well as the ability to leverage native tools for visibility, containment, and evidence retention.

Cloud environments also introduce ephemeral workloads, such as auto-scaling VMs, serverless functions, and short-lived containers, that can vanish within seconds, leaving little trace unless logging is proactively configured. Effective response requires real-time monitoring, automated snapshot policies, and resource-level log collection.

At scale, incidents often span multiple projects, regions, and teams, making investigation more complex. Practitioners must correlate logs across environments, enforce fast containment strategies, and maintain data residency compliance, all while minimizing disruption to business-critical systems.

This chapter provides the tools, workflows, and mindset necessary to respond confidently to incidents in GCP, enabling you to align your response capabilities with the cloud-native scale and security demands.

Structure

This chapter covers the following topics:

- Introduction to incident response in GCP
- Importance of cloud-specific plan
- Defining an incident response plan
- GCP logs for forensic analysis
- VPC Flow Logs
- Isolating resources and limiting blast radius
- Quarantine and evidence preservation
- Using GCP Forensics in real incidents
- Post-mortems and improvement
- Complex made simple

Objective

This chapter will help you develop a structured and practical approach to incident response within Google Cloud environments. You will learn how to define clear roles and escalation paths within your incident response plan, utilize GCP-native tools such as Cloud Logging, Cloud Audit logs, and VPC Flow Logs for forensic investigation, and implement rapid isolation strategies to contain threats while preserving evidence.

By the end of this chapter, you will understand how to conduct structured post-incident reviews to identify root causes, document key learnings, and improve your incident response processes. This will ensure you can confidently handle security incidents in GCP with minimal disruption while maintaining compliance and audit readiness.

Introduction to incident response in GCP

Incident response and forensics within GCP demand a fundamentally different approach compared to traditional on-premises environments. Cloud environments introduce speed, elasticity, and dynamic resource lifecycles, requiring incident responders to adapt their processes, tooling, and mindset to match this agility while maintaining *evidence integrity* during investigations.

A key aspect to understand is the *shared responsibility model in GCP incident response*. While Google is responsible for the security of the underlying infrastructure, including physical security, networking, and foundational compute services, you, as the customer, are responsible for securing your workloads, configurations, and **Identity and Access Management (IAM)** within the cloud environment. This division requires your incident response plan to explicitly cover logging, network segmentation, IAM hygiene, and workload isolation while leveraging GCP-native tooling and APIs for effective detection and containment.

Cloud environments also introduce the complexity of managing ephemeral versus persistent workloads during incident response. Ephemeral resources, such as auto-scaling compute instances, serverless functions, or short-lived containers, can spin up and terminate within seconds, often leaving minimal traces if logging and monitoring are not correctly configured. In contrast, persistent workloads, such as stateful VM instances, databases, and storage buckets, retain data over time, enabling evidence collection but requiring careful handling to preserve integrity during snapshotting or isolation. Effective IR planning must consider automated evidence capture workflows, log collection at the resource-level, and snapshot policies across both ephemeral and persistent resources.

IAM conditional policies for IR readiness

An advanced IR readiness practice in GCP is to leverage IAM conditional policies to enforce access controls during an incident, thereby minimizing the risk of widespread service disruptions.

For example, you can define conditional access policies that:

- *Deny the creation of external IP addresses* unless explicitly allowed during controlled maintenance windows, reducing exposure to external threats.

- *Restrict service account usage* to specific source IP ranges during incident response to limit lateral movement or misuse by compromised credentials.

- *Temporarily block privilege escalation* by applying conditional denial on roles such as **roles/owner or roles/iam.serviceAccountAdmin** during escalation phases. This prevents privilege assignment or modification until incident triage is completed, and trust is re-established through break-glass or approval workflows.

These conditional policies act as programmable guardrails, enabling dynamic access governance in volatile scenarios where static IAM is insufficient.

For example:

```
{
  "condition": {
    "title": "Deny External IP During IR",
    "expression": "!resource.name.startsWith('projects/allowed-
projects')"
  },
  "members": ["allUsers"],
  "role": "roles/compute.admin"
}
```

This allows you to predefine constraints that can be enabled automatically during an incident, reducing manual intervention and limiting attacker options while preserving investigation visibility.

Tags and labels for incident asset tracking

Handling incidents across multiple projects and regions during high-scale incidents requires precise tracking of affected resources. Using tags and labels systematically allows your team to:

- Mark compromised VMs, disks, and buckets with labels like **incident=IR-2025-001** or **status=quarantine**.

- Apply quarantine firewall rules consistently to tagged assets across your entire environment.

- Track resource ownership, project location, and incident identifiers during containment, facilitating rapid post-incident cleanup and audits.

For example, during an incident, applying:

```
gcloud compute instances add-labels vm-name \
  --labels=incident=IR-2025-001,status=quarantine
```

It enables IR teams to query and isolate resources efficiently across multiple projects using these labels.

Serverless incident response with Eventarc

To align with the cloud's speed and scalability, incident response in GCP can leverage automated responder patterns using Cloud Functions and Eventarc to reduce the **mean time to contain** (**MTTC**) incidents. You can build serverless responders that:

- Trigger alerts on log-based metrics or Security Command Centre findings that indicate suspicious activity.

- Automatically tag or quarantine VMs using firewall rules and labels.

- Snapshot disks for evidence preservation.

- Notify incident channels in Slack or trigger PagerDuty for critical escalations.

For example, upon detection of a suspicious IAM escalation, Eventarc can route the event to a Cloud Function that automatically:

- Applies the *quarantine* label to the instance.

- Update firewall rules to block inbound and outbound traffic.

- Takes a disk snapshot for forensics.

- Sends structured notifications for visibility and tracking.

By incorporating IAM conditional policies, systematic tagging and labelling, and automated responders, your GCP incident response processes evolve from manual, reactive steps to automated, scalable, and cloud-aligned workflows that reduce dwell time, enhance visibility, and preserve evidence integrity during high-stress incident scenarios.

Importance of cloud-specific plan

Incident response (IR) in GCP is fundamentally different from traditional on-premises environments, making a cloud-specific plan essential for effective detection, containment, and recovery. The dynamic, API-driven nature of cloud workloads, the elasticity of compute resources, and a distributed, multi-project architecture require incident responders to adopt workflows aligned with cloud-native realities.

Log ingestion latency and log-based metrics

While *Cloud Logging and Cloud Audit logs* provide critical visibility, ingestion latency (ranging from seconds to minutes) can hinder immediate detection during fast-moving incidents if not accounted for. To mitigate this, *log-based metrics and alerts* can be configured to trigger automated workflows as soon as logs are ingested, providing near-real-time detection capabilities.

For example, you can create a *log-based metric* to detect sudden IAM role escalations:

```
{
  "name": "high_impact_iam_change",
  "filter": "protoPayload.methodName=\"google.iam.admin.v1.SetIamPolicy\"",
  "metricDescriptor": {
    "metricKind": "DELTA",
    "valueType": "INT64",
    "unit": "1",
    "description": "Counts IAM policy changes for high-risk escalation
detection"
  }
}
```

Once created, you can set up alerting policies tied to Slack or PagerDuty via Pub/Sub and Cloud Functions to notify your IR team instantly.

Example of Slack notification flow:

Log-based metric triggers | Alerting Policy fires | Sends to Pub/Sub | Cloud Function parses payload | Posts to #incident-response in Slack with resource, actor, and project details.

This approach reduces **mean time to detect** (**MTTD**) while aligning with GCP's event-driven infrastructure.

Cloud Security Command Center custom detectors

Cloud SCC can be leveraged to create custom detectors for your IR workflows, enabling proactive detection of suspicious configurations or behaviors aligned with your environment's context. For instance, you can configure SCC to:

- Detect storage buckets with public access enabled during sensitive projects.
- Alert on newly created service accounts with broad permissions.
- Flag VMs with external IPs spun up in sensitive projects.

SCC custom modules provide organization-wide visibility and alignment with compliance policies, allowing your team to focus on the incidents that matter most.

API quota management during incident response

During containment, IR teams often need to:

- Snapshot multiple disks.
- Modify firewall rules.
- Suspend or stop numerous instances.

GCP enforces API quotas per project and service to ensure platform stability and to prevent abuse. Without proactive quota management, your containment actions may fail or be throttled during high-severity incidents. During security incidents, actions such as snapshotting disks, starting/stopping instances, or updating firewall rules can quickly consume API quotas. To avoid bottlenecks or failure of automated response actions, it is essential to monitor and manage quota limits proactively. The following ways can help with managing quotas:

- **Checking quotas using gcloud:**

```
gcloud compute project-info describe-- project=your-project-id
```

  This command outputs quota usage and limits for Compute Engine, helping you track headroom for snapshot, instance stop/start, and firewall operations.

- **Quota increase request tips:**

  o Identify the relevant quotas in the **IAM & Admin | Quotas** dashboard.

  o Filter for services like Compute Engine API, IAM API, or Cloud Storage API.

  o Submit quota increase requests proactively for high-risk environments to accommodate IR actions, especially for:

    ▪ Snapshots per project

    ▪ Requests per 100 seconds per user

    ▪ API requests per minute

GCP typically processes quota increase requests within 24 to 48 hours; for critical environments, requesting these increases in advance ensures incident readiness without delays.

The following figure represents a Google template on how various teams co-work in an incident readiness plan:

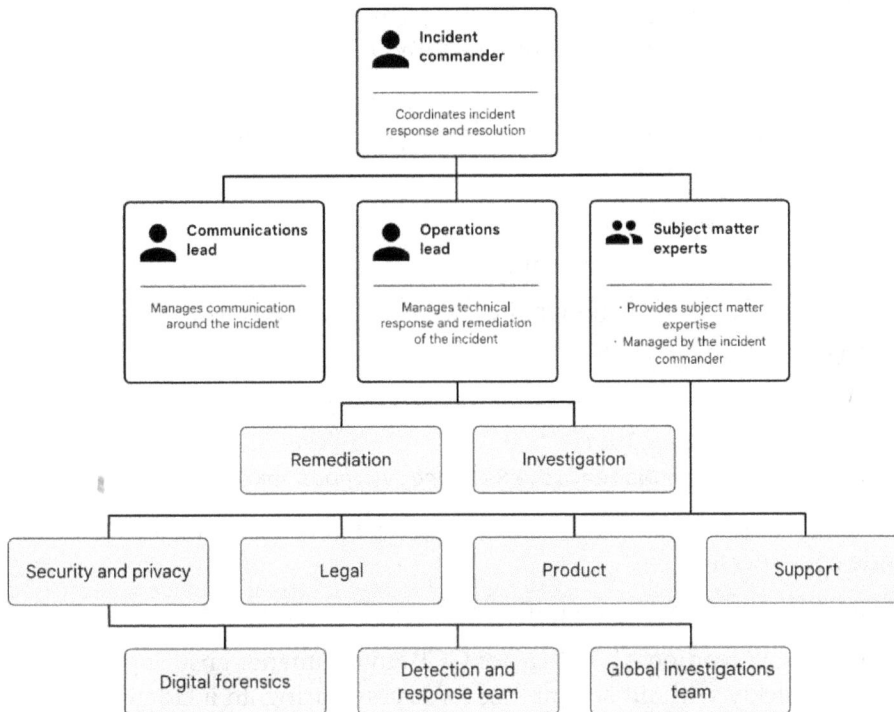

Figure 11.1: Google template on organization readiness for incidents

Key concepts

Effective incident response within GCP requires mastering key concepts that align with the cloud's speed, scale, and API-driven nature, ensuring your team can detect, contain, and investigate threats systematically during security incidents:

- **Real-time vs near-real-time detection**: A critical aspect of GCP incident response is understanding the difference between real-time and near-real-time detection workflows:

    - **Near-real-time detection using Log Explorer:** Cloud Logging and Cloud Audit logs typically introduce minor ingestion latency (seconds to minutes). Log Explorer and BigQuery are excellent for structured threat hunting and post-event investigations, but are not true real-time detection pipelines.

    - **Real-time detection using SIEM and Pub/Sub:** For high-risk, time-sensitive signals (e.g., IAM privilege escalations, suspicious VM creation), integrating log-based metrics with Pub/Sub, Cloud Functions, and your SIEM (e.g., Chronicle, Splunk) enables near-real-time detection pipelines. By pushing logs immediately to Pub/Sub upon ingestion and using event-driven responders, you can reduce your MTTD and MTTC.

Building layered detection with both near-real-time and real-time systems ensures speed without losing the depth of structured forensic analysis.

- **Kubernetes audit logging for IR**: With many GCP workloads running on **Google Kubernetes Engine** (**GKE**), Kubernetes-specific monitoring becomes essential for incident detection and investigation.

- **Kubernetes audit logging captures:**

  - kubectl exec events (potential lateral movement).

  - Configuration changes (create, update, and delete) for critical resources.

  - Unexpected API calls.

For example, to detect suspicious pod execution activities, you can use:
```
resource.type="k8s_cluster"
protoPayload.methodName="io.k8s.core.v1.pods.exec"
```

In Log Explorer or your SIEM, surfacing potential unauthorized shell access attempts inside containers.

- **Practical automation**: Creating IR-specific service accounts with Terraform

Automating IR readiness is critical for GCP environments, ensuring that your team can respond quickly without scrambling for access during an incident. Using Terraform, you can pre-provision IR-specific service accounts with scoped permissions aligned to least-privilege principles.

Example Terraform snippet:
```
resource "google_service_account" "ir_responder" {
  account_id   = "ir-responder"
  display_name = "Incident Response Responder Account"
}
resource "google_project_iam_binding" "ir_logging_viewer" {
  project = "your-project-id"
  role    = "roles/logging.viewer"
  members = [
    "serviceAccount:${google_service_account.ir_responder.email}",
  ]
}
resource "google_project_iam_binding" "ir_compute_admin" {
  project = "your-project-id"
  role    = "roles/compute.instanceAdmin.v1"
  members = [
    "serviceAccount:${google_service_account.ir_responder.email}",
  ]
}
```

Defining an incident response plan

A *clear, actionable IR plan* is crucial for effectively managing security incidents in GCP, ensuring your team can detect, contain, and remediate issues promptly while maintaining compliance and minimizing business disruption.

At its core, your IR plan should define:

- Roles and responsibilities for incident management.
- Escalation paths with clear severity classifications.
- Automated communication workflows.
- Integration with cloud-native tooling for speed and consistency.

Structured incident response unbook snippet

A structured runbook helps standardize IR across your teams, reducing confusion during high-stress incidents.

For example:

```
incident-response-runbook.md:
# GCP Incident Response Runbook

## 1. Detection
- Use Cloud SCC, log-based alerts, and SIEM detections.
- Confirm the incident severity.

## 2. Containment
- Label affected resources: `incident=IR-2025-001`
- Isolate VMs:
  - Remove external IPs.
  - Apply quarantine firewall rules.
- Capture snapshots for forensics.

## 3. Eradication
- Identify root cause.
- Patch vulnerabilities.
- Revoke compromised credentials.

## 4. Recovery
- Restore services in a clean state.
- Monitor for reinfection.

## 5. Post-Incident Review
- Document timeline, impact, and root cause.
- Identify improvement actions.
- Update runbook and detection rules.
```

Note: **Keep your runbook in a central Git repository (e.g., GitHub, Bitbucket) with version control and integrate it with your IR drills.**

Slack message payloads for incident response

Automated notifications ensure the right stakeholders are informed quickly. Using Cloud Functions triggered by Pub/Sub alerts, you can send structured Slack messages to your IR channel.

Example Slack payload JSON:

```
{
  "text": ":rotating_light: *Incident Alert* :rotating_light:\nSeverity: P1\
nProject: your-project-id\nResource: instance-1\nDetected: Suspicious IAM Role
Escalation\nAction: Review and initiate containment.\n<https://console.cloud.
google.com/security/command-center|View in SCC>"
}
```

Escalation paths table

Defining clear escalation paths by severity ensures incidents are handled at the right level with appropriate urgency. To ensure incidents are prioritized and responded to appropriately, it is essential to establish clear escalation paths based on severity. This structured approach ensures that the right stakeholders are notified promptly and that incident handling aligns with business impact and urgency.

The following table focuses on the same:

Severity	Description	Action	Escalation reference paths
P1 (Critical)	Active compromise, customer data at risk, major outage	Immediate containment, notify leadership	Page on-call via PagerDuty, Slack #ir-critical
P2 (High)	Potential compromise, suspicious activity	Triage within 2 hours	Notify the security team, Slack #ir-high
P3 (Medium)	Policy violations, misconfigurations	Triage within 24 hours	Assign to an analyst, track in ticket system

Table 11.1 Incident escalation by severity and response workflow

This structured classification aligns your SLA for MTTD and MTTC with business risk while clarifying who is responsible at each stage.

Optimizing IR with GCP recommender

GCP recommender can provide actionable insights to reduce your cloud attack surface, supporting incident response readiness by continuously analyzing resource configurations and usage patterns across:

- Over-permissive IAM bindings
- Idle or unused resources
- Unused service account keys

During post-incident analysis, integrate *recommender findings* into your IR process to prevent recurrence:

- Review IAM recommender for opportunities to reduce roles.
- Use recommender APIs to export insights:

```
gcloud recommender recommendations list \
   --project=your-project-id \
   --location=global \
   --recommender=google.iam.policy.Recommender
```

- Automate tracking recommender insights post-incident for accountability and continuous hardening.

Sample IAM role bindings for incident responders

To operationalize your IR plan, you can pre-assign IAM roles to your incident response team, enabling swift and secure access during an incident without broad administrative privileges. For example, the following YAML configuration demonstrates role bindings for two incident response roles:

```
bindings:
- members:
  - user:ir_lead@example.com
  role: roles/logging.viewer
- members:
  - user:ir_analyst@example.com
  role: roles/compute.instanceAdmin.v1
```

In this setup:

- The *IR Lead* can view logs across the project to analyze audit events and system activities.

- The *IR Analyst* can manage compute instances (e.g., suspending or snapshotting suspicious VMs) during containment, even without unrestricted admin access to unrelated resources.

Predefined IR roles reduce onboarding delays during incidents and ensure accountability in forensic investigations by avoiding shared superuser accounts.

Slack and PagerDuty escalation paths

Timely communication is critical during an incident. An effective IR plan in GCP should incorporate automated escalation paths using tools like Slack, PagerDuty, or similar platforms to ensure key stakeholders are promptly informed. For example:

- A Slack incident channel (for instance, #gcp-incident-response) can be automatically populated with alerts triggered by Security Command Center or custom log-based metrics detecting high-severity events, such as suspicious IAM escalations or unexpected network spikes.

- PagerDuty can be integrated with these alerts to escalate incidents based on severity, ensuring on-call responders are paged instantly for critical events. At the same time, lower-severity issues are tracked for review.

A typical flow may include:

- SCC detects an IAM anomaly and sends an alert to Pub/Sub.

- A Cloud Function consumes this alert and posts a structured message to Slack, tagging the IR Lead and relevant team members.

- If the event severity is *critical*, the Cloud Function also triggers PagerDuty, paging the on-call security engineer to review and begin containment procedures.

This automated escalation ensures that your response is swift and coordinated, thereby reducing the **mean time to acknowledge** (**MTTA**) and the MTTC.

IR policy to block external IPs

During high-severity incidents, isolating resources to prevent further exposure is critical. Using *organization policy constraints,* you can enforce rules such as *deny external IP address assignment* during active incidents to deter attackers from maintaining external connectivity for exfiltration or command-and-control.

The following is an example of an organization policy JSON that denies external IP assignments for new VM instances during an IR event:

```
{
  "constraint": "constraints/compute.vmExternalIpAccess",
  "listPolicy": {
    "deniedValues": ["projects/*"]
  }
}
```

This policy can be deployed programmatically at the organization or folder level using the Resource Manager API or gcloud CLI during the incident's containment phase. Once the incident is resolved and the environment has been validated, the policy can be lifted under controlled conditions.

Bringing it together

By defining IAM roles tailored for IR workflows, integrating automated escalation paths using Slack and PagerDuty, and preparing enforcement policies such as denying external IPs during critical incidents, your GCP incident response plan becomes operationally effective. These practices ensure that your organization is ready to respond to incidents in a structured, consistent, and rapid manner while maintaining evidence integrity and minimizing business disruption.

A clear IR plan is crucial for ensuring that security events in GCP are promptly contained, thoroughly investigated, and effectively remediated.

This plan should define team roles, escalation paths, and best practices to enable a rapid and organized response.

Roles and responsibilities

The following table outlines key roles within a GCP IR team and their core responsibilities:

Role	Responsibility
Incident commander (IC)	Oversees incident flow, communication, and resource allocation.
Security lead	Coordinates log analysis, forensics, and suspicious activity investigation.
Comms lead	Manages internal and external stakeholder communications.
Platform admin	Executes quarantine, snapshot, rollback, and other resource-level actions.

Table 11.2: Core roles in a GCP incident response team

Escalation paths and communication

Escalation paths ensure incidents are managed efficiently with clear handoffs. The following table summarizes key playbook elements:

Element	Details
Incident classification	Defines severity levels (Low / Medium / High) for consistent triage.
Contact tree	Specifies whom to contact for different incident severities.
Internal vs. external communication	Clarifies when to involve legal, PR, or regulatory teams.

Table 11.3: Incident escalation playbook elements

Best practices

The following best practices help strengthen your GCP incident response capabilities:

- **Frequent drills**: Conduct chaos engineering and tabletop exercises.
- **Automation**: Use Slack or email bots for automated paging.
- **Documentation**: Maintain updated IR runbooks with GCP-specific commands and escalation contacts.

GCP logs for forensic analysis

Comprehensive, structured logging is the backbone of practical forensic analysis and incident response within GCP. Leveraging Cloud Logging, Cloud Audit logs, and BigQuery enables security teams to detect, investigate, and preserve evidence systematically while aligning with compliance and audit requirements.

Advanced Log Explorer queries for detection

For proactive threat hunting and rapid incident triage, advanced Log Explorer queries enable the identification of suspicious administrative activities and credential misuse. The following are high-impact Log Explorer queries that can be integrated into your detection pipelines to surface indicators of compromise quickly and effectively:

- **Detect IAM service account key creations:** Identifying new service account key creations (often used for persistence by attackers):

```
resource.type="project"
protoPayload.methodName="google.iam.admin.v1.CreateServiceAccountKey"
```

- **Detect suspicious role bindings (Escalation)**: Track high-risk IAM role bindings, such as roles/owner or broad editor permissions:

```
resource.type="project"
protoPayload.methodName="SetIamPolicy"
protoPayload.serviceData.policyDelta.bindingDeltas.action="ADD"
protoPayload.serviceData.policyDelta.bindingDeltas.role="roles/owner"
```

- **Detect disabled audit logs (Defense evasion)**: Monitor for any actions disabling audit configurations:

```
protoPayload.methodName="google.logging.v2.ConfigServiceV2.UpdateSink"
```

These queries can be saved and shared within your SOC environment to standardize your IR workflows.

Using BigQuery scheduled queries for IR

Exporting Cloud Audit logs and VPC Flow Logs to BigQuery enables large-scale, structured analysis with powerful SQL queries across your environment. Using scheduled queries, you can continuously monitor for suspicious activities with automated notifications.

For example, a scheduled query to detect new service account key creations:

```
SELECT
  timestamp,
  protopayload_auditlog.authenticationInfo.principalEmail AS actor,
  protopayload_auditlog.resourceName AS targetResource,
  jsonPayload.request.keyType AS keyType
FROM
  `project-id.dataset.cloudaudit_googleapis_com_activity_*`
WHERE
  protopayload_auditlog.methodName = "google.iam.admin.
v1.CreateServiceAccountKey"
  AND _PARTITIONTIME >= TIMESTAMP_SUB(CURRENT_TIMESTAMP(), INTERVAL 1 DAY)
```

This can run daily or hourly using BigQuery scheduled queries, with results:

- Sent to a Slack channel using Cloud Functions.
- Stored for further correlation with VPC Flow Logs for data exfil matching.
- Triggered the page on-call staff for critical patterns.

Compliance-driven log retention

Proper log retention and immutability are essential for maintaining forensic evidence and compliance with frameworks such as **PCI-DSS, HIPAA, and SOC2**:

Framework	Retention Requirement
PCI-DSS	At least one year, with three months online and immediately available
HIPAA	Minimum 6 years for policies, practical logs, often six months to one year
SOC2	Typically, one year to demonstrate monitoring and controls

Table 11.4: Log retention requirements across common compliance frameworks

The following are the best practices in GCP:

- Use centralized log sinks for a dedicated *forensics* project for immutability.
- Configure object lifecycle policies on cloud storage for automated retention and deletion aligned with policy.

- Enable bucket lock for **Write Once Read Many (WORM)** configurations to preserve logs in legal hold scenarios.

- Document retention policies and demonstrate them during audits.

For example, applying a retention policy to the logs storage bucket:

```
gsutil retention set 365d gs://forensics-logs-bucket
```

By aligning your log strategy with compliance frameworks, you ensure your incident response and forensic processes are audit-ready, secure, and operationally effective.

The following figure shows how Google Cloud Logging and Cloud Audit logs enable forensic visibility:

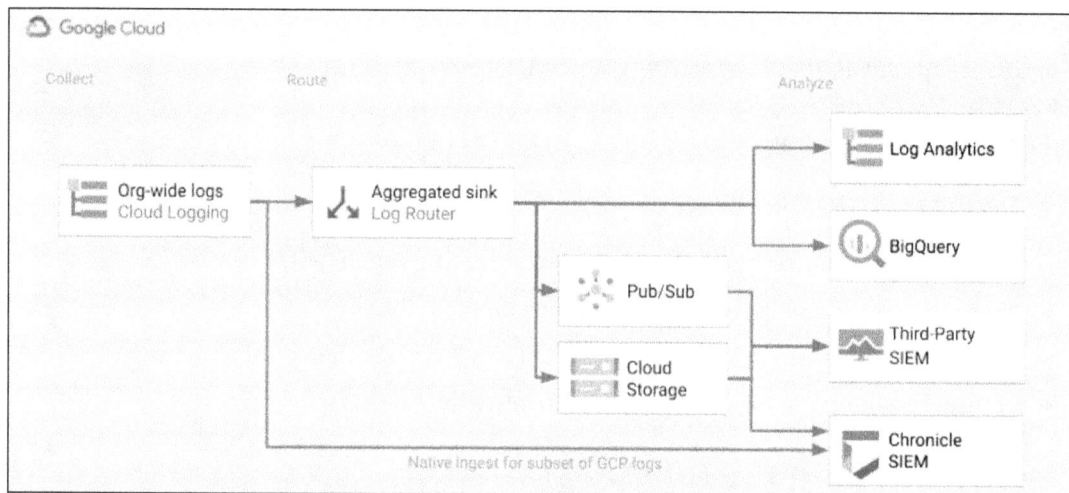

Figure 11.2: *Cloud Logging and Cloud Audit logs enabling forensic visibility and advanced incident analysis in GCP*

VPC Flow Logs

VPC Flow Logs provide detailed visibility into network traffic within GCP, enabling the detection of lateral movement, unauthorized data transfers, scanning activities, and potential exfiltration attempts during incident response and forensic investigations. Flow Logs record metadata about network connections passing through VM instances, subnets, and VPCs, including source and destination IPs, ports, protocols, bytes transferred, and connection states, providing essential context for threat hunting and incident response processes.

Threat hunting with BigQuery and VPC Logs

Exporting VPC Flow Logs to *BigQuery* allows security teams to perform advanced analysis at scale, correlating with threat intelligence feeds and forensic timelines during active incidents.

For example, detect unusual outbound traffic to known malicious IPs:

```
SELECT
  timestamp,
  connection.src_ip,
  connection.dest_ip,
  connection.dest_port,
  connection.bytes_sent,
  connection.bytes_received
FROM
  `project_id.flow_logs_dataset.flow_logs_table`
WHERE
  connection.dest_ip IN UNNEST(['203.0.113.1', '198.51.100.2'])
  AND timestamp >= TIMESTAMP_SUB(CURRENT_TIMESTAMP(), INTERVAL 1 DAY)
```

This query allows responders to:

- Identify instances communicating with known malicious IPs.
- Assess data volumes sent/received for potential exfiltration.
- Prioritize resources for isolation and evidence preservation during the incident.

You can schedule this query to run hourly and trigger Slack or PagerDuty notifications when hits are detected, enhancing real-time threat detection in your IR workflows.

VPC Traffic Mirroring for deep forensics

While VPC Flow Logs provide metadata about network flows, they do not capture packet payloads. For advanced forensic investigations requiring packet-level inspection, VPC Traffic Mirroring enables responders to mirror traffic from VM NICs to packet capture and analysis appliances (e.g., Suricata, Zeek, Wireshark) running on Compute Engine or specialized appliances.

The following are the use cases for VPC traffic mirroring:

- Investigating data exfiltration by reconstructing files transferred over suspicious connections.
- Analyzing malware behavior by inspecting command-and-control traffic.
- Detecting protocol misuse within your VPC environment.

The following are examples of workflow:

- Enable Traffic Mirroring on suspicious VM interfaces.
- Route mirrored traffic to an analysis VM with packet capture tooling.
- Capture, store, and analyze packets while maintaining chain-of-custody practices.
- Disable mirroring post-investigation to optimize costs.

The following are the considerations:

- Traffic Mirroring is resource-intensive; enable it selectively and for a defined duration.

- Combine with *Flow Logs to correlate metadata* and narrow down capture windows, thereby reducing data volumes.

Retention and cost tradeoffs

VPC Flow Logs generate significant data volume, impacting storage costs in BigQuery or Cloud Storage, depending on your aggregation interval and enabled metadata fields. VPC Flow Logs can produce large volumes of telemetry data, so organizations must balance forensic value with cost efficiency. The following strategies help optimize both retention and cost:

- **Retention strategies:**
  - High-resolution, short-term retention (7 to 30 days) for immediate forensic readiness.
  - Lower-resolution, long-term retention (90 to 180 days) for compliance and trend analysis.
  - Utilize partitioning and clustering in BigQuery to reduce query costs.

- **Cost optimization tips:**
  - Adjust the aggregation interval (e.g., five seconds for high-fidelity IR, one minute for baseline monitoring).
  - Filter logs to include only critical subnets or VM tags to minimize noise and storage requirements.
  - Regularly review log volume and prune old, non-critical data.

For example, enabling VPC Flow Logs with high resolution:

```
gcloud compute networks subnets update subnet-1 \
  --enable-flow-logs \
  --logging-aggregation-interval=interval-5-sec \
  --metadata=include-all
```

Using this structured approach ensures that your organization balances visibility, forensic readiness, and cost control, maintaining operational effectiveness while aligning with security and compliance objectives.

The following figure depicts how shared VM-to-VM flows for Shared VPC work:

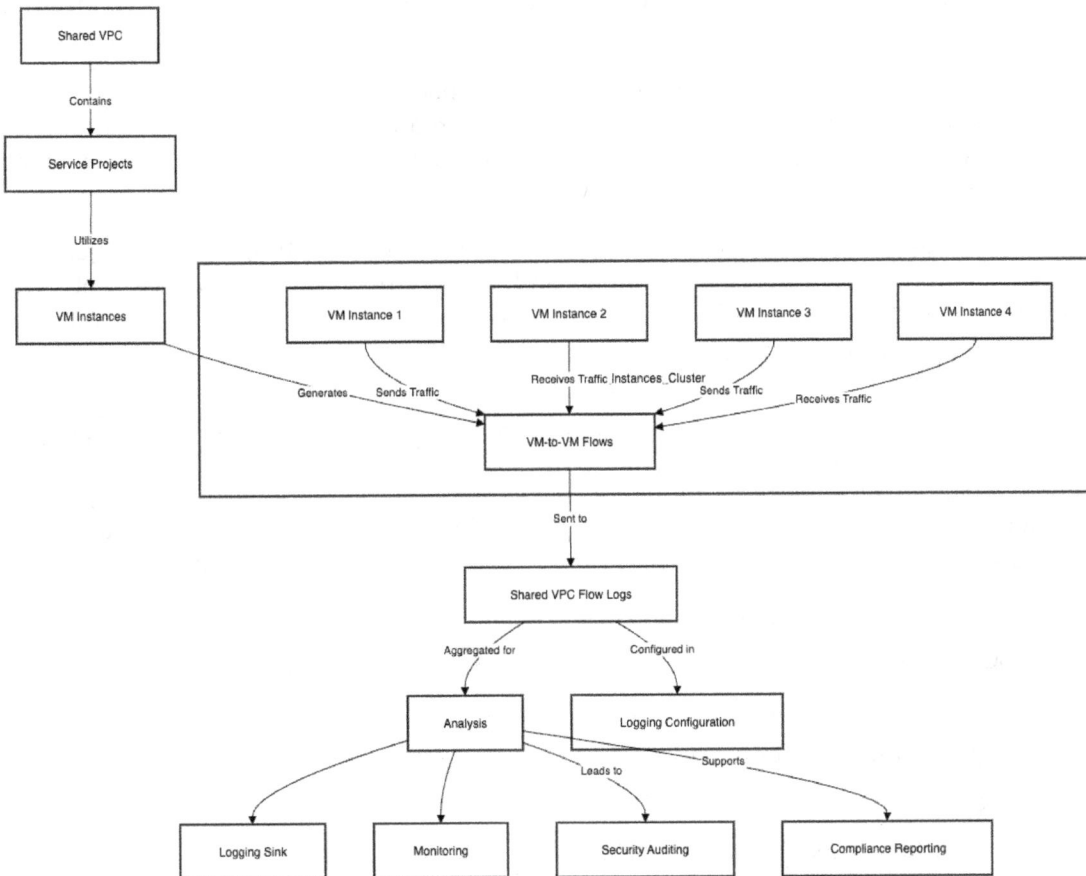

Figure 11.3: *Shared VPC Flow Logs in Google Cloud*

Isolating resources and limiting blast radius

Isolation is a critical containment strategy during incident response within GCP, designed to limit attacker lateral movement, prevent data exfiltration, and preserve evidence for forensic analysis. Effective isolation balances swift containment while minimizing disruption to unaffected services, supporting a measured incident response.

In Google Cloud, isolation can be achieved using a combination of firewall rules, service perimeter enforcement (VPC SC), IAM restrictions, and network segmentation. For instance, security teams can apply deny-all ingress and egress firewall rules to suspect instances or place them into quarantine VPCs with no external access.

You can also leverage tags or labels to dynamically trigger automated responses, such as blocking access, removing external IPs, or re-routing traffic via proxies, using Cloud Functions or Eventarc-based workflows. For managed services (e.g., Cloud SQL or GKE), isolation should include network policies and **access control list** (**ACL**) updates to restrict connectivity immediately upon detection.

Additionally, teams should predefine containment playbooks that account for different resource types and sensitivity levels, ensuring consistent isolation practices even under pressure. These playbooks can incorporate snapshot and disk clone policies to preserve volatile evidence before any intervention, supporting forensic workflows downstream.

Proactively designing your architecture for blast radius control, using project-level segmentation, dedicated service accounts, and scoped permissions, ensures that when incidents occur, their impact remains contained to a narrow surface area, accelerating both recovery and root cause analysis.

Auto tagging and quarantine with Cloud Functions

Manual isolation processes are prone to delays and are error-prone. Leveraging Cloud Functions triggered by Pub/Sub or Eventarc enables automated, consistent, and scalable workflows for isolation, allowing responses to be consistent and near real-time.

For example, you can configure:

- SCC or log-based metrics to detect suspicious activity.
- Forward alerts to Pub/Sub.
- Trigger Cloud Functions to:
  - Apply a quarantine label to suspicious resources.
  - Move resources to a quarantine VPC/subnet.
  - Update firewall rules to block inbound and outbound traffic.

For example, Cloud Function (Node.js) to auto-tag a suspicious VM:

```
const {InstancesClient} = require('@google-cloud/compute').v1;
const computeClient = new InstancesClient();

exports.autoTagQuarantine = async (pubSubEvent, context) => {
  const message = Buffer.from(pubSubEvent.data, 'base64').toString();
  const data = JSON.parse(message);

  const projectId = data.projectId;
  const zone = data.zone;
  const instanceName = data.instanceName;

  console.log(`Tagging instance ${instanceName} in ${projectId}/${zone} for quarantine.`);

  const [instance] = await computeClient.get({
```

```
  project: projectId,
  zone: zone,
  instance: instanceName,
});
const labels = instance.labels || {};
labels['status'] = 'quarantine';

const request = {
  project: projectId,
  zone: zone,
  instance: instanceName,
  instancesSetLabelsRequestResource: {
    labelFingerprint: instance.labelFingerprint,
    labels: labels,
  },
};
await computeClient.setLabels(request);
console.log(`Instance ${instanceName} successfully tagged with quarantine.`);
};
```

The following are the benefits of auto-tagging and quarantine:

- Eliminates manual delays during containment.

- Ensures consistent tagging for tracking and automation.

- Integrates seamlessly with quarantine firewall rules or IAM policies tied to labels.

Project vs. organization-level lockdown considerations

Deciding where to enforce lockdown controls (project vs. organization level) during an incident depends on scope, blast radius, and business criticality. To respond effectively during security incidents, it is essential to evaluate whether lockdown controls should be applied at the project or organization level. This decision depends on the incident's blast radius, criticality of affected assets, and the urgency of containment.

The following guidance outlines the appropriate conditions, capabilities, and considerations for each approach:

- **Project-level lockdown:**
  - Best for contained incidents limited to a single project.
  - Enables:
    - Disabling external IP creation (**constraints/compute.vmExternalIpAccess**).

- Blocking service account key creation (**constraints/iam.disableService AccountKeyCreation**).
- Applying quarantine firewall rules within the project.
  - Less disruptive to the organization's operations while containing risk.

- **Organization-level lockdown:**
  - Required when:
    - The incident spans multiple projects or is suspected to be organization-wide.
    - There is a need to enforce immediate, broad controls across all projects.
    - Legal, regulatory, or critical data exposure is involved.
  - Enables:
    - Enforcing org-level constraints globally (e.g., blocking external IPs, disabling key creation).
    - Temporarily disabling billing or resource creation to halt suspicious activities across projects.
  - Considerations:
    - Organization-level lockdowns may impact legitimate operations across all business units.
    - Should be applied only under high-severity (P0/P1) scenarios with executive alignment.

The following are the best practices for isolation and limiting blast radius:

- Predefine quarantine firewall rules and subnets.
- Use labels or tags for resource identification and automation.
- Implement automated triggers for faster containment using Cloud Functions or Eventarc.
- Maintain clear documentation and runbooks for executing project-level vs. org-level lockdowns.
- Monitor effectiveness through post-isolation validation (e.g., VPC Flow Logs, Cloud Audit logs) to confirm containment.

Quarantine and evidence preservation

Preserving evidence with integrity during incident response requires a structured workflow for snapshotting, memory capture, and log retention. The following table outlines key artifacts and recommendations for collection and storage:

Artifact	Collecting	Storage recommendation
Disk snapshots	`gcloud compute disks snapshot`	Immutable storage bucket
Memory dumps	Serial console, debugging agents	Restricted forensic project
Logs	Logging sinks	Dedicated forensics project

Table 11.5: Recommended collection and storage practices for key digital evidence artifacts during incident response

After collecting these artifacts, validate evidence integrity using *hash verification*:

```
shasum -a 256 snapshot.tar.gz
```

Recording these checksums in your incident documentation maintains the chain of custody while ensuring evidence authenticity.

Additionally, define *retention policies* for forensic data aligned with your compliance requirements. For example:

- Retain critical logs and snapshots for a minimum of 180 days.
- Store artifacts in separate projects with restrictive IAM to limit unauthorized access.

By following these practices, your team ensures evidence is systematically preserved and readily available for regulatory audits, litigation readiness, and root cause analysis during post-incident reviews.

Forensic preservation

A well-structured forensic preservation workflow is essential during incident response in GCP to ensure evidence integrity, compliance, and operational clarity. To ensure consistency and accountability during evidence collection, the following best practices should be applied across snapshotting and chain of custody operations:

- **Snapshotting:** Before detailed analysis, ensure snapshots and memory captures are handled systematically:
  - **Disk snapshots**: Freeze the compromised VM's persistent disk state for later forensic imaging.
  - **Memory dumps**: If possible, gather memory state from live VMs (less trivial in ephemeral container contexts).
  - **Cluster state**: For GKE, export resource definitions, container images, and logs.
- **Preserving chain of custody:** Maintain evidence accountability with clear procedures:
  - **Immutable storage**: Copy snapshots, logs, or images to a separate project with restricted IAM (e.g., security or forensics team only).
  - **Time-stamps**: Label resources with timestamps and the incident ID for clarity.

o **Checksums**: Use cryptographic hashes to verify that disk images and logs have not been tampered with.

These practices ensure your incident response process on GCP remains secure, structured, and audit-ready while preserving the technical depth required for comprehensive investigations.

Quarantine vs. live debugging

An effective isolation and observation strategy is crucial during incident response on GCP to contain threats while allowing investigation when required.

- **Quarantine**: Best suited for clearly malicious activity or high-severity compromise. Isolating the affected instance prevents lateral movement and reduces the blast radius.

- **Live debug**: In controlled IR scenarios, retaining the instance in a live state can help extract volatile data (e.g., C2 callbacks, in-memory scripts). This should be used judiciously, as it risks adversary detection and escalation.

- **Forensic tools**: Purpose-built tools are essential to preserve integrity during evidence collection and facilitate safe analysis:

    o **GCP Compute Engine**: Create disk snapshots of impacted instances and attach them to custom-built forensic VMs in read-only mode to prevent evidence tampering. This approach ensures analysts can safely examine disk contents, including persistence mechanisms, malware droppers, or command history, without altering the original artifact.

    o **Docker-layer analysis**: Investigate container images by unpacking and inspecting individual layers for malicious files, rootkits, or unauthorized binaries. Special attention should be given to public container images pulled from external registries, as these may carry embedded backdoors or tampered base layers. Using tools like *dive* or *syft*, you can examine image contents and **Software Bill of Materials (SBOM)** for indicators of compromise.

These strategies help maintain investigative control, minimize further risk to the environment, and ensure tamper-proof handling of evidence throughout the incident response lifecycle on GCP.

Using GCP Forensics in real incidents

Hypothetical example, if a stolen developer credential can enable attackers to spin up high-CPU Compute Engine VMs for cryptocurrency mining, resulting in cost spikes, alert triggers, and potential reputational damage. Handling such incidents requires a straightforward forensic workflow:

- **Detection:** Use Cloud Logging, billing anomaly detection, and **Event Threat Detection**

(ETD) alerts to identify cost spikes and unusual VM activity.

- **Investigation:** Analyze Cloud Audit logs for unauthorized IAM changes and review VPC Flow Logs for suspicious outbound traffic patterns, correlating with known IOC lists.

- **Isolation:** Enforce firewall rule blocks, remove external IPs, or migrate suspect VMs to quarantine projects using automation scripts.

- **Evidence preservation:** Capture VM disk snapshots, memory dumps (if feasible), and export related logs to immutable storage with timestamping and checksums for integrity verification.

- **Remediation:** Rotate credentials, enforce **multi-factor authentication (MFA)**, adjust IAM policies to least privilege, and add anomaly detection rules for IAM and billing patterns.

The following are the lessons learned:

- Proactive billing monitoring, automated IAM anomaly detection, and pre-defined quarantine workflows are critical for effective incident response in GCP.

- This structured, multi-step approach enables teams to learn and operationalize forensic readiness while reducing MTTD and respond in GCP environments.

Post-mortems and improvements

Post-mortems are essential for transforming incidents into structured learning opportunities while enhancing your GCP IR readiness. A recommended post-mortem structure includes:

- **Executive summary:** Overview of the incident, impact, and outcomes.

- **Timeline:** Clear sequence covering detection, containment, and remediation.

- **Root cause:** Technical and process-level cause analysis.

- **Lessons learned:** Key insights on detection gaps, containment delays, and areas for improvement.

- **Action items:** Concrete next steps with assigned owners and deadlines to track remediation progress.

Tracking incident metrics such as MTTD and MTTR using BigQuery dashboards helps your team visualize and measure IR effectiveness over time. These dashboards can ingest incident metadata, enabling trend analysis across projects and workloads.

By adopting structured post-mortems, aligning them with clear metrics, and updating your IR playbooks with findings, your organization evolves its incident response capability into a continuous improvement process, reducing risk and enhancing resilience within Google Cloud.

Complex made simple

Think of incident response in GCP like running a modern fire department:

- **Pre-planned roles (Fire crew):**
  - Each firefighter (security lead, IC) knows their duty. The fire chief (IC) coordinates the entire response.
  - Everyone has quick access to updated addresses (logs, resource paths) and contact lists (org or project owners).

- **Fire alarms (Cloud Logging and alerts):**
  - A well-maintained fire alarm system (GCP logs and real-time alerts) quickly detects suspicious *fires* (incidents).
  - The moment an anomaly is detected (an unusual IAM role assignment or cost spike), alarms sound in the fire station (the security team's Slack or SIEM).

- **Quarantine and forensics (Isolating the fire):**
  - Firefighters cordon off burning sections to prevent spread; you isolate compromised VMs or subnets, capturing snapshots for forensics.
  - They preserve evidence to determine cause (arson, electrical fault), just like you store logs/disk images for later investigation.

- **Extinguish and remediate (Putting out the flames):**
  - Firefighters cool hot spots and remove flammable materials, just as you mitigate by revoking credentials, patching vulnerabilities, or halting malicious processes.
  - No structure is *safe* until fully verified, *no resource is safe* until logs confirm no more malicious activity.

- **Post-mortem (Fire investigation):**
  - Fire inspectors review the aftermath to identify root causes and propose building code improvements. Your incident post-mortem assesses whether you need new logging rules, stricter IAM, or zero-trust adoption.

The key takeaway is that a thorough GCP incident response mimics a well-trained fire brigade: roles are predefined, alarms (logs or alerts) quickly inform the right teams, and the incident is swiftly contained to protect the environment. Afterwards, thorough inspection leads to building new or stronger defences, just like updating building codes or adding sprinklers after a fire.

Conclusion

This chapter equipped you with a systematic approach to incident response and forensics in Google Cloud, combining preparation, rapid detection, isolation, evidence collection, and continuous improvement. You now have a structured toolkit to manage cloud incidents confidently, ensuring minimal disruption and adherence to compliance.

In the next chapter, we will bring together all the concepts covered throughout this book by applying them to real-world scenarios and certification preparation. You will work through practical challenges simulating real GCP environments, learn to map GCP security features to the Professional Cloud Security Engineer certification blueprint, and explore career pathways while refining your study strategy for continued growth in Google Cloud security.

Exercise

1. Use Cloud Logging to identify an IAM privilege escalation event within your GCP project.
2. Enable VPC Flow Logs on a test subnet, generate traffic, and analyze logs for anomalies.
3. Simulate isolating a suspicious VM using firewall rules and instance tagging.
4. Practice taking a snapshot of a VM and storing it in a restricted project with proper IAM.
5. Conduct a mock incident post-mortem, documenting the timeline, root cause, and action items.

Key takeaways

The following takeaways from the chapter equip security teams to operationalize effective, scalable incident response in Google Cloud environments while continuously improving readiness and resilience:

- **Cloud-native IR mindset:** Incident response in GCP requires a mindset shift from traditional perimeter-focused methods to cloud-native, identity and resource-centric detection and containment strategies.

- **Visibility is critical:** Logging and monitoring (Cloud Logging, Cloud Audit logs, VPC Flow Logs) are essential for maintaining visibility into activities across your cloud environment, aiding in faster detection and effective forensic investigations.

- **Quarantine and containment:** Having pre-defined quarantine strategies using GCP tools, such as firewall rule edits, instance tagging, and organizational policy restrictions, ensures rapid containment to limit the blast radius and prevent attacker lateral movement.

- **Forensic preservation:** Snapshots, memory dumps, and retaining logs with immutable storage and checksums are critical to preserving evidence and maintaining the chain of custody during incident investigations.

- **Post-mortems drive improvement:** Regular post-incident reviews with a non-blaming culture help refine IR runbooks, improve detection and alerting, and strengthen organizational readiness against evolving threats.

- **Automation and drills:** Incorporating automation for containment and detection, coupled with routine security drills, ensures your IR capabilities remain effective as your environment and threats evolve.

- **Metric-driven IR maturity:** Tracking MTTD and MTTR helps teams measure and improve IR effectiveness over time, aligning efforts with organizational risk and compliance goals.

References

1. https://cloud.google.com/security

2. https://cloud.google.com/logging/docs

3. https://cloud.google.com/security/overview/security-design

4. https://cloud.google.com/iam/docs

5. https://cloud.google.com/security/compliance

6. https://cloud.google.com/architecture/security-foundations

7. https://cloud.google.com/binary-authorization/docs

8. https://cloud.google.com/kubernetes-engine/docs/how-to/hardening-your-cluster

9. https://cloud.google.com/vpc/docs/using-flow-logs

10. https://cloud.google.com/architecture/frameworks/google-cloud-trust-foundations

11. https://cloud.google.com/security/command-center/docs

12. https://cloud.google.com/security/binary-authorization

13. https://cloud.google.com/security/threat-intelligence

14. https://cloud.google.com/architecture/frameworks

15. https://cloud.google.com/compute/docs/disks/snapshots

16. https://cloud.google.com/kubernetes-engine/docs/concepts/audit-logging

17. https://cloud.google.com/logging/docs/view/advanced-queries

CHAPTER 12

Real-world Cloud Security

Introduction

This chapter marks the transition from conceptual understanding to applied mastery by guiding you through practical, end-to-end security implementations on Google Cloud. Rather than focusing on isolated tools or configurations, this chapter emphasizes the integration of **Identity and Access Management (IAM)**, **Virtual Private Cloud (VPC)** architecture, encryption strategies, logging pipelines, incident detection, and response workflows into unified security blueprints. These implementations mirror production-grade architectures and reflect the security priorities of real-world organizations.

This chapter emphasizes scenario-driven learning. Each use case reflects a typical organisational environment, ranging from multi-project deployments and hybrid Kubernetes architectures to compliance-oriented analytics workloads. These scenarios are designed to push beyond basic configurations, encouraging the development of layered, context-aware security strategies using tools such as VPC Service Controls, **customer-managed encryption keys (CMEK)**, Binary Authorization, Cloud Armor, and the **Security Command Center (SCC)**.

Beyond technical implementation, this chapter aligns every security task with the exam domains outlined in the *Professional Cloud Security Engineer* certification. You will not only practice configuring access and securing data but also map these tasks to certification competencies, such as detecting threats using Chronicle, enforcing org-level policies with Terraform, or configuring service identity for CI/CD pipelines using **Workload Identity Federation (WIF)**.

By grounding exam prep in realistic cloud scenarios, you gain a working understanding of what secure Google Cloud operations look like in practice.

As the final technical chapter, this section bridges your journey from tactical implementation to long-term security maturity. Whether you're working toward certification, a career pivot into cloud security, or leading architecture decisions, this chapter will equip you with repeatable patterns, diagnostic techniques, and **Infrastructure as Code (IaC)** practices that scale.

In the pages ahead, you will move from isolated skill sets to designing security architectures that are compliant, resilient, and ready for evolving real-world threats.

Structure

This chapter covers the following topics:

- Real-world architectures and exam preparation
- Certification to practice for GCP security
- Sample practice questions and study strategies
- Google Cloud security career paths
- Ongoing security best practices

Objectives

This chapter is designed to help you apply your knowledge of Google Cloud security through complex, real-world scenarios that require architectural thinking, technical precision, and a certification-aligned approach. Rather than isolating individual security concepts, you will be challenged to design and evaluate secure systems end-to-end, spanning IAM, network controls, data protection, workload hardening, and incident response.

You will work through hands-on, scenario-based labs that mirror production-grade environments such as multi-project GCP organizations, hybrid Kubernetes clusters, and regulated analytics workloads. These scenarios are carefully selected to simulate the trade-offs security engineers face in balancing compliance, scalability, and usability in the cloud.

Each exercise directly maps to the domains covered in the Google Cloud Professional Cloud Security Engineer certification. You will explore how to reason through IAM policy design, implement encryption strategies, tune detection tools like SCC, and enforce access guardrails through policy as code, without compromising agility.

By the end of this chapter, you will be equipped to translate theoretical models into practical cloud security solutions and better prepared for certification and on-the-job challenges in cloud security roles.

Real-world architectures and exam preparation

Having delved into IAM, encryption, DevSecOps, container security, threat detection, and more, the final step is to apply these **Google Cloud Platform** (**GCP**) security principles to *real-world, end-to-end use cases*. This chapter bridges the gap between learning individual components and assembling them into cohesive architectures.

You will explore composite scenarios, such as securing a multi-tier web application with Cloud Armor, Cloud NAT, and Identity-Aware Proxy; enforcing VPC Service Controls around sensitive BigQuery datasets; and implementing Binary Authorization in CI/CD pipelines for containerized deployments. These examples mirror real-world production environments, challenging you to design under actual constraints, such as scalability, latency, regulatory compliance, and operational overhead.

This section also maps each hands-on design pattern to the *Professional Cloud Security Engineer* certification domains, helping you see how exam questions translate to practical implementation. You will get tactical advice on interpreting exam scenarios, choosing least privilege designs under time pressure, and navigating overlapping topics (e.g., IAM, DLP, CMEK) in the test.

Whether you are preparing for certification or refining your enterprise security architecture, this part of the chapter ensures you can operationalize what you have learned, securely and confidently, at scale.

Scenario-based threat workflows

This section examines four end-to-end, real-world security scenarios in Google Cloud, integrating IAM, networking, encryption, threat detection, and logging into cohesive implementations. Each scenario maps directly to certification domains and reflects common enterprise patterns. Practical examples, commands, and configuration snippets are embedded throughout to build hands-on intuition.

To reinforce architectural principles and operational best practices, this section presents a series of scenario-driven labs designed to simulate real-world security challenges in Google Cloud. Each scenario includes context, technical goals, policy samples, and practical CLI/YAML examples. Whether you are preparing for certification or advancing your role as a Cloud Security Engineer, these hands-on exercises help bridge the gap between theory and practical implementation:

- **Scenario 1: Secure multi-project deployment:**
    - **Context**: A mid-sized enterprise is migrating apps to GCP across dev, test, and prod environments. Security controls must span IAM, VPC architecture, encryption, and logging.
    - **Goals:**
        - Enforce org policies (e.g., restrict external IPs, require CMEK).

- Evaluate Shared VPC vs. per-project VPC.
- Apply least privilege IAM for DevOps.
- Ensure consistent logging and monitoring.

o **Architecture:**

```
[Org]
 └── [Folder: Applications]
      ├── [Project: dev]  ┐
      ├── [Project: test] ┤ Shared VPC
      └── [Project: prod] ┘
```

o **Sample org policy YAML:**

```
constraint: constraints/compute.vmExternalIpAccess
listPolicy:
  deniedValues:
    - "allUsers"
```

o **gcloud examples:**

```
# Create a subnet in shared VPC
gcloud compute networks subnets create app-subnet \
    --network=shared-vpc \
    --region=us-central1 \
    --range=10.10.0.0/16

# Bind IAM policy for DevOps role
gcloud projects add-iam-policy-binding dev-project \
    --member="user:devops@example.com" \
    --role="roles/custom.devopsMinimal"
```

o **Concern**: Avoid applying broad roles, such as editor; always prefer custom roles with task-specific permissions.

o **Common pitfall**: If each project uses its own VPC, firewall rules, and egress controls may drift over time. Shared VPC centralizes policy.

o **Real-world tip**: Use tools like Terraform with **google_org_policy_policy** resources to enforce guardrails at the org level.

- **Scenario 2: Threat response in a hybrid GKE cluster:**

  o **Context:** An Anthos hybrid cluster exposes workloads to the internet. Cloud Armor detects a DDoS. Malicious containers begin exfiltrating data.

  o **Goals:**

    - Identify and block attacker traffic.
    - Quarantine affected pods/nodes.

- Collect forensic evidence.

- Patch vulnerable workloads.

- **Cloud Armor rule example:**

```
gcloud compute security-policies rules update 1000 \
  --security-policy="prod-waf" \
  --expression=»origin.region_code == 'CN'» \
  --action=deny-403
```

- **Forensics commands:**

```
# SSH into node and export container filesystem
gcloud compute ssh gke-node
sudo docker export <container_id> > /tmp/suspect-container.tar

# Snapshot persistent disk
gcloud compute disks snapshot pd-01 \
  --snapshot-names=disk-snap-incident001
```

- **Isolation via namespace:**

```
apiVersion: v1
kind: Namespace
metadata:
  name: quarantine
  labels:
    quarantine: "true"
```

- **Advanced defense tip**: Enable gVisor on suspicious workloads to limit syscalls and enable deeper syscall-level logging. Use cos-auditd to capture runtime behaviour.

- **Root cause (Post-mortem)**: A Jenkins pipeline pushed unscanned containers with embedded secrets. Secret scanning was disabled.

- **Scenario 3: Compliance-driven BigQuery analytics (HIPAA):**

  - **Context:** A healthcare organization must run analytics in BigQuery while complying with the **Health Insurance Portability and Accountability Act (HIPAA)**.

  - **Goals:**

    - Private IP ingestion only.

    - CMEK encryption and key rotation.

    - PII redaction/tokenization via DLP.

    - Audit-based alerting.

- o **DLP API example in Python:**

```python
from google.cloud import dlp_v2
client = dlp_v2.DlpServiceClient()

item = {"value": "John Doe, SSN: 123-45-6789"}
inspect_config = {"info_types": [{"name": "US_SOCIAL_SECURITY_
NUMBER"}]}

response = client.inspect_content(
    request={"item": item, "inspect_config": inspect_config}
)

for finding in response.result.findings:
    print(f"Found: {finding.info_type.name}")
```

- o **CMEK rotation reminder:**

```
# Schedule key rotation every 90 days
gcloud kms keys update bq-key \
  --location=us \
  --keyring=analytics-ring \
  --rotation-period=7776000s
```

- o **Alerting rule example:** Use log-based metric:

```
resource.type="bigquery_resource"
protoPayload.methodName="tableservice.tables.query"
protoPayload.authorizationInfo.permission="bigquery.tables.
getData"
Trigger an alert when an unauthorised user queries SELECT * FROM
patient_data.
```

- **Scenario 4: Service account misuse in CI or CD:**

  - o **Context:** A developer configures GitHub Actions with long-lived service account keys stored in plaintext. SCC triggers an alert on suspicious GCS access.

  - o **Goals:**

    - ▪ Detect leaked service account credentials.

    - ▪ Replace with short-lived federated credentials.

    - ▪ Alert and revoke compromised accounts.

    - ▪ Audit all workloads using sensitive service accounts.

  - o **WIF setup:**

```
gcloud iam workload-identity-pools create github-pool \
  --location="global" \
  --display-name="GitHub Pool"
```

```
gcloud iam service-accounts add-iam-policy-binding ci-cd-svc@proj.
iam.gserviceaccount.com \
    --role="roles/iam.workloadIdentityUser" \
    --member="principalSet://iam.googleapis.com/projects/123456/
locations/global/workloadIdentityPools/github-pool/*"
```

- o **Detection tip**: Use SCC with Event Threat Detection to identify unusual access patterns, such as **storage.objects.get,** from new IP addresses.

- o **Real-world tip:** Rotate service account keys automatically using tools like *HashiCorp Vault* or disable them entirely via policy.

Certification to practice for GCP Security

The **Google Cloud Professional Cloud Security Engineer** certification covers six core domains: IAM, data protection, network security, logging and monitoring, incident response, and compliance. This section bridges those domains with practical implementations in Google Cloud. Each domain is paired with example tools (e.g., Cloud IAM, VPC SC, CMEK, SCC) and scenarios to illustrate their use in production environments.

Rather than memorizing services in isolation, you will learn how these tools interact, how Cloud Armor integrates with IAP for layered defense, or how SCC findings can trigger alerting pipelines via Pub/Sub and Cloud Functions. You'll also explore trade-offs: for instance, when to use Shared VPC over per-project VPCs in a compliance-heavy setup, or when Binary Authorization adds the most value.

Each mapping calls out critical exam concepts, common misconfigurations, and operational nuances, making your study both certification-relevant and job-ready. This dual focus ensures you're not just prepared to pass the exam—but to apply those principles effectively in real-world cloud security operations.

Domain coverage and GCP service mapping

To successfully prepare for the Google Cloud Professional Cloud Security Engineer certification, it is essential to understand how each domain aligns with specific GCP tools and real-world use cases. The following table offers a concise mapping to help reinforce domain-specific competencies with hands-on relevance:

Certification domain	GCP tools	Use cases or real-world scenarios
Configuring access within a cloud environment	IAM, Workload Identity, service account keys, org policies	CI or CD least privilege, cross-project identity, GitHub Actions federation
Configuring network security	VPC, firewall rules, Cloud Armor, Private Google Access, SCC	Shared VPC design, WAF, IP filtering, restricted egress
Ensuring data protection	Default encryption, CMEK, CSEK, DLP, Secret Manager	HIPAA-bound data, key rotation, customer-supplied key workflows, masking PII
Managing operations	Cloud Logging, Cloud Monitoring, Access Transparency, SCC, Forseti	Audit trails, misconfiguration detection, policy drift analysis
Ensuring compliance	Policy Analyzer, org constraints, SCC compliance dashboard, VPC-SC	FedRAMP or HIPAA validation, environment-wide restrictions
Incident response and forensics	SCC (Event Threat Detection), Chronicle, quarantine workflows, snapshots, logging	DDoS detection, credential compromise, and forensic preservation

Table 12.1: Mapping certification domains to GCP tools and real-world scenarios

Encryption strategy comparison

When selecting an encryption approach in Google Cloud, it is essential to balance control, visibility, and operational complexity. The following table compares default encryption, CMEK, and **customer-supplied encryption keys (CSEK)** across key decision factors to help you make informed choices for different workloads:

Feature	Default encryption	Customer-managed (CMEK)	Customer-supplied (CSEK)
Key visibility	Google-managed	User-managed (Cloud KMS)	User-provided key (no KMS usage)
Audit logging support	Partial	Full (via Cloud KMS logs)	None (outside GCP's visibility)
Key rotation control	No	Yes (automated or manual)	Manual (outside GCP)
Risk of data lock-out	Low	Medium (if keys deleted)	High (loss of key = loss of data)
Recommended for	General workloads	Regulated environments (HIPAA, PCI-DSS)	Niche use cases (ephemeral encryption, advanced control)

Table 12.2: Comparative overview of encryption strategies in Google Cloud

Tip: **CSEK provides maximum control but loses Google's native observability, including no audit logs and no key alerts. Use only when compliance requires full external key custody.**

Feature mapping across scenarios and domains

To effectively prepare for certification and real-world deployment, it is essential to understand how specific Google Cloud security tools align with practical use cases and the broader security domains.

The following table maps core scenarios to relevant tools across access control, network security, data protection, operations, compliance, and incident response:

Scenario	Access config	Net Sec	Data Prot	Ops Mgmt	Compliance	IR and forensics
Secure multi-project deployment	IAM, Org Policy	VPC, FW	CMEK	Logging	Org Pol	-
Threat response in hybrid GKE	Workload ID	Armor	Default	Logging	-	SCC, Chronicle
Compliance-driven BigQuery analytics	IAM	VPC-SC	DLP, CMEK	Audit logs	Constraints	-
CI or CD service account abuse	WIF, SCC	-	SecretMgr	Logs, ETD	Org policies	Chronicle

Table 12.3: Mapping real-world scenarios to security domains and Google Cloud tools

Comparing Workload Identity and service account keys

Choosing the right authentication strategy is crucial for striking a balance between security, operational complexity, and auditability in modern cloud environments.

The following table compares WIF and service account keys across key security dimensions to guide architecture and policy decisions:

	Workload Identity Federation	Service account keys
Rotation overhead	None (short-lived credentials)	Manual or automated via script
Exposure risk	Minimal (JWT or OIDC-based)	High (static credentials)
Auditability	High (Cloud audit logs track access)	Medium (requires external tracking)
Best for	External CI or CD, federated identity	Legacy integrations, on-prem agents
Revocation behavior	Immediate (credentials are short-lived and tied to real-time identity federation)	Manual key deletion required (revocation is delayed if not explicitly performed)

Table 12.4: Workload Identity vs service account keys in GCP

Real-world pitfall, service account keys stored in GitHub, CI/CD pipelines, or other similar repositories are among the most common sources of GCP credential leaks. Always prefer Workload Identity or federation-based approaches.

Integrating SCC with Chronicle workflows

For advanced detection and response maturity, integrate *Security Command Center Premium* with *Chronicle* to create a full-lifecycle threat analytics workflow:

- **Detect**: SCC identifies IAM anomalies or malware-laden containers.

- **Ingest**: SCC findings are exported into *Chronicle* via Pub/Sub.

- **Correlate**: Chronicle links GCP findings with asset inventory, DNS activity, and broader telemetry.

- **Act**: Chronicle alerts trigger workflows (e.g., isolating affected service accounts and updating firewall rules via Cloud Functions).

- **Integration tip:** Use SCC's finding export and Chronicle's **Unified Data Model** (**UDM**) format to unify detection across multiple projects and clouds.

Sample practice questions and study strategies

This section offers a curated set of certification-style questions to reinforce your understanding of Google Cloud security concepts. The questions span all exam domains and feature diverse formats, including multiple-choice, multiple-select, match-the-following, and scenario-based cases. Each question is mapped to its domain and difficulty level, helping you identify areas that need more review.

Exam objective sample question difficulty table

To build exam readiness, it is essential to understand how real-world skills map to exam objectives. The following table breaks down each core domain of the *Google Cloud Professional Cloud Security Engineer* certification, offering representative sample questions, formats, and difficulty levels to help you assess preparedness and study strategically (the below is built of individual perception and the data collected from students prepping for the certification exam, sample size: 30):

Objective	Sample question	Format	Difficulty
Access Configuration	IAM policy for limited access to BigQuery	MCQ	Medium
Network Security	Firewall misconfiguration and Shared VPC	MCQ	Medium
Data Protection	CMEK vs CSEK encryption key choice	MSQ	Hard
Operations Management	Anomaly detection via Logging and SCC	Case-based	Hard

Objective	Sample question	Format	Difficulty
Compliance	Organizational Policy Design for PCI	Match-the-following	Medium
Incident response	Mitigating service account key misuse	Scenario and MCQ	Hard

Table 12.5: Mapping exam objectives to sample questions, formats, and difficulty levels

Question set

1. **IAM policy**: Which role provides minimal read-only access to BigQuery datasets while adhering to PCI-DSS?

   a. roles/bigquery.admin

   b. Custom role with bigquery.tables.getData

   c. roles/viewer at the project level

2. **Network security**: You observe repeated firewall rules allowing 0.0.0.0/0 on a dev subnet. What's the best control to prevent this?

   a. Shared VPC with org policy constraints

   b. Enable Cloud NAT

   c. Cloud VPN to restrict internet access

3. **Data protection (MSQ)**: Which of the following is true about CSEK? (Choose any two)

   a. Full control over encryption keys

   b. No Google audit logging support

   c. Integrated key rotation via Cloud KMS

   d. Automatic key recovery

4. **Compliance (Match-the-following):** Match the compliance goal to the best GCP control:

Goal	Control
Prevent public bucket exposure	Access Transparency and SCC
Restrict external IPs	Cloud DLP VPC
Tokenize PII in BigQuery	Firewall and org policy
Track long-lived credentials	Org policy

5. **Operations monitoring (Case-based)**: Your GCP environment shows unexpected API enablement during off-hours. You want to investigate the source and enforce restrictions.

   Which steps do you take?

   a. Enable Admin Activity audit logs.

   b. Use SCC to surface project-level API changes

   c. Apply org policy: `constraints/serviceuser.services`

   d. Alert on future changes via monitoring log-based metrics

6. **Service account key misuse (consider a scenario):** A security alert indicates that API calls were made from a compromised service account (*a@project.iam.gserviceaccount.com*) using a key stored in a GitHub Actions workflow.

   What should you do to mitigate future risks?

   a. Rotate the key and re-encrypt it in GitHub

   b. Migrate to WIF

   c. Limit the IAM role to `roles or viewer`

   d. Enable Access Approval

7. **Incident response (Chronicle and SCC):** Chronicle detects unusual authentication patterns from a compromised admin account. What is the next step?

   a. Enable VPC Flow Logs

   b. Export SCC findings to Chronicle

   c. Suspend account via IAM

   d. Revoke API key via GCP Console

Answers

1. b

2. a

3. a, b

4.

Goal	Best GCP control
Prevent public bucket exposure	Org policy
Restrict external IPs	VPC firewall and org policy
Tokenize PII in BigQuery	Cloud DLP
Track long-lived credentials	Access Transparency and SCC

5. a|b|c|d

6. b

7. c

Study strategy recommendations

The following are study strategy recommendations:

- **Domain-wise practice**: Split practice sessions by domain, such as IAM, networking, encryption, etc., to identify weak areas.

- **Mock tests with timers**: Simulate real exam conditions with 50 to 60 questions in a two-hour window.

- **Hands-on recall**: Do not just read docs; run **gcloud**, **bq**, and **gsutil** commands in your sandbox project.

- **Understand edge cases**: Many exams' traps test for CSEK quirks, Shared VPC misconfigurations, or IAM scoping nuances.

Google Cloud security career paths

The demand for Google Cloud security professionals continues to rise as businesses adopt multi-cloud strategies, modernize legacy systems, and adhere to stricter regulatory frameworks. Security professionals who understand how to operationalize GCP controls, such as IAM policies, VPC-SC, CMEK, and SCC, are particularly valuable across industries like healthcare, finance, and e-commerce.

Career opportunities span various roles, including:

- **Cloud Security Engineer**: Implements technical controls across workloads, networking, and identities.

- **Security Architect**: Designs scalable security architectures for regulated environments.

- **DevSecOps Specialist**: Integrates CI/CD security, IaC scanning, and secret management.

- **GRC Analyst**: Ensures continuous compliance using GCP-native tools like Forseti and SCC.

- **Cloud Incident Responder**: Investigates alerts using Chronicle, SCC, and logs forensics.

As the cloud security landscape evolves, hybrid skills in automation (Terraform, Python), policy as code, and cloud-native detection will be highly sought after.

To help you chart your path, *Table 12.6* outlines sample roles, essential skills, tools, and relevant certifications (e.g., Professional Cloud Security Engineer, CISSP, CKA). Whether you're shifting from traditional IT or scaling up in your current cloud role, mastering GCP security unlocks future-proof career tracks.

Career role mapping

As you deepen your expertise in Google Cloud security, it is essential to connect the technical skills you have learned with real-world job roles. The following table outlines key career paths in cloud security, mapping essential tools, relevant certifications, and core responsibilities to help guide your career progression and identify areas for further growth:

Role	Key tools	Additional recommended certifications	Key responsibilities
Cloud Security Engineer	IAM, SCC, Cloud KMS, Cloud Armor, Forseti, Workload Identity	Google Cloud Professional Cloud Security Engineer, CKA (optional)	Implement secure architectures, enforce least privilege, automate logging and encryption workflows.
DevSecOps Engineer	Cloud Build, Terraform, Binary Authorization, Policy Controller	DevSecOps, HashiCorp Terraform Associate, GCP ACE	Integrate security into CI or CD, manage policy as code, enforce code-to-prod guardrails.
Cloud Security Architect	Org policy, SCC Premium, VPC SC, Access Context Manager, Chronicle	Professional Cloud Security Engineer, CISSP	Define org-wide posture, architect secure VPC layouts, guide multi-project guardrails, own compliance.
Security Analyst or IR	Chronicle, SCC Event Threat Detection, Cloud Audit logs, BigQuery, Logging	GIAC GCFA, GCP IR specializations (Chronicle or SCC)	Detect threats, triage incidents, maintain dashboards, run playbooks, and conduct forensic investigations.
Compliance or Governance Lead	Org policy, Policy Analyzer, Access Approval, DLP, Cloud Monitoring	CISA, GCP security engineer and compliance focus	Map controls to HIPAA, PCI, or ISO frameworks, generate audit trails, and monitor control drift.

Table 12.6: Mapping cloud security career roles to tools, certifications, and responsibilities

Scenario alignment

To help you connect real-world use cases with professional responsibilities, the following table maps each hands-on scenario from this chapter to a specific cloud security role. This alignment highlights how different personas approach the same security problem from distinct angles, whether it be architecture, operations, compliance, or incident response, reflecting the real team dynamics found in enterprise environments. The following table maps each Google Cloud security role to the most relevant real-world scenario discussed in this chapter. This alignment helps you understand how different responsibilities translate into hands-on tasks and decision-making in GCP environments, preparing you for both the exam and role-based application:

Role	Relevant scenario(s)
Cloud Security Engineer	**Scenario 1**: Secure multi-project deployment
Security Analyst or IR	**Scenario 2**: Threat response in hybrid GKE
Compliance or Governance Lead	**Scenario 3**: Compliance-driven BigQuery analytics
DevSecOps Engineer	**Scenario 4**: (Suggested) Service account misuse in CI or CD Pipelines
Cloud Security Architect	All scenarios (design, review, and enforce cross-cutting controls)

Table 12.7: Aligning security scenarios with role-specific responsibilities

Self-assessment

Ask yourself the following questions before targeting a GCP security role:

1. Do I understand how to set up org policies and IAM roles for a multi-project structure?
2. Can I implement and audit encryption using CMEK or CSEK?
3. Am I comfortable analyzing SCC findings and configuring Chronicle alerts?
4. Have I worked with VPC-SC or network segmentation strategies, such as Shared VPC?
5. Can I design or troubleshoot a secure CI or CD pipeline using Binary Authorization?
6. Do I understand compliance frameworks (HIPAA, PCI) and how to map GCP tools to them?
7. Have I written or reviewed IaC (Terraform, YAML) for security?

If you answered *yes* to at least 5 to 6 of these, you are well on your way. If not, use this checklist to identify which skills to prioritize in your learning path.

Ongoing security best practices

As your Google Cloud environment grows, maintaining a secure posture requires proactive, continuous investment. Security is not just a deployment-time concern; it must be embedded into operational workflows, validated regularly, and automated wherever possible.

The following structured review reinforces the core principles explored throughout the book, linking them to specific GCP tools, monitoring mechanisms, and automation strategies:

- **Best practices checklist**: To translate security theory into daily operational rigour, the following table provides a practical checklist of security principles, mapped to GCP-native tools, monitoring strategies, and automation methods.

  This serves as a tactical reference for implementing secure-by-default guardrails across your cloud workloads, encompassing IAM and network segmentation, container runtime security, and continuous compliance.

Security principle	GCP tool(s)	Monitoring	Automation
Least privilege IAM	IAM, Policy Analyzer, cloud audit logs	Policy Analyzer reports, IAM Recommender logs	Terraform IAM modules and CI checks via gcloud iam policies
Encryption and key rotation	Cloud KMS, CMEK, CSEK	Key usage metrics, KMS audit logs	Rotate keys using KMS lifecycle policies or Terraform rotation_period
Secure network segmentation	Shared VPC, firewall rules, Cloud Armor	VPC Flow Logs, SCC Network Scanner	Firewall automation via Terraform; OPA for network policy validation
Continuous logging	Cloud Logging, SCC, Access Transparency	SCC misconfiguration alerts, log-based metrics	Auto-stream logs to BigQuery or Chronicle for anomaly detection
Compliance control drift	Org policies, Forseti, policy validator	Policy violations tab in SCC	Policy as code with Terraform Validator or OPA
Container runtime security	GKE, Binary Authorization, artifact analysis	Vulnerability reports, admission logs	CI pipeline checks (e.g., gcloud artifacts docker images list-vulnerabilities)

Table 12.8: Mapping GCP security principles to tools, monitoring, and automation practices

- **Policy as code example**: Preventing external IPs; to enforce organization-level security by preventing external IP access on VM instances, you can define a constraint-based policy using **deny-external-ip-policy.yaml**. This policy denies access to all users and can be programmatically validated in your infrastructure pipeline using Terraform Validator to ensure compliance with guardrails before changes are deployed:

```
# deny-external-ip-policy.yaml
constraint: constraints/compute.vmExternalIpAccess
listPolicy:
  deniedValues:
    - "allUsers"
  allValues: DENY
```

To validate using Terraform Validator:

```
terraform plan -out=tfplan.binary
terraform-validator validate tfplan.binary --policy-path=./org-policies
```

- **CI/CD security checklist**: Integrating security into your deployment pipelines helps identify and address misconfigurations and vulnerabilities before they reach production. To build secure CI/CD pipelines in GCP, it's essential to embed security checks at every stage, from code commit to deployment. The following table outlines everyday CI or CD security tasks and the recommended tools or approaches to enforce guardrails and prevent misconfigurations or vulnerabilities from reaching production:

CI or CD security task	Tool or approach
Secrets management	Use Secret Manager or Vault, not plaintext in code
Container scanning	Enable artifact analysis or integrate `gcloud` scans
Deployment gatekeeping	Binary Authorization with signed image enforcement
Infra policy enforcement	Terraform Validator or OPA Gatekeeper
Audit trail for deployments	Enable Cloud Audit logs for Cloud Build
Pipeline segmentation and IAM hardening	Use separate service accounts for each pipeline stage and enforce least privilege via IAM Conditions or custom roles

Table 12.9: CI or CD security tasks and corresponding GCP tools or approaches

- **Case**: Public bucket misconfiguration:
  - **Incident**: A data science team at a mid-sized company created a Cloud Storage bucket with sensitive training data. To share access during a demo, the team added all users with Storage Object Viewer permissions, intending to remove them later. It was not.
  - **Detection**: SCC flagged the bucket with *Publicly Accessible* misconfiguration. Cloud Audit logs showed download events from unknown IPs.
  - **Impact**: Sensitive PII (sampled healthcare data) was accessed and indexed publicly, triggering a compliance investigation.
  - **Remediation**:
    - Enabled org policy; `constraints/storage.publicAccessPrevention`
    - Rolled out the Forseti scanner to detect public buckets
    - Added automation to revoke any new allUsers bindings via Cloud Functions

Conclusion

This chapter served as the capstone to your journey through Google Cloud security, transforming isolated concepts into integrated, real-world solutions. By navigating scenario-driven architectures, ranging from secure multi-project deployments to incident response in hybrid Kubernetes clusters, you have learned how to apply GCP's security primitives with depth, precision, and contextual awareness.

Throughout this chapter, we reinforced the importance of *holistic design*: IAM strategies tied to VPC segmentation, encryption policies aligned with compliance mandates, and threat detection workflows that are actionable, not just observable. These patterns reflect not just what the certification expects, but what production systems demand.

You have also gained a practical lens on how each GCP security service contributes to real outcomes: Cloud Armor halts DDoS traffic, Binary Authorization blocks unverified containers, and Chronicle correlates telemetry into actionable insights. Beyond tools, you learned how to think, how to trace decisions back to business risks, regulatory constraints, and operational trade-offs.

Importantly, we bridged exam prep with practical readiness. Every configuration, policy, and diagnostic step was chosen to align with the *Professional Cloud Security Engineer* domains. The sample questions and career mapping were not just academic—they were designed to prepare you for honest conversations, real interviews, and real production responsibilities.

As you move forward, whether pursuing certification, stepping into a cloud security role, or leading architectural decisions, remember that security is not a checklist to be completed; it is a continuous process. It is a mindset. One that values automation over ad-hoc fixes, principle over convenience, and resilience over assumptions.

This chapter does not just conclude your study. It equips you to begin building *Secure by Design cloud systems* with confidence, adaptability, and purpose.

Exercise

Designing a secure GCP blueprint from scratch

1. **Goal:** Simulate a real-world consulting task where you must design a secure, compliant, and exam-aligned Google Cloud architecture for a fictional client organization. You will integrate multiple concepts, IAM, VPC design, encryption, logging, CI/CD security, and detection workflows, into a single, auditable solution.

2. **Scenario:** Fintech startup launching multi-region GCP platform

3. **Background:** You have been hired as a Cloud Security Consultant for *FinServe*, a startup planning to build a GCP-based payment analytics platform across three regions. The platform must meet PCI-DSS compliance, support real-time fraud detection, and use GitHub Actions for CI or CD.

4. **Requirements:**

   a. **Multi-project setup:**

      i. Projects such as dev, test, prod

      ii. Enforce organization-wide policies via Shared VPC and org constraints.

      iii. Service identity must be federated; no static keys are allowed.

   b. **Data protection:**

      i. All storage must be encrypted using CMEK with 90-day key rotation.

      ii. Tokenize PII in BigQuery using DLP before analysis.

    c. **CI or CD security:**

       i. Use WIF with GitHub Actions.

       ii. Enforce deployment validation using Binary Authorization.

    d. **Detection and response:**

       i. Enable SCC Premium and Chronicle integration.

       ii. Alerts should trigger on:

       iii. External IP access in VMs

       iv. Public buckets

       v. Suspicious service account use

    e. **Logging and auditing:**

       i. Aggregate logs to BigQuery.

       ii. Use log-based metrics to monitor policy violations.

5. **Tasks**: You can perform this in a sandbox project or write pseudo-code/architecture documentation.

6. **Architecture diagram:** Create a high-level diagram that shows the project layout, Shared VPC, and key GCP services.

7. **Org policy configuration:** Write two YAML samples for:

    a. Preventing external IPs

    b. Enforcing CMEK usage

8. **IAM and access strategy:**

    a. Define least privilege custom roles for developers and security engineers.

    b. Write one gcloud or terraform snippet to bind a role with WIF.

9. **DLP tokenization flow:**

    a. Outline how sensitive customer data will be scanned and tokenized before use in BigQuery.

    b. Include a sample DLP API config or pseudocode.

10. **Security logging pipeline:**

    a. Describe the log aggregation and alerting mechanism (e.g., SCC | Pub/Sub | Chronicle | Action).

    b. Write a log-based metric query to detect abnormal IAM activity.

Key takeaways

- **Real-world scenarios bridge theory and practice**: This chapter utilizes four detailed, production-aligned scenarios to reinforce Google Cloud security concepts in a practical context. From multi-project deployments to CI/CD abuse detection, each use case simulates realistic environments, enabling you to translate abstract principles into hands-on implementations.

- **Security architectures must be integrated, not isolated:** IAM, VPC, CMEK, Cloud Armor, Binary Authorization, Chronicle, and SCC are not just standalone tools; they work best when combined into layered defenses. This chapter demonstrates how to compose these into cohesive blueprints for detection, prevention, and recovery across organizational boundaries.

- **Scenario-driven learning reveals hidden trade-offs:** Whether you are debating Shared VPC vs. per-project VPC or WIF vs. static service account keys, the chapter forces you to weigh the trade-offs between maintainability, exposure risks, and operational complexity. This type of decision-making mirrors what is expected in real-world cloud security roles.

- **Certification domains are brought to life through action:** Each exercise in the chapter is directly mapped to the Professional Cloud Security Engineer certification domains. By applying SCC, Chronicle, KMS, Org Policy, and DLP in realistic use cases, your exam preparation becomes anchored in actual workflows, not just documentation.

- **Security maturity requires forensics, not just prevention:** The chapter's forensic exploration of exporting container filesystems, snapshotting disks, or enabling syscall logging with gVisor equips you with the skills essential for modern incident response. You'll learn how to preserve evidence, quarantine compromised resources, and detect root causes via tools like SCC and Chronicle.

- **Data protection is operational, not just regulatory:** Through HIPAA-aligned analytics with BigQuery and DLP API use cases, you learn to move beyond checkbox compliance. Key rotation, PII detection, and alert-based controls enable data protection to be measurable and enforceable across pipelines and analytics environments.

- **CI/CD security is the frontline of modern cloud threats:** service account misuse is one of the most common attack vectors in GCP. The final scenario illustrates how shifting from long-lived credentials to federated identities can remove entire classes of risk from your pipelines. SCC and WIF become essential tools for detection and mitigation.

- **Every role in cloud security has a corresponding use case:** The career mapping and scenario alignment table helps you identify which skills and tools are essential for roles such as Cloud Security Engineer, DevSecOps, Incident Responder, or Compliance Lead. Each role connects to the chapter's hands-on scenarios, helping you find your focus.

- **Best practices must be operationalised through automation:** Security is not *a set-and-forget approach*. The final review consolidates critical principles, least privilege

IAM, encrypted storage, log ingestion, and runtime checks, and maps them to tools, monitoring practices, and Terraform or OPA automation. A single misconfigured bucket can expose **personally identifiable information (PII)**, and automated guardrails prevent such drift.

- **Policy as code and IaC are foundational:** The Terraform Validator, gcloud policy enforcement, and CI/CD integration demonstrate that security guardrails must be shifted left and embedded in code. This ensures consistency, reviewability, and scale, especially across multi-project orgs.

- **Exam success stems from understanding edge cases and patterns:** The practice questions reveal common traps, such as broad IAM bindings or the illusion of security from CSEK, and teach you to reason through real-world outcomes. Memorization alone is insufficient; you must develop a *security reflex* grounded in tool behavior and architecture impact.

- **This chapter is a launchpad, not a conclusion.** Whether you are preparing for certification or transitioning into a cloud security career, this chapter provides you with repeatable diagnostic patterns, architectural reasoning frameworks, and automation strategies to secure Google Cloud environments at scale with confidence.

References

1. https://cloud.google.com/security

2. https://cloud.google.com/iam/docs

3. https://cloud.google.com/vpc/docs

4. https://cloud.google.com/kms/docs

5. https://cloud.google.com/logging/docs

6. https://cloud.google.com/security-command-center/docs

7. https://cloud.google.com/binary-authorization/docs

8. https://cloud.google.com/chronicledocs

9. https://cloud.google.com/dlp/docs

10. https://cloud.google.com/armor/docs

11. https://cloud.google.com/workload-identity/docs

12. https://cloud.google.com/policy-intelligence/docs/org-policy/overview

13. https://cloud.google.com/architecture/security-foundations

14. https://registry.terraform.io/providers/hashicorp/google/latest/docs/resources/organization_policy

15. https://cloud.google.com/certification/guides/cloud-security-engineer

Join our Discord space

Join our Discord workspace for latest updates, offers, tech happenings around the world, new releases, and sessions with the authors:

https://discord.bpbonline.com

Index

H

www.ingramcontent.com/pod-product-compliance
Lightning Source LLC
Chambersburg PA
CBHW061745210326

41599CB00034B/6793